Bridging the Gap

Bridging the Gap

Ethnicity, Legitimacy, and State Alignment in the International System

Cindy R. Jebb

LEXINGTON BOOKS
Lanham • Boulder • New York • Toronto • Oxford

LEXINGTON BOOKS

Published in the United States of America
by Lexington Books
An imprint of the Rowman & Littlefield Publishing Group, Inc.
4501 Forbes Boulevard, Suite 200, Lanham, Maryland 20706

PO Box 317
Oxford
OX2 9RU, UK

British Library Cataloguing in Publication Information Available

Library of Congress Cataloging-in-Publication Data

Jebb, Cindy R., 1960–
    Bridging the gap : ethnicity, legitimacy, and state alignment in the international system
/ Cindy R. Jebb.
        p. cm.
    Includes bibliographical references and index.
    ISBN 0-7391-0591-4 (cl. : alk. paper)
        1. Egypt—Foreign relations—1981—Decision making. 2. Egypt—Foreign
    relations—1970–1981—Decision making. 3. Syria—Foreign relations—1971—
    Decision making. 4. Legitimacy of governments—Egypt. 5. Legitamacy of
    governments—Syria. I. Title.

JZ1670.J43 2004
327.62—dc22   2003065897

Printed in the United States of America

♾™ The paper used in this publication meets the minimum requirements of American
National Standard for Information Sciences—Permanence of Paper for Printed Library
Materials, ANSI/NISO Z39.48-1992.

To Professor Timothy J. Lomperis
My teacher

Ladies and Gentlemen, there are moments in the lives of nations and peoples when it is incumbent upon those known for their wisdom and clarity of vision to survey the problem, with all its complexities and vain memories, in a bold drive toward new horizons. . . . We must all rise above all forms of obsolete theories of superiority, and the most important thing is never to forget that infallibility is the prerogative of God alone.

Anwar el-Sadat
Speech to Israeli Knesset, 1977

Contents

List of Tables

Prologue

This book examines the decisive factors that drive foreign policy decisions, during both the Cold War and post–Cold War eras. Specifically, it examines weak or small states whose legitimacy is inextricably linked to their security. The Cold War and post–Cold War eras provide the contexts for this book's cases; thus, they offer an opportunity to address the level of analysis issue as it relates to states' foreign policy decisions. In brief, this project reveals that ethnically divided states are more constrained by domestic politics than homogeneous states.

Interestingly, there seemed to have been a window of opportunity for the United States, after the Persian Gulf War, to positively influence the Israeli-Palestinian peace process. However, after a decade, the United States seems at a loss in its Middle East policy. This situation is perplexing given that the United States has invested more diplomatic, economic, and military resources in this region than in any other region. However, the United States has not been able to marshal these resources to produce a satisfactory policy to address the current regional instabilities, specifically between Israelis and Palestinians. Moreover, it is unclear how to properly frame this conflict—nationally, religiously, ethnically, etc.[1] Is the United States blinded by an intrastate dynamic, a regional dynamic, or perhaps even their interaction on the global stage? This study examines the interaction of the domestic and international factors while suggesting the possibility of a unique regional dynamic, which may assist with future analyses of both policy and scholarship.

Furthermore, one cannot discuss the current Palestinian-Israeli conflict without discussing other regional actors. This study focuses on Syria and Egypt during the Cold War and the post–Cold War eras, and their roles are evident in today's volcanic climate. Egypt's Foreign Minister, Amre Moussa, recently discussed Egypt's changed diplomatic tenor of the past decade: ". . . the Arab-Israeli conflict, as well as the situation in the Arab world and the

xi

area adjacent to the Middle East, gave Egyptian diplomacy and Egyptian foreign policy a new direction of activism—a role that must be maintained."[2] While Syria's political future is unclear under Hafiz Asad's son, Bashar Asad, Bashar has stood firm on Syria's foreign policy stance toward the Golan Heights. How will Bashar's willingness to introduce more openness domestically affect his foreign policy objectives?[3] While this study focuses on Egypt and Syria, it explores the impact of ethnic cleavages on foreign policy as well as highlighting regional factors. In this post–Cold War age, perhaps it is time to introduce a regional level of analysis.

Domestically, these two countries are fascinating. Syria's political development is a story of ethnic struggles. The political development of Syria has been marked by the displacement of the Sunni civilian elite by successive minority groups, culminating with the Alawis' rise to power. Through the military, the Ba'th Party, and the Asad presidency, the Alawis consolidated their power, although it took eighteen coups between 1949 and 1970. Both Syria's Cold War and post–Cold War cases necessarily examine Hafiz Asad. His skillful and sometimes blunt approach toward gaining regime legitimacy provides much insight concerning the impact of the Sunni-Alawi split on his 1980 decision to sign the Soviet Treaty and his decade-later Persian Gulf War alignment decision.

Egypt's story is one of continuity as compared with Syria. Anwar Sadat described the continuity of the Egyptian identity in his autobiography by stating that:

> our cultural roots are alive, as vigorous as ever after more than 7,000 years. Those who are surprised by what we do cannot simply understand this fact. They cannot grasp the real nature of a people who are working for a modern civilization comparable to the one they erected thousands of years ago in freedom and peace.[4]

The Cold War case examines Sadat's decision to realign with the West in the late 1970s, and the post–Cold War case analyzes Husni Mubarak's Persian Gulf War alignment decision. Each leader devised his own ideology as a means to gain consensus or legitimacy. These attempts were not always successful, especially in the midst of a crumbling economy, but both leaders were able to rely on a reservoir of legitimacy due to the people's strongly felt Egyptian identity.

This project will be of interest to scholars in the international, comparative, and security fields, and it will, I believe, provide insights for Middle East regional experts and practitioners in the policy field, as well. For example, policymakers need to understand the motivations and calculations of foreign leaders as they make state alignment decisions. This study deliberately focuses on nongreat powers so as to reveal current theoretical great power biases. Finally, this project provides an important foundation for further research in other critical areas of current scholarly interest, including democratization, consensus-building, multilateral institutions, and ethnic studies. Specifically, it explores the politically important, yet empirically elusive, concepts of legitimacy and ethnicity, and I believe that further application of this study's adopted model that links domestic variables and foreign policy will enable scholars to better understand this critical connection, while sharpening the model itself.

I chose this project for two reasons. First, I hope to contribute to both the international relations and comparative politics fields. While many international relations scholars have called for the analysis of weak states and their effect on the international system, they have not examined such states with the regional or comparative politics lens. Additionally, many comparativists discuss the effects a lack of legitimacy has on the stability of a regime, but they do not explore such a regime's effect on the international system. I use the comparative politics literature, namely the ethnicity literature, to answer the international relations question of why states behave as they do. A residual effect of this work may be a better understanding of this variable we call ethnicity. Second, I hope to add to the literature concerning state behavior in the Cold War versus the post–Cold War era, as well as explore the relative significance of regionally—versus internationally—based threats on that behavior. Testing cases in the context of a systemic transition while climbing into the black box of elite opinions and attitudes, offers an opportunity for exciting theoretical findings.

The epilogue brings forward the questions and theoretical findings of the Cold War and post–Cold War cases to the post-9/11 world by observing its security environment at the domestic, regional, and global levels. In short, the dynamics observed in this new era seem to validate the theoretical findings based on the earlier cases. It appears that both Egypt and Syria continue to exhibit state alignment behaviors in accordance with the theories; however, each regime's state legitimacy formula has shifted as a result of the driving forces in the domestic, regional, and global security environments. While ethnicity remains a key factor in state legitimacy, other forces have become significant, namely terrorism, continued socio-economic despair, de-liberalization, and regional crises. Subsequently, the epilogue confirms the centrality of state legitimacy for understanding state behavior and its very real regional and global effects. I offer this last chapter as only a beginning; I hope it provokes new questions that will assist future research and thinking in the post-9/11 world.

NOTES

1. Shibley Telhami, "Camp David II: Assumptions and Consequences," *Current History: A Journal of Contemporary Affairs* 100, no. 642 (January 2001), 12. Telhami argues that policy makers use nationalism to frame the conflict, not religion in ibid., 13-14.

2. Tanya Goudsouzian, "'We Are All Angry': Interview with Egypt's Foreign Minister Amre Moussa," *Middle East Insight* 16, no. 1 (January–February 2001): 29.

3. See Neil MacFarquhar, "Syria Reaches Turning Point, But Which Way Will It Turn," *New York Times*, March 12, 2001, A1 and A4.

4. Anwar Sadat, *In Search of Identity: An Autobiography* (New York: Harper & Row, 1978), 313.

Acknowledgments

I could not have completed this book without the tremendous support from family, friends, colleagues, and faculty. I dedicate this to my professor and friend, Tim Lomperis. He epitomizes the academic professional who puts his students first. I have been inspired by his scholarship, his teaching, his integrity, and his friendship. I am especially indebted to Professor Mahmud Faksh who through the years has been a generous colleague, mentor, and friend. Professors Ole Holsti, Alex Roland, and Peter Liotta provided patient guidance, and their example has been important to me as well. Colonel (Ret.) Michael Blythe, my brigade commander, provided excellent editing recommendations, and I appreciate his sense of humor and friendship. First Seargeant Harold Harris and the soldiers of the brigade operations shop always provided great moral support, as well as my long-time friend Col. (Ret.) Maxie McFarland. I have been blessed to work in an organization, the Department of Social Sciences, which supports and encourages research and publication. The faculty in the Department of Social Sciences patiently listened to and provided advice on my developing ideas, most notably, Drs. Ruth Beitler, Jay Parker, and Thom Sherlock. They are wonderful colleagues and friends. Also, collaboration with Ruth Beitler on our Institute of National Security Studies project was instrumental in obtaining some of the research and ideas for the epilogue. I have been honored to serve under the Department's leadership, Gen. (Ret.) James Golden, Gen. Daniel Kaufman, and Col. Russ Howard including his deputies, Col. Mike Meese and Lieutenant Col. (Promotable) Al Willner. As the current Director of Comparative Politics, I am grateful to my predecessors, Colonels (Ret.) Goerge Osborn and Augustus Norton. Thanks also to Lt. Col. (Ret.) Barry Scribner, Jo May and Chris Deitrick. I am grateful to Jim Smith and his organization, the Institute for National Security Studies, and to West Point's Academic Research Division.

I also had the opportunity to serve as a Fellow at the Naval War College, a great institution that encourages and supports research. Ginny Navaro helped me with the research while I was at Ft. Leavenworth. The faculty at the U.S. Army Command and General Staff College (CGSC) encouraged me, most notably Lt. Col. Carey through his expertise and connections. Fred Huxley at the U.S. Information Agency provided critical information and friendly support. My staff group and their spouses at CGSC proofread and discussed the development of this project, primarily Melissa Sorenson. Thanks especially to my friends at CGSC, who provided moral support while I was away from my family, namely Sue Sowers, Karen Hellmeyer, Annie and Peter Baker, Deb Reisweber, Chris and Charlie Pate, Tom Schneider, Scott Sorenson, Joe and Heidi Zacks, Bruce Jones; my staff group—Paul, Joe, Sharon, Rick, Rolf, Al, Don (the Air Force guy), Brian, Dave, Scott, Michael, Jeff (the Navy guy and desk mate), Kirk, and Jay, and many others who were so supportive. I am most indebted to Charlie Keller for his computer expertise and to his family members for their patience. Thanks also to the administrative staff at Duke University, especially Jasmine Jones and Mary Moore. My friend Corinne Bridges, provided terrific editing support. I appreciate the professionalism and fine work of Serena Krombach and Jesse Goodman from Lexington.

My husband, Joel, my best friend and love of my life, has provided not only moral support, encouragement, and love, but he has also raised our children while I have been away on two separate year-long occasions. Additionally, he took care of our—at the time—very small children on many weekends, which allowed me to continue to work on this project. The love, cheer, and happiness of our children—Ben, Alex, and Olivia—sustained me throughout this whole process of "Mommy's book." My parents, Ellen and Jack, and family have been instrumental in this process through their love and support. They have been pillars of strength for me, and they instilled in me the idea that anything is possible.

I have been blessed to work with and know so many good people, not all of whom are listed. I share with them the success of this project, and I am grateful for their assistance and friendship; however, I alone accept the blame for any errors.

The views expressed here are those of the author and do not purport to reflect the position of the United States Military Academy, the Department of the Army, or the Department of Defense.

Chapter One

Introduction

It has been more than a decade since the end of the Cold War, yet scholars are still struggling with how best to explain and predict events that are unfolding before our eyes on the global stage. This is not an easy task, for as Ted Sorenson once remarked:

> The touchstone of our nation's security concept—the containment of Soviet military and ideological power is gone. The primary threat cited over forty years in justification for most of our military budget, bases, and overseas assistance is gone. The principal prism through which we viewed most of our world-wide diplomatic activities and alliances has gone.

There have been many proposed theories since the end of the Cold War, such as clash of civilizations, democratic peace theory, nationalism, etc., which have tried to develop a consensual theoretical world view.[1] Clearly, scholars of international security, in particular, must take a critical look at the theoretical assumptions and premises of the Cold War era and creatively develop sound research approaches to test new ways of thinking about the world. This book is an attempt to provide useful theoretical and empirical insights regarding the gap between the comparative politics and international relations literature. Essentially, this study uses the literature of comparative politics to answer a crucial international relations question: what causes state alignment? It explores the causal significance of ethnic divisiveness and the international system on foreign policy decisions involving state alignment during both the Cold War and post–Cold War eras. Specifically, it deals with two weak states, Egypt and Syria, whose legitimacy is inextricably linked to their security, and examines Egypt's decision to realign with the United States in the late 1970s, Syria's decision to sign the 1980 Treaty of Friendship and

1

Cooperation with the Soviet Union, and both Egypt and Syria's 1990–1991 Persian Gulf War alignments. The different system-level contexts for these cases provide insights concerning the level of analysis issue as it relates to states' foreign policy decisions.

For the past decade, scholars and policy-makers' focus on regions and political regimes has become at least as important as their Cold War era's focus on the international system. With the end of bipolarity, feelings of irredentism, nationalism, religion, and ethnicity have stressed the international system. Bruce Hoffman claims that these sentiments, not ideology, are fueling terrorism and forecasts that these forces ". . . long held in check or kept dormant by the cold war may erupt to produce even greater levels of nonstate violence."[2] The point is that the study of intrastate variables is paramount to the study of the international system. The focus of this project is on ethnicity as a factor for state alignment decisions in the international system, and the core argument of the thesis begins with Donald Horowitz's definition of an ethnically divided state: "In divided societies, ethnic conflict is at the center of politics. Ethnic divisions pose challenges to the cohesion of states and sometimes to peaceful relations among states."[3] An assessment of ethnic divisiveness then is based on the degree to which ethnicity permeates society, especially in the political arena. An ethnically divided state suffers from a low level of state legitimacy, causing it to be more unstable than a homogeneous state. This instability threatens the regime, and leaders of such regimes must often view this internal threat as carefully as external threats posed by other states. We will examine state alignment behavior of an ethnically divided state versus that of an ethnically homogeneous state and measure this behavior by refining Stephen M. Walt's concepts of balancing and bandwagoning through insights gained by Randall L. Schweller and Steven R. David.[4]

In short, this study demonstrates that an ethnically divided state will have different alignment behavior than that of an ethnically homogeneous state. Second, it appears that the post–Cold War era promotes bandwagoning with internal enemies because there is a degree of uncertainty in the international system concerning a superpower's support. Finally, in this post–Cold War era, it seems that the region, as an analytical unit, has become more significant than it was in the Cold War era. Theoretically, this project supports Schweller's critique of Walt, that is that balancing and bandwagoning are not polar opposites; bandwagoning is for profit, while balancing is for security purposes. Extending Schweller's insights with the help of David's concept of omnibalancing, this study reveals that the absence of internal bandwagoning and balancing engenders bold, purposive state alignment behavior, while the presence of internal balancing and bandwagoning fosters cautious, incremental alignment behavior.

The theory appendix comprehensively traces the theoretical foundations for modifying some of the assumptions of realism that underline Walt's theory on state alignment and reassessing the Cold War's focus on the systems-level approach. Systems-level theory and NeoRealism, in particular, failed to predict the change in the international system, that is the change from the Cold War to post–Cold War era.[5] Consequently, scholars of international relations realize that systems theory alone does not fully explain state behavior. For this reason, we must explore other approaches to more fully understand this behavior but without completely discarding the basic tenets of realism, which have formed the foundation of some of the Cold War era theories. We are still operating in an international system, albeit a different one; therefore, we must consider the effects of the international system on state behavior in the current context of the post–Cold War era. However, we cannot ignore the effect of the numerous examples of regime instability on the international system. The republics of the former Soviet Union, the former Yugoslavia, Somalia, and Rwanda are only a few examples of regime instability at work today. This instability not only incites regime failure, but it also greatly impacts the international system. Consequently, scholars must simultaneously analyze the effects of regime instability on the international system, as well as the international system on the regime.

ETHNICITY AS A DETERMINANT FOR INTERNATIONAL BEHAVIOR

Ethnicity is the focus of this study as a potential internal threat because it is more prominent in the new states of Africa, the Middle East, Asia, and the Caribbean than in the comparatively older states of Europe and North America.[6] Additionally, Horowitz states that "Ethnicity is at the center of politics in country after country, a potent source of challenges to the cohesion of states and of international tension. . . . Ethnicity has fought and bled its way into public and scholarly consciousness."[7]

There is a real-world urgency driving this focus on ethnicity as a key variable of international behavior. First, ethnicity is a global, not simply a regional, phenomenon. Second, ethnic conflict can cause great levels of pain and suffering to combatants and noncombatants, alike. Third, the international community is at a loss as to how best to deal with such conflict. For example, the United States, as other nations, has deployed troops as a means to alleviate ethnic tensions, with mixed results. Finally, as this study will demonstrate, ethnic strife or divisiveness as defined by Horowitz can affect international behavior. There is no doubt that ethnicity is a recognized variable for conflict.

Moreover, with the increased number of weak states and transitioning states, internal conflicts, regardless of the cause, can quickly escalate regionally and possibly globally. Michael Brown contends that internal conflicts matter because they are widespread, cause much suffering, involve proximate states, and can indirectly or directly influence the interests of international organizations and "distant powers."[8] In 1994, all thirty-one armed conflicts had intrastate causal origins, with Nagorno-Karabakh and Bosnia-Herzogovina implicating interstate involvement. The United States conducted twenty-seven deployments aimed at addressing ethnic wars or failed states just within the five years after Desert Storm.[9] In the former Soviet Union, ethnicity is a key factor in the undeclared war between Armenia and Azerbaijan. In Georgia, the government is facing challenges from ethnically based movements in South Ossetia and Abkhazia. In Moldavia, the government has faced challenges from the Dniester region, comprising a concentrated Russian minority population. Tajikistan, too, contends with internal ethnic strife.[10] Finally, Chechnya's fight for independence is affecting both its own people and Russian stability.

Ethnic conflict is not limited to any one area or region. In the spring of 1996, ethnic civil wars were occurring in Bosnia, Croatia, Rwanda, Burundi, Angola, Sudan, Turkey, Azerbaijan, Georgia, Chechnya, Tajikistan, Kashmir, Myanmar, and Sri Lanka. Unfortunately, the extreme violence, especially violence directed against noncombatants, prevalent in these conflicts has elicited the need for military intervention. So far, however, such intervention has had ambiguous results.[11] Additionally, Central and Eastern Europe have approximately nine zones or regions afflicted with ethnic hatred or intolerance, the most serious areas being Bosnia and Kosovo, followed by southern Slovakia and Romanian Transylvania.[12]

Contrary to what recent headlines suggest, the effects of ethnicity are not a new phenomenon. The Soviet leadership in 1982 understood the significance of its country's multinational nature and believed that "the successful construction of communism will depend to a significant degree on a correct policy in the realm of national relations." In 1969, the All-Union Council for the Study of Nationality Problems was established in an effort to alleviate potential nationality driven problems, and Soviet president Leonid Brezhnev's concern for such problems seemed to be reflected by his expansion of the activities of the Institute of Ethnography in Moscow.[13] While ethnicity has always been a factor in politics, we cannot ignore the fact that the "revolutions" of 1989 and the end of the Cold War era put ethnic conflict center stage. Iftikhar H. Malik claims that 1989 gave way to "intensified competition between nationalism and ethno-regional/centrifugal forces. Geared to a variety of political, economic and cultural forces, ethnicity is the major challenge to a given state, especially in heterogeneous countries of South and Southwest Asia."[14]

While this study analyzes ethnicity in the states of Egypt and Syria, its findings will provide at least a starting point for understanding ethnicity as a factor for international behavior. For as one scholar asks, "What is it about ethnic nationalism . . . that worries observers concerned with the preservation of international security? [It is] the likely external consequences of policies of internal ethnic exclusion."[15]

The next section provides a brief other-than-great power theoretical journey, ending with an exploration of the ethnicity and legitimacy literature. This theoretical review will not only demonstrate the theoretical precepts of this study, but it will also help explain state alignment and the reasons for this behavior.

THEORETICAL BACKGROUND

Barry Buzan addresses the importance of examining the nature of the state in his book, *People, States, and Fear*. Buzan's work takes elements from Kenneth Waltz and shows the importance of understanding level II, the nature of the state.[16] The importance of understanding the nature of the state, as well as its groups and individuals of the state, stems from his discussion of weak versus strong states. Weak states are fundamentally different from strong states, and this difference is so significant that the idea of national security takes on a whole new meaning for weak states.[17] They must calculate international relations based on internal as well as external threats, whereas strong states primarily look at external threats.[18] Strong and weak states function differently. According to Buzan, " . . . it is probably more appropriate to view security in weak states in terms of the contending groups, organizations, and individuals as the prime objects of security."[19]

Since weak states may base their alignment behavior primarily on internal threats, it is important to understand those threats. Buzan acknowledges the importance of understanding the international system, but not to the exclusion of understanding levels I (nature of man) and II (nature of the state). With the end of the Cold War, Buzan's ideas strike a recognizable chord. Regime instability is a threat to rulers in many Third World states, and it undoubtedly drives foreign policy. Buzan calls for the collaboration of comparative and security studies and awakens us to the need to take the weak state perspective as we advance the security field.[20]

David takes Walt to task by claiming that Walt does not understand Third World alignment. According to David, Walt ignores other considerations that these states have when assessing the threat. These nations must consider internal threats, and these threats then become part of the equation as they determine alignments. His idea of omnibalancing considers internal and external threats.[21] Eric Labs challenges Walt on the same point. He found that weak states will choose sovereignty over security as they make their alignment choices. In other words, weaker states will choose to fight for their territorial or governance rights rather than surrender some of those rights in exchange for physical well-being.[22] Paul Schroeder criticizes Walt's use of history. Schroeder claims that, historically, bandwagoning is a more common behavior, not balancing as Walt claims.[23] In fact, he criticizes NeoRealists in general for approaching history with a theoretical bias.[24] Finally, Schweller also criticizes Walt for his great power perspective. Schweller claims that security is not the only concern for states; there are other reasons for alignment behavior.[25] "Simply put, balancing is driven by the desire to avoid losses; bandwagoning by the opportunity for gain."[26] Clearly, these scholars challenge Walt's interpretation of his case studies, claiming that he analyzed them with a superpower bias.

David claims that his theory of omnibalancing helps us better understand Third World state behavior. His theory calls for the assessment of external and internal threats, with respect to the leader's political survival, not the state's survival.[27] David offers three significant departures from systems theory. "First, rather than just balancing against threats or power, leaders of states will appease secondary adversaries to focus their resources on primary adversaries. . . . [They] must align with one threat to address the other and [they do]."[28] For weak states, the primary threat is often domestic, and the secondary threat is often another state. Second, for Third World states internal threats are more dangerous than external threats. Finally, Third World leaders act in their own interests as opposed to their states' interests.[29] In sum,

> Omnibalancing incorporates both the need to appease secondary adversaries and the need of leaders to balance against both internal and external threats in order to survive in power. It is conditional on regimes being weak and illegitimate, and on the stakes for domestic politics being very high.[30]

David justifies the Third World as an analytic category because all Third World states have a combination of characteristics:

> Their cumulative impact makes virtually all Third World leaders more vulnerable to overthrow—particularly from internal threats—than other leaders. Thus while the leaders of all states must be concerned about threats, in the Third World such concerns assume an urgency and priority that is rarely matched elsewhere.[31]

David limits his test to Third World state—superpower alignments, which necessarily limits him to the Cold War era. Additionally, he does not fully develop or explain internal threats.

THE INTERNAL THREAT:
ETHNICITY AND ITS LINK TO LEGITIMACY

How does one define ethnicity? Although one cannot escape using the term "ethnicity" when describing the post–Cold War, it is not an easily definable term; consequently, it has many, albeit ambiguous definitions.[32] Does one use an inclusive (a very broad definition) or exclusive (a very narrow definition) definition? Robert J. Thompson and Joseph R. Rudolph, Jr. explain that there are problems with both these definitions. The broad, inclusive approach to ethnicity loses analytical usefulness. However, when ethnicity is narrowly perceived, for example just along racial lines, then analysis misses the changing texture, history, and boundaries inherent in the ethnic concept. Thompson and Rudolph explain that "The usual pattern is for a group to possess an overlapping set of traits, such as language, religion, and culture, while sharing others with the rest of the society, with group distinctiveness becoming manifest only in various forms of social, economic, and political interaction."[33]

This study bases the definition of ethnicity on the overlapping set of traits, thereby acknowledging this overlap, but also maintaining some analytical precision. For my purposes, ethnicity is a group identity based on religion, language, and kinship. It does not include such attributes as class, ideology, and region. This definition allows for analysis of ethnicity as a variable, as well as other domestic variables, such as class, mentioned above. While Egypt may be divided along class lines, class does not extensively serve to reinforce other societal cleavages, whereas in Syria, class and region, for example, serve to reinforce the ethnic division between Alawis and Sunnis. However, the Alawai-Sunni cleavage is primarily based on religion and kinship.

It is the reinforcement of ethnic divisions, especially in the political arena, that serves to pose legitimacy problems for the nation. This study assesses ethnic divisiveness based on Horowitz's claims that where ethnicity significantly permeates sectors of social life, we see deeply divided societies.[34] For example, in ethnically divided societies, ethnicity is apparent in land policies, trade union issues, education policy, and tax policy. Issues that are seemingly routine and administrative in nature become ethnically charged.[35] Another indication of a deeply ethnically divided society is the organization of activities, economically and politically, along ethnic lines.[36] Ethnic divisiveness is most dangerous when it enters the political arena and challenges the legitimacy of the state.[37] The institutionalist approach is useful to assess the extent of ethnicity's permeation in the political development of each of the cases; thus, the degree of permeation, based on Horowitz's view, established whether or not the case, or state, is ethnically divided.

An analysis of Syria's political development reveals that ethnic divisiveness was a prominent factor in the political arena. Hafiz Asad ruled, as Patrick Seale observed, with two guiding principles: he worked to gain a public consensus, and in the absence of this consensus, he relied on coercion.[38] Additionally, the Muslim Brotherhood was dangerous in Syria because it was able to exploit these ethnic divisions. Daniel Pipes explains that "the passage of time has hardened the Sunni-Alawi divide to the point that it dominates the way Syrians interpret domestic politics, and the way they anticipate Syria after Asad's passing."[39] Moreover, Pipes explains that the Islamic movement "in Syria . . . is more anti-Alawi and anti-Ba'th, more communal than religious. Muslim Brethern literature, for example, hardly ever brings up the usual fundamentalist concern for applying the sharia. Rather its goals consist of the Sunni public agenda."[40]

Conversely, Egypt's political development reveals an ethnically homogeneous state, and the Muslim Brotherhood did not pose as serious a challenge to Egypt's leaders as it did to Syria's leaders. In Egypt, there were no ethnically defined cleavages that were exploitable. While the Brotherhood challenged the regime in the economic realm by providing social welfare activities, it did not challenge the people's identity. Everyone considered themselves Egyptian. This strong national identity and its resulting legitimacy has allowed Egypt to weather long periods of economic malaise and Islamic fundamentalism. As Fouad Ajami noted:

> Egyptians who know their country so well have a way of reciting its troubles, then insisting that the old resilient country shall prevail. As an outsider who has followed the twists of the country's history and who approaches the place with nothing but awe for its civility amid great troubles, I suspect they are right. The country is too wise, too knowing, too tolerant to succumb to a reign of theocratic zeal. Competing truths and whole civilizations have been assimilated and brokered here.[41]

While the literature on ethnicity reveals its importance as a factor for legitimacy, legitimacy itself is not an easy concept to measure. Because of its centrality in the field of political science, it is critical that we still attempt to discover its significance on the polity and the international system. David Easton explains that "Given its long and venerable history as a central concept in political science, legitimacy has yet to receive the attention it merits in empirical research."[42] It is for this reason that this study is important, if only to lay the groundwork for further study.

Michael Hudson explains that the Arab states experience a legitimacy problem due to their lack of prerequisites for political modernity: authority, identity, and equality. "The legitimate order requires a distinct sense of corporate selfhood: the people within a territory must feel a sense of political community which does not conflict with other subnational or supranational identifications."[43] This point is critical and explains why ethnicity plays such a key role for regime legitimacy. According to Easton, there are three sources of legitimacy: ideology, structure, and personal qualities. Ideology refers to a sense of the regime being morally right; structure refers to the acceptance of norms and governmental apparatus; and personal qualities refers to the acceptance of leaders who fill the structural roles.[44] Max Weber tells us that legitimacy is based on tradition, a leader's charisma, and/or legal statutes.[45] What seems to be a critical component in all these definitions is the idea that the people have a shared sense of community and belief that the regime has the moral right to rule.

RESEARCH DESIGN

This study demonstrates that students of security must reevaluate deductive reasoning, as well as case studies that only represent a certain type of state. The case study method is the appropriate research technique, but we must be careful not to choose unique cases or only certain types of cases. As we increase the number and variety of cases, our ability to eliminate bias and error will improve. Additionally, we must approach our study with an emphasis on level II. The nature of the state does matter, and if we are to understand balancing behavior, we must also modify realism's assumption that the state is a unitary rational actor. Finally, collaborative research by area and security experts will greatly improve our objectivity as we seek to explain and predict state behavior. The more varied and numerous our cases, the more valid our theory. Regionally focused scholarship is a first step towards developing more general theory.

The Cold War era case studies are Egypt's decision to realign with the United States in the late 1970s and Syria's decision to sign the 1980 Treaty of Friendship and Cooperation with the Soviet Union. The post–Cold War era cases are Egypt's alignment with the West during the 1990–1991 Persian Gulf War and Syria's alignment with the West during this same war. I selected these cases for the following reasons: First, they are other-than-the-usual great power cases we find in the international relations literature. Second, they offer the opportunity to hold many, though not all, variables constant, such as the region, time period, and the proximity to the threat. While the case study method cannot possibly hold all variables constant, it nonetheless offers promise for refining theory over time. Third, the Cold War and post–Cold War cases provide some insight on the effects of the international system on state alignment. Fourth, these cases provide a look at the internal variable of ethnic homogeneity (Egypt) and ethnic divisiveness (Syria). Finally, I use the Middle East because it is the region Walt used in his study, and David used a Middle East case, as well. Examining this region provides an opportunity to further enhance both Walt's and David's conclusions regarding state alignment, while taking a closer look at regional dynamics.

This study adopts David's case study methodology and asks similar questions of each case. The case study approach provides an opportunity to give a rich portrayal of each country's political development and test hypotheses. I rely primarily on secondary sources, which allows to, as David says, "not so much . . . [unearth] previously undisclosed material but . . . [interpret] known events in an original way."[46] Additionally, the research for this project has shown that it is extremely difficult to obtain primary sources because the type of information required from interviews and surveys could put respondents in danger. This point will become more evident in the subsequent chapters on Syria.

A comparison of the two country cases reveals that Egypt has a more homogeneous society than Syria. Halim Barakat describes Egypt as relatively homogeneous, with a society that has a shared social identity and a strong consensus on issues involving national identity.[47] He cites Gamal Hamden, who claims that "Egypt is the strongest force among Arab countries twice: once by its mere size, and once by its absolute homogeneity."[48] He also cites Hussein Fawzi, who notes that Egypt's homogeneity explains the continuity of successive civilizations, which has made Egypt "the most ancient of nations on the surface of the planet."[49] Consequently, ethnicity is not as severe an internal threat as it is in Syria. This difference may cause different state behavior; specifically, we may see omnibalancing at work, resulting in either balancing or bandwagoning behaviors.

A review of Syria during the Cold War will allow us to analyze its alignment behavior in three simultaneous contexts: international, regional, and domestic, while an examination of Syria during the Persian Gulf War lacks the international context of a superpower rivalry. The Syrian case reveals the role of ethnicity in state alignment behavior because of ethnicity's prominence and pervasiveness in Syria's political development. As mentioned earlier, I will measure the severity of ethnic divisiveness based on Horowitz's indicators of severely ethnically divided societies.

Using Egypt and Syria as country cases permits us to hold several variables constant. Both countries are from the same region, their alignment decisions occur during the same time periods, and they have similar proximity to external threats. The key difference is their ethnic makeup: Syria is severely ethnically divided, while Egypt is homogeneous. For this study, a multiethnic state is different from an ethnically divided state. Horowitz's criteria establish Syria as an ethnically divided state, that is, a state in which political development occurs along ethnic lines. The significance of ethnic divisions for state legitimacy arises when group loyalties supercede state loyalties.

INDICATORS OF CAUSALITY

Political scientists would like to develop theories that causally link independent variables with dependent variables. Due to the nature of the case study method, however, the best one can hope for is a correlation, accompanied by a good argument. With this point in mind and the nature of the cases, I use the indicators found on table 1.1 to establish a relationship between the independent variables of ethnicity and legitimacy with foreign policy. This methodology expressed in table 1.1 will help reveal the motivations behind foreign policy decisions. Understanding these motivations will, then, provide insight concerning each state leader's threat perception, thereby shedding light on each state's alignment behavior.

James N. Rosenau introduces linkage theory as a way to understand the relationship between the national and international systems. "We wish to identify and analyze those recurrent sequences of behavior that originate on one side of the boundary between the two types of systems and that become linked to phenomena on the other side."[50] The key is empirically establishing that link. William G. Fleming establishes that link with his investigation of elite attitudes. "Social Science theory would specify, generally, that attitudes and opinions precede behavior, though the two phenomena affect each other."[51] He recognizes the challenge of giving empirical meaning to these elite attitudes, and he successfully meets this challenge by using newspapers, legislative debates, and bulletins to assess elite attitudes.[52]

Ole R. Holsti and John D. Sullivan also use this variable to help assess state and alliance behavior. They suggest the link between regime stability and state behavior concerning alliance policy: "It may be that only leaders relatively secure from internal dissent are likely to undertake external policies which violate important bloc norms."[53] In order to assess the link between domestic politics and alliance policy, they look at several indicators, to include elite attitudes, international trade, foreign aid, and treaties and agreements.[54] They then analyze these data to determine their focus based on five issue areas: territory, status (diplomatic recognition and relations, etc.), security, human resources (education or training, etc.), and nonhuman resources (trade, aid, etc.).[55] The authors determine elite attitudes based on documents, newspapers, press conferences, and speeches. Government documents, journals, trade yearbooks, books, and newspapers provided a significant amount of information on trade, foreign aid, and treaties and agreements.

Table 1.1. Indicators and Issues

| | Indicators | | | |
	Elite Attitudes	Foreign Aid	Trade	Treaties & Agreements
Issues				
Security	Is the concern internal or external security?	Is the concern internal or external security?	Is the concern internal or external security?	Is the concern internal or external security?
Territory	Who is gaining territory?	Who is benefiting?	Who is benefiting?	Who is benefiting?
Status	Who is gaining international vs domestic status?	Who is benefiting?	Who is benefiting?	Who is benefiting?
Human Resources	Who is receiving training or education?	Who is benefiting?	Who is benefiting?	Who is benefiting?
Nonhuman Resources	Who is benefiting?	Who is benefiting?	Who is benefiting?	Who is benefiting?

1. a → b
   indicators   issues
2. b → c
   issues   significance of ethnic divisiveness
3. c → d
   significance of ethnic   foreign policy
   divisiveness

I adopt the same indicators discussed above to determine the extent that ethnic divisiveness and the legitimacy problems it causes affect foreign policy decisions; specifically, this allows us to analyze their effects on alignment decisions. The indicators (a) will help determine the issues (b) involved with each case. The analysis of the issues (b) will help us understand the significance of ethnic divisiveness (c). For example, an examination of the beneficiaries of aid and trade will lead to such questions as: Are aid and trade going to a specific ethnic group? Is all of society benefiting? Who is receiving education and training? Is Asad building up his praetorian guard to ensure that he may continue to repress the Sunni majority? Did Sadat ensure that the poverty-stricken benefited from foreign aid? In sum, is the foreign aid used primarily as a domestic policy tool? Finally, did security from other countries play a major role in the decision process? If so, perhaps Walt's argument is strengthened.

From the start of this project, I realized that if I found ethnic divisiveness as an important factor in state alignment, then it would be interesting to see if a pattern of behavior emerges. However, if this project revealed the relative insignificance of ethnicity vis-à-vis other factors, such as security and poverty, on foreign policy, then that too would be an important finding, especially in the midst of recent ethnic studies.

SIGNIFICANT FINDINGS

I have found that these case studies seem to support the idea that a wealth of legitimacy based on ethnic homogeneity provides the leader with more maneuver space in devising foreign policy. The leaders of both Egypt and Syria seemed cognizant of the impact the ethnic make-up of their countries had on the nature and strength of their respective internal support. Consequently, the quality of Egypt's aligning behavior tended to be strong, intense, and purposeful. The nature of Syria's aligning behavior, however, was cautious, tentative, and weak. Also, it appears that a wealth of legitimacy allows a state to put its national interests to the fore. Egypt realigned in order to address its declining economic situation. Syria, meanwhile, was unable to use other countries to help improve its economy because it had to address internal, as well as external, security concerns. Asad's careful balancing of interests prevented him from making bold policy moves. He had to align with the Soviet Union in 1980 because he had already demonized Egypt and its new partners, the United States and Israel. The Soviet Union gave him the tools to repress or balance against his internal enemy, which on one occasion resulted in the brutal Hama massacre. He could rely on external support to prop up his regime — an excellent example of omnibalancing.

What is interesting to me and what gives us an indication of alignment behavior is a comparison of Syria's alignment with its internal enemies in the post–Cold war era versus in the Cold War era. In the post–Cold war era, regarding the Sunnis, Asad chose to bandwagon, as opposed to his balancing behavior in the Cold War era. In the post–Cold War era, he bandwagoned with the Sunnis in order to build the economy and make inroads to western technology, while bolstering Syrian diplomatic clout on the regional and international stages. One may also argue that he also bandwagoned to broaden the support of his regime. In fact, it appears that he had to convince his own circle of fellow Alawis to accept the peace process. Perhaps Syria found itself without the certainty of superpower support, so it felt it needed to develop self-reliance not only in the economic realm, but also in terms of regime support. Consequently, Asad felt he had to look within for such self-reliance and support. There is cause for optimism in the future, if this kind of behavior is indeed a trend with the current leadership of Bashar Asad.

This point leads to the next issue concerning behavioral similarities for Egypt and Syria. Both countries chose to leave the Arab fold during the Cold War for their respective alignment decisions. However, in the post–Cold War era, both countries made deliberate efforts to renew their regional ties and gain regional status. During the Cold War era, Egypt's national sentiment combined with the status it gained in the international arena via its ties with the United States compensated for any lost regional status. For Syria, its ties with the Soviet Union served to compensate for any regional loss of status, as well. Furthermore, Syria's ties with the Soviets allowed it to gain the necessary military hardware to deal with any domestic unrest, so in Asad's view, he was able to use coercion to gain internal support, although the nature of this internal support is debatable.

Why did both states choose to turn their focus to the region in the post–Cold war era? This change in focus supports Waltz's view that there seems to be a degree of heightened uncertainty in the other-than-bipolar world. During the Cold War era, both countries manipulated the Cold War rivalry for their own purposes to gain aid in some form or another. However, in the post–Cold war era, assistance and even alliances are not so certain. Now countries are looking to their own neighborhoods for future economic, security, and cultural arrangements. While Egypt already had ties with the United States, there was some uncertainty concerning future U.S. aid. The Syrians lost their superpower patron altogether, so it was necessary for Asad to look regionally for assistance.

Not only has a state's region become a more important aspect in the post–Cold War era, but leaders now must cultivate domestic support. Syria has resorted to "carrots" (i.e., bandwagoning) in the form of a gradual economic opening in order to improve its economy by sharing economic power with the Sunnis. It will be interesting to see how long this economic power-sharing arrangement will continue without spilling over into the political realm. Egypt, too, has continued its gradual economic and, to some extent, political liberalization. The question for Egypt is whether economically it is doing too little too late. Will it be able to continue economic reform without causing too much hardship on its people? Will such hardship, then, spill into the political realm? The good news is that perhaps the post–Cold War era, with all its uncertainties, is forcing regimes to fix themselves from within. These fixes may be easier for ethnically homogeneous states because ethnic homogeneity provides an easier context in which to deal with opposition groups. For example, currently the Muslim Brotherhood is a greater threat in Syria because of its ability to exploit ethnic divisions than in Egypt where such divisions are nonexistent. Additionally, fixes that come from within will perhaps have long-term effects, as compared to "band-aid" fixes imposed by the international arena.

In sum, this study reveals that ethnic homogeneity does have an impact on foreign policy. It provides a wealth of legitimacy, thereby allowing that state's leader more maneuver room in foreign policy. Consequently, that leader is able to take risks, which leaders of ethnically divided states are unable to do. Such boldness enables leaders to make strong, purposeful alignments, as opposed to tentative, cautious alignments. In other words, the ability to make bold foreign policy causes the nature of alignments, whether they are balancing- or bandwagoning-type alignments, to be different from those alignments stemming from a cautious, tentative foreign policy. It is this legitimacy, based on ethnic homogeneity, that enables leaders to make bold policy and subsequently strong alignments.

Second, it appears that the degree of uncertainty inherent in the post–Cold War era creates a need for bandwagoning with internal enemies because a state cannot depend on a superpower's support. The imperative now is to find fixes from within, which may in the long-term cause a state to better address its real concerns, such as the economy. This point is responsible for what observers call pragmatism in policy-making. Perhaps this pragmatism bodes well for transitioning regimes on the road to democracy, a topic for further study. Third, in this post–Cold War era, it appears that the region has become more significant than in the Cold War era. Emphasis on regional issues may provide added prestige and functionality to regional organizations, which is perhaps also a topic for further research.

I did find that this study made some theoretical contributions to the international relations and comparative politics literature. Generally, this study contributes to the literature that bridges both these disciplines. The concluding chapter discusses in more detail the study's contributions to theory, both in the international relations and comparative politics realms, and presents a more systematic discussion of the findings.

Chapters 2 and 3 discuss the political development of Egypt and Syria. These chapters establish the historical settings for each state's formation, with the following propositions: Artificial state formation tends to negatively influence national identity, whereas the people of a state based on historical precedence and continuity develop a strong national identity. A state that fosters weak national identity tends to weaken state legitimacy, while a state in which the people have a strong national identity will help to strengthen state legitimacy. Also, these chapters examine the role of ethnicity in each state's political development, which provides an understanding of the degree of each state's ethnic divisiveness. Severely ethnically divided states describe states in which ethnicity permeates all sectors of society, and this ethnic divisiveness becomes most problematic when it permeates the political system. As our theoretical discussion demonstrated, political systems created along ethnic lines reflect an ethnically divided society. Ethnic divisiveness critically degrades the legitimacy of a state because, as noted earlier, a critical component of state legitimacy is society's political identity, loyalty, and sense of political community towards the state. A state which has an ethnically divided society suffers from a loss of legitimacy because its society's loyalties, political identity, and sense of political community do not coincide with the state. States which suffer a loss of legitimacy based on this ethnic divisiveness are in danger of regime instability.

Chapters 4 and 5 are the Cold War cases, and chapters 6 and 7 are the post–Cold War cases. For each case, this study poses the question of how a loss of legitimacy based on ethnic divisiveness affects foreign policy decisions. An analysis of each case using table 1.1 helps answer this question; the table helps us examine the impact of the four indicators—elite attitudes, foreign aid, trade, and treaties and agreements—on five issues—security, territory, status, human resources, and nonhuman resources. The research of these indicators helps determine the importance of internal or domestic security concerns versus external security concerns. It also helps determine the identity of the intended recipients of both human and nonhuman resources. These data, then, should help us understand some of the domestic issues, namely ethnic divisiveness, driving foreign policy decisions. Specifically, this project will help us determine the significance of a state's loss of legitimacy, based on ethnic divisiveness, on foreign policy decisions.

Finally, this study concludes by asking the following questions based on the data collected for each case: When do the external threats of the international system override internal threats? When do the external threats of the region take precedence over external threats of the international system, as well as over internal threats? When do internal threats override external threats, both regionally and internationally? How significant are internal and external threats when compared during the Cold War era vs. the post–Cold War era? Does the existence of internal threats based on ethnic divisiveness suggest a pattern of state alignment decisions, such as balancing or bandwagoning? If we cannot distinguish balancing and bandwagoning behavior, will another pattern of foreign policy decisions emerge based on a loss of legitimacy? As noted earlier, no pattern is an interesting finding, too. Clearly, there are many variables that affect foreign policy. This project will hopefully shed light on the significance of ethnicity as one of these variables.

NOTES

1. Ted Sorenson as cited in a Department of Social Sciences briefing to alumni in June 1999 at USMA, West Point, New York. The citation and discussion of proposed theories is taken from Cindy R. Jebb, "Liberal Democracy versus Terrorism: The Fight for Legitimacy," 2. Paper presented at the International Studies Association National Conference, Chicago, February 23, 2001.

2. The citation and the discussion of the forces of ethnicity, nationalism, etc., is found in Jebb, 3, which cites Bruce Hoffman, "Low-intensity Conflict: Terrorism and Guerilla Warfare in the Coming Decades," in *Terrorism: Roots, Impact, Responses*, ed. Lance Howard (New York: Praeger, 1992), 139.

3. Donald L. Horowitz, *Ethnic Groups in Conflict* (Berkeley: University of California Press, 1985), 12.

4. According to Stephen M. Walt, "When confronted by a significant external threat, states may either balance or bandwagon. *Balancing* is defined as allying with others against the prevailing threat; *bandwagoning* refers to alignment with the source of danger." See Walt, *The Origins of Alliances* (Ithaca: Cornell University Press, 1987), 17. For a brief discussion on Randall Schweller's and Steven David's contributions see this chapter's theory section or refer to appendix I (Theory).

5. For a full accounting of the critique concerning the theories of international relations' great power bias, see appendix I (Theory).

6. Horowitz, *Ethnic Groups in Conflict*, 6.

7. Ibid., xi.

8. Michael Brown, "Introduction" in *The International Dimensions of Internal Conflict*, ed. Michael E. Brown (Cambridge: MIT Press, 1996), 3, as cited in Jebb, 3.

9. Pauline H. Baker and John A. Ausink, "State Collapse and Ethnic Violence: Toward A Predictive Model," *Parameters* 26, no. 1 (Spring 1996): 19–20.

10. Mark Webber, "Coping With Anarchy: Ethnic Conflict and International Organizations in the Former Soviet Union," *International Relations* 18, no. 1 (April 1996): 1–2.

11. Chaim Kaufman, "Possible and Impossible Solutions to Ethnic Civil Wars," *International Security* 20, no. 4 (Spring 1996): 136.

12. Sabrina Ramet, "Eastern Europe's Painful Transition," *Current History* 95, no. 599 (March 1996): 100.

13. Gail Warshofsky Lapidus, "Ethnonationalism and Political Stability: The Soviet Case," *World Politics* 36, no. 4 (July 1984): 556–557, and the quote is cited on p. 556 from P. Paskar's "The Soviet People—A New Social and International Community of People," *Kommunist Moldavii*, no. 12 (December 1982): 82.

14. Iftikhar H. Malik, "World Politics and South Asia: Beginning of an End?" *Journal of South Asian and Middle Eastern Studies* 19, no. 3 (Spring 1996): 43, and Mary E. McIntosh, Martha Abele MacIver, Daniel Abele, and David B. Nolle, "Minority Rights and Majority Rule: Ethnic Tolerance in Romania and Bulgaria," *Social Forces* 73, no. 3 (March 1995): 940.

15. Charles F. Furtado Jr., "Nationalism and Foreign Policy in Ukraine," *Political Science Quarterly* 109, no. 1 (Spring 1994): 90.

16. Levels I, II, and III parallel Kenneth N. Waltz's first, second, and third images, which describe approaches to the study on the causes of war. Level I refers to the study of the nature and behavior of man as a primary cause; level II refers to the study of the nature of the state, and level III refers to the study of the international system. See Kenneth N. Waltz, *Man, the State, and War* (New York: Columbia University Press, 1959).

17. Barry Buzan, *People, States, and Fears: An Agenda For International Security Studies In The Post–Cold War Era* (Boulder, Colorado: Lynne Reinner Publishers, 1991), 97.

18. Ibid., 100–101.

19. Ibid., 101.

20. Ibid., 360.

21. Steven R. David, "Explaining Third World Alignment," *World Politics* 43, no. 2 (January 1991): 233.

22. Eric J. Labs, "Do Weak States Bandwagon?" *Security Studies* 1, no. 3 (1992): 407.

23. Paul Schroeder, "Historical Reality vs NeoRealist Theory," *International Security* 19, no. 1 (Summer 1994) takes Walt to task on p. 114 and makes his claim concerning bandwagoning on p. 117.

24. Ibid., 147–148.

25. Randall L. Schweller, "Bandwagoning for Profit: Bringing the Revisionist State Back In," *International Security* 19, no. 1 (Summer 1991): 82, and Walt, p. 86, on the point of security, and p. 7 for the point concerning different alignment behavior.

26. Ibid., 7.

27. Steven R. David, *Choosing Sides: Alignment and Realignment in the Third World* (Baltimore: The Johns Hopkins University Press, 1991), xi.

28. Ibid., 6.

29. Ibid., 6–7.

30. Ibid., 7.

31. Ibid., 15.

32. For a full discussion on the literature of ethnicity, see appendix I.

33. Robert J. Thompson and Joseph R. Rudolph, "Ethnic Politics and Public Policy in Western Societies: A Framework For Comparative Analysis" in *Ethnicity, Politics, and Development* ed. Dennis L. Thompson and Dov Ronen (Boulder, Colorado: Lynne Reinner, 1986), 27–28.

34. Horowitz, 6–7.

35. Ibid., 8.

36. Ibid.

37. Horowitz claims that ethnic divisiveness can threaten the cohesion of the state in ibid., 12.

38. Patrick Seale, *Asad: The Struggle For The Middle East* (Berkeley: University of California Press, 1988), 172.

39. Daniel Pipes, "Syria Beyond the Peace Process," *The Washington Institute Policy Papers*, no. 40 (Washington, D.C.: The Washington Institute for Near East Policy, 1996): 11.

40. Ibid., 12–13.

41. Fouad Ajami, "The Sorrows of Egypt," *Foreign Affairs*, 74, no. 5 (September/October 1995), 88.

42. David Easton, "A Reassessment of the Concept of Political Support," *British Journal of Political Science* 5, no. 4 (October 1975): 451.

43. Michael C. Hudson, *Arab Politics: The Search for Legitimacy* (New Haven: Yale University Press, 1977), 4.

44. Easton, "A Reassessment of the Concept of Political Support," 452.

45. Max Weber, "Politics As A Vocation," in *From Max Weber: Essays in Sociology*, ed. H. H. Gerth and C. Wright Mills (New York: Oxford University Press, 1946), 78–79.

46. David, 27.

47. Halim Barakat, *The Arab World: Society, Culture, and State* (Berkeley: University of California Press, 1993), 16–17.

48. Ibid., 16.

49. Ibid.

50. James N. Rosenau, *Linkage Politics: Essays on the Convergence of National and International Systems* (New York: The Free Press, 1969), 44–45.

51. William G. Fleming, "Sub-Saharan Africa: Case Studies of International Attitudes and Transactions of Ghana and Uganda," in *Linkage Politics*, 120.

52. Ibid., 97, 120.

53. Ole R. Holsti and James D. Sullivan, "National–International Linkages: France and China As Nonconforming Alliance Members," in *Linkage Politics*, 154.

54. Holsti and Sullivan are also examining the intra-bloc environment as a variable linked to alliance policy. Another indicator is action data, which describes France and China's actions over a period of time toward other countries. More information on this point can be found on pp. 169–174.

55. Holsti and Sullivan, 169. Also, the idea of using table 1.1 is from these authors, although I did make some modifications.

Chapter Two

The Political Development of Egypt

The purpose of this chapter is to determine the degree of ethnic pervasiveness in Egyptian society and, more specifically, Egyptian politics. A multiethnic state does not necessarily mean that the state suffers from ethnic divisiveness. What does indicate ethnic divisiveness is the evidence of reinforcing cleavages which so strongly builds loyalties towards a particular group that it diffuses loyalties to the state. How do we assess the existence of such cleavages? As I noted earlier, I will use Horowitz's criteria to establish the presence of these reinforcing cleavages and, thus, ethnic divisiveness, by examining the extent ethnicity permeates society. This chapter will assess the degree ethnicity permeates political development because as Horowitz concludes, ethnic divisions are sharpest when ethnicity shapes the political arena.

As discussed earlier, ethnicity is not an exact science. As a start point, therefore, this chapter will use the characteristics developed in chapter 1 to define ethnicity: kinship, religion, and language. While I will use these characteristics as guidelines, we must not lose sight of two important points. First, as mentioned above, the critical notion about ethnicity is whether or not it creates reinforcing cleavages: does it permeate society and politics, and, therefore, undermine societal members' loyalties to the state? Second, ethnic identity is not necessarily static. It must be assessed in a historical context. Identities can change due to such phenomena as migrations, conquests, or political manipulation.[1]

This chapter begins with a brief discussion of the people of Egypt as a contributing factor to Egyptian homogeneity. Then, I will review the history of the modern state, which will reveal Egypt's historical continuity as a state and society. This continuity helped foster a national identity. Finally, my discussion on Egyptian political development will show that it was not influenced by ethnicity. We cannot ignore other divisions revealed in this discussion, because there are, notably today, under Mubarak, ideological, and some would argue class, divisions. My argument, however, is that due to the lack of ethnic cleavages, there is still great loyalty to the state. Because of Egypt's ethnic homogeneity, loyalty to the state is strong and, therefore, lends legitimacy to the state. Chapter 3 will examine Syria in the same manner, thereby demonstrating its ethnic divisiveness and its society's subsequent lack of loyalty to the state, leading to that state's illegitimacy.

Before we explore the people of Egypt, it is necessary to briefly review the previous chapter's discussion of new institutionalism, because I use an institutional approach to determine the extent to which ethnicity permeates politics in Egypt versus Syria. While there are many arguments for and against institutionalism's viability as an approach to the study of political science, it will help us understand the extent of ethnicity's permeation in each state's political development. As James G. March and Johan P. Olsen claim, an institutional approach cannot be ignored, especially as we examine political life in the context of society.

> This resurgence of concern with institutions is a cumulative consequence of the modern transformation of social institutions and persistent commentary from observers of them. Social, political, and economic institutions have become larger, considerably more complex and resourceful, and prima facie more important to collective life.[2]

Consequently, "the organization of political life matters."[3]

As mentioned earlier, Donald C. Williams explains the importance of the institutionalist approach in examining weak states, such as Egypt and Syria. He explains that institutions

> are viewed as collections of interrelated rules and routines that define appropriate or rational action in the larger context of norms and values. . . . In summary, state-society relations are really an encounter between a structural arrangement of rule-bearing institutions, of which the state is only one.[4]

This institutional approach will be useful for understanding ethnicity as a factor in the political development of our cases. Legitimacy is a key ingredient for regime stability, and when ethnic loyalties coincide with national loyalties, then that sense of a shared political community and values is a great commodity for the regime. Conversely, when these loyalties are in conflict, then the regime is in a tenuous position. A regime in such a position affects its leader's decisions, policies, and actions much differently than does a legitimate, stable regime. In the chapters that follow, I will analyze these differences as they affect the international system. For now, we must establish ethnic homogeneity versus ethnic divisiveness for each case.

March and Olsen remark that "It is interesting to suggest that political institutions and society are interdependent, but that statement needs to find a richer theoretical expression."[5] While my purpose here is to demonstrate ethnic homogeneity and ethnic divisiveness for Egypt and Syria, respectively, the examination of these cases may also help provide insight to the theoretical formulation of institutionalism, as with the concepts of legitimacy and ethnicity. As background, this chapter will describe the people and the formation of the state and discuss the state's political development using a modified version of Roy C. Macridis and Steven L. Burg's institutional framework.[6] This framework will help reveal the degree to which politics does or does not center around ethnicity.

PEOPLE

The population of Egypt is 58 million. There are a small number of Bedouin Arabs, who live in the eastern and western deserts of the Sinai, and fifty thousand to one hundred thousand Nubians who live along the Nile River in upper Egypt.[7] Interestingly, the State Department's *Background Notes* lists Egyptians as both a nationality and an ethnic group. It lists the Nubians and Bedouin Arabs as Egypt's other ethnic groups. Additionally, Arabic is the official language, and 90 percent of the people are Sunnis and 10 percent are Coptic Christians.[8] All Egyptians speak Arabic, with the Nubians and isolated Berbers as the exceptions, and Islam is the state religion.[9] Why are Egyptians listed as both a nationality and an ethnicity? Perhaps it has something to do with the coincidental history of Egyptian society and state—the coincidental development of language, culture, religion, and kinship, as well as state development.

Egypt has existed as a unified state for more than five thousand years, and Egyptian society dates back even further to the pharaohs. Egypt in Arabic is Misr, which means civilization or metropolis.[10] Egyptians, long ago, acquired the sense of being one people, who established a unique social cohesiveness.[11] According to P. J. Vatikiotis, Egypt represents one of the world's most ancient civilizations.[12] One of the themes discussed in Vatikiotis's book is " . . . the continuity in Egyptian society from ancient times to this day."[13] Vatikiotis calls Egypt a "geographical phenomenon." It is at the meeting point of two continents, strongly attached to the Nile River. "To speak of the living

Egypt, therefore, is to speak of the 15,000 square miles upon which 98 per cent of Egyptians live, work, procreate, and die—an area slightly less than five per cent of the total surface of geographical Egypt."[14] He calls "Egyptianity" a product of Egypt's conservatism, isolationism, and well entrenched and traditional social structure. The basis of this Egyptianity is Egypt's rural nation, whose existence has been regulated by the flow of the Nile. Egyptians formed the first unified nation known to history.[15]

Vatikiotis links this Egyptianity to Egypt's unity and characteristic response to foreign influences as having nothing to do with any deliberative thought or action by the Egyptian people. Their common suffering and persistent ties to their traditions, beliefs, arts, and crafts are at the core of their shared historical experience.[16] Anwar Sadat echoed this sentiment. He described the continuity of the Egyptian identity in his autobiography by stating that:

> our cultural roots are alive, as vigorous as ever after more than 7,000 years. Those who are surprised by what we do cannot simply understand this fact. They cannot grasp the real nature of a people who are working for a modern civilization comparable to the one they erected thousands of years ago in freedom and peace.[17]

Furthermore, Ali E. Hillal Dessouki describes the homogeneous nature of Egyptian society and provides a preview to my argument. He claims that:

> There are no fundamental minority cleavages to constrain foreign policy-makers and limit their options. The one major area of anxiety is the Copts' concern about the implementing of Islamic law in Egypt and the status of Copts in an Islamic state.[18]

Sadat relied on this ethnic homogeneous society as he pursued a "purposeful foreign policy," which was not possible for other Arab countries due to their ethnic divisiveness.[19]

I will save the development of the link between domestic and foreign policy for later. For now, it is important that we further establish Egypt's homogeneous nature.[20] The next section examines Egypt's historical state-making process, which further influenced its society's ethnically homogeneous nature. Historical precedence and continuity reinforced the development of Egyptian identity and sense of unity.

BACKGROUND TO THE CREATION OF THE MODERN STATE

I will not dwell on the history of the Ottoman Empire, because I cannot do it justice here, and it is beyond the scope of this study. I only mention it as a means to help illuminate why the Middle East is such a diverse, complex region and to provide a context for the creation of Egypt as a modern state. In the years 1516–1517, the armies of Sultan Selim I captured Syria, Palestine, and Egypt. Ottoman Turkey reached its peak in 1683 when it stretched from Vienna to Iran and southern Russia, North Africa (as far west as Morroco), and the eastern Red Sea coast. The Ottoman Empire included a diversity of groups: Turks, Tartars, Arabs, Kurds, Turkomans, Berbers, Mamluks, Bosnians, Albanians, Greeks, Bulgarians, Hungarians, South Slavs, Rumanians, Armenians, Copts, Georgians, and Jews. Ruling over these groups was the Ottoman hierarchy or Ruling Institution.[21] The sultan was the ruling head of this institution, and the whole government structure depended on him. "The sultan was the crown of the empire. What he did or failed to do influenced every group, not merely the governing hierarchy.[22]

There are three significant periods, which greatly affected the development of modern Egypt. First, there was the Arabic-Islamic conquest in the seventh century. This conquest changed the predominantly Christian Egypt to Islam, as well as changing the language from Coptic and Greek to Arabic. Second, the non–Arab-Islamic conquest between the twelfth and sixteenth centuries (Ayyubids, Mamluks, and Ottomans) was significant because it was a time when Islam grew, and Egypt became the center of Islamic power and civilization. Finally, the period of the European invasions beginning with Napoleon in 1798 was an important influence. The significance of Napoleon was that he discredited the ruling Mamluk Beys, and he introduced France's revolutionary ideas.[23]

Additionally, the French presence was a catalyst for Muhammad Ali's impact on Egypt. Ali, who ruled Egypt from 1805 to 1848, first came to Egypt as an officer in the Albanian detachment of the Turkish expeditionary force, which fought the French.[24] Muhammad Ali, according to Professor Henry Dodwell, " . . . brought Egyptians into closer touch with Europe through his military, educational, economic and other measures, and thus [laid] the foundation of a modern Egyptian state."[25] Muhammad Ali is credited for having laid the foundations for the creation of Egypt as a modern state. He helped build a society whose educated members wanted to emulate many aspects of European civilization. They wanted to establish the basis of modern government, business, and an education system that paved the way for instruction in the modern arts and sciences.[26] According to Nubar Pasha, Muhammad Ali's key role for Egypt's statehood was his ability to establish equality between Christians and Muslims.[27] "In short, Muhammad Ali gave Egypt the organizational basis and the human cadres for the emergence of the modern state."[28]

Egypt's growth as a nation-state continued as the opportunities for politics opened to the notables or agricultural middle class. This opening occurred in three stages. First, the notables entered the National Assembly beginning in

1866, as well as administrative positions outside the village. Experiences outside the village broadened their political aspirations and contacts. In my view, this broadening is critical as it helps foster a national, rather than a village-based identity. Second, the expanding role of the state, especially during the British occupation, occurred through these notables. Finally, notables became critical during competitive elections beginning with the 1923 Constitution for parties seeking mass support.[29]

WESTERN INFLUENCE

Scholars cannot study the Middle East and the West separately because their histories and development are inextricably linked. The Middle East often reflected or influenced the relations among the Western powers; it has been a significant region for the imperialist designs of the West. Undoubtedly, the destinies of the West and Middle East have been linked throughout modern historical times.[30] On the eve of World War I, the Middle East was divided into four spheres: the Ottoman Empire was under German influence, Egypt under British influence, southern and Persian Gulf coasts of the Arabian peninsula under British rule, and Iran was divided between Russian and British spheres of influence. At this time, Western ideas of nationalism began to take root.[31]

After the military failure of the Crusades against the Muslims, the European powers established business relations in the Middle East. The Middle East was a source of exotic fruits, silk, cotton, and spices. Enclaves of merchants, especially from Italy, settled in the Middle East and established semiautonomous settlements. Other European powers challenged Italy's Middle East trade monopoly. Portugal made its first challenge in the fifteenth century. Portuguese explorers Prince Henry the Navigator, Bartholomew Diaz, and Vasco de Gama helped establish a new water route around the Cape of Good Hope, which propelled Portuguese trade and influence in the Middle East.

In the sixteenth century, France joined the fray and developed economic and religious interests in the area. France became a dominant influence and established semi-permanent settlements there. It worked closely with the Ottomans to ensure that their respective subjects could easily pursue their trade interests. Where France had difficulty establishing an economic foothold, the Church went to work. For example, when the French East India Company failed to open up Iran, Cardinal Richelieu encouraged several missions to the area. France became the protector of Lebanon's Maronites. By the seventeenth century, Levantine trade with France was three-fold that of British trade.[32]

BRITISH INFLUENCE

The British occupied Egypt in 1883. This time period is significant because, "To appreciate the legitimizing potential of nationalism in Egypt today, it is important to note the intensified and broadened sense of Egyptian identity that has emerged since the 1880s."[33] From 1883 to 1914, Egypt enjoyed an efficient Egyptian administration, very little corruption, and economic prosperity. Egypt also had a Legislative Assembly, which although it had limited powers, served as a forum for discussion among the elite of educated Egyptians. Secular reformists began to emerge, who called for political emancipation through a gradual process and negotiation with Britain. Among the leading reformists were Ahmad Lufti al-Sayyid and Saad Zaghlul. Up until 1882, Egypt was an independent state ruled by the Muhammad Ali dynasty. It did provide the Sultan with a tribute payment, but it acted as an autonomous state. The British occupation ended all direct ties between Egypt and Turkey. While the British did not initially intend on a permanent occupation, increasing Anglo-German rivalry led to a less than temporary British presence in Egypt.[34]

On December 18, 1914, Britain declared the status of Egypt to be a protectorate. As a result, Britain permanently severed Egypt from Turkey. During the war, the British placed great demands on Egypt and its people in order to support the increased military presence of British, Australian, and other Imperial troops. The peasants, lower classes, and unemployed were the hardest hit, as the prices of consumer goods rose and profiteers took advantage of the situation. The war caused nationalist feelings among a broader spectrum of the population than ever before as many people became disillusioned with the British. At the same time, Britain viewed Egypt as strategically increasing in value, especially after the fall of the Ottoman Empire.[35]

The new leaders of the independence movement viewed political independence as a means of attaining money and power. These new leaders were financiers, landowners, entrepreneurs, etc., and their leader was Saad Zaghlul. He is the 'Father of Egyptians' and the founder of the Wafd Party, the most effective mass party in Egypt's history. The leaders of the Wafd saw the connection between economics and politics. After many frustrating negotiating attempts with the British, the Wafd had secured country-wide support by March of 1919. The Wafd claimed to be the sole representative and spokesman for the Egyptians, especially at the resignation of Egypt's Prime Minister Rushdi. On February 22, 1922, the British unilaterally issued the Declaration of the British Government to Egypt. The Declaration, while acknowledging Egypt's independence, contained four conditions: that Britain still maintain influence over its communications in the area, provide for the defense of Egypt against foreign aggression, protect foreign interests and minorities, and control the Sudan. The Wafd was opposed to these conditions.[36]

POST–WORLD WAR I

The Constitution of 1923 had the potential to liberalize Egypt. It established that two-thirds of the parliament could override the King's veto. However, neither the King nor the British were willing to abide by the Constitution. The King's reactions to forces opposing both him and the British were rigged elections, limited freedom of the press, assembly and speech, and bribery. This situation did not encourage party politics, however some of the parties were part of the problem. The first party was Mustafa Kamil's National Party. It concentrated on a foreign issue, eliminating British control. The Party was not sensitive or interested in social problems. The elites came from well-to-do families and were not interested in the plight of the fellahin.

The Wafd Party was the first truly nationalist party in 1918, under the leadership of Saad Zaghul. Its leadership drew more broadly from society—professionals, landowners, industrialists, intelligentsia. Its focus, too, was on ending British control and limiting the powers of the King. The Wafd Party, after the Anglo-Egyptian Treaty of 1936 helped the party realize somewhat its first goal, divided into several factions. The factions split, based on industrialist or landlord interests, and pro- and anti-British sentiments. Other parliamentary parties that did not recruit broad support included the pro-British and pro-royalist Constitutional Liberal Party and the Union Party. There also existed several anti-parliamentary groups, the most notable being the Muslim Brotherhood.

The army coup of 1952 was designed to wipe away an ineffective and unrepresentative system. While the small group of officers headed by Gamal Abdel Nassar, with General Mohammed Nagib as the intended figurehead, easily toppled the existing regime, the task of establishing a regime proved more difficult. The new regime's goal was to deal with Egypt's social problems while being held accountable by the populace.

Initially, the Egyptian Revolutionary Council tried to build its support on those political parties closest in ideology. The Council developed ties to the Muslim Brotherhood. However, the old parties were corrupt and the newer ones had their own ambitions. As a result, Nassar organized his own political party while banning all other parties. He founded the Liberation Rally in 1953. Its goal was to build support for the regime, " . . . mold a 'new' Egyptian individual and a united, proud, and productive Egyptian society, and mobilize the nation for raising its standard of living."[37]

This discussion of Egypt's historical setting for state formation shows that Egypt has had a history of tying the physical boundaries of the state to its national identity. This historical tie has led to a national identity that bolsters state legitimacy. The next section will use an institutional lens to demonstrate that ethnicity did not play a central role in the development of Egypt's political institutions. First, I will describe the institutional framework, which will help us discern the extent of ethnicity's pervasiveness in politics or lack thereof.

THE INSTITUTIONAL FRAMEWORK

As mentioned earlier, I will modify Macridis and Burg's approach in my analysis of Egypt's and Syria's political development. Specifically, I will show the extent of ethnic permeation in each state's political institutions. Macridis and Burg break down the political regime and its institutions into four major categories: the organization of command, organization of consent, configuration of interests, and organization of rights. First, the organization of command includes the executive, legislature, and judiciary. Their relationship is described by a constitution, and they are the loci for governing. According to Gaetano Mosca, there is "a class that rules and a class that is ruled." The class that rules is "always the less numerous, performs all political functions, monopolizes power and enjoys the advantages that power brings." There are elite in every regime, and as Macridis and Burg tell us,

> the study of the elite will almost always provide us with insight into perhaps the most important characteristic of the command structure: the distribution and the limits of power. Just how much influence elites have over the authoritative decision-making process in any given regime is generally reflected in the organization of consent, the configuration of interests, and the organization of rights; in short, in the relationship between state and society.[38]

Consequently, my examination will center on the elite.

Understanding the elite in our cases is critical for understanding the role of ethnicity, because Egypt and Syria are forms of one-man rule. In each case, the man (and his inner circle) is "bigger" than the institutions themselves. We will examine the role of the elites in the contexts of the organization of command described above, as well as in the organization of consent, which describes how a regime elicits support. To better understand this point, I will examine the institutions of socialization, representation, participation, and mobilization. This examination will center on political parties as well as on ideology in terms of each leader's use of it to gain consensus and mobilize support. I will discuss the configuration of interests, which deal with interests articulated through organizations within a political regime. The organization most significant, in each case, is the military. Finally, I will briefly discuss the organization of rights in terms of individual, social, and political rights.[39] While I refrain from making a value judgment on the type of regime found in each of my cases, I believe that this discussion provides a springboard for students of democratization.

Additionally, because each case involves one-man rule, it is difficult to discuss each political institution separately. It is necessary instead to understand the relationship of each institution, i.e., the military, political party, rights, etc., to the leader. My discussion of Egypt centers on Nassar, Sadat, and Mubarak because of each man's central role in all the other institutions and subsequent political development of his regime. Obviously, Asad is the central figure in chapter 3's discussion of Syria's political development. The purpose for discussing the political development of each regime is solely to discover the extent or lack of ethnicity's permeation in the institutions of each country's political regime.

BACKGROUND TO THE COUP: POST–WORLD WAR II

Before we examine the political institutions of Egypt's political development since Nassar's takeover, it is important to understand the context of his coup, that is, the discontent that stemmed from the country's economic woes. The small but growing middle class was increasingly dissatisfied with the country's political and social conditions; it resented concentration of power in the few, namely landowners, which represented less than 1 percent of the population, and the king. Landowners owning more than two hundred acres were most closely associated with the king. The policies of those in power dissatisfied the nationalists who wanted complete British withdrawal. The loss in the 1948 war against Palestine only inflamed the nationalists. Domestically, the powerful upper class, who lived in the city, lost touch with 80 percent of the population, who lived in the rural areas. Additionally, King Farouk, renowned for his blatantly opulent lifestyle, only served to highlight the have and have-not gap. Egypt's peasants were among the most poverty stricken in the world with per capita income of $55–$65.[40] Doreen Warriner describes their living conditions: "To speak of housing conditions is to exaggerate. . . . The fellaheen inhabit mud huts, built by making a framework of sticks, usually cotton sticks, and plastering it with mud. The hut is in a small enclosed yard, where the family and the buffalo live together, with a small inner room with a roof but no window and a sleeping roof where chickens, rabbits and goats are kept."[41] Disease was rampant. A major factor for this poverty was the tremendous population growth rate of more than one-half million a year.

By the end of the war, the leading political party, the Wafd, lost a great deal of popularity and strength. To regain its power, the Wafd pushed a program focused on getting the British out. The party was somewhat successful, but it could not deal with the country's problems. The military was the only other group capable of action against the old regime.

Until 1936, the army commander-in-chief was British. The Egyptian army was British trained, and merit was not a criterion for promotion. The army attracted lower class youths for its educational opportunities. The Military Academy especially offered great opportunities for these people. It was at this Academy that young officers first came together to share ideas and resentments toward the British. Some of these officers who graduated in 1938, under the leadership of Gamal Abdel Nassar began to plan strategy for tackling the country's woes. The lost war in 1948 served to build support for what is now known as the Free Officers Society. The lost war revealed the ineptitude of the regime.[42]

In 1950, however, the Wafd returned to power in the first free election held in eight years. The King had banished the Wafd Party in 1944, and in the interim eight minority governments attempted to govern. The 1950 Wafd victory instilled some optimism for parliamentary government, since many felt that a majority government would be able to restore some stability and prosperity. Unfortunately, corruption, intraparty feuding, a heavy-handed manner towards political opponents, and appeasement towards the monarchy all served to heighten acceptance for nonconstitutional rule.[43]

In July 1951, the editor-in-chief, Ihsan Abd al-Quddus, of the prominent independent weekly *Ruz al-Yusuf*, proclaimed Egypt a

> country of failure. We in Egypt believe in failure and worship those who fail," he wrote, pointing specifically to Nahhas [Wafd Party leader] and his chief ministers. "Woe to the man of talent who looks to matters with a serious eye and works with determination to succeed. . . . Woe to him, for the doors are shut in front and in back of him, oppressive power pursues him wherever he settles and false charges follow him every day."[44]

Key members of the population were ready for an alternative, even if that alternative was military rule, because of the Wafd's speedy destruction of public trust and the public's growing cynicism towards politics.[45]

GAMAL ABDEL NASSAR: THE INTEGRATION OF ELITES, POLITICAL PARTIES AND THE MILITARY IN ONE MAN

Nassar attempted to cure the country's woes by establishing himself as the focal point of all power. His mostly bloodless coup occurred on July 23, 1952. King Farouk was exiled, and the coup received great support from nearly all political groups to include the Wafd, the Liberal Constitutionalists, Nationalists,

Socialists, Communists, and the Muslim Brotherhood. Initially, the Revolutionary Command Council (RCC) allowed civil authorities to fill top governmental posts, but the RCC, which was the executive committee of the Free Officers Society, soon put its own members in these top positions.

In 1954, Nassar triumphed over General Neguib as the RCC dominating leader after much dispute concerning the direction of the nation. Neguib wanted to reform the existing political institutions and Nassar wanted to create a new political, economic, and social structure for Egypt. Nassar banned all political parties, established censorship, liquidated all opposition, and centralized all power in the RCC. Additionally, he declared a three-year transition period to prepare for the eventual democratic institutions. In place of political parties, the RCC established the Liberal Rally to organize and coordinate the efforts of the people. It actually helped Nassar to control students, labor, and other groups.[46]

Under the monarchy, the nationalists had supported labor militancy because it contributed to the struggle against foreign economic influence. After July 23, 1952, however, the RCC took a different view towards labor militancy. The RCC viewed it as unpatriotic and harmful to national economic development. Moreover, the RCC was better able to put down strikes and other working class protests than the previous regime because of its newly found popularity.[47]

The main goals of the new regime were securing national independence and promoting economic construction. While the RCC did want to improve the lot of the working class and other members of society, its vision for national economic prosperity did not coincide with or complement many of the workers' demands, especially their possible independent role in politics. Additionally, some members of the new regime were blatantly antagonistic towards the interests of the working class.[48]

So why was Nassar popular? Perhaps the people, as already mentioned, were ready for any alternative after King Farouk. Nassar brought with him his own brand of charisma. He was the first real Egyptian to rule Egypt in a thousand years; he came from a village, spoke the language, and lived as the common people. Raymond Hinnebusch claimed that Nassar's "charisma and coercion combined to consolidate a remarkably stable regime possessing a tremendous fund of political capital. Thus Nasir won a free hand to transform Egypt from above."[49] But this achievement had its pitfalls. Namely, the Nassar regime did not feel compelled to create viable political institutions or eliminate its authoritarian rule for two reasons. First the civilians, who struggled with the Free Officers for some authority within the regime, harbored some distrust for the Nassar regime. Second, Nassar translated the tremendous initial popularity into a mandate.[50]

Nassar's regime consisted of an immense authoritarian-bureaucratic structure, headed by a powerful presidency. Together, the power of the office and Nassar's tremendous drive, energy, intellect, and endurance combined to create an activist, intervening, and innovative force. The president's power superceded all other political institutions.[51]

The elite surrounding Nassar as vice presidents, premiers, or ministerial or party officials, primarily came from the military. The outer circle of elites consisted of apolitical civilian professionals and technocrats who provided the inner circle of military elites with the information they needed to implement the regime's policies. The new inner elite represented a marked change from past elites. The king's elites came from the upper class and landlord-lawyers. The leaders of the Free Officers came from modest social backgrounds, mostly from the middle class with roots in the villages and populist outlooks. The technocratic and civilian officials, while having roots in the upper class, were only promoted based on merit.

Participation in the policy process was not institutionalized; Nassar dominated the process. Nassar did work to get a consensus among his inner circle of Free Officers. There were divisions, however, among the inner circle based on personal and ideological grounds. Some officers favored conservative Islamic ideas, some favored technocratic approaches, and others took to left-wing approaches. There were differences regarding Pan-Arabic and Egypt-first philosophies. There were conflicts over bureaucratic jurisdictions. Finally, divisions occurred between the Free Officers and the civilian technocrats as some officers became distrustful of the civilian officials. With all these conflicts, Nassar still had the first and last word. He was able to maneuver through these conflicts and even managed to use them for his own benefit. Nassar centralized and personalized his power.[52]

The bureaucracy consisted of the armed forces, ministries, and a huge public sector. The middle elite who managed these organizations expanded bureaucratic and educational opportunities for the middle and lower classes, thereby democratizing recruitment. While the new regime wanted to eliminate corruption and lethargy rampant during the old regime, the expanding bureaucracy became its own worst enemy. It fell victim to inefficiency, ineffectiveness, and unresponsiveness. The government became the alternative employment, and officials soon exhibited laziness and a lack of a work ethic and motivation. The result was that the political elite did not trust to delegate authority below them, and bureaucratic officials were not used to accepting responsibility. With all these problems, the bureaucracy managed to handle some projects, such as the management of the Suez Canal and the building of the High Dam rather well.[53]

Nassar did make an attempt to create institutions of participation. There was a parliament, but the presidency overwhelmed it. Nassar could legislate by decree, and his cabinet was responsible to him, not to parliament. Parliament did not recruit elites or serve to speak for the people. In 1962, Nassar built the Arab Socialist Union, but it never performed party functions. Interest groups became part of the corporatist structure of the state, and the state manipulated them. Finally, the media became Nassar's tool for shaping public opinion. "The unchecked coercive powers of the regime, combined with a multitude of structural controls and the great personal legitimacy of the leader put a virtual end to pluralistic politics from 1954 onward."[54]

The ideology of Nassarism consisted of several aspects to help shape support from the people. First, he used the language of Islam, even though he and his Free Officers supported a more reformist version of Islam which endorsed their program of secularization and modernization. He appealed to the idea of Arab nationalism and unity.[55] Albert Hourani explains that "Arab unity had been accepted by previous governments of Egypt as an important strand in foreign policy, but the separate historical development of Egypt and the distinctive culture which had grown up in the Nile valley had kept it somewhat distant in its feelings from its neighbors."[56] Nassar wanted Egypt to be the leader of the Arab world, and he focused his leadership on a social revolution based on state ownership and the redistribution of income. Nassar called his ideology "Arab Socialism" which he explained in his National Charter of 1962:

> Revolution is the way in which the Arab nation can free itself of its shackles, and rid itself of the dark heritage which has burdened it. . . . [It] is the only way to overcome underdevelopment which has been forced on it by suppression and exploitation. . . . Ages of suffering and hope have finally produced clear objectives for the Arab struggle. These objectives, which are true the true expression of Arab consciousness, are freedom, socialism, and unity. . . . Freedom today means that of the country and of the citizen. Socialism has become both a means and an end: sufficiency and justice. The road to unity is the popular call for the restoration of a single nation.[57]

Nassar claimed that political democracy first required social democracy, which was public ownership of industry, trade, and public services. He called for equality for all men and women, classes, and Arab countries.[58] His regime stressed social rights over individual rights. It is important to note, however, that his call for equality was based on his concern for class or economic equality. His country's woes were economically based, and the gap between the rich and the poor emphasized his nation's economic plight. Because his plan called for reform from the top, he monopolized the regime's political power at the expense of all other political institutions, as mentioned above, which demonstrates his regime's lack of support for political rights.

Nassarism developed its strongest support from Egyptians and Arabs in general on the regional level. At this regional level, Nassar derived legitimacy that still survives him and continues to mobilize political movements in other Arab states.[59] Nassar exploited the ideas of Arabism, anti-Westernism, and nonalignment to foster Arab unity through diplomacy, propaganda, and insurgency aid throughout the Middle East.[60]

Nassar helped foster a national identity, which was already established due to Egypt's long history as a viable nation-state.[61] While the goals of the Nassar regime were the end of feudalism, the end of monopolization and the dominance of capital over the government, the end of imperialism, the establishment of social justice, the establishment of a strong army, and the creation of democracy, the real mark of Nassarism was its revival of national pride.[62]

Nassar achieved a great deal in spite of the regime's problems. He gained British withdrawal and the seizure of the Suez Canal, which established him and Egypt as the leader of the Arab world with reduced Western influence. As leader of the Arab world, Nassar was able to secure assistance from both the East and the West. Although Nassar's Egypt failed to become the "Prussia" of the Arab world, it did influence the relative independence of the Middle Eastern states from overt Western control.[63]

Nassar shifted economic policies with his goal of economic modernization. His capitalist strategy conflicted with his nationalist foreign policy, populist orientation, and authoritarian rule. Consequently, he embarked on the economic policy called "Arab Socialism." This policy nationalized banks, foreign trade, domestic trade, and a great deal of industry. Nassar established egalitarian policies aimed at opportunities to all segments of society and narrowing class gaps. Private industry was still a player, but these initiatives served to deeply entrench the state in the economy.[64]

The positive aspects of the Nassar regime also proved to be its downfall. The new state bourgeoisie, the heart of the regime, had state power and control over the production of national wealth. Additionally, members of this group did not embrace the ideologies of Nassar. Even some of the Free Officers became "embourgeoisied," rather than embracing Nassar's socialism. The regime also suffered from patrimonialization, which the lack of political institutions fostered. Perhaps the best way to view this patrimonialization is to realize that Nassar was able to use his

authority as one means for running the country. . . . It was, for most of the time, a function of this strangely personal relationship between the [leader] and the people, and not between the [leader], his ministers, bureaucrats and members of parliament, on the one hand, and the masses on the other.[65]

These two phenomena—embourgeoisment and patrimonialization— undermined the regime. Nassar could not overcome the imbalance between resources and commitments. Egypt's poverty and the inefficient and corrupt bureaucracy prevented Nassar from accumulating the required resources for his commitments. Many of these commitments stemmed from his activist foreign policy and the large army required to support it. The final event which ensured the end of the regime was the 1967 defeat by Israel.[66]

ANWAR EL-SADAT: A DEBATABLE ATTEMPT AT BREAKING THE MONOPOLY OF POWER

The political structure which evolved from 1952 to 1970 was marked by a lack of political competitiveness, centralization of power, priority of mobilization rather than participation, primacy of the executive over the legislature, and repression of political dissent. Output institutions (military, police, bureaucracy) were supreme over input institutions (interest groups and political organizations). Political leaders had free reign; the state attempted to penetrate many groups and organizations of society, which would otherwise make up civil society.[67] Just how much Sadat changed this system is debatable. As I will discuss below, he attempted to liberalize the regime, but for myriad reasons, he was not always successful nor that willing to establish these reforms.

Sadat inherited from Nassar a political system in crisis, a demoralized people, and a divided elite. The people had come to rely on the leadership of Nassar, and their grief displayed at his funeral showed how lost they felt without him. The devastating years after 1967, however, readied the Egyptian people for a change. Nassar did leave Sadat a means to cope; his charismatic legitimacy lent the regime enough authority to give it staying power in the face of crisis. The office of the president was well established, as were the habits of compliance born from a bureaucratic state.[68]

The presidency under Sadat remained a powerful force. The key to the power of the presidency was its authority to dismiss and appoint the prime minister, the cabinet, and the chiefs of the armed forces. In a highly bureaucratized state, presidential patronage included a much greater scope of positions in the public sector, media, judiciary, and party. The president could reshape institutions and change the conditions of political participation. These powers enabled the president to act without much restraint because the political infrastructure was incapable of checking his power.[69]

Sadat's first statements as president indicated that he was going to be a president for all the people. Sadat wanted to share responsibility, and he claimed that "the people must not give their full confidence to just one person after Abdel Nassar."[70] Initially, Sadat claimed that the only way to fill the vacuum left by Nassar was "by the rule of the institution representing the unity of the popular forces."[71] He tried to broaden the scope of rights. For example, while Sadat did not remove government control from the universities, he did promise in 1971 to respect their independence. This environment encouraged academic productivity, namely the proliferation of political development research of Egypt itself.[72]

The 1970s under Sadat, however, brought two big changes. First, the Sadat regime greatly increased the civilianization of the political elites. For the first time since 1952, civilians held positions of vice-president (Mahmoud Fawzi) and prime minister (Aziz Sidky, Fawzi, Abdel-Aziz Hegazi, and Mustafa Khalil). Ismail Fahmy became minister of foreign affairs from 1973 to 1977, before Boutros Boutros-Ghali held the post. In the 1980s, Kamal Hassan Ali and Dr. Esmat Abdel Meguid held the post. Second, the regime experienced some gradual democratization. The multiparty system was established in 1976–1977. In 1980, the opposition political parties were the Labor Socialist Party (LSP), the National Progressive Unionist Party (NPUP), and the Liberal Socialist Party. Though the opposition only held 20 out of 390 parliamentary seats, they still had considerable influence through the media.[73]

Hinnebusch provides a basis for better understanding the elite change from Nassar to Sadat through his four categories of elites. First, there was the core elite, who comprised members of the inner circle and were closest to the president. The top elite were those officials, subject to rapid turnover, who were the nonpolitical technicians or administrators. The middle elite consisted of high civil servants, senior military commanders, public sector managers, many newspaper editors, top religious and academic leaders, heads of syndicates and chambers of commerce, and parliamentary committee chairmen. Finally, the sub-elite consisted of local notables of village leaders, party leaders of local branches, and most members of parliament.

Sadat civilianized the core elite. There were still officers present, but not in the same strength as under Nassar. For example, under Nassar, the prime ministers were always officers, while under Sadat, they were all civilian. In place of the officers, Sadat advanced technocrats from the state bureaucracy and economic notables from the private sector. This group from the private sector served to dilute the statist character of the regime under Nassar.[74] "Under Sadat, in short, the inner core changed from a body of relatively like minded 'revolutionary comrades' of similar background into a much more occupationally differentiated and heterogeneous collection of personal confidantes, technicians, bureaucrats, politicians and economic notables."[75] Under Nassar, the criteria for getting to the top were a combination of military service with bureaucratic or political experience or great achievement in academics or technical skill. Under Sadat, the criteria changed to those with professional or academic degrees with bureaucratic or political experience.

Under Sadat, party leadership took on greater significance, and the party started to become a channel of recruitment. Governors under Sadat had party or parliamentary backgrounds, not only bureaucratic backgrounds as under

Nassar. Finally, under Sadat, the elites tended to come from the upper classes because of the movement of state elites into the private sector and private sector elites into the state. The cross fertilization among these groups tended to produce a unified and upper-class political elite.[76]

While Hinnebusch seems to stress the heterogeneous nature of the political elite under Sadat, it is important to note that Sadat still relied on kinship ties for his personal entourage.[77] Two key people (each had sons married to Sadat's daughters) in Sadat's inner circle were Osman Ahmad Osman, who was in charge of reconstructing the canal cities, and Sayyid Marei, a wealthy landowner.[78] Whereas Nassar relied on his personal assistants to fill out his elites, Sadat encouraged family-based networks within the elite as a means of controlling the political system, which he inherited from Nassar.[79] This may not necessarily be problematic. Robert Springborg suggests that in order to make and execute policy, perhaps a small homogeneous inner circle is beneficial.[80] The problem of rapid turnover among the elites caused problems of political institutionalization at the executive level for Sadat, and perhaps this was a greater challenge to the regime than the existence of kinship ties at the personal entourage level.[81]

The second point concerning Sadat's gradual democratization is debatable, but he did make some changes. Michael Hudson claims that the most significant aspect of Sadat's strategy for winning support was his approach towards political participation. He allowed the National Assembly more freedom in its discussions and debates. He gave greater freedoms to the press. In 1975 and 1976, Sadat created forums under the watchful eye of the Arab Socialist Union, which provided politicians an opportunity to express some divergent views. These forums were a step towards the growth of political parties, and they represented the ideas as expressed by the Muslim Brotherhood at one extreme and the Marxists on the other extreme. The middle represented the views of the regime itself, and Mahmoud Abu Wafia, Sadat's brother-in-law, led this forum. "Despite the skepticism expressed by both rightists and leftists, the possibility could not be excluded that President Sadat's cautious liberalization of organized political participation might eventually enhance the structural legitimacy of the political system."[82]

Sadat consistently chose right-wing, conservative, stabilizing, adaptive, pro-Western courses of action, while maintaining a traditionalist character. This traditionalism stemmed from his village past.

> His patriarchal style of rule seemed an extension of village headmanship to the national level. . . . His view of Egypt as "one big family" in which political strife was out of place and his nostalgic image of the village as a place of harmony where men were content with their lot, were artifacts of his village upbringing which in time gave to his outlook a conservative impatience with dissent and insensitivity to inequality.[83]

Sadat was different from Nassar. Sadat was a much more relaxed and tolerant person. He genuinely disliked political repression, and under Sadat, there were hardly any executions, mass imprisonments, and torture [this point is debatable as other scholars discussed below differ on this point]. Sadat wanted peace through negotiation and economic prosperity based on private property. While Sadat wanted democracy, he was unwilling to relinquish any power.[84] Herein lies the problem Sadat faced. He made attempts to liberalize and democratize, but the economic and political challenges he faced caused him to proceed haltingly with some of his domestic initiatives.

In the *October Paper*, Sadat did recognize the significance of the 1952 revolution, Nasser's agrarian reforms, and the *Socialist Charter*. He claimed that "the country was rescued from a violent class struggle, which many other countries have witnessed and are still witnessing. I would not be exaggerating if I say that the Revolution saved the country from civil war."[85] However, the *October Paper* also represented a break with Nassarism. It held that Nassar's socialism and Arabism needed to adapt to a new era. These ideas had to be institutionalized in a constitutional order to preserve their achievements, while correcting deviations. In 1978, Sadat introduced "democratic socialism" as the middle ground between the excesses of liberal capitalism and totalitarianism.[86] In so doing, Sadat moved away from state socialism while opening the Egyptian economy to foreigners. The upper class applauded this move, as they saw opportunities for further enrichment. Luxury items were soon available for those who could afford them. New buses were made available to the poor and helped relieve public transportation's unbearable congestion. Hudson refers to this prosperity as superficial.[87] This strategy, however, contributed to the widening gap between the classes, which, as I will discuss later, manifested itself in the political arena.[88]

While Sadat did not have Nassar's dynamic charisma, he achieved support through his successful crossing of the Suez Canal in 1973 and the unprecedented military successes against Israel.[89] Sadat explained the significance of the October War for the Egyptian people:

> I must put on record that the Egyptian people differ from many other peoples, even within the Arab world. We have recovered our pride and self-confidence after the October 1973 battle, just as our armed forces did. We are no more motivated by "complexes"—whether defeatist "inferiority" ones or those born out of suspicion and hate. . . . With the fighting over, we harbored nothing but respect for one another [he is referring to Mrs. Meir]. Our civilized people know this; it is what induced 5 million citizens to come out to greet me on my return, and the armed forces to salute me in an impressive and quite unprecedented manner.[90]

Building on the support gained from October 1973, Sadat capitalized on a different ideology from Nassar. Sadat's ideology had an "Egypt first" theme, and he challenged the underlying Arab values by challenging Arab causes. He stressed the past sacrifices of Egypt on behalf of the Arab world and its resultant ungratefulness. In fact, by the mid 1970s, middle class educated businessmen expressed a desire to normalize relations with Israel.[91] The Arabic nationalist movement under Nassar, for Sadat, had outlived its usefulness. Others agreed that pan-Arabism was not a reality. Khalid Kishtainy, in his anthology of Arabic humor, tells a story of a trumpeter sitting outside Cairo headquarters of the Arab League.[92] The trumpeter says, "This is my new job to wait for Arab unity and then blow the trumpet to declare it to the world when it is achieved. I get 50 pounds a month." His friend says, "That's a miserable salary." The trumpeter replies, "Yes, but it is a lifetime job."[93] The total renunciation of pan-Arabism, however, did cause problems in Egypt's relations with the other Arab states.[94] I will address this point in chapter 4.

Sadat consolidated his authority against his rivals by "retraditionalizing." He condemned the repressive policies of the former regime. Hamied Ansari calls Sadat's strategy, "retraditionalization behind the liberal mask."[95] His rivals were urban-based, formed around the New Wafd and the Muslim Brotherhood. Sadat faced both liberal and Islamic challenges to his regime. Liberalization of the economy widened the gap between the wealthy and the poor. Calls for political participation increased, and Sadat's response was greater control over the state's institutions and a crackdown on his rivals.[96] Sadat in 1977 clarified his views on liberalization. He said that "politics have no place in our universities" and that "democracy too can have teeth and fangs."[97] Meanwhile, class divisions and gaps worsened.[98]

Exacerbating Sadat's challenges were the social and regional changes over the past thirty years. The tremendous population growth in Cairo, if continued, will have reached 20 million by the year two thousand. The rural population declined from 81 percent in 1960 to 56 percent in 1976. In 1978, 42 percent of the population was under the age of 15. These circumstances combined with Egypt's economic woes manifested themselves in some measure through extremist groups, though many of these extremist groups were not united. For example, the psychological profile of one of these groups, Jama'at, is one of alienation.[99] Religion became a means of consolation and comfort, but Jama'at was not united in purpose or strategy. While extremists justify rebellion against Muslim rulers who would not abide by Islamic law, not all Jama'at were extremists. Sadat responded by arresting all urban dissidents, which in the first week amounted to 1,536 arrests. He arrested bishops, priests, imams, secular leaders, etc. These leaders did not represent an organized opposition; they were just all united in their disapproval of Sadat. When Sadat denounced sectarian violence to the People's Assembly, he received a standing ovation.[100]

Sadat faced many risks with his strategy. Egypt experienced tremendous economic and bureaucratic decay. Ideological cleavage between the Muslim Brotherhood and the Marxists posed challenges to Sadat. Finally, Sadat's turnaround on pan-Arabism and his alignment with the West caused doubt. In 1974, he violently put down a Muslim fundamentalist insurrection. The regime made widespread arrests due to riots spurred on by low wages and a 25 percent inflation rate. The regime blamed these riots on the Marxists. In 1977, the worst riots in 25 years occurred as thousands protested the government's reduction in food subsidies. Eighty people were killed, and the regime arrested fifteen hundred people.[101]

On October 6, 1981, just as Sadat was about to review the military parade celebrating Egyptian successes during the 1973 October War, religious fundamentalists assassinated him. The Egyptian people did not display nearly the amount of grief or sadness as expressed for Nassar's passing. This seeming indifference towards Sadat came as a surprise to the United States, where he had been recently proclaimed *Time* magazine's Man of the Year.[102]

While the extent to which Sadat affected the political regime he inherited from Nassar is debatable, three points are clear. First, his country still faced tremendous economic woes, and unfortunately the economic elites became the governing elites, which accentuated the gap between the haves and the have-nots. Second, his attempt to mobilize his people manifested itself in his Egypt-first ideology, a notable change from Nassar's ideology of pan-Arabism. Finally, he did make attempts to diffuse some of his power to other institutions. In the end, his country's economic plight was the catalyst for renewed repression.

HUSNI MUBARAK: AN INCREMENTAL AND MODERATE ATTEMPT TO DIFFUSE POWER

Just as there are disagreements concerning Sadat's ability or willingness to democratize, there are differences of opinion as to how well the Mubarak regime is democratizing. Hourani is optimistic and believes that under Husni Mubarak the regime seems to be cautiously democratizing. He believes that Egypt has a chance to restore constitutional rule because of its "social and cultural unity."[103] Elections in 1984 occurred in an atmosphere of tolerance, and in a system which ensured a majority government. Even members of the opposition were elected.[104]

There are reasons for such optimism. Upon Mubarak's assumption of the presidency, he vowed that there would be an end to repression. To illustrate this promise, he invited members of the opposition, who were imprisoned during the September 1981 Sadat crackdown, to the Presidential Palace.[105] Mubarak changed the electoral law to one of proportional representation, although parties had to achieve 8 percent to win seats. Opposition parties viewed this change optimistically. Mubarak allowed the reconstitution of the New Wafd Party and established ties with the Muslim Brotherhood, although he did not officially recognize the Muslim Brotherhood.[106]

The smooth transfer of power to Mubarak after Sadat's assassination was significant for the regime. In 1981, Mubarak, in a speech to the People's Assembly, outlined his regime's policy. He wanted to bring economic benefits to the poor and stop the profiteering by wealthy members of society. He wanted to continue the opening, or *infitah*, of the economy, but he wanted to open production, not consumption. He recognized the role of the state to protect the poor. Food subsidies would not disappear. He also began to economically and diplomatically open to other Arab states as long as they did not interfere with Egyptian affairs. Mubarak claimed that "Egypt is for all society—not a privileged few or the chosen elite or the sectarian dictatorship." Additionally, he called for the role of opposition parties in the regime, but they would represent "differences not conflict, without creating confusion; it should be an exchange of views not an exchange of accusations."[107]

Mubarak inherited both the Nassar and Sadat legacies, which may have been a mixed blessing. On the one hand he has inherited an array of institutions, laws, and practices, and on the other, he has inherited policies that have caused problems for the regime. He did inherit an extremely powerful office, the presidency. Sadat added a paternalistic flavor to the office, which connotes even more power.[108] By the end of Sadat's rule, with the president as the head of the dominant party, R. H. Dekmejian described Egypt's political situation: "Egypt had reverted to an institutionalized one-party system."[109]

Mubarak has chosen not to use the extensive powers of the presidency, and he has not made any radical changes to the regime. Nazih N. Ayubi describes Mubarak's style of leadership as "low-key" and "business-like." The Mubarak regime is known for its honesty and reserved approach to issues. The significant problem facing the regime is economic inequality among members of society. While Islamic extremism has not extended a firm grip on the working class, military, or the lumpenproletariat, continued economic woes might spur people to look for an alternative in these extremist groups, especially if political participation does not continue to develop.[110] I will address this point in more detail later.

Mubarak continued Sadat's civilianization of the elite. In 1986, only 10 percent of the fifty ministers serving in Mubarak's cabinet had military backgrounds.[111] Additionally, Mubarak's elite are not powerful or homogeneous. Even his closest advisors have much less power than those from the Nassar and Sadat regimes. Nassar and Sadat, while establishing a heterogeneous elite in both composition and ideology, did have homogeneous inner circles. Members of Mubarak's inner circle do not share the bonds of kinship or friendship, nor do they share similar political ideologies. They gained their positions through the crossing of career paths and chance.[112] The bureaucracy has continued to grow. By the mid-1980s, over 3 million people were employed by the government, in the local, central, or public sector. Also the wages and salaries of these people increased from 19 percent of the nation's expenditures in 1974–75 to 29 percent in 1984–85.[113]

Mubarak has tried to take the best of Nassar and Sadat as he formulates his policies. His regime allows five parties to function, not including the ruling party, the National Democratic Party. The left wing is represented by the National Progressive Union Party and the Socialist Labour Party. The Wafd is back. One religious party is authorized, the Umma, but it is not an extremist party. Although the Marxists, Muslim Brotherhood, and Nassarists are not officially represented, their views are represented in various party factions. By 1990, Egypt was described as having "the most open political system of any Arab state and a determined attempt is being made to foster a democratic society."[114]

Because the courts ruled that there were some irregularities during the 1984 elections, new elections were called for in 1987. The same parties were involved, but some of their alliances changed. For example, the Wafd competed alone and not with the Muslim Brotherhood as in 1984. The Muslim Brotherhood entered an alliance with socialists and liberals, even though the electoral laws banned religious parties. Also, four hundred candidates ran as independents. Mubarak encouraged the secular parties as well as the moderate Muslims, namely the Brotherhood. He was elected in 1987 for a six-year term.[115]

Mubarak has been able to keep his opposition off balance. "Mubarak's political style is akin to a military tactician. He identifies specific threats and tailors countermeasures to confront them."[116] He has not provided the Islamic extremists with a discernible target. He adheres to a simple lifestyle. He has let the courts wrestle with the Coptic extremists. He does allow, for example, the moderate Muslim Brotherhood to function, while maintaining many extremists under detention. Finally, Mubarak has provided many freedoms to political parties, which has provided him with support for his regime.[117]

During the first five years of his presidency, Mubarak was able to counterbalance the secular opposition with the Islamic political activists. The rise of the Wafd Party in the 1984 elections revealed Mubarak's good relationship with this party leader of the secular opposition and his successful supression of the Islamic groups. Additionally, Mubarak helped the moderate Islamic groups dominate the radical groups by establishing a tolerant environment for moderate Islamic views. This tactic seemed to diffuse the appeal of the radical Islamic groups.[118]

Mubarak's toleration of the Muslim Brotherhood seemed beneficial to his regime. First, the Brotherhood's political participation helps lend legitimacy to Mubarak's attempt to create true democracy. Second, the Brotherhood serves to deflect the more extremist groups. Third, the social welfare programs that the Brotherhood established is a benefit to society, lifting some of the burden from the regime. Finally, Mubarak's tolerance for the Brotherhood legitimizes him in light of the Islamic movements occurring in other Arab countries.[119]

By 1987, however, it appeared Mubarak's counterbalancing strategy was failing, and the Islamicists gained strength. Mubarak seemed to have shifted strategies from counterbalancing opposition parties to opening the political arena to the Islamicists. This strategy could perhaps expose their weaknesses, while also allowing Mubarak to keep a better eye on their activities.[120] It is apparent, however, that the Islamicists remain a potent enough force that Mubarak must still rely on his security forces. Will the effort expended on controlling the Islamicists impair the state's ability to manage its economy? Perhaps, the state, while managing organized threats, will have difficulty handling anomie violence, as opposition and the state alike fail to redress economic woes.[121]

The challenge facing Mubarak today is the economy, namely the increasing gap between the rich and the poor. So far, religious groups have not been able to generate political support. The religious groups are split, and Stephen Pelletiere, in his monograph, calls for the United States to exploit this schism as it assesses the wisdom of forcing Mubarak to take measures that may only exacerbate the economic situation.[122] Other studies for regime stabilization exclude U.S. efforts and call upon Egypt to take economic and political measures. The economic measures needed are those that would create jobs, and the political measures include anti-corruption and further democratization measures.[123]

Mubarak has followed moderation in his foreign policy, as well as in his domestic policy. Springborg thinks that Mubarak has done well in the foreign policy realm and that he has the potential to further his legitimacy at home through his actions abroad.[124] We will assess this point in chapter 6.

CONCLUSION

There have been a multitude of approaches taken for the study of Egypt. From pharaonic interpretations, institutional, Weberian, social aggregate, or the domination of class, there is no doubt that Egypt is undergoing tremendous social change that will continue to challenge the regime. Each leader we reviewed faced these challenges in somewhat different ways. Husni Mubarak so far has shown tremendous skill in responding to the challenges he faces.[125]

Institutionally, we have seen attempts to civilianize the elite, while allowing for more political participation both individually and in the form of political parties. Each leader, Nassar, Sadat, and Mubarak, devised his own ideology as a means to gain consensus or legitimacy. These attempts have not always been successful, especially in the midst of a crumbling economy. If any theme has emerged in this discussion of Egypt's political development, it is the constraint of a disastrous economy on the political regime.

This description of Egyptian political development also reveals challenges at every stage, as well as the current problem of Islamic extremism. However, it also reveals the homogeneous character of the Egyptian people. It is a people who identify strongly with the state based on their shared ethnic and national identity. This commonality stems from a shared language and religion combined with the simultaneous, historical, and continuous development of the Egyptian nation-state. And while kinship seemed to play a role in the Sadat regime, it did not significantly impact on the commonality and shared identity of the Egyptian people.

The most divisive factor revealed is the widening gap between the rich and the poor. This gap does not reinforce any ethnic group since the population on a whole is Egyptian. Additionally, the radical Islamic groups represent an ideology calling for a government based on Islamic law. They do not seem to challenge the Egyptianity of the people. For the future, we must evaluate the political situation to see if it does develop along extremist lines, and thereby cause the loyalties of the people to shift from the state. More importantly, we must assess any changes that may occur to the defining criteria of being an Egyptian and how those changes would affect the legitimacy of the regime and its foreign policy. Such an examination is beyond the scope of this book; however, the preceding discussion of Egypt's political development establishes, based on Horowitz's criteria of ethnic divisiveness, that Egypt during the 1970s and 1980s (the timeframe for the cases), was a homogeneous state. What Nassar and Sadat have done "is to preserve through several wars and two unexpected changes of president—Nassar's fatal heart attack in 1970 and Sadat's assassination in 1981—the fundamental stability of the country. Compared with other developing countries, this was a remarkable achievement."[126]

NOTES

1. This instrumentalist approach and the dynamic nature of ethnicity is found in Dale F. Eickelman, *The Middle East: An Anthropological Approach*, 2nd ed. (Englewood Cliffs, New Jersey: Prentice Hall, 1989), 209, when he cites Frederick Barth, "Introduction," in *Ethnic Groups and Boundaries: The Social Organization of Cultural Difference*, ed. Frederick Barth (Boston: Little, Brown and Company, 1969), 10–15.

2. James G. March and Johan P. Olsen, "The New Institutionalism: Organizational Factors in Political Life," *American Political Science Review* 78, no. 3 (September 1984): 734.

3. Ibid., 738, 747.

4. Both quotations are from Donald C. Williams, "Reconsidering State and Society in Africa: The Institutional Dimension in Land Reform Policies," *Comparative Politics* 28, no. 2 (January 1996): 208, 210.

5. March and Olsen, 742.

6. See Roy C. Macridis and Steven L. Burg, *Introduction to Comparative Politics: Regimes and Change* (New York: HarperCollins Publishers, 1991).

7. *Background Notes*, United States Department of State, Bureau of Public Affairs, Office of Public Communication 5, no. 7 (August 1994): 1–2.

8. Ibid., 1.

9. Ali E. Hillal Dessouki, "The Primacy of Economics: The Foreign Policy of Egypt," in *The Foreign Policies of Arab States: The Challenge of Change*, ed. Bahgat Korany and Ali E. Hillal Dessouki (Boulder: Westview Press, 1991), 159.

10. *Background Notes*, 2.

11. Dessouki, 159.

12. P. J. Vatikiotis, *The Modern History of Egypt* (New York: Frederick A. Praeger, 1969), 3.

13. Ibid., xiv.

14. Both quotations are from ibid., 3.

15. Ibid., 10.

16. Ibid.

17. Anwar Sadat, *In Search of Identity: An Autobiography* (New York: Harper & Row, Publishers, 1978), 313.

18. Dessouki, 160.

19. Ibid., 160.

20. Joel Migdal, *Strong Societies and Weak States: State-Society Relations and State Capabilities in the Third World* (Princeton: Princeton University Press, 1988), 37, describes Egypt's society as an "unusually homogeneous one."

21. Don Peretz, *The Middle East Today*, 5th ed. (New York: Praeger Publishers, 1988), 51.

22. Ibid., 59.

23. Vatikiotis, 10–16, 37.

24. Ibid., 49.

25. Ibid., 55.

26. Ibid., 56.

27. The point about establishing equality between Christians and Muslims is from F. Robert Hunter, "Self-Image and Historical Truth: Nubar Pasha and the Making of Modern Egypt," *Middle Eastern Studies* 26, no. 2 (April 1990), 364. Please note that this point on establishing equality is debatable. Peretz quotes a Turkish official at the time who sums up the religious divisions during the Ottoman Empire: "Once," said the Vali . . . "I was a very young man, and went [for] a ride with my old father. I was foolish then, and my head was stuffed with silly notions and liberal ideas. . . . I told my father we ought to reform our constitution, systematize our administration, purify our family life, educate our women, introduce liberal ideas, and imitate Europeans. And my father answered never a word. So we rode on along the banks of the Bosphorus. At

last we came to a Christian village, and round the Christian village were many pigs. Then my father said to me, 'My son, what seest thou?' I replied, 'Pigs, my father.' 'My son,' he said, 'are they similar in size and color, or do they differ?' 'They differ, my father. There are big pigs and little pigs, white pigs and black pigs, brown pigs and mottled pigs.' 'But they are all of them swine, my son?' 'All, my father.' 'My son,' he said, 'it is with the Christians even as with the pigs. There are big Christians and little Christians, Russian Christians and English Christians, French Christians and German Christians; they are all of them swine, and he who wishes to imitate the Christians, wishes to wallow with swine in the mire.' . . . I was very young then, and my brain was full of nonsense—so I thought my father was a fool. But now that my own beard is getting grey—by God, I think the old gentlemen was right!" in Peretz, 74.

28. Vatikiotis, 56.

29. Nathan Brown, "Peasants and Notables in Egyptian Politics," *Middle Eastern Studies* 26, no. 2 (April 1990): 148-149. Brown's argument is that the notables deliberately misrepresented the peasants to further their own interests.

30. Peretz, 75.

31. Ibid., 96.

32. Ibid., 75–78.

33. Michael C. Hudson, *Arab Politics: The Search for Legitimacy* (New Haven: Yale University Press, 1977), 237.

34. Vatikiotis, 239–241.

35. Ibid., 243–248.

36. Ibid., 248–265.

37. Prior to the quotation is a summary from Manfred Halpern, *The Politics of Social Change in the Middle East and North Africa* (Princeton: Princeton University Press, 1963), 304–309. The quotation is taken from p. 309.

38. Macridis and Burg, 5–9. The quotations are from pages 6 and 8, respectively.

39. Ibid., 8–14.

40. Summary of Peretz, 224–225.

41. Perez cites Warriner in ibid., 225.

42. All after last citation is a summary of ibid., 225–230.

43. Joel Gordon, "The False Hopes of 1950: The Wafd's Last Hurrah and the Demise of Egypt's Old Order," *International Journal of Middle Eastern Studies* 21, no. 2 (May 1989), 193.

44. Ibid., 210.

45. Ibid.

46. Peretz, 230–236.

47. Joel Beinin, "Labor, Capital, and the State in Nasserist Egypt, 1952–1961," *International Journal of Middle East Studies* 21, no. 1 (February 1989): 88.

48. Ibid.

49. Raymond A. Hinnebusch Jr., *Egyptian Politics Under Sadat: The Post-Populist Development of an Authoritarian-Modernizing State* (Cambridge: Cambridge University Press, 1985), 14.

50. Ibid., 13–14.

51. Ibid., 15.

52. Ibid., 16–17.

53. Ibid., 17–18.

54. Ibid., 20. The previous section came from ibid., 18–20.

55. Albert Hourani, *A History of the Arab Peoples* (Cambridge, Massachusetts: The Belknap Press of Harvard University Press, 1991), 405.

56. Ibid.

57. Hourani citing the National Charter in ibid., 406.

58. Ibid., 406–407.

59. Hudson, 240.

60. Ibid., 241.

61. Halim Barakat, *The Arab World: Society, Culture, and State* (Berkeley: University of California Press, 1993), 166.

62. Ibid., 166–167.

63. Hinnebusch, 21–22.

64. Ibid., 21–24.

65. The quotation only is from Anthony McDermott, *Egypt From Nasser to Mubarak: A Flawed Revolution* (London: Croom Helm, 1988), 280. The rest of the ideas in this paragraph are noted below.

66. Hinnebusch, 29–35.

67. Dessouki, 164.

68. Hinnebusch, 38.

69. Ibid., 78–79.

70. Hamied Ansari, *Egypt: The Stalled Society* (Albany: State University of New York Press, 1986), 153.

71. Ibid., 154.

72. Thomas Mayer, *The Changing Past: Egyptian Historiography of the Urabi Revolt, 1882–1983* (Gainesville, University of Florida Press, 1988), 58–59.

73. Dessouki, 165.

74. Hinnebusch, 91–100. Hinnebusch provides detailed statistics on the elite during the Nassar and Sadat periods.

75. Ibid., 100.

76. Ibid., 100–109.

77. Ibid., 80.

78. Hudson, 247–248.

79. Robert Springborg, "Approaches to the Understanding of Egypt," in *Ideology and Power in the Middle East: Studies in Honor of George Lenczowski,* ed. Peter J. Chelkowski and Robert J. Pranger (Durham: Duke University Press, 1989), 156–157.

80. Robert Springborg, *Mubarak's Egypt: Fragmentation of the Political Order* (Boulder: Westview Press, 1989), 32–33, suggests that Mubarak's regime, due to a lack of homogeneity of the inner circle, might be less effective.

81. The point about rapid turnover and institutionalization is found in Marc N. Cooper, *The Transformation of Egypt* (Baltimore: The Johns Hopkins University Press, 1982), 151.

82. The quotation and the points above are from Hudson, 248.

83. Hinnebusch, 80.

84. Ibid., 81–86.

85. Ansari, 178.

86. Hinnebusch, 112–113.

87. Hudson, 248–249.

88. Ansari, 208–209.

89. Hudson, 248.

90. Sadat, 312.

91. Hudson, 248.

92. Thomas W. Lippman, *Egypt After Nasser: Sadat, Peace, and the Mirage of Prosperity* (New York: Paragon House, 1989), 184.

93. Ibid.

94. Ibid., 185.

95. Ansari, 195.

96. Ibid., 195, 208–209.

97. James A. Bill and Robert Springborg, *Politics in the Middle East* (New York: HarperCollins College Publishers, 1994), 224.

98. Ibid., 222.

99. This alienation is a phenomenon called "anomie" as explained by Emile Durheim and Bernard Brown, mentioned in the theory annex.

100. Ansari, 212–213, 229–230.

101. Hudson, 250.

102. Raymond William Baker, *Sadat and After: Struggles For Egypt's Soul* (Cambridge: Harvard University Press, 1990), 1–2.

103. Hourani, 456.

104. Ibid., 456–457.

105. Ansari, 241.

106. Ibid., 243–244.

107. Derek Hopwood, *Egypt: Politics and Society 1945–1990* (London: Harper-Collins, 1991), 184. The quotations are from Mubarak's speech.

108. Nazih N. Ayubi, *The State and Public Policies in Egypt Since Sadat* (Reading: Ithaca Press, 1991), 226–227.

109. Ibid., 227.

110. Ibid., 227–236.

111. Nazih N. Ayubi, "Government and the State in Egypt Today," *Egypt Under Mubarak*, ed. Charles Tripp and Roger Owen (London: Routledge, 1990), 5.

112. Springborg, *Mubarak's Egypt*, 32–33.

113. Ayubi, "Government and the State in Egypt Today," 7.

114. The quotation and the above points are from Hopwood, 185.

115. Ibid., 186–187.

116. Springborg, "Approaches to the Understanding of Egypt," 158.

117. Ibid., 159.

118. Springborg, *Mubarak's Egypt*, 186.

119. Gregory L. Aftandilian, *Egypt's Bid For Arab Leadership: Implications For U.S. Policy* (New York: Council on Foreign Relations Press, 1993), 57–58.

120. Springborg, *Mubarak's Egypt*, 184, 186.

121. Ibid., 244–245.

122. Stephen C. Pelletiere, *Shari'a Law, Cult Violence and System Challenge in Egypt: The Dilemma Facing President Mubarak* (U.S. Army War College, Carlisle Barracks: Strategic Studies Institute, April 5, 1994), v.

123. Casandra, "The Impending Crisis in Egypt," *Middle East Journal* 49, no. 1 (Winter 1995): 26–27.

124. Springborg, "Approaches to the Understanding of Egypt," 159.

125. For all the detailed interpretations of Egyptian politics, see Springborg, "Approaches to the Understanding of Egypt," 137–159. The other idea reference Mubarak is from Springborg, p. 158.

126. McDermott, 274.

Chapter Three

The Political Development of Syria

This chapter extends Donald L. Horowitz's criteria for ethnic divisiveness to Syria. In the last chapter, we established Egypt's "Egyptianity." Contrary to Egypt, an analysis of Syria will reveal Syria's lack of "Syrianess" because of strong, reinforcing group loyalties, which do not coincide with the state. The basis for these group loyalties is ethnicity. As described earlier, the commonality of the characteristics of religion, culture, kinship, and language is the basis of ethnicity.

In order to establish Syria as an ethnically divided state, I will follow the same format as the last chapter and begin with a discussion of the Syrian people. I will pay particular attention to the roots of the Sunni-Shi'a split to better understand the significance of the religious, cultural, and kinship differences that affect group identity among the Sunnis and Alawis (as I will explain later, Alawis are a Shi'a sect). Next, I will discuss the history of the modern state because the artificial creation of this state does not foster, but rather weakens, a sense of national identity. Syria does not have the historical continuity of a shared society and state as we found in Egypt. Finally, my discussion of Syria's political development, using Roy C. Macridis and Steven L. Burg's framework, will show its basis in ethnicity. According to Horowitz, this is the key criterion for determining a state's ethnic divisiveness. My discussion of Syria's political development, as well as its people and state history, will show that the state of Syria has a weak national identity because of the competing and reinforced group or ethnic loyalties. My argument is that because of Syria's ethnic divisiveness, loyalty to the state is weak and, therefore, undermines legitimacy to the state.

PEOPLE

The population of Syria is 14.3 million. The nationality of Syria is Syrian (as listed by the U.S. State Department), and the ethnic groups (based on the State Department's view of ethnicity, not mine) are Arabs (90 percent), Kurds (9 percent), Armenians, Circassians, Turkomans. The religions are Sunni Muslim (74 percent), Alawis (12 percent), Christians (10 percent), Druze (3 percent), and a small percent of other Muslim sects, Jews, and Yazidis. The official language is Arabic. English and French are widely known, and a small percentage of the population speak Kurdish, Armenian, Aramic, or Circassian.[1]

There have been attempts to create a Syrian identity. The idea of a Syrian fatherland stems from the writings of Butrus al-Bustani (1819–1883). He expressed Syria as a "well defined historical unit, with a distinctly Arab culture and in the process of adopting certain Western characteristics deemed essential for its survival."[2]

In 1863, al-Bustani founded an all-boys school that taught European languages, history, math, and geography. This school established a close association with the Syrian Protestant College (later known as the American University in Beirut). From these schools, al-Bustani encouraged publications and writings on the topic of Syrian nationalism.[3]

Syrian national identity strengthened during the aftermath of the young Turkish revolt in 1908. This identity reached a peak after World War I when King Faisal, in 1920, became the ruler of the kingdom of Syria. However, French intervention broke the kingdom into smaller parts, creating Greater Lebanon and four other smaller states. King Faisal's compensation for the loss of Syria was that he became king of a new Iraqi state under British control. France's defeat of the Syrian revolt in 1925 effectively squelched the nationalist movement in Syria except for small areas in which lived minorities such as the Alawis. In the 1930s, Arab nationalism replaced Syrian "localism." Syrian identity seemed to only indicate a reactionary response encouraged by the British and anti-Arab parties.[4]

While Syrian identity seems weak and transitory, the ethnic identities seem enduring. Based on our definition of ethnicity, this enduring quality is a result of the reinforcing characteristics of primarily religion, culture, and kinship. Horowitz explains why religion and ethnicity can be almost synonymous:

> For many groups, religion is not a matter of faith but a given, an integral part of their identity, and for some an inextricable component of their sense of peoplehood. . . . For groups like the Syrian Alawi, descendants of mountain dwellers who blended Shiite doctrine with nature worship, religion and ethnicity is coterminous.[5]

Additionally, kinship helped cement this identity. An observer of Syria in the 1850s described the lack of patriotism as follows:

> Patriotism is unknown. . . . There is not a man in the country whether Turk or Arab, Mohammedan or Christian who would give a para (penny) to save the Empire from ruin. The Patriotism of the Syrian is confined to the four walls of his own house; anything beyond them does not concern him.[6]

In Syria, ethnic and religious boundaries coincide, and this coincidence defines the nature of "a people."[7]

Syrian society, as a result of its heterogeneous character, contains numerous divisive forces. Loyalties to religious sects, social classes, tribal groups, agro-cities, and families replace those loyalties one might expect towards a nation.[8] While under French rule, these divisions were encouraged as part of the French's divide-and-rule practice.[9] In the midst of all the different group loyalties, which compete with state loyalties, Syria has further detracted from national loyalty when it has emphasized Arab nationalism rather than Syrian nationalism.[10] How does one reconcile all the different loyalties? According to Alasdair Drysdale,

> A Syrian officer may act like an officer in a restaurant if he feels this will get him quicker service; he may be very conscious of his kin group in choosing a marriage partner; he may act as a member of a particular Alawi tribe during an intra-Alawi dispute within the armed services; he may act as an Alawi, villager, peripheral non-Sunni or Ba'thi—or all five—during a coup d'etat, as a socialist during regime economic policy formation and as a Syrian during a war with Israel.[11]

To better understand the strong identities of Syria's ethnic groups, primarily the Sunnis and Alawis, we must first understand the formative roots of these groups. Consequently, it is important to understand the most significant schismatic movement in Islam that is Shi'ism.[12] There are five pillars of Islam, to which most Muslims adhere: declaration of faith, the five daily prayers, almsgiving, fasting, and the pilgrimage to Mecca.[13] Sunnism is " . . . the belief in a unity which includes differences in legal opinion, and in the importance of the Qur'an and the practice (sunna) of the Prophet as the bases of it. . . ."[14] Sunnis believe that all Muslims should live peacefully and unified, and accept the past. Sunnis accept the legitimacy of the first four caliphs, i.e., community leaders, though claims of their authority and lineage are the root of much debate and schisms within Islam. While the later caliphs might not have always acted justly, they are still regarded as legitimate because they did not violate God's basic commandments. There are indications that some of the Umayyad (Sunni) caliphs claimed to expand their community leadership role to successors of the Prophet and even vice-regents of God on earth, who interpret

God's law. Sunnism in its developed form, however, does not believe the caliph to be a prophet nor an infallible interpreter of the faith, but rather a community leader who ensures peace and justice. The caliph, according to the Sunnis, should be a descendent from the Prophet's tribe.[15]

Shi'a movements challenged the authority of the first three caliphs. They believed that 'Ali ibn Abi Talib was solely the legitimate and appointed imam successor of the Prophet.[16] The division stemmed from a political dispute between the Shi'a (party or faction) of Ali, who was the cousin and son-in-law of the Prophet Muhammad, and the Sunnis, who opposed the Shi'a view that the caliphate was divine in nature. The Sunnis view the caliphate as a constitutional office. The person assuming this office is selected by leaders of the community and through an acclamation or *bay-a* of the general public. The Sunnis base their identification with the Sunna, which are the precedents set by Muhammad, and their respect for the "Golden Age" of Islam under the first four caliphs, the successors of Muhammad.[17]

The dispute originated in 661 when Ali's first son, Hasan, gave up his claim to the caliphate to Mu'awiya, the governor of Damascus. Mu'awiya created the Umayyad dynasty, and his son, Yazid, assumed the caliphate. Ali's son, Husain, challenged Yazid's claim, and the subsequent clashes resulted in the massacre of Husain and many of his followers. From that point, the supporters of Ali's line of succession became a religious sect, called Shi'a. What began as a dispute concerning the succession of the caliphate, expanded to include disputes over ritual, legal, and theological matters. The division gradually took on ethnic and geographical qualities. Most Shi'as reside in Iran, Iraq, Bahrain, Kuwait, the United Arab Emirates, the Eastern Province of Saudi Arabia, as well as large communities in Lebanon, North Yemen, and Syria.[18]

With the domination of the Umayyads, the Shi'a went underground and remained in a secretive but active status. The sect not only provided a means of political dissent, it continued the local beliefs and practices that were contrary to the Sunni ways. Many non-Arabs of Iraq, Syria, and Persia were followers of this secretive sect, which was like a popular cult.[19] There are four subsects within Shi'ism. They are the Isma'ils (Seveners), the Nusairis (Alawis), the Imam Shi'ites (Twelvers), and the Zaidis. For purposes of this study, I will focus on the Alawis, who live today in northern Syria, and in areas of Lebanon and Turkey. Alawis primarily live in rural areas, and their practices are steeped in secrecy and an esoteric interpretation of the Quran.[20] In fact, some Sunni and Shi'a do not even accept Alawis as Muslims because of Alawi beliefs and rituals stemming from this esoteric interpretation.[21]

The rise of the Alawis in the regime, which I explain later, only exacerbates this source of friction. As mentioned earlier, some Sunnis even regard Alawis as non-Muslim. Ahmad ibn Taymiya (1268–1328), a highly influential Sunni writer, claims that "the Nusayris are more infidel than Jews or Christians, even more infidel than many polytheists. . . . They are always the worst enemies of the Muslims."[22] Perhaps this disdain is a result of the secretive nature of the Alawi sect. Their religious books are kept hidden, and only a select few are allowed to read them. They practice religious dissimulation (*taqiya*) which allows them to hide their true intent and beliefs.[23] Additionally, governments historically have had trouble subduing the Alawis. It was not until 1850 that the Alawis came under Ottoman control. This control led to Sunni economic inroads and to an Alawi underclass. The Alawis, poorly educated, lacking political and military strength, frequently worked on the Sunni farms. Alawis even sold their own daughters.[24] Reverend Samuel Lyde in 1860 wrote that "the state of (Alawi) society is a perfect hell on earth."[25]

This description of the roots of the Sunni-Alawi division in Syria partially explains the strong identities of the members of each group based on differences in religion and kinship. Regional and class divisions further reinforced this ethnic division. As the next sections will show, the artificial creation of the Syrian state and its political development only helped to cement these identities.

BACKGROUND TO THE CREATION OF THE MODERN STATE

According to James A. Bill and Robert Springborg, "The more artificial the country, the more difficult are the challenges of nation- and state-building."[26] The British and French created states in the region of the Middle East known as the Fertile Crescent, based on British and French divide-and-rule desires. Consequently, national sentiment and identities of the people did not coincide with state boundaries. To the peoples of the Middle East, the idea of a nation was synonymous with their ethnic groups. The new state boundaries imposed by the French and British did not accommodate the Middle Eastern view of a nation, and therefore state boundaries and ethnic groups were not coterminous.[27]

Daniel Pipes adds: "Not only does Syria have no history as a state, but its residents historically did not consider themselves as a Syrian nation." The geography of the region contributed to this sentiment. It is an area that has experienced many conquering armies. Its mountainous terrain serves to isolate its residents and offers a refuge for the oppressed. Additionally, its religious holiness makes it an area of pilgrimage. All these factors contribute to the region's great ethnic diversity.[28]

This great diversity has made a tremendous impact on public life in Syria. Historically, each community has enjoyed strong internal bonds and has lived separately from other communities. Communities only cooperated based on specific commercial or political interests, but, in general, communities did not cooperate. They did not share any sense of common identity as Syrians. People living in Syria "directed their first loyalties to the family; then came other genealogical relations, as well as religious, ethnic, regional, linguistic, ecological, and class ties."[29]

The idea of nationalism in Syria came in the 19th century from Europe with the Middle East Christians who viewed nationalism as a tool to increase their power.[30] From 1516 to 1918, Syria was a small region within the Ottoman Empire. The rulers of the Empire divided Syria into several administrative districts. After 1864, these districts became three *vilayets*, known as Aleppo, Damascus, and Beirut; the Jerusalem province; and the *mutasarrifiya* of Mount Lebanon. Except for the Maronites around Mount Lebanon, these regions were not significant in any way besides their administrative function; they held little political significance, and people, as well as communications and goods, moved freely throughout the region.[31]

After World War I, the British controlled most of the region, the French occupied the Mediterranean coast, and Amir Faisal's Arab army controlled the interior, namely Damascus, Aleppo, Homs, and Hama. France justified its claims to all of northern Syria by the Sykes-Picot Agreement, while Amir Faisal justified his claim of the area on the basis of the Husein-McMahon correspondence.[32] Faisal and France were on a collision course.[33]

The French have a record of discouraging democracy in the Middle East. They deposed King Faisal, who was popular with his people, and replaced him with a puppet government in 1920. In 1925, the French put down a revolt against their installed government. Additionally, they exacerbated the ethnic tensions by employing divide and rule tactics as a means of discouraging any nationalist sentiment.[34]

France employed this tactic of divide and rule during its almost two decades of control under the French mandate. The French carved up Syria into five regions: The Territory of the Alawites, the independent government of the Jabal Druze, the State of Aleppo, the State of Damascus, and the State of Greater Lebanon. In 1925, Damascus and Aleppo united to form the State of Syria, and the Alawite and Druze states were consolidated in 1937 and again in 1942. The seeds of separatism which were sowed and nurtured could not quickly dissolve. Opposition arose even after the French treaty, though never ratified, offered an attempt to reintegrate Syria along nationalist demands. Brigadier Longrigg, who studied this period, observes:

> The failure to make good the 1936 decision in favor of unity in Syria was due to the strength of local autonomist feeling which during sixteen years, an un-

happy policy of planned fragmentation had allowed—or encouraged—to build up: to the resulting lack of confidence between these minorities and the main body of Syrian opinion: to the provocation on the spot by French officials with convinced localist preferences: and to the absence of firm French backing, at all levels, for the policy which their own new decisions and statutes implied. To these causes of failure must be added a lack of tact in the Syrian officials directly concerned.[35]

Hudson suggests that there is less tension among the different communities, at least as far as the mid-1970s, but he came to this conclusion before Asad's big crackdown on his opposition in the late 1970s and his brutal attack on his own country's village of Hama.[36] The point here is that Syria's political history is a story of political division.

POST–WORLD WAR II AND INDEPENDENCE

Both Great Britain and France's admission to the United Nations signaled their recognition of the end of the mandate. Both countries evacuated Syria on April 17, 1946, which resulted in Syrian self-government.[37] Syria had free elections in 1943, and Shukri al-Kuwatli, from the Nationalist Bloc Party, was the first Syrian president. However, the whole political structure collapsed by 1949. There were many factors contributing to this collapse, including defeat in the Palestinian War, rising dissension among the leaders, rising cost of living, and general dissatisfaction. This situation set the stage for an army coup and military domination in politics for the next five years.[38]

Hudson explains that Syrian politics was family politics, including the early nationalists who struggled against French rule. These post–World War II early nationalists included the Jabiris, Kikhias, and Qudsis of Aleppo; the Azms, Barazis, and Kaylanis of Hama; the Atasis of Homs; the Asalis, Haffars, Mardams, and Quwatlis of Damascus. These leaders' failure to establish a stable regime after the French withdrawal stemmed from their narrow support base. They were unable to build national constituencies even among themselves, given that they were faced with an increasing threat to their position as a ruling class. The significance of kinship to politics proved detrimental to opposition groups, as well. Hudson suggests that the limited success of some of these groups in the 1940s and early 1950s was perhaps due to their ability to exploit kinship, ethnic, sectarian and regional identities, rather than to overcome them.[39] This approach is in contrast to the constitutional compact in 1943 among ethnic groups in Lebanon, as mentioned earlier.

Horowitz explains that postwar Syrian politics did not originally center on ethnicity. However, he claims that

> Gradually, ethnic affiliation became the servant of ideological, organizational, and personal rivalries. Once deployed in these struggles, however, ethnicity itself became the struggle. . . . Once politics had become both military and ethnic, the ethnic group most favorably placed in the armed forces found itself able to defeat all other contenders. In the process, the ethnic "complexion of the officer corps" and of the regime was transformed.[40]

THE RISE OF THE ALAWIS: THE MILITARY AND THE PARTY

I will examine the rise of the Alawis by demonstrating how this ethnic group used its power in the military, the Ba'th Party, and later the presidency to establish its political hold in the Syrian regime, by exclusively becoming the regime's sole political elite. Table 3.1 demonstrates the extent of Alawi dominance in key political positions, thus revealing the ethnic nature of the political elite. Some scholars believe that the Alawis are politically powerful primarily due to their dominance in the military.[41] It is important to note, however, that there are competing views on the nature of Syrian politics. The first school of thought is that the violence and instability of Syria is

> . . . the product of a unique cultural environment, in which "primordial loyalties" and tribal ethics predominate. It portrays the Baathist regime as little more than an Alawi cabal, which holds power by virtue of religious solidarity and command of the military. [The other school of thought claims that Syrian politics is a result of] . . . struggles to establish or resist state authority, and to consolidate or attenuate the power of ruling elites.[42]

The latter is common to most Third World states.[43] However, as this section will show, for Syria one can only understand its political development in an ethnic context.

How did such a minority catapult itself to power, even though the majority of the population views it with such disdain? To understand the Alawi rise in power, we must examine the institutions of the Ba'th Party and the military because the Alawi rise to power occurred through these institutions. The Ba'th Party's secular, socialist ideology attracted minorities from the rural area, for both political and economic reasons. Politically, the Party's secular ideology posed a threat to the Sunni-dominated political system. Economically, the socialist ideology was more appealing to the poverty-stricken rural areas than it was to the more affluent urban areas.[44] Alawis constituted the core of the Ba'th Secret Military Committee in 1959. This committee attracted disaffected officers who were to play a

Table 3.1.   Provisional Classification of Syrian Nomenklatura[91]

Name	Functions	1	2	3	4	5	6	7	8
Hafiz al-Asad	President								
Bashar al-Asad	Officer in Presidential Guard	x	x	x	x	x		x	
Rif'at al-Asad	Vice President	x	x	x	x			x	x
Muhammad Nasif	Chief of Internal Security		x	x	x	x		x	
Ghazi Kan'an	Head of Intelligence Service in Lebanon		x	x	x	x		x	
Shaqif Fayyad	Division Commander		x	x	x				
'Adnan al-Asad	Brigade Commander	x	x	x	x			x	
'Ali Aslan	Division Commander			x	x	x		x	x
'Ali Duba	Chief of Army Intelligence Service				x	x		x	x
'Ali Haydar	Chief of Special Forces				x	x		x	x
Ibrahim Safi	Division Commander				x	x		x	x
Muhammad al-Khuli	Chief of Air Force				x		x	x	x
Jamil al-Asad	Vice President of al-Majlis al-Milli	x	x	x	x				
Hikmat al-Shihabi	Army Chief of Staff					x		x	x
'Adnan Makhluf	Chief of Presidential Guard		x		x			x	
Ibrahim al-Huwayji	Chief of Air Force Intelligence				x		x	x	
Muhammad Salman	Minister of Information			x	x				x
'Abd-al-Halim Khaddam	Vice President					x			x
Faruq al-Shar'	Foreign Minister					x			x
Mustafa Talas	Defense Minister							x	x
Husan Turkmani	Division Commander							x	x
Majid Sa'id Muhammad	Chief of External Security					x		x	
Ghubbash	Governor of Damascus				x				x
Mahmud al-Zu'bi [Muhammad]	Prime Minister								x

Name	Functions	Criteria*							
		1	2	3	4	5	6	7	8
Zuhayr Mashariqah	Vice President								x
'Abdallah al-Ahmar	Secretary General of the Ba'th Party								x
Muhammad Harba	Interior Minister								x

Table 3.1.   Provisional Classification of Syrian Nomenklatura[91] *(continued)*

*Criteria

1. Direct family ties with the president
2. Collateral family ties with the president
3. Membership in the president's tribe or confederation
4. Membership in the Alawi community
5. Regular and frequent access to the president
6. Membership in the air force
7. Membership in the army
8. Membership in the central committee of the Ba'th party

key role in the March 1963 military coup. Membership of the Party allowed the Alawis to act as Ba'thists, rather than Alawis. These military officers further advanced Alawis in the military by regulating admission to the military academy, shuffling command posts, and gaining control of key military units such as the air squadrons, missile detachments, armored brigades, intelligence and counter-intelligence units.[45]

The Ba'th (Resurrection) Party emerged in the 1950s and 1960s as a response to the divisive political forces of that time. Specifically, it presented a challenge to the dominating and ruling urban families and their followers. A new emerging educated class, who came from the less-powerful classes in society and from communities other than the Sunni community, found the Party attractive and meaningful. These followers, as mentioned earlier, primarily came from the Alawis, Druze, and Christians.[46]

Its origins lay in intellectual debates about the identity of the Syrians, and their relations with other Arabic speaking communities: a debate which was more urgent in Syria than elsewhere, because the frontiers drawn by Britain and France in their own interests corresponded less than in most Middle Eastern countries to natural and historical divisions.[47]

The Ba'th Party offered new governments a means to assert an ideological umbrella in the midst of competing loyalties and identities. Both Syria and Iraq saw Ba'thist ideology as a means to legitimate themselves by elevating the ideals of Arab nationalism and unity above all other competing group sentiments. The concept of *al-qawmiyyat al-Arabiyya*, which refers to loyalty to the Arab nation, was ideally, in Ba'thism, supreme over *wataniyya*, which refers to loyalty to a particular state. Ba'thist terminology for Arab states is *aqtar* or *iqlim*, which refers to regions, not states. The term "nation" refers to the Arab world as a whole, but this terminology now has little meaning in practice. Since the mid- to late-1970s, the leaders of both Iraq and Syria have increasingly emphasized their particular state, rather than the Arab nation.[48] Syrian leaders have emphasized "Greater Syria, a historical-geographical unit centered on today's Syria, Lebanon, Jordan, and Israel. In short wataniyya is displacing qawmiyya in Ba'thist ideology."[49] The significance of the Ba'th Party, however, is that it provided a vehicle for mobilizing the minorities against the ruling Sunnis, who monopolized political, as well as economic power. As I will discuss in the next section, the Party continues to help mobilize the public, based on Asad's agenda. Whether or not it will continue to serve Asad's son, Bashar, and the Alawis' needs is an interesting consideration and beyond the scope of this study.

The Alawis rose to power as political elites in three stages. The first stage occurred during the French mandate from 1920 to 1946. As previously mentioned, the French used divide and rule methods to ensure their control. Consequently, the French recruited minorities for the military as a way of keeping the nationalist forces in check. Sunnis did not cooperate with the French and refused to enlist. Additionally, the Alawis gained legal autonomy in their region. The second stage occurred during Sunni dominance from 1946 to 1963. While the Sunnis did not want a strong military involved with domestic affairs, the Alawis gained a foothold in the military and party through the Ba'th Secret Military Committee described above. Also, minorities could not afford the fee required for military exemption, although for them military life did offer a great deal in terms of social advancement. Military life, in general, appealed more to those in the rural area than in the urban centers.[50] The combined effect of all these factors was that Sunnis entered the military as individuals, whereas Alawis entered as a sect.[51]

The history of Syrian politics is a story of ethnic strife. The political development of Syria is marked by the ability of some minorities to displace the Sunni civilian elite, until finally the Alawis became the dominant ruling political elite. In the 1940s and 1950s, Syria had a parliamentary regime, with the Sunnis dominating. The major parties were the National Party, which represented primarily Damascus, and the People's Party based in the North in the vicinity of Aleppo and Homs. There were eighteen coups from 1949 to 1970. The leader of the first coup was a Kurd, Husni Za'im. A small group of Druze officers assassinated Za'im in August of 1949, and they established a civilian regime dominated by the People's Party. This regime was overthrown in December of that same year by Kurdish officers led by Adib Shishakli. He instituted civilian rule for two years, before he retook his power and became an autocrat. Another Druze officer overthrew Shishakli in 1954.[52]

The coup of 1954 set a precedent for Syrian politics. First, the military and politicians learned to plot the overthrow and the establishment of regimes. Second, the Kurds were eliminated from the officer corps. Akram Hourani became the leader of the Arab Socialist Party and later the Ba'th Party. The military plotted with the Ba'th Party, until it finally took over the Party. As I mentioned earlier, the Ba'th Party attracted Druze and Alawi, but not the Sunni. The Sunni were more attracted to the Muslim Brotherhood and President Nassar. While theoreticall, the Ba'th favored the Arab union with Egypt, reality proved different.[53] "[The] . . . experience of partnership with Nasser, beginning in 1958, and the special reservations Druze and Alawis had about smothering Syria in a Sunni Egyptian embrace soon led these officers to conspire against the union."[54]

Finally, in 1963 the Ba'th Party became the dominating force in the regime. The Ba'th Military Committee eliminated all competing factions, until it consisted of a "minority among minorities, [and] the Ba'th officers became masters of Syria."[55] The Committee continued purges of Sunni officers. It recalled to active service all family, clan, or sectarian-connected Ba'thist reserve officers, which created a minority-filled officer corps, consisting of Alawi, Druze, and Isma'ili officers.[56] The Sunnis also lost positions in the civil service, and they were replaced by Alawis. The Sunnis reacted at times violently. They looked down on the Alawis' backward ways, and they sided with Nassar, who did not consider Alawis and Druze as Arabs. In 1966, two leading generals, Salah Jadid and Hafiz Asad, maneuvered to win over their enemies' supporters. This alliance soon experienced its cracks between Druze and Alawis, and under the leadership of both Asad and Jadid the Alawis dominated. Asad assumed control over the army, whereas Jadid was leader of the party. Finally, in 1970, Asad emerged as the sole leader.[57]

Asad's emergence as leader marked the height of the third stage of the Alawi rise to power. The Alawis consolidated their power during the Ba'th coup d'etat of March 1963, the February 1966 coup, and Asad's coup in November 1970.[58] Asad's rise to power and takeover in 1970 secured the Alawis a dominant place of power in Syria.[59] But to understand Syria since Asad's rise to power, it is necessary to understand Asad. He was the consummate political animal who turned seemingly bad situations to his advantage. His intense desire to survive gave him an acute political instinct. He knew how to get people of varied backgrounds to work together, as well as how to play different factions off one another. The Syrian regime reflects Asad's very personal leadership style.[60]

HAFIZ AL-ASAD: AN ALAWI MONOPOLY OF THE PRESIDENCY, MILITARY, AND PARTY

Asad, unlike his predecessor Salah Jadid, never shared power. Once he assumed power, he realized full authority. He was briefly the prime minister and defense minister before he formed his new presidential system in 1971. The 1973 Permanent Constitution authorized sweeping powers for the presidency to include legislative and military authority as well as executive powers. Asad exercised his unlimited control of the country through the presidency, cabinet, the bureaucracy, the military, and the Council of People. He was also the leader of the Ba'th Party, as well as of the National Progressive Front, which is a coalition of the Ba'th Party and three left-wing and national parties or groups. He used his advisors as another channel of influence. These advisors helped wield power through the political, military, security, and bureaucratic systems. An unofficial group, the Jama'a (Company), was a critical tool for Asad's power, which helped to safeguard the regime against enemies by meeting domestic and foreign policy challenges. Members of the Jama'a were loyal to Asad, although there have been rifts among members, such as that between Rif'at Asad (Asad's younger brother) and Mustafa Tlas, the defense minister. The Jama'a consists of elite military units designed to protect the heart of the regime, such as the presidential palace, airports, radio and television stations, etc. The high profile units are the Defence Companies and Special Forces stationed near Damascus. Asad's brother commands one of these units.[61] As commander of the army, Asad selected his primary officers for key positions. The criteria for selection are personal; those chosen were Alawi and Ba'ath friends of Asad and his relatives. While there were some Sunnis filling key positions, their loyalty was unquestionably to Asad.[62]

Asad ruled with two guiding concepts. First, he did not allow challenges to his rule. Second, he sought a popular consensus for his policies because he did want public support and an overall broad base of support among the population.[63] When he first assumed control, he set out to broaden support for his regime. He held parliamentary and presidential elections, granted permits to parties to work with the Ba'th Party, and instituted economic liberalization.[64] Asad's economic policies reflect his political maneuverings in an attempt to placate competing groups. Initially, the policy of economic liberalization benefited high ranking officers in the Ba'th Party and military as well as the Damascene import-export merchants by consolidating political power and stimulating the commercial and industrial economic sectors. This economic relaxation also benefited independent farmers who took advantage of cash crops. A new class of "nouveaux riches" farmers emerged, creating a schism with the old landowning elite, who in turn supported dissident urban forces fighting the regime.[65]

Moreover, this economic liberalization hurt the public sector. The regime dismantled state farms, leaving the peasant's federation and other state affiliated associations vulnerable to market forces. This move alienated the peasants from the regime and reduced the regime's influence in rural areas. Aware of these problems, Asad introduced a bonus system for public employees, pay raises, and increased autonomy at the local level. Taxes imposed on private enterprises paid for these changes. Additionally, Asad called a series of emergency congresses of workers, students, and peasants. Each group created a paramilitary brigade to defend the regime. These brigades were only part of the military and security build-up against the Islamic fundamentalists.[66]

Asad continued to manipulate and take advantage of the power position of the economic classes as a tool towards consolidating and securing his own power. Asad's regime was a "presidential monarchy presiding over three main institutions of rule—the Syrian Army, the Ba'th Party and the state bureaucracy."[67] Fred H. Lawson claims that societal shifts were just a lucky phenomenon for the Asad regime, but I contend that Asad's ability to use those shifts to his political advantage characterizes his regime.[68] Political cunning, not luck, marks the Asad regime. When he was not using his praetorian guard to impose his will, he did try to gain a consensus, that is build his legitimacy, namely in the eyes of the Sunnis.

Asad not only handled class divisions, but he was acutely aware of the perception of Alawi power domination. Asad tried to mask Alawi dominance in several ways. His statements stressed the importance of the nation and the importance of its people. He tried to establish institutions to increase political participation. In 1973 and 1977, the people elected their first National Council (parliament). He down-played the role of the Ba'th Party, although it is a major tool for mobilizing support. He tried to establish ties with the middle class and gave special attention to improving the quality of life of the lower classes. Additionally, he tried to appease the Sunnis by, for example, changing the secular format for the oath of office to a religious one. Also, he stressed Arabism and Syrian patriotism as the bases for a common identity among Syrians.[69]

Additionally, he responded to protests in 1973 concerning the constitution's omission regarding the requirement for a Muslim president. Asad corrected this omission, only to be confronted with the question of whether an Alawi was a Muslim. He answered this question by appealing to a prominent Shi'i cleric, Imam Musa al-Sadr, who declared that the Alawis were Muslims.[70] He had non-Alawi high officials in his regime. His first three prime ministers were Sunni, but the clannish character of those in power was evident.[71] Hanna Batatu describes this clannish nature, especially conspicuous during the military buildup from 1979 to 1983:

. . . that the ruling element consists at its core of a close kinship group which draws strength simultaneously, but in decreasing intensity, from a tribe, a sect-class, and an ecologic-cultural division of the people.[72]

This buildup was a response to internal (Muslim Brotherhood) and external (Lebanon and Camp David Accords) reasons. Perhaps it also reflected the domination of Alawis in the ruling coalition.[73] During that time, the military and security forces mushroomed. From 1979 to 1983, Syria was the leading weapons importer of the Third World. The number of soldiers in the regular army increased from 200,000 in 1979 to 300,000 in 1984. The reserves increased from 100,000 to 270,000 in that same time period.[74] Rifaat al-Asad, Asad's brother, commanded the 50,000-man Defense Companies. These units possessed the finest equipment, their own intelligence services, their own uniforms, better pay than the other services, and engaged in smuggling operations. They took part in the bloody destruction of Hama in 1982. These forces, led by Rifaat, were feared and hated by Alawis and non-Alawis alike.[75]

The Alawi officers held several key military commands, notably the Chief of Staff for the Air Force, the command of three armored divisions, and command of the Special Units.[76] During Asad's illness, much infighting arose among the high ranking Alawi officers. Three factions developed: Rifaat al-Asad's defense companies and Jamil al-Asad's Alawi Black Shirt organization; special units, chiefs of military intelligence and air force intelligence, the Third Armored Division, and the Presidential Guard; and the regular army's chief of staff, Foreign Minister and Minister of Defense.[77] Asad dealt with this infighting and jockeying for power in a number of ways.

First, Asad appointed each leader of the factions a vice president. The duties of the vice president remained intentionally vague, leaving Asad some flexibility as to the fate of these new appointees.[78] Asad removed the autonomy of the security force and subordinated them to the regular army, demoted officers who used these forces for their own political purposes, broke up the smuggling operations, and dissolved their intelligence services.[79] Additionally, Rifaat and other threatening officers were sent to Moscow and Geneva. Rifaat did not return with the others but stayed in exile for a period of time before his eventual return. There is still much speculation as to the terms of his exile and its purpose.[80] In the end, Asad had to take the necessary steps to diffuse the infighting as well as the dangerous growth of the armed services.

Asad managed to handle every challenge to his regime. Fred H. Lawson sees the future as one of stability for the Asad regime, especially in light of the economic progress during the early 1990s. He claims that

developments in the Syrian economy over the last several years generally reinforced the collective position of the social forces that constitute the al-Asad coalition, leaving them better able to resolve conflicts of interest among themselves and to fend off actual or potential challenges from their primary opponents.[81]

Raymond A. Hinnebusch optimistically views the future of Syria, with the possibility of democratization. He bases his argument on evidence of a growing civil society in Syria, spurred by a growing bourgeoisie. If Bashar, Asad's successor, nurtures and encourages these developments, then, according to Hinnebusch, democratization is possible.[82] However, the strength of Bashar's legitimacy as Asad's successor is still uncertain. Hinnebusch recognized the criticality of the struggle for succession as he claims that, "The test of civil society in the shorter term may come with the inevitable succession struggle."[83] So far, succession does not appear to have been much of a struggle and, therefore, perhaps, not much of a test.

The question on Syria's future is interesting, but it, too, is beyond the scope of this book. The future direction of Syria's domestic politics, however, I would argue will impact on its future foreign policy. I will show this link to the past in chapters 5 and 7, which may serve as a springboard for research on future cases. For this study, we must focus on Asad's regime in light of the ethnic divisions in Syrian society.

Asad was a clever politician who was able to manipulate the situation to his advantage.[84] "He used a combination of kin and sectarian solidarity, Leninist party loyalty, and bureaucratic command to concentrate power in a presidential monarchy, while a praetorian guard commanded by Alawi clansmen shielded him from challenges."[85] He spent a tremendous amount of resources on the military, which employs one-fifth of the labor force.[86] "In deploying Alawi asabiyya in its primitive power accumulation, it stimulated primordial identities and de-legitimized itself in the eyes of many Sunnis."[87] Additionally, both the regime and its opposition reflected the coinciding of communal and class divisions, which greatly reduced room for compromise or civility. Opposition groups saw violence as a credible means for expression, and, in turn, the regime repressed violence harshly and without any lawful restraint.[88]

Even with Asad's determined effort to diffuse ethnic divisions, he was not successful. Moshe Ma'oz claims:

> Indeed, it appears that the appointment of Sunni Muslim personalities to senior positions in the Syrian government does not alter the fact or the awareness of the majority of the population that Alawi army officers control the centres of power in the country. Similarly, the public gestures and tributes which have been made by Assad towards Muslim ulama and Islamic values have apparently

failed to satisfy the misgivings in conservative circles lest Islam be divorced from the Syrian state and society.[89]

Asad could not escape the fact that the people in Syria have ethnic loyalties that do not coincide with the state. His minority-rule regime exacerbated this situation and caused him, at times, to rely on his praetorian guard for stability.

CONCLUSION

There are a number of ways to approach the study of Syria. Yahya Sadowski mentions two approaches, explained earlier. I agree with those scholars who argue that Syria can only be understood in an ethnic context, though I recognize that other variables can constrain its leaders, such as economic variables and regional instabilities; however, Asad was forced to address the ethnic divisions in his country (albeit there is much controversy on how he addressed those issues). Also, I focused my discussion on Asad because he was the leader during each of my cases. Interestingly, he met many of the challenges to his regime, but not without a heavy cost. In the following chapters, I will examine how he used foreign policy to address a critical domestic challenge: ethnic divisiveness.

My discussion of the people, the history of Syria's state formation, and its political development all point to the fact that Syria is an extremely divided country. Ethnic loyalties are strong because group members share a common religion, culture, kinship, and language. Additionally, these components of ethnicity are further strengthened or reinforced through region and class. The artificial creation of the state further exacerbated ethnic divisiveness because state boundaries were made without considering the ethnic dimension of the people. Finally, and most importantly, Syria's political development occurred along ethnic lines, and the Alawis emerged as the wielders of political power by capturing the institutions of the military, Party, and presidency; therefore, according to Horowitz, it is a state indicative of ethnic divisiveness. Consequently, ethnic loyalties supersede state loyalties.

The above description of Syrian political development addresses the challenge of Islamic extremism. The danger of this challenge, is that unlike Egypt it is conducted in the context of a country that does not have a sense of a strong national identity. Extremist groups pose a greater danger in this context because they can serve as a wedge to further divide members of a society who lack a strong national bond. If these groups incite the Sunni majority, then they will pose a great danger to the Alawi-dominated regime. In this situation, extremist groups who manipulate ethnicity for political gain pose a great danger.[90] In Egypt, where ethnicity and nationality coincide, these groups are not afforded the ethnic dimension in their quest for power.

For the future, we must continue to evaluate Syria's political development, to include the effects of Islamic fundamentalism as well as other forces on the loyalties of the people toward their ethnic group vice the state. This analysis will be extremely interesting now that Asad has passed away. For this project, however, we have established, based on Horowitz's criteria, that Syria during the 1970s and 1980s, the time-frame for my cases, was an ethnically divided state. In the following chapters, we will examine how Egypt's ethnic homogeneity and Syria's ethnic divisiveness were variables in their respective foreign policies, specifically in their choices in state alignment.

NOTES

1. *Background Notes*, United States Department of State, Bureau of Public Affairs 5 no. 13 (November 1994): 1.

2. Y. Choueiri, "Two Histories of Syria and the Demise of Syrian Patriotism," *Middle Eastern Studies* 23, no. 4 (October 1987): 496.

3. Ibid., 498–501.

4. Ibid., 508.

5. Donald L. Horowitz, *Ethnic Groups in Conflict* (Berkeley: University of California Press, 1985), 50–51.

6. Moshe Ma'oz, "The Emergence of Modern Syria," in *Syria Under Assad: Domestic Constraints and Regional Risks*, ed. Moshe Ma'oz and Avner Yaniv (New York: St. Martin's Press, 1986), 13.

7. Horowitz, 492.

8. Joseph Pincus, "Syria: A Captive Economy," *Middle East Review* 12, no. 1 (Fall 1979): 49.

9. R. D. McLaurin, Don Peretz, and Lewis W. Snider, *Middle East Foreign Policy: Issues and Processes* (New York: Praeger Publishers, 1982), 239.

10. McLaurin, Peretz, and Snider, 241.

11. Yahya M. Sadowski, "Ba'thist Ethics and the Spirit of State Capitalism: Patronage and the Party in Contemporary Syria," in *Ideology and Power in the Middle East*, ed. Peter J. Chelkowski and Robert J. Pranger (Durham: Duke University Press, 1988), 163.

12. Daniel Bates and Amal Rassam, *Peoples and Cultures of the Middle East* (Englewood Cliffs: Prentice Hall, 1983), 60.

13. Dale F. Eickelman, *The Middle East: An Anthropological Approach*, 2nd ed. (Englewood Cliffs: Prentice Hall, 1989), 266.

14. Hourani, 37.

15. Ibid., 61.

16. Ibid.

17. The differing views of the caliphate between the Sunnis and the Shi'as came from a discussion with Dr. Mahmud A. Faksh on February 22, 1997. The discussion of the Sunna and "Golden Age" came from James A. Bill and Robert Springborg, 54.

18. The historical discussion on the roots of the split are from Peretz, 33, and the discussion on the expanding nature of the division is from Bill and Springborg, 54–55.

19. Bates and Rassam, 60–62.

20. Ibid., 67–68. Dr. Faksh clarified the four sub-sects and areas in which Alawis live. Peretz, 33 clarified the name of the Twelvers.

21. Eickelman, 275.

22. Daniel Pipes, "The Alawi Capture of Power in Syria," *Middle Eastern Studies* 25, no. 4 (October 1989): 434.

23. Ibid., 431, 433.

24. Ibid., 435–437.

25. Ibid., 437.

26. Bill and Springborg, 39.

27. Ibid.

28. Daniel Pipes, *Greater Syria: The History of an Ambition* (New York: Oxford University Press, 1990), 16.

29. The discussion of the diversity of communities and the quotation is from Pipes, *Greater Syria*, 18.

30. Ibid., 21.

31. Ibid., 16.

32. The Sykes-Picot Agreement stemmed from a series of notes exchanged among the governments of Britain, France, and Russia from 1915 to 1916. These notes explained the future status of the Ottoman Arab lands. France was promised the Syrian coast north of the city of Tyre, the Ottoman province of Adana, a majority of Cilicia. Additionally France would create an independent Arab zone under French protection, which included Syria and northern Iraq, as well as the Mosul's oil fields. The Husein-McMahon Agreement stemmed from a series of exchanged letters between Sir Henry McMahon, the British high commissioner for Egypt and the sherif. The Agreement formed a military alliance based on a vague political understanding. The Allies wanted to prevent a delay in the Arab uprising against the Ottomans, so the details of the agreement were to be finalized at a later date. Great Britain agreed to Arab independence in the regions from the Mediterranean and the Red Sea, eastward to Iran and the Persian Gulf. Great Britain retained supremacy in Aden. The districts of Mersina and Alexandretta and the regions in Syria west of Damascus, Homs, Hama, and Aleppo were excluded from the agreement because the British believed that these areas were not purely Arabic, a claim the sherif disputed. This information about the Sykes-Picot Agreement is from Peretz, 98, and the information about the Husein-McMahon Agreement is from Peretz, 139.

33. Ibid., 397–398.

34. Bill and Springborg, 230.

35. Hudson, 255.

36. Ibid., 255–256.

37. Philip K. Hitti, *Syria: A Short History* (New York: The MacMillan Company, 1959), 249–250.

38. Peretz, 406–407.

39. Hudson, 253–254.

40. Horowitz, 492.

41. Bates and Rassam, 67–68.

42. A review by Yahya Sadowski of *Authoritarian Power and State Formation in Ba'thist Syria: Army, Party, and Peasant,* by Raymond A. Hinnebusch, in *Middle East Journal* 45, no. 2 (Spring 1991): 341.

43. Ibid.

44. Mahmud Faksh, "The Alawi Community of Syria: A New Dominant Political Force," *Middle Eastern Studies* 20, no. 2 (April 1984): 140–141.

45. Hanna Batatu, "Some Observations on the Social Roots of Syria's Ruling Military Group and the Causes for its Dominance," *The Middle East Journal* 35, no. 3 (Summer 1981): 343.

46. Hourani, 404.

47. Ibid, 404.

48. Springborg and Bill, 39–40.

49. Ibid., 40.

50. McLaurin, Peretz, and Snider, 242–243.

51. Pipes, "The Alawi Capture of Power in Syria," 437–441.

52. Horowitz, 492–493.

53. Ibid., 493–494.

54. Ibid., 494.

55. Horowitz cites Petran in ibid.

56. Ibid., 494–495.

57. Ibid., 495–496.

58. Pipes, "The Alawi Capture of Power in Syria," 443–446.

59. Ibid., 446.

60. Patrick Seale, *Asad: The Struggle For The Middle East* (Berkeley: University of California Press, 1988), 172, 178.

61. Ma'oz, 27–28.

62. Ibid., 28.

63. Seale, 172.

64. Yosef Olmert, "Domestic Crisis and Foreign Policy in Syria: The Assad Regime," *Middle East Review* 20, no. 3 (Spring 1988): 19.

65. Fred H. Lawson, "From Neo-Ba'th to Ba'th Nouveau: Hafiz al-Asad's Second Decade," *Journal of South Asian and Middle Eastern Studies* 14, no. 2 (Winter 1990): 1–6.

66. Ibid., 5–7.

67. Ibid., 20.

68. Ibid., 2.

69. Ma'oz, 29–30.

70. Seale, 173.

71. Seale, 182, and Batatu, 331.

72. Batatu, 331.

73. Lawson, "From Neo-Ba'th to Ba'th Nouveau: Hafiz al-Asad's Second Decade," 6–8.

74. Ibid., 8.

75. Alasdair Drysdale, "The Succession Question in Syria," *The Middle East Journal*, 39, no. 2 (Spring 1985): 248.

76. Lawson, "From Neo-Ba'th to Ba'th Nouveau: Hafiz al-Asad's Second Decade," 8.

77. Ibid., 12.

78. Drysdale, 249.

79. Lawson, "From Neo-Ba'th to Ba'th Nouveau: Hafiz al-Asad's Second Decade," 12–13.

80. Drysdale, 250–257.

81. Fred H. Lawson, "Domestic Transformation and Foreign Steadfastness in Contemporary Syria," *Middle East Journal* 48, no. 1 (Winter 1994): 51.

82. Raymond A. Hinnebusch, "State and Civil Society in Syria, *Middle East Journal* 47, no. 2 (Spring 1993): 256–257.

83. Ibid., 256.

84. See Seale, 169–184.

85. Hinnebusch, "State and Civil Society in Syria," 246.

86. Ibid.

87. Both the idea about the military and the quote are from ibid. Note that the term asabiyya is defined by Albert Hourani as a "corporate spirit oriented towards obtaining and keeping power," in Albert Hourani, *A History of the Arab Peoples*, (Cambridge: The Belknap Press of Harvard University Press, 1991), 2.

88. Hinnebusch, "State and Civil Society in Syria," 246. Ibid.

89. Ma'oz, 31–32.

90. For a discussion on political ethnicity see Joseph Rothschild, *Ethnopolitics : A Conceptual Framework* (New York: Columbia University Press, 1981), 4–5 and 248, and for political entrepreneurship and for ethnicity see pages 87–96. Also, see chapter 2 in which I discuss Rothschild's theory of ethnopolitics.

91. This table is taken from "Power and 'Alawi Cohesiveness," *FBIS*, NES-95–191-S, October 3, 1995, 15–17.

Chapter Four

Cold War Case: Egypt

The purpose of this chapter is to explore the relationship between ethnic divisiveness and foreign policy. I will examine four indicators: elite attitudes, foreign aid, trade, and treaties and agreements—in light of five issues: security, territory, status, human resources, and nonhuman resources (see table 1.1). These indicators will help us determine the significance of ethnic divisiveness to foreign policy decisions. Specifically, I will look at alignment decisions and the effect of a loss of a state's legitimacy based on ethnic divisiveness. This chapter will examine Egypt's realignment with the United States in the late 1970s, while chapter 5 will examine Syria's decision to sign a treaty with the Soviets in 1980. These Cold War–era cases are revealing because the Camp David Accords affected Syria's decision to reaffirm its relationship with the Soviets. My focus will be the internal factor, ethnic homogeneity and ethnic divisiveness for Egypt and Syria's decisions, respectively.

The most challenging indicator is elite attitudes, and to best meet this challenge, I will use opinion polls of students and noted intellectuals' opinions as indications of elite attitudes. While I will focus on Sadat, I will expand my elite category to include prominent government officials, intellectuals, students, and commentators. I do this for three reasons: First, we may never know exactly what a leader is actually thinking or what is motivating him. Even memoirs or interviews may not reflect the true thoughts of the individual. By examining other key members of society, we may better understand the thoughts and motivations of its leaders. In Ole R. Holsti and John D. Sullivan's discussion of the socialization of political elites, they explain the significance of examining cultural factors: "They may . . . be viewed as background factors which have contributed to the political 'education' of present leaders, and which provide at least latent support for current foreign policies."[1] I will use this idea in my analysis of elite attitudes based on the attitudes of certain members of society from which these leaders came. Second, I extend the notion of elites to these elements of society because of the availability of that data. Finally, I use expert opinions and analyses to help understand the motivations and thoughts of leaders. The most valuable opinions are from those experts who worked with the leaders in some capacity. The sources for my data on elite attitudes include speeches, memoirs, student opinion polls, and noted experts' observations and analyses.

After a brief recounting of the case, I will discuss the realignment story based on the indicators noted earlier. By using this framework, I feel that we may better analyze these cases in terms of the linkage between the domestic and foreign policy realms. The tradeoff is that we might lose some meaning of the story if it is not told in total. By briefly recounting the story before fully discussing it using the framework, I believe that the tradeoff does not diminish our analysis. My conclusion will attempt to put everything back together, but analysis, at times, requires us to break the whole into its components, i.e., indicators and issues. We must remember, therefore, that the components are related, and only when we put them back together do they tell the story. I will follow this organization for both my Cold War era and post–Cold War era cases. Finally, we will explore these cases for any differences or similarities that may shed light on the significance of ethnic divisiveness to alignment decisions in the Cold War versus post–Cold War contexts.

BACKGROUND TO EGYPT'S ALIGNMENT CHANGE

From 1955 to 1973, Egypt was the largest noncommunist recipient of Soviet economic and military assistance. However, at the peak of its support from the Soviets, Egypt turned to the United States. According to Steven David, in order to understand the realignment, we must understand the following: Sadat's decision to maintain the Soviet alignment following his rise to power in 1970; his formalization of the alignment in the Treaty of Friendship and Cooperation in 1971; the expulsion of Soviet advisors in 1972; and the partial rapprochement with the Soviets in 1973. Additionally, we need to examine the reasons behind the 1973 war.[2]

At first, Nassar claimed that he had neither Eastern nor Western leanings. This would soon change when the West refused to sell Egypt arms unconditionally. Czechoslovakia agreed to sell arms, and it was the first time a Soviet bloc nation had made such an agreement with an Arab nation.[3] For Arab nations, this was viewed as a move away from Western influence and the reminder of colonialism. With the Soviet Union's lack of a colonial past in the region and the United States' refusal to fund the Aswan Dam, Nassar chose the Soviets as an ally. The soviets, in turn, welcomed Nassar's anti-West rhetoric and wanted influence in the region. Consequently, they agreed to sell arms to Egypt in the spring of 1955. This was the first major arms deal for the Soviets with a Third World country. The Soviet-Egyptian alignment expanded to include economic and political assistance. After Egypt's 1967 defeat, the alignment further strengthened, and the Soviets supplied Egypt with more arms, while Egypt gave the Soviets naval and air bases. Soviet pilots and air defense crews directly participated in the fighting during the War of Attrition in 1969–1970 in a demonstration of Soviet commitment, which was the first time Soviet forces participated in a Third World conflict in substantial numbers. While there were still cracks in the alignment, for example Nassar was angry that the Soviets would not supply offensive weapons needed to win back the Sinai, it was overall mutual dependence that marked this relationship.[4]

The United States thought Sadat would not rule for long. Henry Kissinger said that Sadat "was an interim figure who would not last more than a few weeks." (Later he retracted that claim and called that earlier prediction as "among my wildest misjudgments.") According to David, Sadat initially maintained alignment with the Soviets because the American-Israeli alliance posed a great threat, and internally Sadat needed the support of his military. Also, Egypt faced great economic hardship. Since the mid-1960s, the growth rate averaged 4 percent annually. The 1967 War made this worse because of the revenue lost from the Suez Canal, Sinai oil fields, and tourism. Saudi and Kuwaiti grants could not fully compensate for this loss. Economic problems stimulated student, intellectual, and journalist unrest. The Soviet alignment ensured that assistance would continue.[5]

Internally, Sadat faced a challenge to his rule from Ali Sabri, the vice president, who led a group of leftists in the Arab Socialist Union, the primary political party. Sadat represented a moderate position, which Ali Sabri believed was too divergent from Nassarist policies. Sadat responded by not only purging the government of the leftist supporters of Ali Sabri, but also by successfully removing those members of the military who were extreme Rightists.[6] Ironically, in the midst of the Ali Sabri affair, Sadat signed the Treaty of Friendship and Cooperation with the Soviets on May 27, 1971. The treaty was a bit surprising because Sadat was suspicious that the Soviets might have supported the Sabri affair, and Sadat tended to view the Soviets as a threat.[7]

While the Americans had thoughts of approaching Sadat, Kissinger argued that "no Arab leader, however moderate, could accede to Israel's demands and survive in the climate of humiliation, radicalism, and Soviet influence of the period." For Sadat, the Soviets still provided the means to deal with the Israeli threat, as well as with the domestic economy. Still, it is not clear who initiated the Treaty. According to Sadat, it was a Soviet initiative. In any case, the treaty reflected a tenuous relationship between Egypt and the Soviet Union.[8]

EXPULSION OF SOVIETS

In 1972, Sadat took a dramatic step by expelling the Soviets from his country. Between fifteen and twenty thousand technicians and instructors left, as well as Soviet pilots and two hundred aircraft. Additionally, the Soviets lost their exclusive use of six airfields. The Soviets' quick compliance with Sadat's expulsion demand reflected their lack of control and influence. Sadat felt certain that the Soviets would not resist his demand because they feared losing influence in other Third World countries, and if they were to invade, then they would face Egyptian resistance. Although earlier it had appeared that Sadat had depended on Soviet assistance, it was evident in 1972 that he retained a great deal of autonomy regarding his relations with the Soviets.[9]

Why did Sadat expel the Soviets? A prominent view is that he expelled them to actually further the alignment. He demonstrated his autonomy and signaled to the Soviets that they would have to meet his demand for offensive arms in order for the Soviets to remain in Egypt. Sadat did make a last effort to secure such weapons before announcing his decision. While this is an important factor, there were also domestic considerations. David suggests that Sadat was concerned about appeasing his own military, which was primarily anti-Soviet.[10] Raymond A. Hinnebusch agrees that Sadat recognized the importance of the military for his success, and he worked hard to reform the military and change its role of political player to professional fighting force.[11] I will elaborate on this point when I discuss the October 1973 war. Additionally, the role of the military in politics is debatable. Robert Springborg claims that "empirical and theoretical reevaluation of the role of the Egyptian military in politics suggests that it was less profound than previously thought." Sahrough Akhavi claims that "The notion of praetorian solidarities binding a military elite together is simply not an accurate description of the Egyptian political system."[12] My point is that while the military may have been a key player, which Sadat wanted to appease, it was not so politically powerful as to prevent Sadat from purging elements of it from his political elite, as described in chapter 2, nor could it prevent Sadat from overseeing real military reform, which I will explain in the next section.

Another domestic consideration for the expulsion was that it paved the way for other sources of aid from Libya, Saudi Arabia, and Western investment. This economic imperative will become evident as a key factor in Sadat's decisions in the following sections of this chapter and in chapter 6. Additionally, the decision was extremely popular with the Egyptian people.[13] "The elite and the masses rejoiced in the prospect of getting back at the Soviets, while hopes were raised that the years of international inaction had at last come to an end."[14]

Sadat's decision occurred without any evidence of a changed external environment. The Israeli threat did not change, the level of Soviet aid was constant, and the United States remained a staunch Israeli ally. While the expulsion brought temporary domestic support for Sadat, he still faced many domestic challenges. There were still dissatisfied members of the military, student protests, and a continued economic slump. The oil-rich Arab nations withheld assistance until Sadat showed more aggressive intentions towards Israel. Sadat did send Hafez Ismail to Washington to see if there were possibilities of American diplomatic support for Egypt's desire to peacefully remove Israel from the Sinai. Ismail left Washington convinced that the United States stood firmly behind Israel.[15]

THE OCTOBER WAR

Egypt turned to the Soviets, and this time the Soviets responded with offensive weapons. Why did Sadat decide to go to war? According to David, Sadat initiated conflict because both the military and the Egyptian people were impatient with the continuing stalemate, and the oil-rich Arab states demanded Egyptian action against Israel before they provided assistance to Egypt.[16] Sadat decided to use his military in a limited manner to support his political aims, and he viewed the 1973 war as a means to gain political leverage. According to Colonel T. N. Dupuy,

> the disruption of war was certain to force the superpowers to turn their attention back to the Middle East. . . . In essence, then, Sadat's decision to go to war was a political gamble designed to end a political stalemate, since for Egypt and for Sadat any change was likely to be better than the stalemate.[17]

Sadat based his decision to go to war on limited aims by combining force and diplomacy in the pursuit of political objectives.[18]

Another reason Sadat was able to launch this war was due to his ability to oversee real military reforms that created an improved fighting force. The homogeneous nature of Egyptian society contributed to these successful reforms. According to J. C. Hurewitz, "A major reason why neither the Iraqi nor the Syrian officers contrived to work as a team could be found in the heterogeneous societies of these two states, which contrasted with the relatively homogeneous society of Egypt."[19] The army was not fragmented along religious lines. The Copts were an integrated and contributing factor to the force and many filled key roles in positions of responsibility.[20] This cohesiveness is a significant point of departure as compared with the composition of the Syrian forces, described in chapters 3 and 5.

Sadat's generals understood the relationship between politics and the military. General Ismail, in particular, understood this relationship and realized that while complete victory over Israel was not achievable, political gains were. Ismail ensured skillful staff planning and recognized the importance of training, discipline, and indoctrination. According to Dupuy, "The professional competence of the Egyptian planning for Operation 'Badr' . . . could probably not have been excelled by any other army in the world." The soldiers were ready; they were highly motivated and well trained for this operation.[21] Major General Chaim Herzog observed that

> Many of the Israeli commanders noted a marked improvement in the standard of fighting of the Arab forces, and particularly of the Egyptian infantry. . . . Because of the emphasis that had been placed on the intellectual ability of the officers and men, the Israeli forces faced an Egyptian Army better led at the tactical level than any they had known before. Added to this was a marked increase in the standard of discipline and outward smartness, which very naturally reflected itself also in the execution of orders on the battlefield.[22]

Also, Herzog claims that the Egyptians did well strategically and made great strides in their military intelligence.[23] Sadat trusted his military leaders with good military intelligence, which was, and still is, not the case in Syria, as we will see. While David argues, as mentioned earlier, that there was dissatisfaction within the military, it was not critical enough to disrupt Sadat's ability to encourage real military reform without fear of reprisals. Consequently, on the battlefield, his forces performed well.

During the course of the War, Sadat once again became disenchanted with the Soviets. They evacuated their civilians from Egypt, which demonstrated their lack of confidence in his army. They requested a cease-fire based on Asad's request, and not on Sadat's. There was a delay in Soviet arms deliveries, and the United States technologically outpaced Soviet support for Egypt with U.S. support for Israel.[24]

After initial success, Sadat faced the threat of the destruction of his Third Army. The Soviets failed to ensure Israel's cease-fire compliance, so Sadat turned to the United States. The Americans had leverage over the Israelis and were able to save the Third Army. The October War was a turning point for the Americans, also. They realized that their past policy of undisputed Israeli superiority as a deterrent for conflict needed adjustment. Now they had to be receptive to Egyptian interests as well in order to better deter conflict.[25] Alfred Leroy Atherton Jr., a senior diplomat who worked Middle East issues, remarked that, "Even I was skeptical of Sadat's sincerity. We didn't take him seriously enough as an institution until the 1973 war."[26] Apparently, Sadat's decision to go to war grabbed the attention of the superpower that could help him. His political gamble paid off.

Meanwhile, according to Mohamed Hassanein Heikal, relations between Egypt and the Soviet Union deteriorated for three reasons: First, Egypt felt that the Soviets were not providing enough arms as compared to what Israel was receiving from the United States. Second, there was personal animosity between Sadat and the Soviet leaders. Finally, the Soviets felt that they were not included in the Middle East issues. Consequently, Sadat reached the following conclusions:

1. The United States was the only power that could make Israel withdraw. According to Sadat, "That man [Kissinger] is the only person who can order that woman [Golda Meir] to get out—and be obeyed."[27]
2. The United States had to be convinced that Soviet influence in the region was insignificant.
3. The October War was the last war with Israel.
4. Egypt needed a Marshall Plan that could only be funded by the U.S. government and private investment, as well as money from Arab oil-producing states.
5. As a result, two new alliances would emerge: regionally, the Tehran-Riyadh-Cairo axis replaced the Cairo-Damascus-PLO axis, and globally, the United States and Western Europe replaced the Soviet Union and the Third World.[28]

In March, 1976, Sadat abrogated the Treaty of Friendship and Cooperation with the Soviets. He ended all Soviet naval privileges in Egyptian naval ports, repudiated his $11 billion debt to the Soviet Union, and publicly criticized Soviet influence in the Third World. According to David, Sadat was able to do this because Western, especially American, aid more than made up for the lost Soviet aid. Additionally, he received aid from oil-rich Arab countries. By November 1977, Sadat surprised everyone with his visit to Jerusalem, and a year later he signed the Camp David Accords. The formal peace treaty occurred in 1979.[29]

It was Sadat's journey to Israel and the events leading up to the 1979 treaty that seemed most risky for Sadat. Why did he choose such a risky move? According to David, the United States saw the importance of economic assistance as the key for Sadat's popular approval. Consequently, by the fall of 1985 the United States had poured more economic assistance into Egypt than the Soviets had in its twenty years of assistance to Egypt. In five years, the United States became Egypt's principal provider of arms, trade, aid, and food.[30]

The following sections will examine the motivations of Sadat's realignment decision by focusing on his historic Jerusalem visit, the Camp David Accords, and finally the treaty signed in 1979. Sadat himself understood the risks involved with this decision. In his speech to the Israeli Knesset he said,

> But to be absolutely frank with you, I took this decision after long thought, knowing that it constitutes a great risk, for God Almighty has made it my fate to assume responsibility on behalf of the Egyptian people, to share in the responsibility of the Arab nation, the main duty of which, dictated by responsibility, is to exploit all and every means in a bid to save my Egyptian Arab people and the pan-Arab nation from the horrors of new suffering and destructive wars, the dimensions of which are forseen only by God Himself.[31]

Why was Sadat able to make this decision? Did the homogeneous nature of the Egyptian people provide enough of a reservoir of legitimacy to enable Sadat to take risks? According to Ali E. Hillal Dessouki,

> Sadat used to contrast Egypt's deep-seated unity with the sectarian, familial, and communal fragmentation of most Arab countries. According to Sadat, this unity allowed Egypt to pursue a purposeful foreign policy and to make hard decisions (e.g., peace with Israel) impossible for most Arab countries because of their domestic fragmentation.[32]

My task is to determine the truth of this statement.

INDICATOR: ELITE ATTITUDES

To begin, we will examine elite attitudes as defined earlier in light of the issue areas described in table 1.1 and attempt to uncover the motivations for Sadat's decision to realign. For example, we will ask whether Sadat and other elites were concerned about internal versus external security, or perhaps both. Additionally, we will explore these attitudes in the contexts of the domestic, regional, and international levels. Heikal explains that "After 1973, Egypt's foreign policy appears to have been formulated largely on the basis of assumptions that the Egyptian decision-maker drew from his reading of certain variables he saw on the internal, regional and global fronts."[33] Our framework allows us to explore these different contexts. As noted earlier, I derived these data from speeches, memoirs, polls, Foreign Broadcast Information Service (FBIS), and other such documents. The key to this analysis on Egypt, our null set, will be its comparison to the analysis on Syria, which will follow. If my hypotheses are correct, then we will not see ethnicity as a factor driving foreign policy, although we will see other domestic factors having an influence on this particular case.

ISSUE: SECURITY AND TERRITORY

How did elites view the issues of security and territory? I combine these two issues because of their interrelationship in this area of the world. The issue of security focuses on military aid, bases, weapons, military actions, boundaries, etc.[34] Sadat explains that at the heart of the Middle East question is the Palestinian problem. He offers a peace strategy recognizing the State of Israel: "A peace agreement should provide for the establishment of a Palestinian State on the West Bank of Jordan and the Gaza Strip, and Israel should withdraw from the territories occupied in 1967 . . . [thereby] ending the state of war."[35] He continues to state that, "We cannot have any bargaining over the rights of the Palestinian people or over one inch of the Arab territories seized in 1967. Only thus can a permanent and just peace be achieved."[36]

In an interview, Boutros Boutros-Ghali, the Minister of State for Foreign Affairs of Egypt, echoed Sadat's view that the Palestinian issue was a key factor for peace. When asked if peace could exist without a resolution on the Palestinian issue, Boutros-Ghali replied, "No, absolutely not. There will be no peace in the Middle East without a solution to the Palestinian problem." He continued to claim that the agreement with Israel is not a bilateral agreement, but instead an all-inclusive agreement for the region. When asked about the possibility of war in the Middle East, Boutros-Ghali said, "I don't think war in the military sense is possible, but you can easily imagine other forms of tension, such as the use of the oil weapon by the Arab powers in an attempt to get certain concessions necessary for maintaining the peace process." Additionally, he added that "I think we can say that there'll never be a war between Egypt and Israel again."[37]

A 1980 editorial in the Al-Ahram newspaper praised President Ronald Reagan for continuing the peace process as laid out in the Camp David Accords. The editorial claimed that Reagan's message of retaining the Camp David framework had three meanings. First, it was a sign that the United States realized the importance of peace and stability in the Middle East and its tie to world peace and security. Second, Reagan understood that the gains of the peace talks will continue without delay. Finally, the peace process was a result of the United States recognizing its vital interests in the region and commitment to peace.[38] The Deputy Prime Minister and Foreign Minister Kamal Hasa 'Ali also indicated the importance of stability and security as reasons for Egyptian and American cooperation. He claimed that the Egyptian military facilities used by the United States are a means for ensuring peace and stability in the region. Additionally, the facilities allowed the United States to build modern Egyptian forces so that Egypt may defend its territory and contribute to the region's security and stability.[39]

Globally, the United States seemed to be the only power that could deliver peace. According to Kissinger, "the Soviets can give you arms and this means war, but only the United States can give you back your occupied territories and this means peace."[40] Peace appears to have been a motivating factor for this agreement. Was peace pursued for the purpose of security or were there other reasons for peace? According to Marc R. Cooper, the Egyptians add the following to the phrase stated by Kissinger: "and the Soviets cannot give you economic development."[41] We will discuss the economic issue later.

ISSUE: STATUS

Holsti and Sullivan's meaning for this issue of status included diplomatic recognition, consular and diplomatic relations, status of representatives, etc.[42] They only looked at this issue as it related to the international realm. I will extend the idea of status to the domestic and regional realms. In other words, did Sadat make decisions based on his desire to gain status internationally, regionally, and/or domestically? This domestic or internal status incorporates our discussion on legitimacy based on national identity. Remember, however, we limited our discussion on legitimacy based on this link. Legitimacy, a key factor of this "domestic status," is a key ingredient for the regime, and when ethnic loyalties coincide with national loyalties, then that sense of a shared political community and values is a great commodity for the regime. Was this commodity responsible for Sadat pursuing "a purposeful foreign policy"? We will find that there are other domestic considerations, primarily the economy, that may also have an effect on Sadat's domestic or internal status.

As early as 1970–1971, Sadat felt that he had the support of the Egyptian people and that the United States failed to recognize this point. He said that he "enjoyed the support of my entire people, and that I was capable of saying and doing things no other Arab leader had yet dared to do for the past twenty-two years."[43] Sadat recounts U.S. Secretary of State William Rogers's surprise on hearing of Egypt's peace initiative in 1971. Secretary of State Kissinger's reply to the peace initiative echoed the prior secretary's surprise when he said that he admired Sadat's courage: "He is a man who, for the first time in your part of the world . . . has taken steps never before attempted by any other Arab leader."[44] Sadat's reply to such surprise was, "You are dealing with a people more than 7,000 years old. Isn't it about time you know the Egyptian people?"[45]

It was clear that Sadat did risk a great deal of regional status with his steps towards realignment with the West, and in particular with Israel. President Jimmy Carter discussed Sadat's risks of alienation in the Arab world as he recounts a meeting with the Shah of Iran:

> That same day I had my first meeting with the Shah of Iran. I urged him to support Sadat, which he did, but he warned me not to expect the Saudi Arabians to favor the visit. I did what I could to get foreign leaders to refrain from criticism until the results of Sadat's visit could be assessed. However, it became apparent that Sadat's announcement had made him very vulnerable. His greatest danger came from the accusation that he would seek only bilateral Israeli-Egyptian agreement—that Sadat would betray his Arab brothers and abandon the Palestinian cause merely to get back the Egyptian territory in the Sinai. Vituperative attacks on the Egyptian President continued to mount, in spite of repeated assurances from Egypt, Israel, and ourselves that a comprehensive peace was our goal.[46]

Carter's description of Sadat confirms Sadat's willingness to take risks: "It soon became apparent that he was charming and frank, and also a very strong and courageous leader who would not shrink from making difficult political decisions. He was extraordinarily inclined toward boldness and seemed impatient with those who were more timid or cautious."[47] Additionally, he felt that Sadat was unlike other Arab leaders.

> The more I dealt with Arab leaders, the more disparity I discovered between their private assurances and their public comments. They would privately put forward their ideas for peace and encourage us in any reasonable approach. However, the peer pressure among them was tremendous. None of them—apart from Sadat—was willing to get out in front and publicly admit a willingness to deal with Israel.[48]

Why was Sadat different? Why did he feel that he could risk his status on a regional level among many of the Arab leaders?

I find this especially interesting in light of Heikal's view that the Arab system greatly influences any Arab leader's decisions. Decision-makers derive their moral authority from the Arab world, and Heikal believes this is especially true for Egypt's leaders:

> Together with his ability to attune his decisions to the mood of the whole region, this moral authority is what gives any Arab ruler, especially in Egypt with its central role in the Arab system, stature and importance.[49]

Based on Heikal's view, then, we are left with the same question: Why did Sadat risk his status in the Arab region in order to realign with the West, and even more dramatically seek peace with Israel?

An examination of elite attitudes towards the Arab world will help answer this question. According to Hinnebusch, "By the late seventies a radical cosmopolitanism and an unprecedented anti-Arabism dominated elite circles. Egypt's close foreign policy alliance with the US was one expression of the new mood."[50] Many elites embraced the Western view of the Arab-Israeli conflict, that it was a psychological problem, and dismissed the Arab one, which viewed the struggle as a residue of Western imperialism. They took pride in the West's approval of Egypt's peace initiatives, which proved, as Sadat himself claimed, that unlike other Arabs, Egyptians were civilized. Tawfiq al-Hakim, Egypt's foremost playwright, echoed this view as he claimed that Egypt and Israel were linked as civilized islands in a sea of barbarism. Sadat further distinguished Egyptians from the rest of the Arab world through his efforts for democracy, because Egyptians could claim that they did not share the instability and repressive characteristics of the rest of the Arab world.[51] This point is debatable as chapter 2 suggested, as did the following sections, particularly those dealing with the economy. However, it is important to note how the elites felt about their regime, especially vis-à-vis other Arab regimes.

It appears that there was a strong sense of Egyptian nationalism that was separate from the Arab world. Among elites, there was a strong anti-Arab sentiment. They viewed the Arabs as the cause of Egypt's problems: Egypt had sacrificed both blood and the economy fighting for them, but they had never shown any gratitude. "The signing of the separate peace with Israel was, of course, the most decisive and concrete manifestation of the low priority given by the elite to Egypt's role in the Arab world." Of course, not everyone agreed with this view. Some elites did want Egypt to focus its foreign policy on its role in the Arab world shop. This faction believed that "the break with the Arab states was viewed as transitory since the other Arab leaders had no practical alternative to the course set by Egypt and because, while Egypt could do without them, the Arab world could not do without its heart."[52] Others saw normalization between Israel and Egypt as a means for Zionists to pave the way for Israeli domination of Egypt, while the dean of the Egyptian Lawyers

Table 4.1. Foreign Policy Attitudes[55]

Question	Agree		Disagree		Mixed Feelings		No Opinion		N/A
	%	N	%	N	%	N	%	N	N
1. Which best describes your view of Egypt's proper strategy toward Israel?									
a. Egypt should join the rejectionists and continue to struggle against Israel because she is an illegitimate intrusion by foreigners into the Arab world.	7.9	11							
b. Egypt should make peace with Israel only on condition that she returns all the occupied Arab territories, including the Golan Heights of Syria and permits creation of an independent Palestinian state on the West Bank of the Jordan.	60.0	84							
c. Egypt should make peace with Israel if Israel returns all Egyptian territory, but it doesn't matter about Syrian or Palestinian lands.	29.3	41							
d. Egypt should make peace with Israel even if Israel won't return all Egyptian lands.	2.9	4							
e. NA		5							
2. President Sadat's visit to Israel was a good thing.	64.3	92	10.5	15	21.0	36	4.2	6	2
3. Egyptians and Israelis can live in peace if only they overcome the psychological barriers between them, since there are no irreconcilable conflicts of interest or principle between them.	27.5	39	38.7	55	25.4	36	8.5	12	3
4. President Sadat should continue his negotiations strategy more with the other Arab states.	44.7	63	24.8	35	22.0	31	8.5	12	4

Table 4.1.   Foreign Policy Attitudes [55] (continued)

Question	Agree		Disagree		Mixed Feelings		No Opinion		N/A
	%	N	%	N	%	N	%	N	N
5. Egypt can do without the Arabs who have only caused trouble for her.	23.9	34	38.7	55	33.1	47	4.2	6	3
6. It was a mistake for President Sadat to fight with the Russians.	22.0	31	51.1	72	16.3	23	10.6	15	4
7. It is silly for Egypt to rely on the Americans, friends of Israel.	16.3	22	50.4	68	27.4	37	5.9	8	10
8. What position do you think Sadat should take toward the great powers?									
a. Strongly pro-USSR	0.7	1							
b. Non-aligned but leaning toward the USSR	2.9	4							
c. Absolute non-alignment and neutrality	42.1	59							
d. Non-aligned but leaning toward the USA	50.7	71							
e. Strongly pro-USA	3.6	5							
f. N/A		5							

Association stated that, "the Arab lawyers, with the Egyptian lawyers in the forefront, will maintain their solid stand in rejecting any cooperation under the occupation [occupation here refers to Israeli control of previously Arab held land to include Jerusalem]."[53] While not all elites favored Sadat's policy, it does appear that generally he did have a great deal of support.

Tables 4.1 and 4.2 support this view. The tables reflect answers to a survey given to 145 students at the American University at Cairo between 1977 and 1978. They reflect elite perspectives because, in contrast to students at national universities, they come from the highest strata of Egyptian society. They tend to reflect their parents' opinions and not some student subculture's opinions. As Hinnebusch explains: "This method is not technically rigorous but in the absence of a research climate tolerant of opinion surveys, it was adopted as a plausible substitute." Additionally, students are probably more honest about their opinions than their parents. While scientific sampling was not possible, Hinnebusch concludes that the ". . . responses seem congruent enough with what is known about the group studied to be taken as suggestive indicators of attitudes."[54]

Based on the above tables, it appears that generally the responses supported peace with Israel, as well as Sadat's trip to Jerusalem. Even ethnic Arabs supported his trip to Jerusalem, although their support was the lowest among the other groups. Interestingly, there was great support for Sadat's policy on the international level, as most respondents supported Egypt's break with the Soviet Union and his turn to the West. International status for Sadat seems to have been an important influence on his decisions. Even before the peace process, Sadat explained the importance of international status behind his decision to expel the Soviets:

> I wanted to put the Soviet Union in its place — in its natural position as a friendly country, no more, no less. The Soviets had thought at one time that they had Egypt in their pocket, and the world had come to think that the Soviet Union was our guardian. I wanted to tell the Russians that the will of Egypt was entirely Egyptian; I wanted to tell the whole world that we are our own masters. Whoever wished to talk to us should come over and do it, rather than approach the Soviet Union.[57]

Generally, it appears that elites supported Sadat's policy of peace, although there were some reservations to his dealings with the Arab world. Even this point, however, did not attain totally overwhelming responses.[58] The opposition's criticisms of his trip to Jerusalem paled in the face of mass enthusiasm. Sadat was welcomed home with jubilation. All the state institutions, including the military, bureaucracy, and the media praised Sadat's bold visit. Arab leaders who chastised him only served to increase Sadat's status and increase

Table 4.2. Ethnic Background and Foreign Policy Attitudes[56]						
	Trip to Jerusalem			Silly to Rely on U.S.		
Ethnic Background	*Agree (%)*	*Disagree (%)*	*N*	*Agree (%)*	*Disagree (%)*	*N*
Egyptian Only	69.7	6.1	66	15.6	45.3	64
European Blood	60.0	6.7	15	7.1	50.0	14
Arab Blood	38.1	33.3	21	36.8	36.8	19
Turkish Blood	78.6	0.0	28	4.0	68.8	25

Note that % of mixed feelings and no opinion are omitted

the antiwar sentiment in Egypt. Al-Ahram answered Sadat's critics by claiming that without Egypt, there was no Arab world. The October magazine called Mu'ammar Kaddafy of Libya and Houari Boumedienne of Algeria "mice and monkeys dwarfed by Sadat's presence."[59] Sadat was hailed as the "master of decision," even though only a few months before there were riots over price increases.[60]

President Carter, Prime Minister Menachem Begin, and Sadat's observations indicate widespread support for Sadat's realignment decision. Although we should be wary of the possibility of staged events, their observations corroborate the evidence presented earlier. President Carter describes his visit to Egypt:

> The remainder of our visit was delightful, designed to let the Egyptians and the rest of the world know the closeness between us, the ties between our nations, and the overwhelming support of the Egyptian people for the peace process. We particularly enjoyed a trip from Cairo to Alexandria, moving slowly through the beautiful farming regions of the Nile delta on a fine old train built in 1870. Our car was completely open on both sides, and we felt that we were right in the midst of the hundreds of thousands of people along the way. There were no apparent worries about security. In Alexandria we were welcomed by the largest and most enthusiastic crowds I have ever seen. As I told Sadat, describing my reception would be one time a politician would not have to exaggerate.[61]

Prime Minister Begin had a similar experience during his trip to Egypt. He told Carter that

> I had a wonderful visit to Cairo! The people of Egypt opened their hearts to me. In the morning, tens of thousands lined the streets on both sides, and cheered and waved, and took me to their hearts. I am very moved. I left my car for a while, to the disturbance of the Egyptian secret service, and went into the crowd, which was crying, 'We like you, we love you!' It was absolutely wonderful. Yesterday's reception was at the Qubba Palace. The evening was a 'thousand nights into one.'[62]

Sadat, himself, described the popular support at his homecoming after his trip to Jerusalem. "On my return nearly 5 million Cairenes were out to welcome me, staging an unprecedented demonstration of support."[63] Sadat seems to have had internal support for his realignment decision based on a legitimacy derived from a strong national identity as he claimed that

> the Egyptian people differ from many other peoples, even within the Arab world. We have recovered our pride and self-confidence after the October 1973 battle, just as our armed forces did. We are no longer motivated by 'complexes'—whether defeatist 'inferiority' ones or those born out of suspicion and hate. . . . With the fighting over, we harbored nothing but respect for one another [Israel and Egypt]. Our civilized people know this; it is what induced 5 million citizens to come out to greet me on my return, and the armed forces to salute me in an impressive and quite unprecedented manner.[64]

It does seem as if there was a reservoir of internal status based on a legitimacy linked to national identity, which enabled Sadat to take some risks regarding his status on the regional level. Thomas Lippman supports this view as he claims that

> Sadat wanted to seize the moment. He was not crippled by the domestic weaknesses that hindered other Arab leaders—Egypt was not a precarious artificial state with an imposed monarchy, like Jordan, nor a pit of unrest run by a despised minority, like Syria—and he had reestablished Egypt's freedom of action by breaking with the Soviet Union and attacking Israel in 1973.[65]

Internationally, he was able to cut ties with the Soviets and lean towards the West, because, again, he had support from home. I think we will find in the next section, however, that the hope for prosperity was a driving force for such leanings.

ISSUE: HUMAN AND NONHUMAN RESOURCES

According to Holsti and Sullivan, the issues of human and nonhuman resources include cultural activities, training, travel, education, etc. (human resources), as well as trade, foreign aid, transportation, and other nonmilitary goods (nonhuman resources).[66] I combined these two issues because the literature tends to discuss them together. Did elites believe these issues were important to the realignment decision?

According to Lippman, Sadat went to Jerusalem because Egypt was economically desperate. The economy shaped Sadat's agenda, and he recognized that he inherited an economy that was "below zero." He viewed a peace with

Israel, private enterprise, and an influx of Western capital and technology as instruments of an economic revival that he believed necessary for the dignity and stability of the regime. Some critics point out that Sadat's economic reforms did not bring prosperity to the masses, only to the few parasites. One must look at the dire conditions Sadat inherited. It was clear that Sadat and the government wanted a more even distribution of wealth. The "Planning for Economic Development" summary of the ministry's development plan for 1978–1982 states that

> political wisdom and simple justice call for the alleviation of the burdens of the masses. They deserve respite, for they have given much when Egypt has required it of them, socially, politically and militarily. Political wisdom further recognizes the inherent danger in allowing the standard of living of the majority to deteriorate, when they can see around them luxurious consumption and special privileges. It is only human that they should feel discontent, fear and envy.

The summary reflects the awareness of the government to the political implications of the economic situation.[67]

Using foreign policy as a tool for economic gain was not a new phenomenon to Sadat. He learned this technique from Nassar. Both leaders realized that Egypt could not develop without external help. Economics was an influential variable for the decision to launch the October War. Sadat suggests the primacy of the economy in a speech he gave to his National Security Council on September 30, 1973:

> Let me tell you that our economy has fallen below zero. We have commitments (to the banks, and so on) which we should but cannot meet by the end of the year. In three month's time, by, say, 1974, we shan't have enough money for bread in the pantry! I cannot ask the Arabs for a single dollar more; they say they have been paying us the aid in lieu of the lost [Suez] Canal revenue, although we didn't, or wouldn't fight.[68]

Cooper also claims that the economy played a key role for Sadat's decision to go to Jerusalem. According to Cooper, "Mid-1977 begins to look a great deal like mid-1973. The economy was under a severe strain and going nowhere. There was nothing left to be tried in the polity."[69] Additionally, the regime was faced with mounting criticism from within, strains in the military, an Israeli threat, and superpowers who were unwilling to break the deadlock. Consequently, for Sadat all this meant that "It was back to the well of foreign affairs; one more effort to pull off the international miracle that will solve the domestic problems and ensure the legitimacy of the regime. This is the key link between the domestic and foreign situations."[70] Cooper outlines a three-legged strategy as the basis for Egypt's realignment. First, the moderates had to show the radicals that their view of the solidarity of Israeli and American interests was wrong. In other words, American and Egyptian interests can coincide and create a stability to ensure that the material gains from the October War would not be sacrificed in a future war. Second, Egypt wanted a nonhostile environment in which to receive American and moderate Arab aid that would allow its economy to flourish. Finally, it was clear that Arab dollars would not be enough for Egypt to acquire the essential material, expertise, factories, and food; Egypt needed American aid.[71] While Cooper's three-legged strategy includes both internal and external security factors, it seems that they all hinged on the economy. The desperate situation culminated in the food riots. A realist perspective would support this conclusion because by ensuring peace, the external security issue was resolved. Once security is resolved, other issues may gain precedence. Egypt could now look at resolving other issues, i.e., the economy. Cooper claims that the following Egyptian phrase sums up the three-legged strategy: "the Soviets can give you war, only the Americans can give you peace, and the Soviets cannot give you economic development."[72]

R. D. McLaurin, Don Peretz, and Lewis W. Snider also claim that the economy took on great significance for Sadat:

> With the termination of the war and newfound wealth from the Arab oil-producing states, a new set of priorities emerged. Regaining the rest of the Sinai and the liberation of the other occupied territories were relegated to a secondary or tertiary objective, while an intense, new emphasis was placed on economic and social development.[73]

The realignment gave Egypt access to U.S. and European investment capital and technology. The Egyptian people viewed Sadat's policy of *infitah* to the West as a means to bolster the Egyptian economy. Moreover, the Egyptian people viewed Sadat's trip to Jerusalem as a means for securing economic benefits.[74] Egypt realized that although the Soviets could provide arms, they could not provide the capital or the technology to revive Egypt's dismal economy.

Egypt realigned on the regional level as well in order to gain economic benefits. The Cairo-Riyadh-Tehran axis replaced the Cairo-Damascus-PLO axis that was in place since the October War. American aid to Egypt increased from $250 million in 1974–1975 to $750 million in 1975–1976, and exceeded $1 billion in 1976–1977. This aid represented more economic assistance than any country had received from the United States since the Marshall Plan.[75] The United States provided enough aid to offset the loss of $300 million to $400 million in Arab economic commitments.[76]

Not everyone felt that Sadat was taking the correct steps economically by realigning with the United States. The journal, *Economic Aharam*, provided a forum for academic analysis of Egyptian economic policy. Galal Amin, a noted and internationally renowned economist, provided a critique of the Sadat era. While the popular view of Sadat's assassination was a reflection of religious fanaticism that would threaten the regime, Amin believed that the real danger was the Western technological approach that guided the Sadat regime. In other words, economic rationality that directed Western thought was not suited for Egypt.[77]

While not everyone agreed that infitah was the best policy, it does seem that most elites favored Sadat's economic opening and privatization. Even those students whose fathers experienced upward mobility in the public sector favored capitalism (see tables 4.3 and 4.4). It seems to follow, then, that these elites saw the realignment with the West as an opportunity to further their favored economic policy.

INDICATOR: FOREIGN AID AND TRADE

I combined the foreign aid and trade indicators because together they help us understand the economic imperative in light of the issue areas described in table 1.1. We will need to determine both the quantity and quality of the aid and trade as well as determining the beneficiaries. Did Egypt receive military aid, and if so, was it directed for internal or external security? Was there a particular group in society that benefited economically from this aid and trade? I derived this data from a variety of sources, in particular documents found in the *Middle East Economic Handbook*. The key to this analysis on Egypt will be its comparison to the analysis on Syria, which will follow. The reader should remember that Egypt is our null set. If my hypotheses are correct, we should not see ethnicity as a factor driving foreign policy, although we will see other domestic factors having an influence on this particular case.

ISSUE: SECURITY AND TERRITORY

A legacy of the fifteen-year-old Camp David peace accord between Egypt and Israel is the enormous share these two countries receive of U.S. foreign aid. The current total is $5.6 billion in U.S. military and developmental assistance each year.[80] At the time of the realignment, the United States delivered a great amount of military assistance. The United States compensated for Saudi Arabia's decision to withdraw financing of the purchase of U.S. F-5E fighters with military credits that enabled Egypt to purchase F-4Es.[81]

Table 4.3. Socioeconomic Attitudes[78]

Question	Agree		Disagree		Mixed Feelings		No Opinion		N/A
	%	N	%	N	%	N	%	N	N
1. What in your view, should Egypt's economic policy be?									
a. Increase the size of the public sector, reverse the open door policy and build socialism.	13.4	18							
b. Keep the present balance between the public and private sectors and keep the current open door policy.	37.3	50							
c. Decrease the public sector, expand the private sector, and broaden the open door policy.	49.3	66							
d. N/A		11							
2. There is too much inequality in the distribution of wealth in Egypt.	77.0	111	7.0	10	12.6	18	2.8	4	3
3. The open door has caused the rich to get richer and the poor poorer.	50.0	71	16.9	24	25.3	36	7.7	11	3
4. Egypt never really gave socialism a chance to work.	26.5	36	27.2	37	21.3	29	25.0	34	9

Table 4.4.   Economic Policy Preferences by Employment Sector* and Social Mobility[79]

	N	Policy Preference (%)		
		Socialism	Current Infitah	More Capitalism
Public Sector + Upward Mobility	10	30.0	20.0	50.0
Private Sector + Upward Mobility	12	8.3	50.0	41.7
Public Sector + Stable Status	26	15.4	30.8	53.8
Private Sector + Stable Status	27	18.5	25.9	55.6
Public Status + Downward Mobility	12	8.3	41.7	50.0
Private Status + Downward Mobility	12	8.3	41.7	50.0

*Those reporting careers spanning the public and private sectors are excluded.

In December 1980, Vice President Mubarak and U.S. Defense Secretary Harold Brown agreed to the following:

1. The M-60 tanks, which were scheduled to be delivered by the end of 1981, will be delivered immediately.
2. The completion of the Phantom program will be speeded up by the immediate delivery of the complementary equipment.
3. Some types of weapons for the army, including TOW anti-tank missiles, will be increased.
4. Permission will be given for the supply of some special types of ammunition, particularly sophisticated air-to-air missiles and television-guided bombs, and the supply of all equipment pertaining to paratroopers within 2 months.
5. Training programs will be speeded up and scheduled periods will be reduced in order to increase the number of pilots, technicians and air defense officers.
6. The present administration will recommend to the new administration that Egypt be treated as a friendly country when the U.S. military program for the next five years is drawn up.
7. The preparation and development of the Ra's Banas area on the Red Sea, to enable it to receive all types of aircraft, was discussed. A U.S. expert committee is expected to visit the area within a few days and prepare a report on the requirements in the area.

8. Agreement in principle was reached on the dispatch of an Egyptian military unit to the United States in the second half of next year in order to conduct joint exercises similar to those held in Egypt by U.S. and Egyptian units several weeks ago.[82]

Egypt benefited from the peace treaty with Israel in the area of its military spending. From 1973–1975, Egypt spent 32 percent of its GNP on military forces. By the late 1980s, Egypt was spending only 8–12 percent. Additionally, in 1973–1975, Egypt spent over 50 percent of its central government expenditures on the military, but by 1986–1988, this expenditure dropped to 22 percent. While Egypt's military spending decreased, its military in terms of hardware and personnel increased, as shown in table 4.5. Even with this good trend, Egypt's economy still struggled.[83]

ISSUE: STATUS

Though the U.S. has kept the Egyptian economy afloat and Egyptian prominence in Middle East diplomacy since the 1970s, Egypt still faces many challenges, the most prominent being its society's economic and social welfare.[85] According to Fouad Ajami,

> The gift of Egypt to other Arabs is the gift of its example and moderation and of the skill with which its custodians manage some formidable tasks that lie ahead of them: the economy that has to be privatized and reformed, the task of making livable once again a capital city now choking under the weight of urban blight and ecological degradation, the social peace that has to be vigilantly kept between its substantial Coptic minority, the opening up of more democratic space while still keeping in check the theocrats who tear asunder the country's peace and national unity.[86]

Table 4.5. Military Spending Trend: Egypt (U.S. dollars: millions)[84]

	Manpower (1,000s)	Tanks	Aircraft	Defense Spending ($ millions)	Arms Imports ($ millions)	Arms Exports ($ millions)
1967	220	530	400	0.3	204	1
1973	390	1,880	620	11.4	741	14
1982	447	2,100	429	7.2	1,900	360
1988	452	2,425	517	6.1	725	170
1991	420	3,190	495	5.2	—	—

Economic growth is a means of attaining status, both internally and externally. Ajami cites other variables that affect status, such as religious divisions; however as mentioned earlier, these divisions alone are not ethnic divisions. The Copts still consider themselves as Egyptians because they are the descendants of the first Egyptian Christians who were the original Pharaonic inhabitants.[87] I think it is fair to say that economic growth can enhance the status of a country.

ISSUE: HUMAN RESOURCES AND NONHUMAN RESOURCES

At first glance, the economy seems to have improved under Sadat. Egypt's gross domestic product (GDP) grew at an average annual rate of 8.1 percent from 1970 to 1980. Agriculture contributed 19 percent, mining 17 percent, and manufacturing, wholesale and retail trade, and services each contributed 12 to 13 percent.[88] These statistics, however, do not capture all aspects of Egypt's economic situation.

During the 1970s, there was a great consumption boom. The infitah policy was not the primary cause; rather, it was the coincidental occurrence of Egypt's economic opening and the OPEC countries' price fixing capabilities. These countries experienced a surge in economic development and its markets, which in turn created a manpower need. The Egyptians fulfilled this need. More than one million Egyptians worked in these countries and sent their earnings home. In addition to money, these workers brought back all kinds of goods, such as stereos, toys, watches, cigarettes, etc. Those that brought back these goods for resale were known as "suitcase millionaires." The government encouraged this migration of workers because it not only brought in dollars, but it also reduced unemployment.[89]

There were negative effects of this worker migration. First, many who left were important for Egypt's struggling domestic economy. According to an Egyptian journalist who covered economic affairs for the Middle East News Agency, there were four potential purchasers of goods in Egypt. "First, thieves and smugglers. Second, butchers. Third, doctors. And, fourth, anyone who owns an apartment." Smugglers became rich because they evaded customs and resold goods at a high price. Butchers or more accurately meat producers profited by using subsidized bread rather than the more expensive hay as cattle fodder. Doctors charged high fees to private patients who wanted to escape from the dirty crowded public clinics. Finally, apartment owners became rich by filling their homes with cheap, tacky furniture, known as "Louis Farouk" style and renting them out to foreigners.[90]

There was legitimate money circulating as well. Egypt had been under such an austere economy during the 1960s and early 1970s that it is quite understandable that there would be a spending frenzy after the people had gone without for so long. Also, spending was an outcome driven by high inflation and low domestic interest rates; the incentive to save was just not there.[91] The authors of the 1978 five-year plan explained that their intentions did not support the private sector's use of the infitah to import foreign luxury comsumer goods. They certainly did not intend ". . . to promote class divisions, but this has happened. . . . There are indications of a societal trend toward class divisions in Egypt now, which can only mean a weakening of national solidarity"[92]

Egypt, however, did receive critical aid from a number of sources that seemed to have helped and at least offset any aid Egypt lost from many Arab countries as a result of the 1979 peace treaty.[93] The U.S. Agency for International Development (USAID) and the World Bank supported the infitah, although both organizations have worked with Egypt in the past. Egypt, by 1979, was receiving $2,000 million a year in aid and credits. The United States provided $970 million annually of which $750 million came from the USAID and $220 million through Public Law 480 wheat shipments. The World Bank provided $270 million of which $150 million was loans and $120 million was credits. Finally, Japan provided $184 million, while West Germany provided $163 million. Egypt received aid from other sources as well, but now it looked to the West rather than the Eastern bloc or the non–oil producing Arab states. While it did receive aid from countries such as Saudi Arabia, it was still the West that had the most money and technology required by Egypt.[94] Why was the West offering all this aid? According to Alan Mackie, "Thanks in large part to Egypt's pivotal role in the Arab-Israeli conflict, its vital military and commercial position and its big domestic market, the West, Japan, and Iran have been more willing to offer development aid."[95]

The USAID program is significant because it represents a strong political commitment from the United States. It supports such programs as sewerage improvement and demands adherence to regulation, which helps teach business practices. The critics contend that such practices only serve to teach Egyptians how to work with the United States and not their own bureaucracy. The USAID may also help improve efficiency within the bureaucracy, for example by insisting that the Ministry of the Economy and Economic Cooperation adheres to commercial rates when lending money and by encouraging private sector participation.[96]

The World Bank has helped with Egypt's progress and offers prestige because it is an apolitical institution. The program director for Europe, the Middle East and North Africa, Martijn Paijmans, said, "Our assessment was that after opening up the economy, we saw much better prospects for growth. Egypt has a much stronger resources base now than it did five years ago."[97] The World Bank provides finances for development, advice on economic and sectoral policies, and chairs the Consultative Group for Egypt, which is a twenty-six-member group of Egypt's creditors. Paijmans explains that the Bank focuses on ". . . rural poverty, population, education and projects that increase foreign exchange."[98] Even with all this assistance, it is not an easy task to learn and restructure the economy. For example, Egypt ran into trouble with the International Monetary Fund (IMF) for not controlling its deficit as directed. As a result, the Finance Minister Ali Lutfi agreed to study ways to implement sales tax, combat tax evasion, and cut losses by public sector companies.[99]

As mentioned earlier, the major challenge Sadat faced, and Mubarak is still facing, are the dire economic straits which Sadat inherited. The biggest drain on the economy has been Egypt's historically burdensome population growth rate (see table 4.6), which is projected to reach 68 million by the year 2000. Additionally, the population is concentrated around the Nile River Valley, which only comprises 3.6 percent of the country's total area.[100] Agriculture seems to be a no-win situation because of the continual increase in population and the limited (only 3 percent) arable land in the country. As a result, Egypt has had to import 40 percent of its grain.[101] Additionally, as noted earlier with the IMF discussion, inefficiency and corruption have been major problems. Table 4.7 shows the trade deficit that Egypt experienced during Sadat's rule as discussed earlier, as well as major trading partners.

INDICATOR: TREATIES AND AGREEMENTS

I have already discussed, at least indirectly, the effects of Sadat's Jerusalem visit, Camp David Accords, and the Egyptian-Israeli peace agreement. Consequently, I just want to point to the fact that while Egypt did gain territory, security, and the prospects of peace because of the peace agreement, it also

Table 4.6. Economic Data: Egypt[102]

	1971	1973	1975	1977	1979	1981	1983
GNP per capita (U.S. $)	250	270	310	400	420	540	600
Population (thousands)	33,690	34,864	36,289	38,253	40,401	42,672	45,084
GDP (millions of Egyptian pounds)	3,241	3,806	5,218	8,344	12,705	17,320	24,170

Table 4.7. Foreign Trade By Region: Egypt (1983) (Egyptian pounds, 1,000's)[103]

	Imports	Exports	Trade Balance
Arab Countries	256,947	103,879	−153,068
Eastern Europe	1,100,357	403,728	−696,629
Western Europe	3,239,568	934,174	−2,305,394
Asia	751,215	449,532	−301,683
Africa	27,946	16,588	−11,358
North America	1,207,577	149,695	−1,057,878
South America	44,966	—	−44,966
Central America	101,208	10	−101,198
Oceania	135,099	152	−134,947
Others	327,778	192,537	−135,241
TOTAL	7,192,657	2,250,295	−4,942,362

Source: Central Agency for Public Mobilization and Statistics

saw the reacquisition of the Sinai as a great economic opportunity. Israel had developed the Sinai's roads, airfields, and tourist sites, and Egypt viewed these assets, as well as the possibility of redistributing its overpopulated areas, profiting from the oil and mineral resources of the land, and encouraging foreign investment as peace dividends.[104] While the visit, accords, and agreement emphasized peace between historical adversaries, Sadat also saw the potential for other gains as discussed in previous sections.

PRELIMINARY CONCLUSIONS

What did this examination uncover in terms of the relationship between the domestic and foreign realms? First, it is important to realize that the issues in our framework are interrelated. For example, the discussion in the security section concerning the Palestinian problem can be interpreted as a means of gaining regional status. Clearly, we saw an erosion of regional status, so it is not a great leap of faith to look at the Palestinian issue as a means for Egypt to regain some of its status at the regional level. Another important point that was mentioned is that once external security concerns were alleviated, Egypt was able to put primacy on trying to resolve its economic problems. If one domestic variable emerges in this case as influential in foreign policy it is the economy. Finally, internal status, that is legitimacy based on a shared national identity, seemed to figure prominently in Sadat's willingness to take risks.

Each indicator uncovered some of the significant factors influencing Sadat's decision to realign. The elite attitudes reveal both the motivations for the realignment decision and as the widespread support Sadat enjoyed. First, the elite attitude indicator suggests that while security and peace were a concern, there were also other factors influencing Sadat's decision. This indicator reveals that Sadat understood the legitimacy he enjoyed due to his people's shared national identity. We know this based not only on his own words, but also on other elites' attitudes. This legitimacy seemed to have given him the maneuver room to make risky decisions, particularly his realignment decision. In this case, an ethnically homogeneous state was recognized by its leader and entered into his foreign policy calculations.

Second, elites shared the view that economics was a driving factor for Egypt's turn to the West. Elites supported the infitah; they wanted economic prosperity for the country and relief for the masses. Sadat realized that he could not economically develop Egypt without external support. Unfortunately, the outcome of Sadat's economic policy based on the realignment did not necessarily match his intentions. The authors of the 1978 economic program clearly stated this point. Unfortunately, Sadat inherited such a desperate economy that even well intentioned policies could not produce good results. Consequently, widespread corruption and the lack of a strong economic foundation sparked consumerism and a widened gap between the rich and the poor. This ever-widening gap exacerbated class divisions in society, and it appears that Sadat recognized this point. Government officials saw the political impact of the food riots, and even the Muslim Brotherhood tried to boost its appeal by offering an economic plan.[105] The divisions in society appear to have been economically based, and Sadat's foreign and domestic policies attempted to mitigate those divisions.

The foreign aid and trade indicator also suggests the importance of the economy in Sadat's realignment decision, even with the tremendous amount of U.S. military hardware and assistance Egypt received. As mentioned earlier, perhaps with this influx of military aid Egypt no longer had to worry about an impending war and could focus on economic issues. Egypt received a great deal of economic aid, such as U.S. food aid and projects funded by the USAID and the World Bank, which was primarily directed towards alleviating the plight of the masses. However, the infitah still managed to exacerbate the gap between the rich and the poor.

This case revealed that Sadat relied on a reservoir of legitimacy that was based on a shared national identity. Consequently, he was able to risk losing regional status, which he did, because he had support from home; he repeatedly referred to the greatness of the Egyptian people as a tremendous resource. Other elites shared his view concerning the significance of this shared identity, and they supported his risky foreign policy moves, even when those moves opposed a majority of the Arab world. Legitimacy, as we defined it, is a subset of our discussion on domestic or internal status. The other component of internal status for this case was the economy, and I would argue that this was Sadat's focus for his decision to look westward, as well as his decision to seek peace with Israel. Because Egypt had an ethnically homogeneous population at this time, Sadat was able to make his realignment decision even though he risked losing regional status, as well as third world status. He was able to do this because he had such wide-spread legitimacy based on a national identity free from ethnic divisions. The evidence suggests that Sadat realized this point.

NOTES

1. Ole R. Holsti and James D. Sullivan, "National-International Linkages: France and China as Nonconforming Alliance Members," in *Linkage Politics: Essays on the Convergence of National and International Systems*, ed. James N. Rosenau (New York: The Free Press, 1969), 151.

2. Steven R. David, *Choosing Sides: Alignment and Realignment in the Third World* (Baltimore: The Johns Hopkins University Press, 1991), 55.

3. *The Middle East*, 8th ed. (Washington, D.C.: Congressional Quarterly Inc., 1994), 198.

4. David, 56–57.

5. The quotations are found in ibid., 57, and the reasons for Egypt's alignment are from ibid., 58–59.

6. Don Peretz, *The Middle East Today* (New York: Praeger: 1988), 241, and David, 60–63.

7. David, 63–64.

8. The quotation is from ibid., 65, and the discussion on the treaty is from ibid., 65–67.

9. Ibid., 76.

10. Ibid., 76–78.

11. Raymond A. Hinnebusch Jr. *Egyptian Politics Under Sadat: The Post-Populist Development of an Authoritarian-Modernizing State* (Cambridge: Cambridge University Press, 1985), 125.

12. Both quotations are taken from Robert Springborg, "Approaches to the Understanding of Egypt," in *Ideology and Power in the Middle East: Studies in Honor of George Lenczowski*, ed. Peter J. Chelkowski and Robert J. Pranger (Durham: Duke University Press, 1989), 147.

13. David, 76–78.

14. Ibid, 78.

15. Ibid., 78–82.

16. Ibid., 81 and 84.

17. Colonel T. N. Dupuy, U.S.A. Ret., *Elusive Victory: The Arab-Israeli Wars 1947–1974* (Fairfax: Hero Books, 1984), 388.

18. Ibid., 602.

19. J. C. Hurewitz, *Middle East Politics: The Military Dimension* (New York: Praeger Publishers, 1969), 152.

20. George W. Gawrych, "Jihad in the Twentieth Century," in *Book of Readings: Modern Military History of the Middle East*, ed. George W. Gaurych, Combat Studies Institutes (Fort Leavenworth: U.S. Army Command and General Staff College, 1996), 5.

21. The idea about the relationship between the military and politics is taken from Dupuy, 389–390; the quotation is taken from Dupuy, 393, and the description of the soldiers is from Dupuy, 394.

22. Major General Chaim Herzog, *The War of Atonement, October 1973: The Fateful Implications of the Arab-Israeli Conflict* (Boston: Little, Brown and Company, 1975), 273.

23. Ibid., 274–275.

24. David, 84–86.

25. Ibid., 86–91.

26. Robert D. Kaplan, *The Arabists: The Romance of an American Elite* (New York: The Free Press, 1995), 167.

27. Heikal, 725–726.

28. Ibid., 726–727.

29. David, 91–95.

30. Ibid., 95–96.

31. Anwar Sadat in a speech to the Israeli Knesset on November 20, 1977, in William B. Quandt, *Camp David: Peacemaking and Politics* (Washington, D.C.: The Brookings Institution, 1986), 346.

32. Ali E. Hillal Dessouki, "The Primacy of Economics: The Foreign Policy of Egypt," in *The Foreign Policies of Arab States: The Challenge of Change*, ed. Bahgat Korany and Ali E. Hillal Dessouki (Boulder: Westview Press, 1991), 160.

33. Mohamed Hassanein Heikal, "Egyptian Foreign Policy," *Foreign Affairs* 56, no. 4 (July 1978): 724.

34. Holsti and Sullivan, 169.

35. Anwar Sadat, *In Search of Identity: An Autobiography* (New York: Harper & Row, 1978), 297.

36. Ibid., 298.

37. "Minister of State Ghali Interviewed in Paris," *Foreign Broadcast and Information Service (FBIS)* NES (16 October 1979): D2–D4.

38. "Al-Ahram Praises Reagan Support of Camp David," *FBIS*, NES (8 December 1980): D1–D2.

39. "Ali Denies Coordination With U.S., Israel," *FBIS*, NES (8 December 1980): D3.

40. Heikal, 725.

41. Marc N. Cooper, *The Transformation of Egypt* (Baltimore: The Johns Hopkins University Press, 1982), 252.

42. Holsti and Sullivan, 169.

43. Sadat, 281.

44. Ibid., 288.

45. Ibid., 281.

46. Jimmy Carter, *Keeping Faith: The Memoirs of a President* (Toronto: Bantam Books, 1982), 296–297.

47. Ibid., 282.

48. Ibid., 286.

49. Heikal, 727.

50. Hinnebusch Jr., *Egyptian Politics Under Sadat*, 116.

51. Ibid., 116–117.

52. The quotations and ideas are from Ibid., 117.

53. The warning about Zionism comes from "Ash-Sha'B Fears Zionist Influence," *FBIS*, (30 January 1980): D7, and the quotation is from "Lawyer Denounces Normalization," *FBIS NES* 30 January 1980): D8.

54. The quotations and explanations of the survey data are found in an endnote in Hinnebusch Jr., *Egyptian Politics Under Sadat*, 307.

55. Hinnebusch Jr., *Egyptian Politics Under Sadat*, 232.

56. Hinnebusch Jr., *Egyptian Politics Under Sadat*, 233.

57. Shaheen Ayubi, *Nasser and Sadat: Decision Making and Foreign Policy, 1970–1972* (Wakefield: Longwood Academic, 1992), 171.

58. Please note that my observations do coincide with those from Hinnebusch Jr., *Egyptian Politics Under Sadat*, 233 and 235.

59. Raymond William Baker, *Sadat and After: Struggles For Egypt's Political Soul* (Cambridge: Harvard University Press, 1990), 181–182.

60. Ibid., 182.

61. Carter, 418–419.

62. Ibid., 428.

63. Sadat, 310.

64. Ibid., 312.

65. Thomas W. Lippman, *Egypt After Nasser: Sadat, Peace and the Mirage of Prosperity* (New York: Paragon House, 1989), 9–10.

66. Holsti and Sullivan, 169.

67. The ideas and quotations are from Lippman, 90 and 91.

68. R. D. McLaurin, Don Peretz, and Lewis Snider, *Middle East Foreign Policy: Issues and Processes* (New York: Praeger Publishers, 1982), 34–35.

69. Cooper, *The Transformation of Egypt*, 250.

70. Ibid., 251. Note that here legitimacy refers to the economic effectiveness of the regime, not the national identity link with ethnicity as we defined for this project.

71. Ibid., 252–253.

72. The quotation is taken from ibid., 252.

73. McLaurin, Peretz, and Snider, 35.

74. Ibid.

75. Ibid., 51.

76. Ibid., 52–53.

77. Baker, 228–230.

78. Hinnebusch Jr., *Egyptian Politics Under Sadat*, 238.

79. Hinnebusch Jr., *Egyptian Politics Under Sadat*, 239.

80. John Lancaster and Dana Priest, "U.S. Assures Egypt on Foreign Aid: Defense Secretary Makes No Promises About Cuts After 1996," *Washington Post*, January 9, 1995, sec. 1A, p. 8.

81. McLaurin, Peretz, and Snider, 52–53.

82. "Cairo Papers Report U.S. To Speed Arms Delivery," *FBIS*, NES (8 December 1980): D1.

83. Anthony H. Cordesman, *After the Storm: The Changing Military Balance in the Middle East* (Boulder: Westview Press, 1993), 328–329.

84. Cordesman, *After the Storm*, 322.

85. Fouad Ajami, "The Phantoms of Egypt," *U.S. News and World Report*, 10 April 1995, 55.

86. Ibid.

87. The origins of the Copts are from Derek Hopwood, *Egypt: Politics and Society* (London: HarperCollins Academic, 1991), 164.

88. *Compton's Interactive Encyclopedia* (Compton's NewMedia, Inc., 1994).

89. Lippman, 106–107.

90. Ibid., 107–108.

91. Ibid., 109–110.

92. Ibid., 114.

93. The loss of Arab aid is taken from *Compton's Interactive Encyclopedia* (Compton's NewMedia, Inc., 1994).

94. Alan Mackie, "Cairo is Now Looking to Washington as a Major Source of Aid," *Middle East Economic Digest*, January 5, 1979, 5.

95. Ibid., 5.

96. Ibid., 5–6.

97. Ibid., 6.

98. Ibid., 7.

99. "Egypt," *Middle East Economic Digest*, February 23, 1979, 24–25.

100. "Egypt," *Middle East Economic Handbook* (London: Euromonitor Publications Limited, 1986), 113–114.

101. Ibid., 120.

102. *World Tables, 1989–90 Edition: From the Data Files of the World Bank* (Baltimore: The Johns Hopkins University Press, 1990), 224–225.

103. "Egypt," *Middle East Economic Handbook* (London: Euromonitor Publications Limited, 1986), 126.

104. Eliyahu Kanovsky, "Egypt's Economy Under Sadat: Will the Peace Agreement be Followed by Prosperity?" in *Middle East Contemporary Survey 1978–1979*, ed. Colin Legum, Haim Shaked, and Daniel Dishon (New York: Holmes and Meier Publishers, 1981), 369.

105. As discussed in chapter 3, according to Gregory L. Aftandilian, *Egypt's Bid For Arab Leadership: Implications For U.S. Policy* (New York: Council on Foreign Relations Press, 1993), 56, the Muslim Brotherhood established social welfare institutions, such as workshops, health clinics, daycare centers, etc. As a result of this work, the Brotherhood increased its popularity.

Chapter Five

Cold War Case: Syria

The purpose of this chapter is to explore the relationship between ethnic divisiveness and foreign policy by exploring the motivation for Syria to sign the 1980 Treaty of Friendship and Cooperation with the Soviet Union. As with Egypt, I will examine four indicators: elite attitudes, foreign aid, trade, and treaties and agreements—in light of five issues: security, territory, status, human resources, and nonhuman resources (see table 1.1). These indicators and issues will then reveal the significance of ethnic divisiveness as motivation for Syria's state alignment choice. Specifically, I will look at Syria's alignment decision with the Soviets in light of Syria's lack of legitimacy due to ethnic divisiveness.

The most challenging indicator is elite attitudes. Unfortunately, I found such data as interviews with elites less available on Syria than on Egypt. In fact, most interviews are with Asad himself. The few Syrian high officials noted in open sources are non-Alawites, who I believe were deliberately exposed in the press to give Asad's policies more credibility among the largely non-Alawi population. Additionally, I found no survey data during this time frame concerning views on politics and society in Syria. Fortunately, some surveys were finally conducted in the post–Cold War era, which I will present in chapter 7. I still found a wealth of information, although my examination of elite attitudes will rely heavily on field experts' views combined with official interviews of Asad and some high governmental officials.[1] This elite attitude indicator, along with the foreign aid and trade indicator, will show us the significance of domestic considerations, namely ethnicity, on Asad's foreign policy.

As with the previous chapter's format, this chapter begins with a brief summary of the case and a description of its global, regional, and domestic contexts. I then analyze Asad's decision to sign the 1980 treaty based on the table 1.1 framework and conclude with some preliminary findings.

BACKGROUND TO THE 1980 TREATY OF
FRIENDSHIP AND COOPERATION

Asad's longevity as Syria's ruler reflects his political deftness in both the domestic and foreign policy realms. Some scholars believe that his policies are a reflection of his overwhelming concern for regional security and his deep-seated desire for independence in his decision-making process. When Asad came to power in 1970, he wanted to end Syria's regional isolation, a condition the neo-Ba'th's extremist policies had created.[2] However, Asad's policies often did regionally isolate Syria. As Syria played the balancer role in the region, it helped to achieve regional stability by balancing against external threats.[3] For example, Syria allied itself with Iran against Iraq in the Gulf War and intervened in Lebanon against the Palestine Liberation Organization (PLO) and the Leftists. The former action was to avert the threat of Iraq in the region and the latter to avoid war with Israel. This last policy happened to be quite unpopular at home.[4] These policies are just examples of Asad's many complex policies that cannot escape global, regional, and domestic causes and effects. It is important, then, that we examine the global, regional, and domestic contexts in which Asad operated so that we may better understand the motives driving his foreign policy. Of course, as we describe one context, we cannot ignore the others because, as we shall soon see, they are linked.

THE GLOBAL CONTEXT: SOVIET-SYRIAN RELATIONS

Feelings of regional isolation appear to have been a key motivator for Syria's alliance with the Soviet Union. Regional concerns were of great importance in Asad's decisions concerning Syria's alliances.[5] It was the Soviets, however, who helped Syria play the balancing role in the region. The Soviets looked at this alliance globally. Syria offered the Soviets a foothold in the Middle East, which grew in importance when Anwar Sadat ejected the Soviets from Egypt.[6] In 1972, Syria and Moscow completed an arms deal that provided for the enlargement of Syrian ports to accommodate Soviet ships, the building of air bases, and the improvement of the Soviet image in the Arab world in light of the recent Soviet ejection from Egypt. Not only did Syria gain a more critical regional role through increased military wares, but it also made gains on the domestic front because the Soviets persuaded the local Communist Party in Syria to join the Ba'th Party. However, in a bid to prove his independence in decision-making, Asad refused to sign any type of treaty.[7]

Although the Soviets supported the Syrians in the October 1973 War, relations were strained in the aftermath of the war. The Soviets wanted a settlement that would serve Soviet interests by formalizing and legalizing the Soviet presence in the Middle East, thus enhancing their superpower status. The Soviets felt that their participation as coequals with the United States in the peace process would help them achieve their goals. Consequently, the Soviets cooperated with the United States in establishing the Geneva Peace Conference.[8] The Syrians, however, refused to participate due to the Soviets' implicit recognition of Israel and lack of support of the notion of a Greater Syria. A divergence of opinion concerning the use of military force versus negotiations resulted, with the Syrians and Soviets pressing for each option, respectively.[9]

Since the Soviets did not want their ally to fare worse than the United States's allies, the Soviets backed down. They supported Syria by endorsing Syria's War of Attrition and providing a great deal of military equipment to include coveted Mig-23s. Additionally, the Soviets granted Syria a twelve-year moratorium on repayment of its military debt. Syria wanted to build its power position based on its military, leadership of a militarily based coordination on the Eastern front, and political leadership over Jordan, the PLO, and Lebanon. The accomplishment of these goals would free Syria of dependence on Egypt, but Syria realized that it needed Soviet military aid to accomplish these goals.[10]

Relations between the Soviets and Syrians grew warmer as a result of the Egyptian-Israeli agreements. However, the Soviets and Syrians disagreed on diplomatic strategies. The Syrians introduced the Palestinian issue to the U.N. Security Council, as opposed to using the Soviet-preferred Geneva Conference as a forum. Relations further deteriorated when Syria intervened in Lebanon against the PLO and Leftists.[11] As mentioned earlier, Syria's motivation was to prevent a possible conflict with Israel, but Galia Golan and Itamar Rabinovich claim that "the explanation (for this policy in Lebanon) seems to lie in the great importance Hafiz al-Asad attached to the sovereignty of the decision-making process in his political system."[12]

Relations once again improved in 1977 because of the temporary end of the Lebanese conflict and, domestically, the need of the Ba'th Party to change its conservative image.[13] By 1979, it was the Syrians who wanted a bilateral treaty with the Soviets. Asad was experiencing domestic problems with the Muslim Brotherhood. More importantly, the American intention to sign a defensive pact with Israel threatened Syria. The Egyptian-Israeli Treaty signed in March 1979 pushed the Soviets and Syrians towards a large-scale arms deal. Syria's determination for a bilateral treaty continued and manifested itself through Syria's regionally unpopular support for the Soviet invasion of Afghanistan in 1980. Finally, on October 8, 1980, the Soviets relented, and the Soviet-Syrian Treaty of Friendship and Cooperation was signed. However, different interpretations of this treaty would lead to more problems.[14]

Efraim Karsh calls the relationship between Syria and the Soviet Union a "marriage of convenience."[15] He further claims that

> the Soviet-Syrian interrelationship should be portrayed in terms of a mutually beneficial strategic interdependence between two allies: a relationship favoring each partner in accordance with the vicissitudes of regional and global affairs.[16]

Syrian policy occurred on two levels: policies tended to have an independent character tempered by Arab-Israeli and inter-Arab relations and, secondly, policies based on cooperation occurred only when Soviet and Syrian interests converged.[17] Surely, the Lebanon intervention, attacks on the PLO, support of Iran in the Gulf War, and preference towards a military solution in the Arab-Israeli conflict show Syrian defiance towards the Soviets.[18] Once again, Asad based his policies on the security interests of Syria even if they antagonized his strongest ally. However, when he was most threatened, regionally, either by Israel or other Arab countries such as Egypt or Iraq, he relied especially on the Soviets. Syria's desire to balance against regional threats for security purposes seemed to be the primary rationale for Syria's alliances.

THE REGIONAL CONTEXT

The significance of Camp David on Syria is unmistakable. Egypt's decision to seek relations with the West served to initially move many of the Arab states into the Syrian camp. Syria received diplomatic support through the Steadfastness Front, which included Libya, Algeria, and Democratic Yemen. Syria and Jordan established an alliance in 1975 as a means to reject the westward-looking Egyptians. Syria also established a "strategic alliance" with the PLO. Even Syria and Iraq temporarily aligned, and at the 1978 Baghdad Conference, they spearheaded Egypt's ostracism in the Arab world, while promoting Arab financial support for Syria's military buildup.[19]

Syria's policy was soon in disarray. Its alliance with Iraq collapsed over the Iran-Iraq war because Syria aligned with Iran and was not pleased with Iraq's other-than-Israeli focus. King Hussein of Jordan defied Syria's wishes when Jordan aligned with Iraq and pursued peace initiatives regarding the West Bank. Saudi Arabia and the Gulf States turned their attention to the threat of Iranian expansionism, and the Arab-Israeli issue assumed a second priority for them. Consequently, Syria's alliance with Iran alienated these oil states whose political and financial support Syria needed. Interestingly, Syria turned its back on its role as leader of the Arab cause and strongly supported Iran, who did make up the financial losses Syria incurred due to its alienation from the Arab states. Meanwhile, Syria found itself engaged in a protracted struggle with Israeli-backed Maronite forces in Lebanon. By 1980, Syria was regionally isolated, bankrupt diplomatically, and seemed to be all alone in the event of an Israeli attack. Asad also faced internal rebellion, and he was convinced that the United States could not offer him anything. Asad now turned to the Soviets for new arms and guarantees as stipulated by a Soviet friendship treaty that it signed in 1980. He saw Israel's 1981 "annexation" of the Golan as the end of a chance for settlement, and he was afraid that the Golan would be left out of further Arab-Israeli negotiations. Under these conditions, Asad felt political settlement with Israel was possible only if the Arabs gained a more favorable balance of forces and Syria achieved military parity with Israel. Syrian policy in the 1980s rejected the U.S.-sponsored peace process.[20]

THE DOMESTIC CONTEXT: TROUBLE AT HOME

Syria's main asset, as opposed to Egypt's preeminence and Saudi Arabia's wealth, was its penchant for mischief. Syria derived its power from its proximity to Israel, its Soviet ties, its army, and its presence in Lebanon and hold on the PLO. However, one cannot measure Syria's power without examining its trouble at home. Since the mid-1970s, the base of the Syrian regime had greatly narrowed, causing the regime to be more repressive. Near civil war described the state of some of Syria's key cities, and the regime spent a great deal of its efforts in maintaining power. In the long run, it is questionable how such a regime survives at all, especially when it uses heavy artillery on its own cities; this cannot be the modus operandi for long.[21]

Asad was dealing with a Sunni majority that had begun to demonstrate a cohesive determination to rid itself of Alawi domination. Sunni resentment was undeniable. Interestingly, the Sunnis often opposed the regime on nonreligious issues, even though the opposition was based on its desire to return Syria to Sunni rule. Conservative Sunnis led the opposition, while the Sunni Sheikhs and the Muslim Brotherhood played prominent roles in the anti-regime demonstrations. The Muslim Brotherhood, founded in Egypt in 1928, has long appealed to certain Syrian Sunni groups. Asad identified the Muslim Brotherhood as the scapegoat for rising opposition to Alawi rule after the Aleppo school massacre. Yet, there were other anti-Alawi groups and fundamentalist Sunni groups besides the Muslim Brotherhood. The Brotherhood has ties to many like-minded groups, but it is also split into four factions. Still, majority Sunni opposition to Alawi rule resulted in support for the Brotherhood, including support from secular Syrians.[22]

R. D. McLaurin, Don Peretz, and Lewis W. Snider claim that

> More recently, the sectarian conflict between Alawis and Sunnis have impinged directly and importantly on Syrian foreign policy, and [the] separation of domestic from foreign policies is arbitrary and misleading, in that foreign issues frequently are of domestic significance.[23]

John C. Campbell also claims that domestic unrest contributed to Asad's foreign policy, specifically his decision to sign the 1980 treaty with the Soviet Union. According to Campbell, ". . . the regime of Hafez al-Assad, weakened by opposition at home and close to war with Israel in Lebanon, felt more need for the Soviet connection and finally agreed . . . to conclude a security treaty with the Soviet Union.[24]

Clearly, Asad was balancing many competing and complicated interests. According to McLaurin, the two main objectives of the Syrian regime are Israel's return of the Golan Heights and the maintenance of the regime to include popular support for the regime. McLaurin observes that

> It is unlikely that the unpopular Alawi minority can continue to control Syria indefinitely. It is even more unlikely that Hafez Assad, given the level of domestic opposition that has developed over the past few years, fails to recognize this fact. He is an astute political leader who mastered the complex political machinations traditional in the country. . . . Assad recognizes the end of Alawi leadership is near.[25]

As we shall see, domestic issues are frequently of foreign significance.

Our task is to explore this link between the domestic and foreign policy realms. Specifically, we will see how the ethnic divisiveness, which literally exploded in the streets of several Syrian cities, threatened the regime and contributed to Asad's decision to sign the 1980 treaty. Did the ethnic divisiveness of Syrian society decrease Asad's legitimacy, thus constraining his foreign policy decisions and actions? Using the table 1.1 framework, we begin our analysis by looking at the indicator, elite attitudes, in terms of the issues of security and territory, status, and human and nonhuman resources.

INDICATOR: ELITE ATTITUDES

As mentioned earlier, I derived elite attitudes primarily from leading experts in the field, as well as from interviews (namely with Asad), official statements, and observations from world leaders. As with the Egypt case, I use this indicator to try to understand the motivations for the decision to sign the 1980 treaty and further explore these attitudes in the international, regional, and domestic contexts. Based on this indicator alone I found evidence that both internal and external concerns motivated Asad's decision to sign the 1980 treaty. Asad justified his actions towards other states based on his belief of their potential to cause trouble within his regime. Second, there was a tremendous coincidence of timing between the signing of the treaty and the violent domestic unrest in Syria. We will also see that for Asad there were external security concerns, but in order for us to understand the full reason for his signing the treaty with the Soviet Union, we must examine the relationship between the domestic and foreign realms.

ISSUE: SECURITY AND TERRITORY

The elite attitudes indicator will help uncover the relative importance of internal versus external security concerns, which influenced Asad's decision to sign the treaty. Asad and other high officials viewed Syria's foreign policy with other states as a consequence of domestic unrest. For example, Asad explains his view towards Israel and the United States in terms of their part in his regime's internal situation. Asad explains that

> We regret to say that the United States and Israel were able to find some agents in our country during the recent stage. We regret to say that the United States and Israel were able to use many of those who belong to the Muslim Brotherhood and to exploit some other Arab parties to serve their interests. Those agents and parties committed numerous acts of sabotage and assassination, something which opposes our national, moral and pan-Arab values and traditions and, most of all, contradicts our religious teachings. Such acts are unprecedented in our history. When the objectives of sabotage became clear to our people, . . . when it became clear that all this constituted a serious threat to Syria's firmness and confrontation against the aggression and a threat to the Arab interests and national aspirations and when the link between these agents and some other parties abroad was completely disclosed, our people—in their various forces, parties and popular organizations—hurried to strike at this misguided group which has linked itself to the foreigners.[26]

Asad does see Israel and the United States as the forces behind the domestic unrest at home. Whether or not he truly believes that these nations are instigating this unrest, it does seem that the internal situation is a factor for Asad's foreign policy, at least in terms of how he views other states.

Asad repeats this theme in many of his speeches and interviews. According to Patrick Seale, "The war against the terrorists convinced Asad that he was wrestling not just with internal dissent but with a large scale conspiracy."[27] Asad explains that

> We were not just dealing with killers inside Syria, but with those who masterminded their plans. The plot thickened after Sadat's visit to Jerusalem and many foreign intelligence services became involved. Those who took part in Camp David used the Muslim Brothers against us.[28]

Asad felt that this conspiracy to unseat him included Iraq, Jordan, Israel, and the United States. He saw himself as the victim of a "terrible alliance of external and internal enemies.''[29] As mentioned earlier, it is not just the Muslim Brotherhood that is unhappy with the regime. We will further explore this discontent in the status section.

He accused Iraq of inciting Syria's internal dissent. Asad said, "The hangman of Iraq was not content to kill tens of thousands of his own people. He came to Syria to carry out his favorite hobbies of killing, assassination and sabotage. That man has been sending arms for the criminals in Syria ever since he took power." He also recounted,

> We told the Americans that we had proof and they asked us to produce it, which we did. They denied giving the Muslim Brothers this equipment. "All right, then," we said, "here are the serial numbers. Perhaps you can tell us to whom you did sell it." The Americans refused to say. Finally I said to them, "Your involvement is clear and nothing can prove your innocence, but I'm prepared to let the matter rest."[30]

At a meeting of the Progressive National Front (PNF) with Asad as chairman, discussion focused on "crimes committed by the agent Muslim Brotherhood gang against the sons of Hamah in implementation of the imperialist and Zionist schemes which are hostile to Syria and to the Arab nation."[31]

In an interview, Asad accused Jordan of harboring saboteurs. He identified the Muslim Brotherhood as responsible, but he claimed that Syria's internal dissent was externally driven by the United States and supporters of the Camp David Accords. Asad claimed that

> At any rate, what is the aim behind all this? We do not need to exert any great effort to know the aim. Syria is against the Camp David accords, separate solutions and As-Sadat's visit to Jerusalem. Syria is also against the clear U.S.-Israeli policy in the region which, if achieved, would place the entire Arab region under Israeli hegemony.[32]

Asad told King Hussein,

> These incidents [acts of violence in Syria] are annoying us in Syria. However, we are not worried because they constitute no danger to us. In light of the nature of our regime, the national apprehension of the masses, and the nature of the popular and party organizations here in Syria, we can absorb and overcome such developments. We shall liquidate the Muslim Brotherhood gang in Syria because this is a gang which has been condemned throughout history and is rejected by our masses because it is a suspicious gang. Yet, how can we deal with those who collaborated with this gang? With those who were behind the murdering of innocent people in our country? We in Syria, as I mentioned before, can endure such crises.[33]

In 1980, Syria massed 35,000 troops along the Jordanian border to destroy Muslim Brotherhood sanctuaries. Saudi mediation ended the confrontation, but other such conflicts with Jordan followed. In 1985, King Hussein read a letter apologizing for his harboring of the Muslim Brotherhood.[34]

Several scholars' examination of Syrian policy towards Lebanon highlight the blurred boundaries between the domestic and foreign realms. According to Mahmud Faksh, Syria's role in Lebanon is based on three concerns: the unity and independence of Lebanon, the two countries' special relationship, and Syria's national security.[35] A fractured Lebanon could threaten "Syria itself because of the mosaic nature of its population."[36] Faksh continues to state that, "Indeed, the Syrian fear of possible spillover is rational in light of the nature of the makeup of the Syrian populace and the regime's own base in a religious minority group, the Alawites."[37] Alasdair Drysdale concurs and explains the domestic ramifications of Asad's Lebanese policy:

> This action [Syria's sending of troops into Lebanon in 1976] was deeply unpopular with the Sunni majority in Syria. . . . To the regime's most incorrigible critics, it was further proof that the Alawis were not Muslim at all. . . . With a civil war raging next door, refugees streaming into Damascus, and soldiers returning from tours of duty, it was only a matter of time before some of Lebanon's sectarianism would be transmitted to Syria.[38]

Asad acknowledges the special relationship between Lebanon and Syria and why they do not have embassies:

> The contacts between the two countries are beyond the resources of any embassy. Anyway, this is a reality which appeared when the two countries gained their independence. I do not see any reason for thinking of another form of relationship. Naturally, this is a symbol of the warm fraternal relations between the two countries.[39]

Press commentary in Syria reflects this special relationship. One article refers to Lebanon as "Fraternal Lebanon." Another article explains that "Lebanon will not be outside the pan-Arab framework politically or socially. This makes Syria a sister of Lebanon: Its prosperity stems from Lebanon's prosperity and its security stems from Lebanon's security."[40] One has to wonder if these "warm fraternal or sisterly relations" are really another way of acknowledging the two countrys' shared regime instabilities based on ethnic divisions and minority rule.

Umar F. Abd-Allah explains Asad's superpower relations as a means to ensure his power at home. "The chief purpose of the Soviet-Syrian 'friendship pact' was to strengthen Asad's position in Syria in the face of mounting popular opposition, not to further the struggle against Zionism."[41] According to the Action Committee for the Liberation of Syria, the pact was primarily a military alliance, and "the purpose of the agreement was to protect Asad from the wrath of the Syrian people."[42] The Syrian representative to the United Nations, Hammud ash-Shufi claimed that Syria's reception of both French and Soviet aid "is like a war against the Syrian people to oppress and humiliate them, to absolutely annihilate their role in the Arab world, while providing the full benefit to Israel in Lebanon just as it is used to contain the Palestinian resistance."[43] Asad's regime could not survive without outside support due to its minority rule and subsequent lack of popular support. Asad's actions in Lebanon are merely in the name of the superpowers, which has helped Asad gain their support.[44]

According to Abd-Allah, the Lebanese intervention allowed Asad to focus his attention at home. The red-line agreement, which was the clear demarcation of the Syrian and Israeli perimeter in Lebanon, ensured the safety of the Jawlan front (Golan Heights) and allowed Asad to send the Defense Squadrons and the Special Elite Units of the Syrian armed forces to the major Syrian cities in order to suppress popular unrest. Asad did not use these elite units, essential to government security and regime stability, in Lebanon. Instead, he relied on his predominantly non-Alawi secondary units in Lebanon under predominantly Alawi leadership. Furthermore, Asad wanted to control the internal affairs of Lebanon. Maronite-dominated Lebanon mirrored his own Alawi-dominated regime. The overthrow of this Lebanese microcosm of Syria could only spell doom for his own regime.[45]

Asad's ever-changing policies in Lebanon reflect internal and external security concerns. First, he supported his traditional allies, that is, the leftist Palestinians and Muslim factions versus the rightist Maronites. He then switched sides and supported the Maronites because he was afraid of Lebanon's partition. Why did he have this fear? First, the partition of Lebanon could influence Syrian cohesion in his sectarian state. Second, he did not want the Maronite forces going to the Israelis for help. Third, Asad had personal ties to Lebanon's president, Sulayman Franjiyyah. Fourth, his Alawi-minority rule understood and experienced Sunnite hostilities. Finally, Asad's perception was that leftist leaders such as Kamal Junblatt "were engaged in sectarian vendettas." Asad did not want a radical Lebanon that would provide Israel with an excuse to attack.[46] Asad's Lebanese policies reflect his internal as well as external security concerns.

According to Fouad Ajami, Asad holds the Palestinian issue hostage. He secured that power through his intervention in Lebanon. Consequently, Asad has linked the Palestinian claim to the West Bank and Gaza Strip to Syria's claim to the Golan.[47] For Asad, the Palestinian issue is complex, having links to both his internal and external security concerns. He explains that

the conspirators against the Palestinian question tried to strike inside Syria by using the murderous gangs which have been liquidated by our people. Syria has always understood that the target has been Palestine, which they tried to reach
through Syria. Syria will not permit and will not keep silent on this. Syria, whose
destiny has been linked with that of the Palestinian question, was and will be the
heart, the mind, the shield and the sword of the issue against all conspirators.[48]

According to one Syrian merchant, the centrality of the Palestinian issue is
clear: "Settle the Palestinian question and the whole conflict will lose its
energy . . . all of us Syrians feel that way privately." He continued this thought:
"Of course there will be a period for a shakedown within the Arab world as
many people have built careers on the old war with Israel." John Edwin Mroz
claims that for some Syrians, this shakedown would be destabilizing for the
Syrian regime. Additionally, other Syrians express concern over Israel's ability to stir up internal strife to destabilize the established regimes. According to
a senior Syrian diplomat, the Syrian leadership have the following concerns:

1. developing close ties among Israel, United States, and Egypt;
2. economic well-being;
3. the Palestinian issue.[49]

The Palestinian cause is again given great importance by 'Abd al-Halim
Khaddam, deputy prime minister and foreign minister, who explains that the
conditions for peace are a return of all occupied lands, recognition of Palestinian rights, and their right to return to their land and establish an independent state.[50]

During Asad's meeting with President Jimmy Carter on May 9, 1977, Asad
agreed that there were three issues: borders, Palestinian rights, and the prerequisites for peace. The centrality of the Palestinian issue was clear as he explained his position to Carter and the importance of evacuation of all occupied territories. Without full evacuation, the conflict would persist. Beyond
this point, however, his position on the Palestinian issue was evasive. He did
favor a demilitarized zone, as long as no armies were close to Damascus.[51]
Perhaps he was not only fearful of foreign armies, but also concerned about
having his own regular forces close to the capital.

The complexity of the Palestinian issue is highlighted in the following passage as Asad asserts that

we in Syria will not allow anyone to attack the natural rights of the PLO, the sole
and legitimate representative of the Palestinian people and to which the right of
representing the Palestinian people and the right to negotiate over all that relates
to this right should be confined. At a time when we are working to put an end to

the Jordanian regime's involvement in the acts of sabotage inside Syria, we are also working to put an end to other aspirations, the aspirations of the Jordanian regime, in particular, to supplant the leaders of the Palestinian people. In my assessment, the two matters are linked.[52]

Here, Asad acknowledges the fragile links between his domestic and foreign well-being.

These links appear in Asad's views on Israel, as well. Mroz explains several reasons why Syrians believe Israel would attack and claims that Syrians do consider Israel a threat, not only because of its ability to militarily confront Syria, but also due to its ability to instigate regime instability inside Syria.[53] Of course, Asad emphasizes the external threats, and he explains that he signed the treaty with the Soviets because

> Egypt departed [from the Arab fold]; Israel's military capabilities are increasing; some Arab countries support As-Sadat; U.S. bases are increasing in the region; and the Arab efforts—even if serious—are not able to achieve the balance which will enable them to defend the Arab nation in the face of these developments in the near future. At the same time Israel threatens and bullies. And signs appear that some other Arabs are marching toward a new Camp David. As a result of this the way to the greater Israel does not appear to be impossible. . . . In light of these developments from this standpoint, we had to look hard for sources of strength to help us face this great and dangerous Zionist advance. . . . In strengthening the existing relations with the USSR, we found the strength we were looking for.[54]

As we have seen, however, Asad's domestic and foreign policies are so intertwined that we must examine both. Even Asad himself talks about the domestic-foreign connection. According to John F. Devlin, the treaty reflected Asad's internal and external security concerns: "Serious domestic troubles, near isolation in the Arab world, and the need to ensure a flow of arms all played their part [in Syria's signing of the treaty]."[55]

Martha Neff Kessler explains the conditions in which Asad had to make a choice concerning the treaty: "as the 1980s began, Assad, beleaguered at home and without a convincing plan for either regaining the Golan or protecting against Syria's exposure to Israel on the ceasefire line or in Lebanon, turned to the Soviet Union.[56] Alasdair Drysdale concurs that Syria's internal security problems were a significant factor for Asad's decision to sign the treaty:

> Another consequence of the Syrian regime's internal problems, its regional isolation, and its frustration over the Arab-Israeli dispute has been the forging of even closer ties with the Soviet Union. . . . The signing of a 20-year Treaty of Friendship and Cooperation in October, 1980, a goal long sought by the Soviet Union, merely codified and formalized the existing relationship.[57]

Kessler claims that the treaty was actually a warning for both Syria's domestic and foreign enemies. "Politically, it was a warning to Assad's regional and domestic enemies that he had a backer possibly prepared to help ward off continued pressures on the regime."[58] As we have established, these pressures were a result of Syria's ethnic divisiveness. The next section will highlight this point.

ISSUE: STATUS

As we have already seen in the above section, Asad recognizes internal threats, based on the ethnic divisions and his minority rule as well as external threats of other states. He walks a tightrope as he balances competing interests and justifies his policies to a global, regional, and domestic audience. This clever balancing is a result of careful calculation and caution. According to Yahya Sadowski, Syria has been "balancing relations with the USSR by an 'opening' to the West, supporting the Palestinians while not provoking an Israeli assault, and proceeding with the socialist transformation at home while steadily strengthening ties to the monarchies of the Arab Gulf." As a result, Asad's first focus is maintaining rather than gaining power. According to Shlomo Avineri, "Syria is at the moment a status quo power, despite its belligerent and radical public image."[59] Asad's first instinct, therefore is defensive, not expansionist.

Asad cleverly manipulates external and internal status, and I will examine, specifically, how the lack of legitimacy, which is a key component of internal status, may have contributed to Asad's decision to sign the treaty with the Soviet Union. Consequently, this section focuses on those events that took place within the regime leading up to and following the treaty and examines how Asad justified this treaty to his global, regional, and domestic audiences.

Asad, however, is not an easy man to understand. President Carter's diary of May 9, 1977, says the following of a meeting with Asad:

> It was a very interesting and enjoyable experience. There was a lot of good humor between us, and I found him to be very constructive in his attitude and somewhat flexible in dealing with some of the more crucial items involving peace, the Palestinians, the refugee problem, and borders. He said that a year or two ago it would have been suicide in his country to talk about peace with the Israelis, but they have come a long way and were willing to cooperate.[60]

Carter later observes that "This was the man who would soon sabotage the Geneva peace talks by refusing to attend under any reasonable circumstances, and who would still later, do everything possible to prevent the Camp David accords from being fulfilled." Carter observes that only Sadat was willing to admit that he could cooperate with Israel. He felt the other Arab leaders, Asad included, were constrained by factors, namely shaky regimes, which prevented them from publicly admitting their willingness to cooperate with Israel.[61]

Raymond Hinnebusch agrees that "A 'public mood' does seem to define certain bounds outside which decision-makers dare not tread without risk to their legitimacy." He claims that this point is especially significant in a regime in which its minority (Alawi) dominated elite are vulnerable to attack and its opponents question the regime's Arabism.[62] Asad seeks public consensus on issues, and public opinion constrains regime options. According to Seale, Asad governs with two principles in mind: "first was that he would allow no challenge to his rule, the second that wide popular backing for his policies were nevertheless necessary."[63] It appears then that Asad is aware of the importance of legitimacy and formulates policy with this in mind.

Until Camp David, the regime did attempt to satisfy a strong pro-Egyptian public sentiment. The regime, under the Ba'th Party, lost the Golan Heights, and it feels a special responsibility to recover it without compromise. This issue remains, in large part, due to the some 100,000 Syrians expelled from the area, who remain a permanent constituency keeping the issue on the regime agenda. Syrian opinion sympathizes with the Palestinian cause. Regime policy on core issues such as the Israeli conflict and international alignments, largely reflects public opinion. According to Hinnebusch, the commercial bourgeoisie would have liked to follow Sadat's course, which would have opened the possibilities to greater prosperity and a lesser role for the military and government in society. This segment of society also opposed the Soviet alliance because of its conflict with its religious ideals and material interests. As mentioned in chapter 3 and later emphasized through data available in the post–Cold War era, this commercial bourgeoisie reflect primarily the Sunni population in Syria.[64] However, nonalignment seems to be the dominant trend in public opinion, yet the public considers ties with the Soviets to be indispensable.[65] As one Syrian merchant said, "our fears are as much over subversion by the Soviets or Americans or other Arabs, particularly the Iraqis, as they are about the Israelis. . . . We all know the Israeli intentions, so it makes it easier to know how to deal with them."[66] There was not a strong positive sentiment towards the Soviet Union vis-à-vis the United States. Prior to 1980, we see that Asad tried to assert his independence as much as possible in his "marriage of convenience" with the Soviets, as mentioned earlier.

Asad's use of the "carrot and the stick" as means to gain support of the population for his regime reflects his desire to legitimize and stabilize his regime. His actions and policies reflect his acknowledgment that his legitimacy and stability rely heavily on his ability to either mitigate or oppress ethnic divisiveness. For example, Asad publicly discharges Alawis who perform poorly, and he appoints non-Alawis to high-visibility positions; however, Alawis still hold the key positions. Asad takes steps to blur ethnic distinction, i.e., he changed the presidential oath, highlights his activities with the Islamic community, and encourages Islam leadership to portray Alawis as Muslims.[67] While Asad's work to improve relations with the majority Sunni sect has been somewhat successful, the tensions and periodic eruptions of violence demonstrate that the conflict is deep-rooted. The culminating event reflecting the ethnic divisions was the massacre of the young army cadets at the Artillery School near Aleppo in June 1979 by a fanatically religious army captain. The captain was a member of the Muslim Brotherhood, and his actions resulted in a series of governmental reprisals.[68]

Asad is acutely aware of the perception of Alawi power domination. Consequently, he responded to protests in 1973 concerning the constitution's omission regarding the requirement for a Muslim president. Asad corrected this omission, only to be confronted with the question of whether an Alawi was a Muslim. He answered this question by appealing to a prominent Shi'i cleric, Imam Musa al-Sadr, who declared that the Alawis were Muslims.[69] He did have non-Alawi high officials in his regime. His first three prime ministers were Sunni, but the clannish character of those in power was evident.[70] Hanna Batatu describes this clannish nature, especially conspicuous during the military buildup from 1979–1983:

> the ruling element consists at its core of a close kinship group which draws strength simultaneously, but in decreasing intensity, from a tribe, a sect-class, and an ecologic-cultural division of the people.[71]

Drysdale claims that "the more threatened and vulnerable the regime, the more it is cemented by primordial loyalties and the less it is united by a sense of ideological mission."[72] Alawis do benefit from the regime's power structure, especially through favoritism to one another. Of course, not every Alawi engages in such activity, but even the innocent Alawis are tainted by this behavior. The regime became more repressive as discontent mounted, which in turn bred more discontent. Although Asad initially liberalized political life, he undermined the Party and gave more power to the military. To many Syrians during the late 1970s and early 1980s, the twenty-thousand-man Special Defense Forces led by Rifa't al-Asad, the President's brother, was a symbol of the illegitimacy of the regime. These forces, primarily Alawi in composition, are equipped with their own intelligence apparatus and the most modern equipment available. Moreover, it gave Rifa't al-Asad, who is known for his corruption and cruelty, a seemingly unchallenged power base. Rifa't al-Asad had once said that "We are prepared to exterminate a million citizens in order to ensure the safety and defend the revolution."[73] The President tolerated his brother's behavior because it was these defense forces that provided the regime with vital protection.[74]

Syria's intervention in Lebanon sparked the first widespread indications of organized opposition to the Asad regime, when a series of bombings and assassinations struck prominent supporters of the regime. Nearly all these victims were Alawi.[75] In March 1980, massive demonstrations broke out in Aleppo, Hama, and Hums, where citizens not affiliated with the Brotherhood took to the streets to protest the violence, the lack of civil liberties, and the decreasing prospects for democracy. The regime would not have lasted long if these large-scale demonstrations had continued. It was the regime's military superiority that quelled these demonstrations.[76] The attack on the sixty artillery academy cadets in June 1979 in Aleppo and the subsequent demonstrations led to the regime's dispatching 10,000 of its best troops. Two hundred Syrians lost their lives in this confrontation.[77] The Voice of Lebanon reported that

> Our correspondent reports that three Soviet embassy officials were killed last Saturday when gunmen opened fire on them near the Aleppo Club. The Muslim Brotherhood issued a statement denying responsibility after having been accused by Syrian intelligence of having committed the incident. Our correspondent also reports that intelligence units in Latakia, Aleppo and Tartus have raided and blown up liquor stores. Curfew is still in force in Latakia, Aleppo and Tartus from 0600 to 1800.[78]

During this civil war, Asad also used patronage in its most extreme form: "In the heat of the civil war, the regime risked the crassest abuses of patronage in an effort to improve its security."[79]

The peak of the instabilities based on the population's resentment of Asad's minority rule came in 1982. Early that year, Asad assaulted the city of Hama. Prior to Asad's assault, the Muslim Brotherhood had killed the governor and several hundred other officials. Asad's forces were 12,000-strong, and after three weeks of fighting with artillery, tanks, and helicopters, 30,000 Sunnis lost their lives. One government official claimed that "the city was reduced to the status of a village."[80] Daniel Pipes explains that although the Muslim Brotherhood was defeated, the Sunni danger did not go away. In other words, the illegitimacy of Asad's minority rule was ever-present, and Asad felt that he needed at this point to increase his bodyguards to a 12,000-strong force.[81]

The timing of this domestic unrest and Asad's signing of the treaty is not pure coincidence. In my view, Asad ran out of "carrots" as a means to gain consensus, and instead he resorted to repression. The treaty, as we will see in the next indicator section, provided Asad with the means, i.e., "sticks," to deal with this lack of legitimacy. Perhaps his Lebanese foreign policy is what caused his carrot bankruptcy, and thus he resorted to repression. Or perhaps he ran out of economic carrots when further economic liberalization challenged the existing Syrian social fabric and power structure. In any case, the motivation behind the treaty might have stemmed from challenges Asad's minority-ruled regime faced from the majority Sunni population.

How did external status affect Asad's decision to sign the treaty? As we saw in the previous section, by 1980 Syria was regionally isolated. The Soviets understood the diminishing status of Syria at this time. By the late 1970s, the Soviets were not pursuing a bilateral treaty with Syria due to Syria's weakened domestic and regional status. As Karsh claims, "A treaty with a confident and strong Syria that was playing a leading role in the Arab world was one thing, but an accord with an isolated leader, who faced imminent threat of overthrow, was a completely different matter."[82] From 1979 onward, Syria pursued the treaty and supported Soviet causes to include the unpopular invasion of Afghanistan. The two countries, however, interpreted the treaty differently; for Syria, the treaty was a means to redress a strategic imbalance due to Egypt's abandonment (Asad's view) of the Arab cause. The Soviet Union viewed the treaty in terms of crisis management, stressing its international, not bilateral, nature.[83] In any case, it was not just the Syrians who recognized the fact that by 1979–1980 Syria had lost a great deal of status both regionally, domestically, and perhaps globally. It would seem that a treaty with a superpower could only enhance one's overall status.

Asad seemed eager to explain the regional benefits of this treaty as he stressed its importance for Arabs, not just for Syrians:

> Thus, we consider this an Arab not a Syrian matter. That is, this treaty constitutes a source of strength as Arabs and not only as Syrians. . . . The treaty stresses the increase of Syria's military capability, support for Syria and the Arabs in their just struggle against occupation, for the Palestinian question and the continued struggle against imperialism, Zionism and racism and support for Syria's policy and its position in the nonaligned movement and for other such stands.[84]

Additionally, descriptions of high level Soviet visits to Syria stressed the regional importance of Syria-Soviet relations:

> This visit [of Soviet Foreign Minister Andrey Gromyko] comes at the invitation of the Syrian political leadership. This invitation clearly shows that the Soviet role in supporting and backing the Arab right is unlimited, since this role has strengthened the Arab position in the Middle East conflict and has provided the means for maintaining steadfastness and continuing the comprehensive battle of liberation. . . . Indeed, Gromyko's visit to Damascus cannot be separated from

the general framework of the extensive, effective Syrian move in the Arab and international arenas, a move aimed at entrenching the pan-Arab Confrontation and Steadfastness Front—which rejects the Camp David accords and the separate peace treaty—and strengthening the Arab nation's positions of attack while confronting the most savage Zionist-imperialist plots at this stage.[85]

For Asad, the treaty was an indication of Syria's increasing status both regionally and globally.

Asad's ability to mix and match ideologies as a means for gaining support is not surprising. For example, when Asad wanted to justify his actions in Lebanon he claimed in an article "Behind the News" in *Tishrin*, that

> Fraternal Lebanon is resisting the joint U.S.-Israeli pressure for normalization and subsequent capitulation. . . . Syria's national stand today is a true translation of the will of the Arab people everywhere. The Arab masses cannot remain silent when a knife is being held at the throat of the Arab nation. The first Arab duty requires extending support to Lebanon, which is confronting the invaders and their schemes with deeds, not with words. It also requires backing up Syria's steadfastness. This is the first step on a long, difficult road that will eventually lead to the victory of Arab rights.[86]

The Damascus Domestic Service reported that Syria

> responded to Lebanon's request because of Syria's commitment to Arabism. . . . Now that our Arab people in Lebanon are suffering from the Zionist occupiers' injustice and viciousness, the principle and creed of pan-Arab Ba'th aspirations make the Syrian Arab forces presence in Lebanon more necessary than ever before.[87]

It is interesting that Asad stresses Arabism in this case. One must wonder how he justified his support of the Maronite Christians? Of course, Asad even found a way to explain his support of the Maronites. He claimed that his intervention on the side of the Maronites was to preserve the Arab cause in the face of misguided adherents.[88]

He also understood the importance of Islam as a legitimizing force. He assured the Arab Muslim states as well as the Muslims in Syria that his alliance with the atheistic state of the USSR did not reflect a commitment to its values.[89] Additionally, he emphasized Islam as the justification for his support for Iran vis-à-vis his Arab neighbor Iraq. Asad congratulates Iran's Bani-Sadr:

> I would like to express my confidence that the relations of friendship and cooperation between the Syrian Arab Republic and the Islamic Republic of Iran, along with the common struggle against imperialism and Zionism that we are waging together for the sake of the issues of all peoples, will become, even

stronger. I would like to express my confidence that the Iranian Islamic Revolution's support for the Arab issues and the holy Palestinian issue, support which we highly appreciate, will remain one of the foundations of Iranian policy.[90]

Asad responds to his support of Iran, and is asked whether Iran reproaches him for his treatment of the Muslim Brotherhood.

Why should Khomeyni reproach us because of that? Islam is one thing and the Muslim Brotherhood is another. The Muslim Brotherhood is nothing but a party bearing that name. . . . We will permit none to speak alone in the name of Islam, and most of all not the Muslim Brotherhood.[91]

It will be interesting to see if these relations will remain stable in the context of the on-going peace process (but that is another project). In any case, he is well aware of the importance of status evidenced by his careful use of ideology as a means to rally support, both internally and externally.

It appears that Asad is well aware of and concerned about his regime's internal and external status. He views the treaty as a means to gain regional and global recognition. However, internally, his illegitimacy breeds further dissension. Drysdale tells us that

Syria's "illegitimacy" has had at least two major consequences. First, supra- and sub-national political loyalties have often been stronger than national loyalties, and this has impeded national unity. Second, there has seldom been a clear distinction between the foreign and domestic.[92]

Perhaps, then, Asad is looking to use the treaty with the Soviets as a means to gain consensus at home. Interestingly, he seems to only use non-Alawis in the press. The primary high officials named are the deputy prime minister and foreign minister, 'Abd al-Halim Khaddam; Ba'th Party assistant secretary general, 'Abdallah al-Ahmar, and the deputy commander-in-chief of the army and the armed forces and defense minister, Gen. Mustafa Talas. The press links many of the Soviet visits to the Ba'th party, and specifically to 'Abdallah al-Ahmar.[93] Perhaps using non-Alawis to punctuate Syrian foreign policy, Asad hopes to gain some domestic, Sunni support for those policies. As mentioned in chapter 3, Asad uses his non-Alawi officials as a means to bolster Sunni support for his regime. Perhaps also, by associating the Ba'th Party with a superpower, the USSR, Asad hoped to bolster the Party's status. The decision to sign the treaty appears to have been influenced by both external, as well as internal events, and clearly those internal events, or the internal dissension fueled by Syrian ethnic divisions, played a key role in that decision.

ISSUE: HUMAN AND NONHUMAN RESOURCES

The elite attitudes described above indicate that the Alawis in charge of security and the armed forces received the most benefits from the treaty. Economic liberalization did not blossom with Syria's partnership with the communist USSR; therefore, it appears that the economic elite or the Sunnis were not the key beneficiaries. In fact, many Sunnis died because of the increased military hardware as a result of the treaty. As explained above, Asad ruthlessly used this equipment on his own Sunni population. The beneficiaries of human and nonhuman resources from the treaty will be more evident in the following sections.

INDICATOR: FOREIGN AID AND TRADE

As with my earlier case, I combined the foreign aid and trade categories because they will help us understand the economic imperative, or lack thereof, in light of the framework's issue areas described in table 1.1. This indicator will focus more on military aid than on economic aid because, as we have already discussed, Asad's focus was on the military, and as this next section will show, the treaty focused on military aid. We must determine if that military aid was directed for internal and/or external security. Was there a particular group in society that benefited from this aid? My data for this section come from a variety of sources and documents. If my hypotheses are correct, we will see ethnic divisiveness as a factor driving Asad's decision to sign the treaty. It is important to note how Asad deals with the domestic unrest, which we have established as a manifestation of the Alawi-Sunni divide.

ISSUE: SECURITY AND TERRITORY

As Asad faced internal opposition, as well as a declining regional position in the late 1970s, i.e., with his adversarial position vis-à-vis Egypt, Iraq, Jordan, the PLO, to include Syria's involvement in Lebanon Asad sought Soviet aid during his visit to Moscow in October 1979. At that time, the Soviets forgave $500 million of Syria's debt, and the two countries reached their largest arms deal to date. As a result, Syria received approximately 1,400 tanks (including advanced T-72s), 200 combat aircraft (including MiG-25s), 2,000b armored vehicles, and 1,700 artillery pieces. In order to demonstrate its goodwill towards the Soviets, Syria agreed to support the Soviet invasion of Afghanistan, which was a very unpopular stand in the Arab world.[94]

Syria's military buildup from 1979–1983 was a response to internal (Muslim Brotherhood) and external (Lebanon and Camp David Accords) reasons. Perhaps it also reflected the domination of Alawis in the ruling coalition.[95] During that time, the military and security forces mushroomed. From 1979–1983, Syria was the leading weapons importer of the Third World. The number of soldiers in the regular army increased from 200,000 in 1979 to 300,000 in 1984. The reserves increased from 100,000 to 270,000 in that same time period.[96] Rif'at al-Asad, Asad's brother, commanded the 50,000-man defense companies. These units possessed the finest equipment, their own intelligence services, their own uniforms, better pay than the other services, and engaged in smuggling operations.[97] It was Rif'at's forces, however, that took part in the bloody destruction of Hama in 1982, which caused them to be feared and hated by Alawis and non-Alawis alike.[98]

After 1980, one of Rif'at al-Asad's more powerful lieutenants, 'Adnan Makhluf (an Alawi), assumed command of a newly formed Presidential Guard consisting of 10,000 elite troops stationed in central Damascus. In addition, such covert organizations as Military Intelligence (al-Mukhabarat al-'Askariyyah), Air Force Intelligence (Mukhabarat al-Quwwah al-Jawiyyah), and Political Security (al-Amn al-Siyassi) broadened the scope of their operations. Military Intelligence infiltrated political associations banned by the regime, including medical and engineering professions, as well as the diplomatic service.[99]

According to Anthony H. Cordesman, "Syrian intelligence seems biased toward peacetime political problems rather than toward the support of combat operations. The transfer of technical intelligence to operational units remains poor."[100] This point greatly contrasts with Sadat's trusted use of his military intelligence for operational purposes in the 1973 war. Asad seems to only trust such intelligence with his Alawi praetorian guard.

Black Shirt units formed in the Alawi regions of Latakia and Tartus, which were state sanctioned private organizations led by Asad's brother, Jamil. This larger use of military and paramilitary forces at home coincided with the massive buildup of the Syrian armed forces in the late 1970s, following the Camp David accords between Egypt and Israel. Syria's number of main battle tanks went from 2,300 to 4,050, and its helicopters from 56 to 148. Syria was the leading Third World country in weapons importing, and by 1979, Syria spent $4.7 billion on the military which was 16 percent of GDP. In 1984, military spending reached 16.7 percent of GDP.[101] During this year, military spending reached 24 billion Syrian pounds, which was the value of the entire Syrian GDP in 1980. This military buildup made the military the most dynamic, if not the largest, sector of the Syrian economy.[102]

The military hardware found its way to both those forces dealing with internal security, i.e., Rifa't al-Asad's units, and the regular armed forces. This military buildup of both these types of forces indicates an external as well as internal security concern. During this time of military buildup, there was a marked increase of the regime's use of the state security forces to suppress domestic uprisings. For example, in March 1980, commandos belonging to the Special Units (al-Wahdat al Khassah) surrounded the northern town of Jisr al-Shughur and forcibly suppressed demonstrations directed against local headquarters of the Ba'th Party and the People's Army. Furthermore, the Special Units used its helicopter-borne paratroopers in Hama in late April 1981 hunting for a team of Mujahidin (holy warriors) that ambushed a checkpoint outside the city. In order to perform these missions, the Special Units were doubled in size during the early 1980s, reaching a peak of almost 8,000 in 1982–83.[103] As we have already discussed, other such operations occurred within Syria between 1979, culminating in 1982 with the massacre in Hama.

As noted earlier, Syria and the USSR had different interpretations of the treaty. Syria considered the treaty a Soviet guarantee for Syria's security, and the Soviets viewed the treaty as a crisis management tool and downplayed any bilateral traits. The treaty was tested twice within the following six months. In November 1980, Syria threatened to invade Jordan to destroy Muslim Brotherhood sanctuaries; however, Moscow feared that hostilities would provoke an Israeli intervention, so Moscow worked hard to contain the crisis. In April 1981, a missile crisis in Lebanon threatened a Syrian-Israeli confrontation, which the Soviets did not want. As the Syrians soon found out, however, the Soviets would not match the U.S. aid provided to the Israelis. While the United States signed a Memorandum of Strategic Understanding in November 1981, the Soviets rejected Syrian requests to respond in kind.[104]

It took the confrontation in Lebanon to spur the massive military buildup between 1982–1984. The Soviets provided Syria with 800 T-72 tanks, 160 fighter aircraft which included MiG-23s and MiG-27s, SAM-5s, SAM-6s, SAM-9s, SSC-1 and SS-21 missiles, APCs, guns, and rocket launchers (see table 5.1 for a summary of military hardware buildup). Yuri Andropov, who succeeded Leonid Brezhnev, favored closer military ties with Syria and pro-

Table 5.1 Trends in Military Equipment and Dollars: Syria. (U.S. dollars)[125]							
	1978	*1979*	*1980*	*1981*	*1982*	*1983*	*1984*
Main Battle Tanks		2600			3990		4100
Combat Aircraft		389			450		503
Arms Imports (in current $)	120	0	3200		2600		2200
Military Expenditure		1463	1936	1959	2289	3340	3462

vided it with weapons never before available to Third World countries. With this technologically advanced weaponry, however, came an increase of required Soviet advisor presence and less autonomy for the Syrians. Consequently, Syria could no longer consider initiating hostilities. Under Chernenko and Gorbachev, relations became even more tense.[105] We will explore this changing relationship in chapter seven.

ISSUE: STATUS

According to Fouad Ajami, "Syria's main asset, in contrast to Egyptian preeminence and Saudi wealth, is its capacity for mischief. Its location in relation to Israel, its Soviet connection, its army, and its presence in Lebanon and therefore its hold on the PLO give Syria a measure of power."[106] For Syria, this treaty provided the means for it to achieve mischief, and thus enhance its power.

Syria wanted to achieve strategic parity with Israel. Asad realized that he needed the superpowers, but with the United States firmly in the Israeli camp cemented by the Camp David Accords, he had to look towards the Soviets. When he was asked if the superpowers were necessary to have peace, Asad said, "Nobody can ignore the big powers. For this reason I would like to see not only the big powers participate in this solution but the whole world."[107] Unattributed commentary from Damascus Domestic Service on Asad's visit to Moscow reported the following: "Arab considerations with regard to this visit lie in freeing the region from the grip of the Camp David Accords and bolstering Syria's defense capabilities in order to achieve a strategic balance."[108]

Perhaps Asad's ties with the Soviets at this time helped to achieve some international status because he had lost status on a regional level. His quest for strategic parity had its ups and downs, and he realized he could not gain parity through a regional coalition. In 1978, Syria did attempt to build an Iraqi-Syrian alliance to counterbalance Israel. This endeavor eventually failed. Other events such as the end of Iraqi-Syrian unity in 1979, Syrian support for the unpopular Soviet invasion of Afghanistan, and Iraq's invasion of Iran in 1980, which led to Saudi Arabian requests for U.S. assistance, all contributed to Syria's view of an ever-expanding U.S. sponsored peace process. As a result, Syria rejected the idea of an Arab coalition to balance Israel and, instead, sought strategic parity by itself and signed the Treaty of Friendship and Cooperation with the Soviet Union.[109]

One may argue that Asad's bolstering of his internal security forces secured some status for himself because he was able to, albeit cruelly, repress the domestic uprisings. Once the domestic uprisings ceased, he perhaps was in a better position to deal with other states in both the regional and global contexts.

ISSUE: HUMAN AND NONHUMAN RESOURCES

Syria's relationship with the Soviets is primarily based on its need for military wares. Asad's emphasis on the military buildup beginning in the late 1970s caused him to set aside many developmental projects. Asad, however, from 1970 to 1976 did improve the economy with his limited privatization.[110] The 1970s had a vast improvement of growth rate as compared to the 1960s. Syria, which had been an agriculturally based economy until 1970, by 1973 had an economy in which the commercial, mining, and manufacturing sectors took the lead. While the growth rate in the 1960s was 5.7 percent, it increased to 9 percent during the 1970s. The reasons for this increase were, as mentioned earlier, the privatization and the increase in oil production and exports. It is important to note that the growth rate was far from consistent on an annual basis. Trade increased from 20 percent of the GDP in 1970 to 23.7 percent in 1977–1980. Mining and industry increased from 12.6 percent in 1963 to 18 percent in 1980. Interestingly, the state sector also increased, from 10.2 percent in 1963 to 16 percent in 1970–1980.[111]

The growth of the economy in the 1970s may be partly due to Asad's economic policy, a Syrian version of infitah, which expanded the scope of the bourgeoisie and merchant class in particular. As compared to its Egyptian counterpart, however, Syria's open-door policy remained limited. In Syria, the state played the key role in industry and foreign trade even as it opened the country to the world market. In other words, Syrian infitah was actually a tremendous program of public economic investment. The October War and the political and economic changes following the war provided the financing for this program. Syria did well financially because of the Arab petrodollar assistance and profits due to the rise in oil prices. Also, Syria took advantage of the readily available cheap credit during the 1970s from the international money market.[112]

This combination of inegalitarianism and authoritarianism was not accidental; rather, it reflected the political, social, and economic interests of the dominant social forces. These dominating forces included alliance among the top of the civil and military bureaucracy, as well as with the new, and parts of the old, commercial bourgeoisie. It was this alliance of the old and new elites that helps explain the limits Asad placed on the liberalization program. Too much liberalization would have led to greater political reform and greater popular participation. Instead, Asad limited privatization of public resources so as to favor the commercial bourgeoisie, while the rest of society bore the burdens of an ineffective economy.[113] As we discussed in chapter three and in the previous indicator section, this limited liberalization was a "carrot" for Asad to help broaden his support among Sunnis.

According to Kais Firro, "There is no one conclusion that can be drawn from this study of the Syrian economy over the years of the Assad regime. The country's economic performance between 1970 and 1984 has been both positive and negative."[114]

By 1976, Syria began to suffer from balance of payments deficit, which seemed to have stemmed from the West's abrupt withholding of aid, a bad harvest, and a decrease of oil revenues.[115] However, by the end of the decade Asad could still feel satisfied with an economy that had a GDP growth rate of 8 percent over the previous ten years, and Syria's economy was beginning the new decade of the 1980s with twice the volume it had in 1970.[116]

Syria had been dependent on aid from the oil-rich Arab states, although this aid had not been consistent. The Arab states at the Baghdad Conference in 1978 pledged $1,850 million per year for ten years for Syria's military effort; however, the recession and the Arab states' disapproval of Asad's support for Iran vis-à-vis Iraq resulted in a lower amount of aid. In 1983, due to Syria's role in terrorism and its 1980 friendship treaty, the United States halted all aid to Syria. The European Community and individual European states also reduced their aid for Syria. Due to Syria's slow rate of developmental projects, multilateral institutions have withheld aid. The USSR followed up its friendship treaty with an agreement to increase bilateral trade to approximately $2,600 million for five years ending in 1985, which was renewed for another five years in 1985. The Soviets were involved with Syria's transport, oil, phosphate, agriculture, and power generation industries and the search for water reserves. In 1980, socialist countries accounted for 16.1 percent of Syria's exports, and in 1986 they accounted for 46.4 percent of the exports. However, Syria's exports did decline between 1980 and 1986 due to both a decline in oil prices and volume of exports. There was also a decline in the value of imports from 1981's 19,781 million Syrian pounds to 1985's 15,570 million Syrian pounds. In 1986 the value of imports declined by 31.9 percent to 10,611 million Syrian pounds.[117] See table 5.2 for further breakdown of Syria's imports and exports by country.

Syria's focus on military development reflected the regime's reliance on the army "as the single most important source of legitimacy and to the high level of military involvement in Syrian domestic politics. There was, however, a price paid for the government's increased military spending: a relative decline in welfare spending."[118] Estimates put Syria's military spending at 50 percent of its central government budget. Military growth stifled any economic expansion. During the 1980s, military spending was 8 to 23 percent of the GNP and 35 to 70 percent of the central government's expenditures.[119] It was only due to Soviet military assistance and Kuwaiti aid that Syria could sustain high levels of imports during the early 1980s.[120]

Table 5.2. Principal Trading Partners: Syria (Syrian pounds, millions)[127]

	Imports				Exports		
	1982	1983	1984		1982	1983	1984
Belgium	284.5	291.5	326.1	Austria	.4	113.5	0.7
China, PRC	292.2	272.9	14.3	France	773.1	769.2	876.8
Czechoslovakia	354.4	324.7	212.5	GDR	118.2	123.3	83.3
France	920.7	1,355.7	824.2	Germany	135.6	84.3	146.0
GDR	271.9	394.9	685.0	Greece	314.1	70.5	89.9
Germany	916.0	1,511.9	947.7	Iran	161.5	402.9	163.7
Greece	270.5	294.3	223.6	Italy	2,461.2	1,212.5	1,438.2
Iran	3,094.0	4,661.5	3,664.8	Jordan	89.5	133.9	78.0
Iraq	1,159.4	0.1	0.0	NE	174.2	68.3	4.1
Italy	956.2	1,293.2	773.0	RA	1,667.1	2,240.8	2,053.3
Japan	710.2	1,198.2	749.4	SA	134.4	115.3	138.7
Netherlands (NE)	365.4	449.2	455.5	Spain	13.1	274.4	240.2
Romania (RA)	441.6	332.0	409.0	USSR	898.6	811.2	837.6
Saudi Arabia (SA)	983.0	26.1	34.5				
Spain	425.6	363.9	431.3				
USSR	315.9	471.4	558.2				
United Kingdom	351.4	424.7	478.7				
USA	646.4	779.2	556.6				
TOTAL (incl others)	15,757.2	17,828.7	16,154.5		7,953.6	7,547.5	7,274.8

Syria, however, always relied on external aid, even during the limited liberalization in the 1970s. This reliance grew somewhat more apparent when Syria had to rely on itself. The decline in Arab aid from about US $1.3–1.8 billion a year between 1979 and 1983 to US $600–700 million in subsequent years significantly affected the Syrian economy. Although Iran tried to compensate for the loss of Arab aid, it could not equal the Arab countries' reduced financial support. Even during the height of Arab aid in the early 1980s, Syria still suffered from an unsatisfactory output of its state industries, it's high dependency on imported material, the increased need for agricultural imports, and the ever-widening gap in Syria's trade balance. The economic strategies developed during the 1970s depended on foreign aid. According to Volker Perthes, "When from 1983 on it was forced to rely partly on its own resources, Syria's economy revealed its structural deficits."[121]

From 1970 to 1982, Syria exhibited one of the highest population growth rates (3.4 percent) increasing from 6.3 million to 9.66 million, respectively.[122] See table 5.3. Even with this population burden, Asad still invested heavily in the military vis-à-vis developmental projects. Who benefited from this practice? As we have seen,

> the Syrian army remains the guarantor of the Assad regime . . . [and there is a] pervasive presence of Alawis throughout the armed services. They occupy key positions in every major element of the army, and constitute the true command and control network, bypassing (when necessary) the official unit commanders. Although the army has been infrequently used for domestic purposes [except from 1979–1982], it retains a primary capability for regime security.[123]

The treaty benefited the regime's survival and those people interested in that survival, namely the Alawis and those Sunnis who had been coopted. The economic effects of the treaty cannot be specifically determined other than to note that the economy declined in the 1980s after the signing of the treaty. While no leader wants a downturn in his or her economy, the treaty

Table 5.3. Economic Data: Syria[126]								
	1971	*1973*	*1975*	*1977*	*1979*	*1981*	*1983*	*1984*
GNP per capita (U.S. $)	390	460	890	1,010	1,240	1,660	1,640	1,580
Population (thousands)	6,475	6,942	7,438	7,959	8,510	9,101	9,745	10,091
GDP (billions of Syrian pounds)	8.04	9.95	20.60	27.01	38.97	65.78	73.29	75.34

seemed to indicate a focus on the health of the military, rather than the economy. Tables 5.1 and 5.3 indicate the beginnings of this trend, as punctuated by the preceding discussion. According to R. D. McLaurin, Don Peretz, and Lewis W. Snider, any developmental projects during this time were for the benefit of the Alawis:

> With Syria under Alawi control, disproportionate attention was paid to their welfare—internal investment and foreign assistance projects were heavily oriented toward the improvement of the Alawi area around Latakia. . . . Alawis continue to follow military careers in large numbers, and under Assad they continue to hold virtually all real power in the country.[124]

Chapter 7 will show an Asad with an eye on the economy. While it is difficult to assess the Syrian economy, it appears that there was a decline; this downturn in the Syrian economy during the 1980s may have caused Asad to refocus his efforts as the Persian Gulf War approached. This is a matter for chapter 7.

INDICATOR: TREATY AND AGREEMENTS

I have already discussed this indicator in terms of the issues of security and territory, as well as human and nonhuman resources. The treaty and the agreements which followed were primarily military in nature.

PRELIMINARY CONCLUSIONS

As with the Egyptian case, we must realize that the issues in our framework are interrelated. Syria's involvement in Lebanon is as complex as any policy could ever get, and it highlights the interrelationship of the issues. As we have seen, this complexity is a result of the interconnection among the issues described here, namely that of security, territory, and status. It also involves relations with states within the region, as well as the superpowers. Finally, Asad's Lebanese policy also involves domestic considerations. What does all this mean for Asad's foreign policy calculations? As cited earlier, Yahya Sadowski remarked that Syria has been

> balancing relations with the USSR by an "opening" to the West, supporting the Palestinians while not provoking an Israeli assault, and proceeding with the "socialist transformation" at home while steadily strengthening ties to the monarchies of the Arab Gulf.

Avineri claimed that "Syria is at the moment a status quo power, despite its belligerent and radical public image."[128] Basically, compared to Sadat, Asad follows a much more constrained and cautious foreign policy. He cannot afford to take risks, because, unlike Sadat he does not enjoy a wealth of legitimacy due to the ethnically divided nature of his state.

My research shows that Asad, indeed, must consider the effects of these ethnic divisions as he plans his foreign policy moves. The elite attitudes demonstrate for us how Asad's actions towards other states reflect his motives for undermining his enemies at home, i.e., his actions towards Jordan were based on destroying Muslim Brotherhood sanctuaries. The timing of the treaty and the tremendous unrest at home, culminating with the massacre at Hama, is not a coincidence. Clearly, Asad could not ignore and did not ignore his internal enemies. Perhaps the treaty with a superpower could help him gain legitimacy on a global level to help make up for the legitimacy he was losing at home. We saw that Asad takes great pains in justifying his actions to his global, regional, and domestic audiences. He uses a mixture of "carrots and sticks" to build support for his regime. He does want a public consensus; this matters to him, but he will not tolerate challenges to his regime's survival.

The foreign aid and trade indicator demonstrated the treaty's role in not only building his regular forces, but more importantly in strengthening his security forces—his praetorian guard. When T-72s, helicopters, and artillery pieces are making their way to the forces earmarked for regime security, then, in my view, there is evidence that the leadership is concerned about its survival. The treaty ensured that Asad could successfully thwart the challenges to his minority-ruled regime. Additionally, the Alawis as a sect control the military, so it was mainly members of that sect who benefited from the treaty.

The treaty focused on military wares, not economic tools. Developmental projects were put on hold, and we saw a glimpse of the downturn the economy will take in the 1980s; however, as Firro claims, "There is no one conclusion that can be drawn from this study of the Syrian economy over the years of the Assad regime."[129] The key point, however, is twofold. First, the Syrian economic situation was not as pressing as the Egyptian economic situation described in the last chapter. For Asad, the economy did not pose a threat, but Asad still felt his regime under fire because of the ethnic divisions in his country. Consequently, he took action in the foreign policy realm to quell that threat. Second, it is interesting that while his economy was sound as compared with Egypt's economy, it did not mitigate the ethnic divisions even when he tried to liberalize the economy. The ethnic divisions still came to the fore. Sadat, however, in the midst of a crumbling economy was still able to rely on the sense of national unity stemming from ethnic homogeneity to pursue bold foreign policy. While we cannot hold the economic variable constant for these two countries for the purposes of analysis, I think these Cold War era cases reveal the criticality of ethnic divisions versus ethnic homogeneity. One leader, Sadat, was able to rely on a reservoir of legitimacy due to ethnic homogeneity even while facing grave economic conditions, as he pursued purposeful foreign policy decisions. The other leader, Asad, who did not face such grave economic conditions, still had to address the problems of a Sunni majority in his minority Alawi-ruled regime. Asad's lack of legitimacy due to ethnic strife seems to have led him towards a policy of caution and careful calculation that helped him address his internal security concerns. The economy did not seem to play a key part in his alignment with the Soviets. Will the economic factor become more prominent in the post–Cold War era for Asad? Chapter 7 will help us determine this point when we examine Syria's alignment decision concerning the Persian Gulf War.

While the data on Syria were not as plentiful as those on Egypt, the combination of primarily observations and analyses from field experts, as well as some interviews and press releases reveal that while Asad did have external security concerns, he also had to worry about regime survival because of the ethnic divisions that precluded a national loyalty in the midst of his minority-ruled regime. He was a clever ruler and was always able to maneuver within the tight constraints placed on him. In chapter 7, we will analyze Asad's alignment decision without the Cold War era framework. Will the post–cold War era framework lessen or increase these constraints?

NOTES

1. My search for surveys and interviews led me to conversations with Monte Palmer, Augustus Norton, Mahmud Faksh, Fred Huxley, and several analysts at Defense Intelligence Agency, Foreign Broadcast Information Service, and U.S. Information Agency who explained that the best way to analyze elite attitudes was to examine scholarly opinions. The nature of Asad's regime combined with the Cold War time-frame created an environment that made surveys and interviews too dangerous, especially those that tried to discern sectarian differences. For this case, I have taken the advice of the above scholars and analysts; therefore, I rely heavily on scholarly opinion to determine elite attitudes.

2. Yosef Olmert, "Domestic Crisis and Foreign Policy in Syria: The Assad Regime," *Middle East Review* 20, no. 3 (Spring 1988): 21.

3. The balance of threat theory is found in Stephen M. Walt, *The Origins of Alliances* (Ithaca: Cornell University Press, 1987), 17.

4. Olmert, 22.

5. The importance of regional concerns in forming alliances is from Walt, 270.

6. Galia Golan, *Soviet Politics in the Middle East from World War II To Gorbachev* (Cambridge: Cambridge University Press, 1990), 146.

7. Galia Golan and Itamar Rabinovich, "The Soviet Union and Syria: The Limits of Cooperation," in *The Limits to Power: Soviet Policy in the Middle East*, ed. Yaacov Ro'I (London: Croom Helm Ltd., 1979), 214–215.

8. Dina Spechler, "The Soviet Union in the Middle East: Problems, Policies and Prospective Trends," in Ro'i, ed., *The Limits to Power* 337.

9. Golan, 149.

10. Golan and Rabinovich, 217–223.

11. Ibid., 223–226.

12. Ibid., 226.

13. Ibid., 228.

14. Efraim Karsh, "A Marriage of Convenience: The Soviet Union and Asad's Syria," *The Jerusalem Journal of International Relations* 11, no. 4 (December 1989): 15–20.

15. Ibid., 1.

16. Ibid., 21.

17. Golan and Rabinovich, 228.

18. John P. Hannah, "At Arms Length: Soviet-Syrian Relations in the Gorbachev Era," *The Washington Institute Policy Papers*, no. 18 (Washington, D.C.: The Washington Institute for Near East Policy, 1989), 7–8.

19. Raymond A. Hinnebusch, "Revisionist Dreams, Realist Strategies: The Foreign Policy of Syria," in *The Foreign Policies of Arab States: The Challenge of Change*, ed. Bahgat Korany and Ali E. Hillal Dessouki (Boulder: Westview Press, 1991), 401–402.

20. Ibid.

21. Fouad Ajami, "The Arab Road," in *Pan-Arabism and Arab Nationalism: The Continuing Debate*, ed. Tawfic E. Farah (Boulder: Westview Press, 1987), 125.

22. R. D. McLaurin, Don Peretz, and Lewis Snider, *Middle East Foreign Policy: Issues and Processes* (New York: Praeger Publisher, 1982), 257.

23. Ibid., 261 and 271.

24. John C. Campbell, "Soviet Policy in the Middle East," *Current History* 80, no. 462 (January 1981): 42.

25. McLaurin, Peretz, and Snider, 271; for a complete list of all the objectives, see McLaurin, Peretz, and Snider, 270.

26. "Al-Asad Interviewed by Kuwaiti Newspaper," *FBIS*, NES (8 December 1980): H17.

27. Patrick Seale, *Asad of Syria: The Struggle for the Middle East* (Berkeley: University of California Press, 1988), 334.

28. Ibid., 335.

29. Ibid., 334–335.

30. Ibid., 336.

31. "Progressive National Front Meets Under Al-Asad," *FBIS*, NES (17 March 1982): H1.

32. "Al-Asad Interviewed by Kuwaiti Newspaper," H2.

33. Ibid., H3.

34. Alasdair Drysdale and Raymond Hinnebusch, *Syria and the Middle East Peace Process* (New York: Council on Foreign Relations, 1991), 68–72.

35. Mahmud A. Faksh, "Syria's Role and Objectives in Lebanon," *Mediterranean Quarterly* 3, no. 2 (Spring 1992): 82.

36. Ibid., 84.

37. Ibid., 87.

38. Alasdair Drysdale, "Syria's Troubled Ba'thi Regime," *Current History* 80, no. 462 (January 1981): 33.

39. "Damascus Radio Carries Al-Asad's Der Spiegel Interview," *FBIS*, NES (30 August 1979): H2.

40. The first quotation is taken from "Al-Ba'th: Syrian Presence in Lebanon Necessary," *FBIS*, NES (19 November 1982): H2. The second quotation is taken from "Tishrin Scores Lack of Arab Support For Lebanon," *FBIS*, NES (4 January 1983): H1.

41. Dr. Umar F. Abd-Allah, *The Islamic Struggle in Syria* (Berkeley: Mizan Press, 1983), 75.

42. Ibid., 76.

43. Ibid.

44. Ibid., 77.

45. Ibid., 78.

46. Drysdale and Hinnebusch, 74–76; the quotation is on p. 76.

47. Ajami, "The Arab Road," 126.

48. "Al-Asad Interviewed by Kuwaiti Newspaper," H19.

49. The quotation by the merchant and the Syrian diplomat's concerns are from John Edwin Mroz, *Beyond Security: Private Perceptions Among Arabs and Israelis* (New York: Pergamon Press, 1980), 79.

50. "FRG Foreign Minister, Economic Delegation Visit," *FBIS*, NES (28 August 1979): H1.

51. William B. Quandt, *Camp David: Peacemaking and Politics* (Washington, D.C.: The Brookings Institution, 1986), 56–58.

52. "Al-Asad Interviewed by Kuwaiti Newspaper," H5.

53. Mroz, 74.

54. "Al-Asad Interviewed by Kuwaiti Newspaper," H15.

55. John F. Devlin, *Syria: Modern State in an Ancient Land* (Boulder: Westview Press, 1983), 114.

56. Martha Neff Kessler, *Syria: Fragile Mosaic of Power* (Washington, D.C.: National Defense University Press, 1987), 108–109.

57. Drysdale, "Syria's Troubled Ba'thi Regime," 38.

58. Kessler, 109.

59. Both these quotations are from Ajami, "The Arab Road," 125–126.

60. Jimmy Carter, *Keeping Faith: The Memoirs of a President* (Toronto: Bantam Books, 1982), 286.

61. The quotation and the comments which followed are from ibid.

62. Hinnebusch, 391.

63. Seale, 172.

64. This analysis is fleshed out in chapter 7, but I believe that the correlation holds true during this time-frame for two reasons. First, chapter 3 discusses the Sunnis as the economic elite, and second, I do not see evidence of a great socioeconomic change from the Cold War to post–Cold War eras.

65. Hinnebusch, 391.

66. Mroz, 72.

67. McLaurin, Peretz, and Snider, 257.

68. Mroz, 72.

69. Seale, 173.

70. Ibid., 182, and Hanna Batatu, "Some Observations on the Social Roots of Syria's Ruling Military Group and the Causes for its Dominance," *The Middle East Journal* 35, no. 3 (Summer 1981): 343.

71. Batatu, 331.

72. Drysdale, "Syria's Troubled Ba'thi Regime," 33.

73. Derek Hopwood, *Syria 1945–1986: Politics and Society* (London: Unwin Hyman, 1988), 64.

74. Drysdale, "Syria's Troubled Ba'thi Regime," 33.

75. Ibid., 34.

76. Yahya M. Sadowski, "Ba'thist Ethics and the Spirit of State Capitalism: Patronage and the Party in Contemporary Syria," in *Ideology and Power in the Middle East: Studies in Honor of George Lenczowski,* ed. Peter J. Chelkowski and Robert J. Pranger (Durham: Duke University Press, 1988), 177.

77. Drysdale, "Syria's Troubled Ba'thi Regime," 34.

78. "(Clandestine) Voice of Lebanon," *FBIS*, NES (30 January 1980): H2.

79. Sadowski, 177.

80. Daniel Pipes, *Greater Syria: The History of an Ambition* (New York: Oxford University Press, 1990), 182.

81. Ibid., 183.

82. Karsh, 16.

83. Ibid., 17–19.

84. "Al-Asad Interviewed by Kuwaiti Newspaper," H16.

85. "Damascus Domestic Service," *FBIS*, NES (30 January 1980): H3.

86. "Tishrin Scores Lack of Arab Support For Lebanon," H1.

87. "Al-Ba'th: Syrian Presence in Lebanon Necessary," H2.

88. Michael C. Hudson, *Arab Politics: The Search for Legitimacy* (New Haven: Yale University Press, 1977), 267.

89. Hopwood, 76.

90. "Al-Asad Congratulates Iran's Bani-Sadr," *FBIS*, NES (30 January 1980): H5.

91. "Yugoslav Paper Rilindja Interviews President Al-Asad," *FBIS*, NES (29 August 1979): H4–H5.

92. Drysdale, "Syria's Troubled Ba'thi Regime," 35.

93. See "Ba'th Party Delegation to Visit GDR, USSR," *FBIS*, NES (30 January 1980): H2; "Ba'th Moroccan Socialist Party Delegations Hold Talks," *FBIS*, NES (30 January 1980): H2; "Ba'th Official Receives Visiting Soviet Delegation," *FBIS*, NES (30 January 1980): H4; "Defense Minister Meets with USSR Deputy Minister," *FBIS*,

NES (17 March 1982): H1; "Foreign Minister Khaddam Returns From Iran," *FBIS*, NES (17 March 1982): H1; "Damascus Reports Khaddam's Cyprus Speech," *FBIS*, NES (20 July 1982): H2; and "FRG Foreign Minister, Economic Delegation Visit," *FBIS*, NES (28 August 1979): H1.

94. Drysdale and Hinnebusch, 157.

95. Fred H. Lawson, "From Neo-Ba'th to Ba'th Nouveau: Hafiz al-Asad's Second Decade," *Journal of South Asian and Middle Eastern Studies* 14, no. 2 (Winter 1990): 6–8.

96. Ibid., p. 8.

97. Alasdair Drysdale, "The Succession Question in Syria," *The Middle East Journal* 39, no. 2 (Spring 1985): 248.

98. Ibid.

99. Lawson, 7.

100. Anthony H. Cordesman, *After the Storm: The Changing Military Balance in the Middle East* (Boulder: Westview Press, 1993), 278.

101. Lawson, 8.

102. Ibid., 11.

103. Ibid., 7.

104. Drysdale and Hinnebusch, 157–158.

105. Ibid., 159–161.

106. Ajami, 125.

107. "Yugoslav Paper Rilindja Interviews President Al-Asad," H9.

108. "Damascus Radio on Significance of Al-Asad's Visit to Moscow," *FBIS*, NES (16 October 1979): H1.

109. Nadav Safran, "Dimensions of the Middle East Problem," in *Foreign Policy in World Politics: States and Regions,* ed. Roy C. Macridis (Englewood Cliffs: Prentice Hall, 1989), 410–411.

110. Valerie Yorke, *Domestic Politics and Regional Security: Jordan, Syria, and Israel* (Aldershot: Gower, 1988), 144–148.

111. Kais Firro, "The Syrian Economy Under the Assad Regime," in *Syria Under Assad: Domestic Constraints and Regional Risks*, ed. Moshe Ma'oz and Avner Yaniv (New York: St. Martin's Press, 1986), 44–45.

112. Volker Perthes, "The Syrian Economy in the 1980s," *Middle East Journal* 46, no. 1 (Winter 1992): 37–38.

113. Ibid., 56.

114. Firro, 65.

115. Ibid., 59 and 62.

116. *Middle East Contemporary Survey, 1979–1980,* eds. Colin Legum, Haim Shaked, and Daniel Dishon (New York: Holmes and Meier Publishers, 1981), 780.

117. *The Middle East and North Africa, 1995* (London: Europa Publications Limited, 1995), 848 and 854.

118. Ze'ev Ma'oz, "The Evolution of Syrian Power, 1948–1984," in *Syria Under Assad: Domestic Constraints and Regional Risks*, ed. Ma'oz and Yaniv 74.

119. Cordesman, 260.

120. *The Middle East and North Africa, 1995,* 260–261.

121. Perthes, "The Syrian Economy in the 1980s," 57.

122. Firro, 37.

123. McLaurin, Peretz, and Snider, 284.

124. Ibid., 256–257.

125. Cordesman, *After the Storm,* 256.

126. *The Middle East and North Africa, 1987* (London: Europa Publications Limited, 1988), 769.

127. Ibid.

128. Both quotations are from Ajami, "The Arab Road," 125–126.

129. Firro, 65.

Chapter Six

Post–Cold War Case: Egypt

This chapter examines Egypt's post–Cold War alignment, that is, its alignment with the Persian Gulf War coalition. I want to make three points before we begin this case. First, this case is difficult to present because it is essentially our null set case. In other words, we will be examining how the lack of ethnic divisiveness (or, rather the positive effect of ethnic homogeneity) influenced Mubarak's pro-coalition alignment decision. What will become clear, however, is how another domestic variable, the state of the Egyptian economy, influenced Mubarak's foreign policy behavior. While Mubarak's pro-coalition alignment was not as surprising as Sadat's realignment decision discussed in chapter 4, Mubarak, nevertheless, took a pro-U.S. stance in the midst of an opposition that was anti-West and during which his country faced short-term economic costs that would be felt throughout the population. Even in the face of such a seemingly unpopular decision, Mubarak had relatively strong support among his elite, the opposition parties, and the people. His cooperative approach towards the United States, and to some extent towards Israel, was much different than Asad's antagonistic approach towards both the United States and Israel. We will examine these differences. Second, I will reference the peace process, not only because of its immediacy after the crisis, but because the Egyptian leadership throughout the crisis looked beyond it and planned for the post–Gulf War period. Finally, we will also begin our examination of the systemic variable for this decision, now that the analysis brings us to the post–Cold War era.

BACKGROUND

In 1981, Mubarak outlined his guiding principles for both domestic and foreign policy, and this interrelationship will be evident throughout this case. Specifically, the economy seems to be linked with almost every aspect of Egyptian policy. When Mubarak assumed the presidency in 1981, he wanted to provide economic benefits to the poor. He wanted the continuation of the infitah, but with the focus on production, not consumption, although food subsidies, the root cause of the food riots, would remain. Politically, he wanted to uphold the peace with Israel and retain ties with other Arab states. Derek Hopwood recalls parts of Mubarak's 1981 speech to the People's Assembly:

> Sadat's death was a warning to Egypt to "cleanse itself of the plague of religious extremism." This could only be achieved with social justice. "Egypt is for all society—not a privileged few or the chosen elite." Opposition parties would be allowed but opposition should be about "differences not conflict, without creating confusion; it should be an exchange of views not an exchange of accusations."[1]

Mubarak, as we will see, could not talk about domestic policy without talking about foreign policy, and vice versa.

Mubarak's main success in the first five years was restoring balance in Egypt's foreign policy. He restored ties with the Soviets, and he gradually worked his way back into the Arab world. The 1980–1988 Iran-Iraq war did much to pull Egypt into the Arab camp because of Mubarak's support of the Arab state of Iraq. The war deflected attention from Egypt's treaty with Israel, and Egypt made the case that there were other threats to the Arab region, besides Israel. Mubarak's assistance to Iraq with military aid and civilian workers was important for Egypt's acceptance in the Arab world because it was Iraq that had hosted the Arab summit in 1978 and led the Arab boycott of Egypt. Also, Egypt advocated a renewal of ties with the PLO and supported an international peace conference, which brought Egypt in line with the Arab consensus.[2] In January 1984, Egypt was readmitted to the Islamic Conference Organization. In November 1987, Iraq and Morocco restored relations with Egypt, and in 1989, King Fahd of Saudi Arabia gave his approval to Egypt by visiting Cairo. In May 1989 at the Arab summit meeting in Casablanca, Mubarak said, "The Arab people of Egypt are very happy in the unification of the ranks after separation." The Arab League headquarters returned to Cairo, and ties with Syria resumed.[3]

This feat was not without its challenges. Egypt lost regional status when Israel invaded Lebanon in 1982, which led to Egypt's withdrawal of its ambassador from Tel Aviv. The Egyptian Foreign Minister stated that Israel's acts towards another Arab country affected Israeli and Egyptian normalization. The Minister's remark about the invasion was that "Normalization was no longer normal." Moreover, the strategic pact between Israel and the United States further made this time period for Mubarak "a catastrophe for him and a humiliation before other Arabs."[4]

With the massacres of Palestinians by Christian Lebanese, an action that was unobstructed by Israeli forces, Egypt's relations with Israel were mostly frozen, and a cold peace ensued. Israel's continued settlement in the occupied territories, repression of the Palestinian infitada on the West Bank and in Gaza, and the influx of Soviet Jews angered Mubarak. When the Palestinian National Council in November 1988 decided to announce the establishment of a Palestinian state revealing a guarded recognition of Israel, Mubarak called for a peace conference with the PLO, the United States, and Israel. While the United States did talk with the PLO, Israel would not follow suit. Again, Mubarak was embarrassed by Israel's actions. Hopwood contends that "all these Israeli actions embarrassed Mubarak, although to date, despite opposition and external Arab pressure, he has refused to go back on the peace treaty."[5] Perhaps this refusal reflects a certain amount of risk Mubarak accepted in order to reap, as we will soon see, economic benefits from the United States.

Harold H. Saunders believes that Mubarak realized that he would have more influence with the United States and Israel if he had a greater leadership role in the region. This added influence could compensate for Egypt's lack of military power relative to Israel by making it a key leader of a wider political base for an eventual peace in the region. The Egyptians, by the mid-1980s, realized that they needed this broader political base to be an effective player in regional negotiations. Egypt had failed to negotiate on behalf of the Palestinians during the post–Camp David era. Saunders claims that the Egyptians "recognized the need to build the Arab negotiating group with Jordanians and Palestinians that we Americans failed to assemble after Camp David. By late 1984, they had made progress in paving the way for their own reentry to the Arab world." Mubarak was a key player in the [King] Hussein-Arafat negotiations, and he helped to bring the United States back to the negotiation table with the Jordanian-Palestinian delegation.[6]

On the global level, the Cold War era came to a close. The collapse of the Soviet Union was not viewed favorably among Arab governments for three primary reasons. First, the Arabs viewed the Soviet Union as a supporter of Arabs in general and Palestinians in particular. Second, the Soviet Union allowed pro-West governments that had ties with it to project a nonalignment stand. Third, the Cold War rivalry benefited many Arab governments by "allowing individual states the room to maneuver politically in regional and world politics."[7] Finally, as a result of the above points, many Arab leaders see the need for regional cooperation because they are fearful of a sole superpower in the form of the United States for two reasons. First, without a Soviet Union, the United States will impose itself and its ideology on the Arab world. Second, in contrast with the first reason, some Arab leaders fear that the United States will ignore the region with the end of Cold War era politics and competition.[8]

The end of the Cold War has contributed to a new sense of "pragmatism" for the Arab states in their dealings concerning the Arab-Israeli dispute. According to Gregory Aftandilian, this pragmatism may be a good sign for the peace process. Aftandilian claims, however, that ideology has changed, as well. State nationalism and Islamic nationalism have overtaken Pan-Arabism. How governments will respond to this new change remains to be seen.[9] Additionally, Aftandilian argues that besides the perception that the end of the Cold War does not bode well for the region, the idea of "Western cultural imperialism" evolved into the view that, primarily among Islamists, a Western bias against Muslims and Arabs greatly influences U.S. policy in the Middle East. While many opposition parties in Egypt are divided on various issues, opposition to U.S. policies unifies them.[10] It appears then, that it is in Mubarak's interests not to be seen as dependent on the United States, but Mubarak knows that the United States provides valuable economic and military aid. Consequently, Mubarak wants the Arab world to rely on Egypt's ties to the sole superpower and acknowledge Egypt's leadership so that the region may continue to benefit from the world's sole superpower.[11]

It is interesting to me that faced with an opposition with an anti-Western sentiment, Mubarak was able to take a firm pro-American stand. The opposition, in fact, strongly supported Mubarak's words and deeds at the beginning of the conflict. We will examine this situation in the status section.

While Mubarak seemed to be faced with the dilemma of whether to oppose Iraq in the midst of his attempts to bring Egypt back into the Arab fold, in my view there was not much of a true dilemma here. It did mean that Egypt's opposing Iraq would make it side against an Arab county just as Egypt was trying to reassert itself within the Arab community; however, failing to side with the coalition would anger the Gulf Arabs, weaken relations with the United States, and invite further Iraqi aggression. Egypt proved instrumental to the coalition, especially when Mubarak said that he would not withdraw if Israel did retaliate against Iraq.[12] Such a statement is a clear example of Egypt's boldness in foreign policy as opposed to Syria's cautious approach, as we will see in chapter 7.

Mubarak hosted a meeting of the Arab League on August 10, 1990, eight days after the invasion. The meeting concluded by having most of the Arab countries condemning Saddam Hussein. Egyptian troops were in Saudi Arabia the next day. Egypt worked to gain broad Arab support for the anti-Iraq coalition. Egypt sent 30,000 troops and 400 tanks as part of the coalition, more than any other Arab state.[13] Military cooperation continued between the United States and Egypt after the war, and the United States promised Egypt preferential treatment regarding Egypt's receipt of sophisticated military equipment. By 1991, Egypt's debt was reduced from $50 billion to $36 billion. Mubarak also hoped for increased aid and investment from the Gulf countries, but the GCC countries did not deliver on what was promised. "Nevertheless, Egyptian prestige in the Arab world rose dramatically because of its leadership during the Gulf War. In March 1991 the Arab League transferred its headquarters back to its original location in Cairo."[14]

Iraq's invasion of Kuwait angered Mubarak on a personal level because Saddam had assured Mubarak that he would not invade. On a strategic level, the invasion threatened Saudi control of oil reserves from which Egypt anticipated benefits from its revenues. Iraq's bellicose rhetoric concerning Israel threatened Egypt's lead in building a moderate consensus in the region. "Moreover, the Egyptians perceived Saddam Hussein as trying to usurp Arab leadership by portraying himself as the Arab strongman, and they believed that no other state other than Egypt had the right to claim the leadership mantle."[15] The Gulf crisis posed an opportunity for Egypt to take the leadership role in the Arab world. "Mubarak's strong leadership in forming the anti-Iraq Arab coalition, and the strenuous efforts by Egypt's religious and intellectual establishment to counter Iraqi propaganda, therefore, helped to scuttle Saddam Hussein's plans to turn most of the Arab world to his side."[16]

It appears that Mubarak's immediate objective for his Persian Gulf alignment was to bolster his status both internationally and regionally. In my view, he felt he needed this status in order to secure economic benefits. He realized, as we will see, the dire economic straits Egypt was in, and the only way to improve the economic situation was to secure benefits from the region and the world. It is this economic imperative that drives his policies, both in the domestic and foreign realms. We will find that the economic situation is the root of Egypt's domestic unrest, as opposed to the ethnic divisions, which for Egypt, makes finding an answer to Egypt's economic woes that much more critical. Egypt's pro-coalition stand was a means to find that economic answer. We will see, as Nazih N. Ayubi argues, that

> The most important foreign policy dilemma for Egypt is the incongruity between the country's objectives and its capabilities, between its roles and its resources, or, put more bluntly, between its aspirations for power and the reality of its poverty . . . there can be no doubt as to the "primacy of economics," as a shaper of the country's foreign policy in recent years.[17]

INDICATOR: ELITE ATTITUDES

I will rely heavily on elite attitudes as an indicator for the issues of security and territory, status, and human and nonhuman resources. Generally, I will use expert analyses of elite views, but I will also examine some recent studies conducted in Egypt that may help us understand the reasons behind Mubarak's alignment decision. We will explore these attitudes in the contexts of the domestic, regional, and international levels. Again, the key to this analysis of Egypt will be its comparison to the analysis of Syria, as well as a comparison to the analyses of our Cold War era cases conducted in the previous chapters.

SECURITY AND TERRITORY

Egypt emerged from the war as the strongest military power in the region. Mubarak wanted to demonstrate Egypt's commitment to the Gulf states, as well as have Egypt lead the main effort in the GCC security plan. The Egyptian Defense Minister Mohamed Tantawi in March 1992 said, "the Arab countries should depend on their own security. They should coordinate among themselves to compensate for any shortage in their military capabilities. . . . Assistance from some friendly countries could be used whenever necessary and only for a limited time." Moreover, he stated that "any threat to the Arab national security or the Gulf security reflects on the Egyptian security. That necessitates coordination between Egyptian, Gulf, and Arab security systems." Additionally, he explained that Egypt's response to the Iraqi invasion was based on the idea that "Egyptian national security is not only linked to Arab national security, but it is one of its main supports."[18]

Egyptian leaders identified a lack of regional strategic balance with Israel because of Israel's military power. However, these leaders did not feel a direct threat from Israel; they just felt that a military imbalance is an unhealthy state of being. This strategic situation gave Israel more latitude to take reckless actions, such as its 1982 Lebanese invasion. Additionally, these leaders identified Israel's nuclear capability as a regional threat. According to Edward B. Atkeson, after the Gulf crisis, Egypt looked "primarily to the U.S./C.I.S.-sponsored peace process for [solutions] to most of its difficulties with Israel. Egyptian leaders are enthusiastic about the concept of a 'new world order,' and embrace the notion that the age of naked force is over."[19]

It is also evident that Egypt is concerned about the regional balance of power beyond the Arab-Israeli issue. For Egypt, Iran posed a threat to the balance in the region. Egypt's support for Iraq during its 1980–1988 war with Iran confirms Egypt's position concerning Iran. Moreover, in an interview with U.S. News and World Report, Mubarak said, "I do not trust the Iranians. More than once they asked to restore diplomatic relations, but I turned down this request."[20] Muhammad 'Abd-al-Halim Abu Ghazalah, the assistant to the president, also stressed the need for an Arab security arrangement in the post–Gulf War period. In an interview, Abu Ghazalah was concerned about looking beyond the Gulf crisis to ensure a balance in the region, namely keeping a check on Iran.[21]

Interestingly, Mubarak was asked of any possible link between Iran and the fundamentalists inside Egypt. His reply was that "as for fundamentalists, we have some in Egypt, and we cannot say that the media have exaggerated in depicting this phenomenon. We know well where they are, what their names are, and how many there are. We are in full control as far as they are concerned." He further explained that the law forbids religious-based parties; therefore, the Muslim Brotherhood is not a legitimate political party.[22] It appears that the fundamentalists may pose a security threat to Mubarak, but he plays this threat down. As we will see in the following sections, however, the root cause of any domestic unrest is the dire economic situation. In fact, it seems that the Gulf War alignment served to secure stability in the region so that Egypt could look forward to the peace process and economic benefits stemming from its regional and international status.

During the Gulf crisis, Egypt played a proactive role in setting the stage for the peace process in the hopes of gaining economic benefits and diffusing any threat posed by fundamentalist groups, who could only exploit class divisions and not nonexistent ethnic divisions. For Egypt, security in terms of the peace process was, and still is, a means for obtaining economic benefits. 'Abd-al-Majid, the deputy prime minister and foreign minister, in his talk with the Consultative Council's Foreign Relations Committee, stated: "Ladies and Gentlemen: Our region needs peace and the consecration of resources for construction and development for the sake of a better future for all our peoples."[23] Mary Morris suggests that the long term prognosis for the peace process

> is that the rewards of a more stable and rational regional environment will sap the power of radical groups, especially if economic conditions improve both within Egypt and across the region. With resolution of the Arab-Israeli dilemma—and the removal of excuses for tackling endemic political, economic and social problems of individual states—such improvement will at least be possible.[24]

Mubarak saw the peace process as an opportunity to resolve many regional problems. He wanted broad participation, including the United States, the Soviet Union, the European Community, and the United Nations. President

Mubarak clearly expressed his desire to organize the peace conference as he offered, "We are ready to help and ready to be very active with all parties in order to achieve peace."[25]

Egypt saw the peace process as a means to gain status both in the international and in regional communities. Consequently, Egypt would have a say on prioritizing agendas for both communities in a way that would benefit Egypt. According to Boutros Boutros-Ghali, "It is no exaggeration to say that Egypt's main concern during the end of the 1980s has been the economic plight of the Third World and the ever-increasing burden of interest on debts" which has risen to threaten development and deterioration.[26] In an address to university students, Mubarak commented on the peace process: "We are helping as much as we can because our position and Egypt's status in the region are basic and pivotal. We can help and we were the ones to help convene the Madrid conference. We cannot abandon our role because this constantly highlights Egypt's importance."[27]

While the Gulf crisis did not immediately seem to pose external threats to Egypt, there was a great deal at stake for Egypt at home. Primarily, it seems that the Gulf War provided an opportunity for Egypt to unequivocally assert itself in the regional and international communities in a quest to secure economic benefits at home. Security, in the classical sense, became a means for regional peace and stability, which in turn, could lead to prosperity. This is what Egypt craved the most. According to Stephen Pelletiere, "Egypt's security problem must be seen in context of its economic plight."[28] The following sections will develop the linkage of all these issues in greater detail, but for now, in terms of the issues of security and territory,[29] they were stepping stones for the eventual peace process—a process from which Egypt anticipated greater status and prosperity.

STATUS

As discussed in the background section, Egypt was working its way back into the Arab fold. The Gulf crisis solidified its efforts as the key leader in the region. Additionally, Egypt maintained a cooperative relationship with the United States, which enhanced Egypt's leverage within the region. Finally, Mubarak initially gained a great deal of support among his elites, opposition parties, and the people for his alignment decision. As with the issue of security, status became a means for economic gain. Here we will focus on the issue of status on all levels. Additionally, we will examine Mubarak's internal status as motivation for his alignment decision. As we saw with Sadat, Mubarak's internal threat that had the potential to erode his internal status was the dire economic situation at home. This is what the fundamentalist groups, namely the Muslim Brotherhood, tried to exploit. However, what we will find is that Mubarak also enjoyed a wealth of legitimacy due to Egypt's ethnic homogeneity and strong national identity. In fact, this legitimacy greatly weathered the prospect of economic crises, and once again proves to be the more powerful variable when it comes to the issue of internal status. Finally, we will find that the peace process serves as an umbrella for all issues, and Egypt saw it as an opportunity to further its status on all levels.

Egypt saw its Gulf alignment as a means for increasing its international status, and it viewed the peace process as a means for attaining that status. An Egyptian source, commenting on Rabin's visit to Cairo, explained the significance of Egyptian-Israeli relations in facilitating regional peace: "Egypt will stress during . . . these talks the bases it believes can establish a just and comprehensive peace in the region, bases that stem from the resolutions of international justice and legitimacy that the international community passed."[30]

Egypt wanted to take advantage of international forums to help resolve key issues in the region. When asked about the possibility of an international conference, Boutros-Ghali responded: "We certainly think that immediately after the war a new peace process must be started, especially on the Palestinian problem."[31] It appears that Egypt was able to look beyond the Gulf crisis and plan for Egypt's continual engagement in the international and regional arenas. Boutros-Ghali explained that Egypt's intention is to find an answer to the Palestinian problem once the Gulf crisis is over. Moreover, he advocates the use of an international forum as a means to address this regional issue.[32]

From the U.S. perspective, Egypt's actions before, during, and after the Gulf crisis bolstered Egypt's international status, primarily by Egypt's continued close ties through diplomatic channels with the United States. These ties helped to secure benefits for Egypt by linking Egypt's actions in the region to economic rewards. For example, Boutros-Ghali described the three objectives of a visit to the United States by three high Egyptian officials: First, the visit aimed to discuss bilateral relations. The second objective was to discuss the post–Gulf War situation. Finally, the two countries were to discuss economic relations, as well as Egypt's efforts with the IMF and the World Bank to reform the economy.[33]

A report prepared by Dr. 'Abd-al-Majid, deputy prime minister and foreign minister, links the importance of Egypt's international role to its regional and domestic status. An article noted that the report highlighted the world community's appreciation for Egypt's civilized role, its abidance by international legitimacy, and its vanguard Arab role; for President Mubarak and his principled and responsible stance in support of right and justice; and for the efforts to reform the Egyptian economy in light of democratic practices aimed to preserve stability. The report also outlined the timetable agreed upon to sign the final agreement with the IMF in light of the serious steps taken by Egypt concerning economic reform.[34]

Boutros-Ghali explained how the Gulf crisis highlighted the importance of the region to the West, as well as demonstrating that it is in Egypt's best interests to broaden its perspective beyond the Nile. He applauded the efforts of the United Nations as a viable international mechanism for addressing regional issues.[35] Egypt followed up on its international diplomatic efforts by organizing and hosting the world's first "anti-terrorism" summit on March 13 in support of the peace process. Steve Negus explains that this deed was "an enormous diplomatic coup for President Hosni Mubarak. . . . The summit is a new lease of life for Egypt's supply of foreign aid—Egyptian diplomats openly admit that as their diplomatic utility wanes, the money will start to dry up."[36] Again, we see the link between international status and economic benefits.

Egypt continued to build upon its status in the peace process that followed the War, both on the international and regional levels. According to Farwaz A. Gerges, Egypt is an instrumental player. "Alienating Cairo will irreparably damage the cause of peace in the region. Egypt holds the key to the Arab world. Without its consent and active participation, Arab-Israeli peace agreements will remain just so much ink on paper."[37] Egypt continues to parlay this status into economic benefits.

As discussed above, Egypt used its international status to help bolster its regional status. Egypt also took action to bolster its regional status directly, which did not necessarily conflict with Egypt's international outlook. For example, Dr. Usamah al-Baz, Egyptian foreign ministry first under secretary and director of the president's office for political affairs, explained that the Egyptian-Saudi-Syrian coordination is not a "tripartite axis in the sense of a warlike grouping or a bloc that is separate from other Arab parties." Instead, it is seeking a solution to the crisis. This regional effort did not conflict with the broader international coalition. Dr. al-Baz claimed that foreign intervention, "for which Iraq's rulers alone are responsible," was necessary because without it the crisis would have become more critical, and the region would have had worse experiences than without a foreign presence.[38]

Throughout the conflict, Egypt looked for regional tools to fix regional problems. We have already mentioned Egypt's deliberate actions to reassert itself in the Arab fold as it made amends with countries such as Syria. The press in Cairo reported that "on the topic of Egyptian-Syrian relations, President Mubarak stressed that there is full agreement between him and President Hafiz al-Asad and also between Egyptian and Syrian stands on Arab issues in general and the Gulf crisis in particular."[39] The defense minister, General

Yusuf Sabri Abu-Talib, emphasized the importance of the region to the Egyptian soldier. The article reported that Gen. Abu-Talib "Praised the role of the Egyptian soldier throughout history and said the Egyptian soldier never saw his role as concerning Egypt alone. His role always extended into the region around him."[40]

Mubarak, while speaking to a group of writers and intellectuals, linked Egypt with the region. The article explained that

> The president asserted that the Egyptian stand is guided by its Arab and pan-Arab principles. . . . President Mubarak affirmed that he always keeps in mind Egypt's dignity, prestige, and weight, as well as the dignity of each Egyptian on his own land. He noted in this respect that the Arab nation appreciates the role played by Egypt and the Egyptians.[41]

As a result of linking Egyptian national status with regional status, Mubarak simultaneously increased both, thereby reaping economic benefits and solidifying the regime at home.

Morris claims that Egypt gained a great deal from its participation in the coalition, including military and economic benefits. However, the increased status and potential increase of status for the future on all levels is the critical outcome for Egypt. Morris states that "Egypt emerged from the Gulf War as one of the big 'winners' and expected to reap both military and economic benefits from its participation in the coalition against Saddam Hussein."[42] Diplomatically, Egypt regained prominence with the Arab League's move to Cairo, the Arab League's election of Egypt's foreign minister, Ismet Abdul-Meguid, as the League's secretary general, and the selection of Boutros Boutros-Ghali as secretary general of the UN. Morris further claims that Egypt can parlay this increased regional and international stature into domestic stature because the success of the peace process would bolster the acceptance of a moderate regime throughout the region. "Accordingly, the Mubarak government has moved the peace process to the top of its foreign policy agenda. The success of the talks would enhance Egypt's credibility as a regional leader and underscore the success of moderate politics in the Middle East."[43]

The problem is that if the peace process fails, Morris believes that Egypt would lose its standing in the region as well as its leadership of moderates in the Middle East. Such a failure would renew the radical fundamentalist charge that Mubarak had sold out to the West, which might precipitate a rise of radicalism in the region. Morris contends that: "The prognosis for the long-term, however, is that the rewards of a more stable and rational regional environment will sap the power of radical groups, especially if economic conditions improve both within Egypt and across the region."[44]

On a domestic level, Mubarak, I believe, felt that he could count on support for his decision, even in the midst of threats of Islamic fundamentalism. Admittedly, Mubarak did not avoid all problems, but relative to other Arab countries, namely Syria, he had great support, especially when he first made the decision to play an active role in the coalition. An examination of legitimacy, that is, internal status, in terms of elite attitudes, including opposition parties, and the views of the public-at-large will provide insight concerning Mubarak's domestic support. Additionally, I will address the Muslim Brotherhood because it is the most prominent Islamic group.

On an institutional level, Mubarak enjoyed support for his decision. The People's Assembly approved a draft resolution that declared

> its full support for His excellency President Muhammad Husni Mubarak in all his efforts and steps to tackle the crisis in order to achieve peace, avert bloodshed, prevent the outbreak of hostilities, safeguard legitimacy, repulse aggression, and liberate the State of Kuwait. Likewise, the Assembly declares its support and backing for his excellency the president in all the steps and measures that he might take in this regard. Second, the assembly endorses the farsighted policy being pursued by the government on the Arab and international scene in this regard.[45]

Opposition parties also declared their support for Mubarak. In my view, this is extraordinary due to the anticipated economic hardship caused by the Gulf crisis. Egypt would lose money on foregone remittances, Suez Canal revenue, tourism, loss of bank deposits in Kuwait and Iraq, developmental assistance from Kuwait, and trade with Iraq. The estimated loss was $9 billion. There was some hope that part of this burden would be offset by sending workers to Libya and the GCC states, money from oil-rich regimes, emergency funds from the West and Japan, and significant debt forgiveness.[46] With all this economic burden to bear, the public and opposition groups supported the regime even at a time of an unsettled domestic political situation. Ann Lesch explains:

> Nonetheless, virtually all non-governmental politicians denounced the Iraqi invasion. The general guide of the Muslim Brotherhood, Muhammad Hamid Abu al-Nasr, termed the invasion "Terrifying" and urged Muslim leaders to convince Iraq to withdraw its forces before Israel and the West could exploit the situation to their benefit. [Note how the Muslim Brotherhood in Syria used this opportunity to denounce the regime.] The liberal secular Wafd Party's editor sounded more hawkish than the government when he declared that Saddam had committed a "barbaric crime," and "treacherously stabbed Egypt in the back."[47]

The Wafd Party approved of Mubarak's decision because of its pan-Arab basis and "its belief in the unity of Arab national security." In a statement following the Iraqi aggression against Kuwait, Wafd leader Fua'd Siraj-al-Din announced that the party supported Mubarak based on the following principles:[48] First, Iraq's aggression was against a fraternal Arab state. Second, the Egyptian forces were not the aggressive invading force, but instead they went to defend at the request of the United Arab Emirates and Saudi Arabia. Finally, Egypt is responding to its duty as outlined in the Collective Defense Pact signed by member states of the Arab League.[49] On the other end of the political spectrum, the left-wing Tagammu Party also condemned the occupation of one Arab country by another and called for an immediate Iraqi withdrawal. Lesch states that "Such unanimity across the political spectrum was unprecedented."[50]

Finally, the elites declared their support for Mubarak's decision. According to Lesch,

> Egyptian officials maintained that the basic principles of their policy were the renunciation of force to resolve Arab differences, nonintervention in the domestic politics of Arab countries, and the need to settle Arab differences within an Arab framework. Egypt, therefore, rejected Iraq's invasion and annexation of Kuwait and called for a peaceful solution under the auspices of the Arab League.[51]

Furthermore, Aftandilian explains that the Egyptian elite wants a lead role in the peace process in order to enhance Egypt's status. "Egyptian leaders believe such a role will enhance Egypt's importance in both regional and international affairs, resulting in economic and political benefits."[52] Mubarak says that Egypt must be a key player in the peace process "because our position and Egypt's status in the region are basic and pivotal. . . . We cannot abandon our role because this constantly highlights our importance."[53]

Egyptian elites have strong positive views of Kuwait and Saudi Arabia. Three-quarters had positive views of the United States, Germany, and Japan (see tables 6.1–6.3) based on a June 10–July 4, 1991, survey of 202 Egyptian business executives conducted by RadaResearch, an Egyptian marketing research firm. Although the response trend is rather predictable for this sample, its intensity is not. The (United States Information Agency) report continues to highlight the significance of the survey results because "so many of these Egyptians give three Gulf states the highest possible rating on a five-point scale—and that virtually none of them do the same for any of the other regional countries in question."[54] In my view, this favorable rating reflects economic expectations from these Gulf countries, which supports the economic imperative of this alignment decision.

David Pollock conducted surveys in Morocco and Egypt, and he found that during the Fall of 1990, both Egyptians and Moroccans were more sympathetic with Kuwait than with Iraq. Furthermore, there was overwhelming support for economic sanctions against Iraq in Egypt and strong support for these

Table 6.1. Egyptian Elite Views of Mideast States (June 1991)[55]

Elite Views of	% Very Favorable	% Fairly Favorable	% Neutral	% Fairly Unfavorable	% Very Unfavorable
Saudi Arabia	67		13	7	2
U.A.E.	69	13	8	6	1
Kuwait	64	1	11	8	12
Syria	0	26	44	20	10
Jordan	0	21	18	18	16
Iraq	0	4	34	37	25
Libya	0	8	37	38	17
Iran	0	20	38	19	22

Table 6.2. Egyptian Elite Views of Foreign Countries (June 1991)[56]

"What is your overall impression of the following countries, on a 5-point scale, where 5 means very favorable and 1 means very unfavorable:"

(Number of cases – 202)

	% Very Favorable	% Favorable	% Neither/Nor	% Fairly Unfavorable	% Very Unfavorable
U.S.	75	16	5	2	1
U.K.	51	35	11	2	—
France	47	40	9	1	1
Germany	66	24	5	3	—
Japan	65	19	10	2	2
USSR	17	48	10	14	10

Table 6.3. Expectations of U.S. Aid to Egypt (June 1991)[57]

"Thinking about the future, do you expect that U.S. help to Egypt will be more, less, or remain the same in the following areas:"

(Number of cases: 202)

%	Financial	Economic	Military
Increase	17	50	24
Remain the Same	35	43	68
Decrease	48	6	8

sanctions in Morocco. "The 'street' in both Cairo and Casablanca mostly rejected Saddam's claims to be acting on behalf of Islam, the Arabs, the have-not Arabs, or even just the Palestinians."[58] However, "if it came to war, . . . these two Arab publics parted ways: in Egypt, a plurality was prepared to back—and to participate—in hostilities against Iraq if necessary." The closer you are to Saddam the less you like him.[59]

Pollock did find a difference between the street or mass opinion and elite opinion. "The elite, on the whole, seems clearly to have a 'moderate' foreign policy orientation," which differs from street opinion.[60] Pollock explains that "while there are no current polling data from that country, results from 1991 showed signs of sharply diverging views between the elite and the street: the former generally supported broad moves toward peace with Israel; the latter were noticeably more noncommittal, at best." In a survey taken in Cairo and Alexandria just before the Madrid Conference, 50 percent of those with more than a secondary education believed that the peace talks with Israel were acceptable to Islam. However, only 25 percent of Egyptians with intermediate or secondary education concurred with that moderate view, while two-thirds of those with just primary or less education felt "strongly" that these peace talks were not acceptable to Islam. Additionally, on the issue concerning Egypt's further participation in the Arab-Israeli peace talks, two-thirds of those with at least an intermediate education said yes, yet fewer than one-third of the less-educated urban "masses" agreed, even after more than ten years of formal peace with Israel. Although this survey is barely within statistical validity (500 sampled), the gap is extremely wide between the street and the elites. While this gap only affected policy on the margins, it affects the quality of peace.[61]

The question, then, is whether this gap presents a problem for the regime or internal status. In a relative, that is in the regional context, sense I do not believe it is a critical problem for three reasons. First, the people have a patrimonial view towards politics. According to Ayubi, "By political and legal tradition, both the State and the President/Boss (rayyes) are invested with much power and respect. One result is that both in domestic and external matters, 'regime' and 'policy' are often presented and/or perceived of as one and the same thing. The political instinct of most Egyptians would be first to support the state and then to find out why!"[62] Remember that Asad did not seem to have this immediate support from his people, and he had to devote a great deal of effort to build a consensus. (This will be true for the post–Cold War era too as we will see in the next chapter.) Ayubi explains that

> other Arabs have repeatedly expressed surprise at the way many Egyptians will take criticism of certain policy options of a certain Egyptian leader as an attack on Egypt herself. And the leadership has used the same inclination for its own benefit often by implying that a disagreement with one of the policies of the President is almost tantamount to national treason.[63]

Furthermore, Ayubi explains, "Another aspect of this veneration of the State is the linkage some Egyptians establish between the strength of the State domestically and its strength externally."[64] This linkage helps to explain the importance at a domestic level for Mubarak to increase his standing on the regional and world stages. Finally, Hopwood observes that even with "Sadat's mistakes the fact that the transfer of power was so smooth showed a great stability in the system."[65] Again, this point supports the view that the "street" still had great respect for authority and its leaders, even in the midst of great adversity.

Second, Egypt has dealt with the issue of religion and politics in the past, so it is important to consider the context in which Egyptian politics is operating. Paul Salem explains that secularism was a key factor in the pre–1952 period of the Egyptian nationalist movement, led by the Wafd party and writings of Ahmad Lutfi Sayyid, Taha Husayn, and others. A separation of religion from politics was necessary to deter Muslim-Christian (Coptic) tensions in Egypt and, "to foment a unifying nationalism, as well as in order to move closer to the European model of polity, economy and society that the Wafd and the social strata it represented held in high regard."[66]

Later, Arab Communists and Marxists emphasized the idea of secularism and blamed religion for the ills of Arab society. They directly opposed the Islamic parties in Egypt and in other countries.[67] Ideas of class struggle, socialism, antiimperialism found their way to Arab nationalist thought. "Communist and Marxist thought, therefore, which . . . [is rooted in] a profoundly secular outlook, has had more of an influence in the Arab world than a quick current survey of political parties would suggest."[68] However, the demise of the Soviet Union affected the Arab political culture. The West no longer represented an alternative ideology; it now represented the only ideology, one that was perceived by many Arabs as ". . . monolithic, dominant, Christian and aggressive."[69]

While Mubarak took a firm stand against Iraq and recognized the Gulf states' right to ask for U.S. support, he did create some distance with the United States, perhaps realizing some groups' perception of the West. Perhaps with the post–Cold War era and the lack of a counter-ideology to the West, anti-secularism, I believe, seemed to be more prominent—but was it really? Even in this context, Mubarak seemed able to override this sentiment. At times, Egypt even praised the United States for its diplomatic efforts, which seemed to be much different than Asad's bellicose rhetoric towards the United States. An editorial commented that

> Washington's offer to hold a dialogue with Iraq and the support expressed for this offer by other capitals shows that the United States has finally managed to lead the chorus of the anti-Saddam coalition without allowing for any discordant voice to be heard, and that it can project a defiant front on behalf of the international community in its separate talks with Iraq.[70]

Additionally, Lesch explains that Mubarak frankly talked about those short-term economic sacrifices Egypt was making in terms of lost trade, bank deposits, and remittances from Kuwait and Iraq, as well as lost revenue from the Suez Canal and tourism, as a result of his decision.[71] Even with this economic hardship at the microeconomic level, Mubarak still had support.

Again, admitting these economic woes is risky for Mubarak because acknowledging his inability to fix them opens a door for his opposition. Pelletiere explains that religious forces have been able to exploit the dire economic situation as a way to build public support. While Egyptians are known for their tolerance for suffering, there are limits.[72] Yet, Mubarak was able to keep the opposition at bay even in the midst of a failed economy.

Third, the opposition did not pose a unified bloc. As mentioned earlier, opposition leaders favored Mubarak's initial anti-Iraq stand, but divisions among the opposition arose with the U.S. presence.[73] There were some demonstrations against the regime. For example, a group of journalists staged a sit-in protesting U.S. action in the Gulf: "Today's issue of AL-SHA'B reports that the State Security Prosecution Office yesterday began interrogating Naji al-Shiyahbi, a member of the Labor Party's Executive Committee, on charges of printing leaflets entitled: 'No to the Gulf war'"[74] Another report claimed that "On Sunday, students burned three effigies: one of U.S. President George Bush, one of King Fahd of Saudi Arabia and one that was faceless."[75]

Generally, it does not appear that the prominent opposition Islamic group, the Muslim Brotherhood, resorts to such tactics. According to Pelletiere, there are two different approaches by antigovernmental groups. One approach adopted by the Muslim Brotherhood is basically peaceful; the wealthy and well-connected Brothers are attempting to use the system, namely the ballot box, to gain power. The other approach, used by groups of anarchists, is one of violence. Pelletiere does not think the Brotherhood encourages violence. "The psychology of the 'shooters' (as one U.S. Embassy official described the radicals) is so at variance with that of the Brotherhood leaders, it seems unlikely there would be a link. Whatever else, the leaders of the Brotherhood are men of property, who respect authority as exemplified by the ulama [religious leaders]. They would hardly countenance the kind of anarchic behavior that the 'shooters' carry on."[76]

In fact, both groups fear and loathe each other. It appears that the shooters do not have widespread support, and they are only supported by their home communities in the Upper Egypt area. Pelletiere admits that it is hard to characterize the anarchists in Cairo. "At the same time, they do not appear to have struck a responsive chord in the wider polity, [and] it is hard to envision how, in its present stage, this sort of behavior poses a threat to Mubarak."[77]

According to Robert Kaplan, the Brotherhood does have a following, but it is due to the Brotherhood's ability to provide basic services for the people. "Many Egyptians see the Brotherhood as a benevolent neighborhood force, operating clinics, welfare organizations, schools and hospitals."[78] The Brotherhood in Egypt appears to be trying to exploit class divisions, not ethnic divisions as we saw happening in Syria. Kaplan explains: "The issue I slowly began to realize was less the Brotherhood than modernity and the contradictions associated with it. Egypt is rapidly changing. There are not only more slums but also more cordless phones, Mercedes Benzes, and boutiques. . . . Not just the poor but the wealthier classes, too, are impatient for better government."[79]

Finally, while there were increased clashes of Copts and Muslims in 1990, they were limited to the Upper Nile. These clashes were not a new phenomenon.[80] Although this is not a good thing for Mubarak, there are several factors, in my view, that differentiate these clashes from the Sunni unrest in Syria. First, and I believe most importantly, unlike the Sunnis who comprise three-quarters of the Syrian population, the Copts are only 6 percent of the Egyptian population.[81] Second, Egypt's sense of nationalism is a strong unifying factor. George W. Gawrych points out that in the modernist state of Egypt, patriotism and nationalism are more influential than Islam. For example, the Egyptian army developed along national, not Islamic lines. There is compulsory national service for all Egyptians, and several Copts have moved into positions of responsibility. The highest religious leader in Egypt in 1973, Shaykh al-Azhar, declared that

> al-Jihad is an obligation for all, without distinction between Muslims and Christians. It is the duty of all who live under the sky of Egypt, the motherland of all. . . . Being martyred for the sake of the motherland gives access to Paradise. This is confirmed by divine laws that have been revealed to the People of the Book.[82]

Gawrych explains that "the integration of Christians into the armed forces reflects a moderation in the Egyptian practice of war. Egyptians have tended to depict their struggle with Israel in more national and ideological than religious terms."[83]

Undoubtedly, there are Muslim-Coptic tensions, however the critical issue facing all Egyptians is the challenge of democratization in the midst of enormous economic challenges. It is Mubarak's dilemma of how much democracy he may introduce in an unstable economic context. Mona Makram-Ebeid claims that the 1995 elections revealed chaotic political participation with no clear opposition voice. A mechanism that links the citizenry with the national decision-makers is nonexistent, and she contends that "What has occurred is a pluralization of public space, yet it has been liberal neither in intent nor outcome."[84] I believe Makram-Ebeid's point is correct concerning the undemocratic nature of the regime, however, I do feel that her criticisms are harsh. Instead, I believe we need to examine Mubarak's efforts within the regional and economic context in which he is operating. Morris explains that Mubarak has said that he does intend to make constitutional changes when the economic picture has stabilized. She cites Mubarak as saying, "No one has the right to claim [he has] a mandate from the people. I live with the pulse of the street, and its basic demand is to get out of the economic crisis we have confronted and to set right the accumulated problems of the past."[85]

It is not an easy task to transition from an authoritarian regime to a democratic one. Even Makram-Ebeid acknowledges the difficulties of such a transition.[86] The point is that setbacks along the democratic process do not necessarily mean that the leader does not intend for a democratic outcome. In fact, Mubarak's heightened concern for the country's economic health can be considered a stepping stone for democracy. Morris describes Egypt as a moderate nation that will most likely continue to democratize, but it is a country that faces many challenges: the economy, bureaucracy, inflation, unemployment, rising population, etc. The causal factors for regime instability are present.[87] I believe that the main ingredient for instability is the exploitation of these economic problems by the opposition groups.

According to Lesch, Mubarak's alignment decision benefited him in several ways, to include increasing status on all levels. Mubarak emerged from the Gulf War with great domestic support, while the opposition lost influence. He secured economic benefits from the (International Monetary Fund), Iraq—a rival—was almost annihilated, and Egypt revived its diplomatic role in the region.[88] Robert Springborg agrees with this assessment and believes that Mubarak's international and regional diplomacy will help him at home: "Mubarak has, in a relatively short time, converted many of Sadat's foreign policy liabilities into net assets. While he has not yet converted this foreign policy capital into a significant legitimating factor at the domestic level, it seems likely that he will be able to do so in the not-so-distant future."[89]

While we may argue over the normative aspect of insufficient democracy in Egypt, it is still apparent that Mubarak was able to rely on support for his decision, at least initially, from the elites, opposition, and society. His increased international and regional status helped him on the domestic front. Again, we should not judge Mubarak with a Western bias. Fouad Ajami observes that "Contempt for the government there is aplenty in Egypt today, but the political and cultural continuity of the place has not ruptured. . . . Most important, unlike the shallow roots of the Algerian state—a postcolonial entity that rose in the 1960s—central authority in Egypt reaches back millenia."[90] As we have touched on already, it is this increase in status which Mubarak hoped to parlay into economic benefits. It is the sickly health of the economy that most threatens the regime. It is this failing which encourages antigovernment sentiment and is the greatest challenge to Egypt's chance for democracy.

HUMAN AND NONHUMAN RESOURCES

This section will reveal the beneficiaries of human and nonhuman resources. This is a critical issue because it appears that the primary objective for Egypt in its decision to align with the coalition was to gain economic benefits. While we will assess economic benefits of the alignment, we must also remember that the outcome does not necessarily reflect intentions. For example, we will see that there were some developmental projects promised as a result of Egypt's alignment, but Egypt still faces a tremendous gap in wealth between the haves and the have-nots. In this case, the intention was to bring some benefits to the majority of the population; however, the outcome may not have had an effect on this wide gap.

It does appear from the beginning of the crisis that Egypt saw an opportunity to achieve economic benefits. There is also evidence that the purpose of these benefits was to reduce the economic burden of the masses. For example, 'Abd-al-Majid, the deputy prime minister and foreign minister in his statement on the Gulf War to the Consultative Council's Foreign Relations Committee, said: "Ladies and Gentlemen: Our region needs peace and the consecration of resources for construction and development for the sake of a better future for all our peoples."[91] This emphasis on developmental projects reflects a desire to lessen the economic plight of the majority of Egyptians. Boutros-Ghali also saw the importance of the alignment to Egypt's future. When asked about the postwar situation in the Middle East, he responded:

> It will be a unique opportunity for the Arab world to create a new impetus in favor of a general awareness and a renewal of Arab solidarity. The postwar period in the Arab world should correspond to the postwar period in Europe which gave rise to the Marshall Plan and the EEC. We have a similar opportunity 50 years later. In addition, in the past 45 years, Europe has never been willing to help the integration of the Arab world. Now, Europe and the United States realize that it is in their interest to encourage a minimum of solidarity in this Arab world to prevent this Balkanization, these contradictions which weaken this region.[92]

Notice how Boutros-Ghali has put the Arab region and Egyptian interests on the international agenda, as discussed in the last section.

Egypt has crafted its foreign policy along economic interests in the past. In fact, in the late 1980s, Egypt improved its relations with Libya in order to gain opportunities for Egyptian workers, as well as acquire technical expertise and products. So far, this alliance produced such benefits as increased trade, Libya's acceptance of many Egyptian workers, and political cooperation, namely Libya's opposition to Iraq's invasion.[93] As chapter four demonstrated, the bases for U.S.-Egyptian ties are U.S. security and economic assistance for Egypt, which expanded greatly after 1979. In fiscal year 1993, Foreign Military Sales (FMS) grants were $1.3 billion and $815 million in Economic Support Fund grants.[94]

Springborg claims that "at the regional level it is also the economic rather than the military dimension that is increasingly seen as exerting the greatest influence on Egyptian decision making." Furthermore, when compared to other countries in the region, Egypt is woefully falling behind.[95] On the global level, one may argue that Egypt is just becoming a more dependent country, which would again explain the constant economic problems facing Egypt. According to an Israeli expert, however, this dependence can be reversed because "The revocability of the process ensues from its two inevitable attributes: the fact that growing dependence creates, in any society imbued with a nationalist spirit, its own antidotes; and the fact that the efforts of the assisting power are bound to frustrate the assisted society."[96] In the meanwhile, Egypt continues with the problem of increasing foreign earnings and is in constant dialogue with the IMF and World Bank. The problem is that the IMF establishes conditions, such as economic reform, liberalization, lifting or reduction of subsidies, promotion of private sector, which Egypt favors in principle, but they are all hard to do in practice. Moreover, Mubarak remembers the food riots under Sadat.[97]

The unfortunate situation that Egypt finds itself in is that any economic progress pales in comparison to the alarming population growth, which increases one person per 30 seconds or 1.25 million people per year. Cairo grows at 300,000 per year. The fertility rate per mother is 5 children, which is ironically an increase due to better medical care. There is not enough housing, and unemployment is at 20 percent. The end of the Iraq-Iran war made the situation worse when Iraqi soldiers returned to take jobs held by Egyptians. After August 1990, this situation worsened again when many of the Egyptian workers in Iraq and Kuwait came home penniless. Additionally, Egypt experienced reduced aid from Kuwait and trade with Iraq, as well as declining revenues from tourism and the Suez Canal. Egypt lost $9 billion that year. Later, Egypt's role in the coalition led to $14 billion of debt canceled, with additional help promised.[98] It is this state of economic affairs that I feel most inhibits economic improvements for Egypt. It is also the reason why I believe that the outcome of economic reforms or programs do not necessarily match intentions. It is an enormous challenge for Mubarak. As

Hopwood says, "Whatever the answers may be, the future development of Egypt presents a challenge which will tax to the utmost the ability and wisdom of its leaders."[99]

It is without question, that the Egyptian economy was in shambles at the start of the Gulf crisis; however, the crisis did provide Egypt with economic possibilities. Tim Niblock believes that Egypt may have been the only Arab country to have economically benefited from the war. Fifteen billion dollars of a $50 billion debt Egypt owed to foreign debtors in July 1990 has been forgiven, including $7 billion in military debt to the United States and the rest of the debts to the Gulf states. Niblock acknowledges, however, that even with the forgiven debts, Egypt's losses may not be overcome. Egypt still suffered from losses after the war because there was a sharp decline of remittances from Egyptian workers in the Gulf, as well as reduced earnings from tourism. These two sources of revenue lost $5 billion in the first three months after the invasion of Kuwait. Niblock concludes, however, that the close ties forged between Egypt and the Gulf states will most likely benefit Egypt in the long term.[100]

President Mubarak, in January of 1991, acknowledged Egypt's uneasy economic situation, but he also felt that his reforms were of some benefit. He explained that the cancellation of Egypt's military debt relieved Egypt's financial difficulties during December and January, which enabled Egypt to secure basic necessities. Mubarak admitted that Egypt faced financial difficulties as a result of the war, but the article concludes that, "in the long run only right will prevail."[101]

According to Carlyle Murphy, Egypt began to realign its political system and private sector because the fall of communism gave great impetus to global trade with an increase of opportunities for economic development and integration, especially with the beginnings of a reconciliation of Arab-Israeli relations. Moreover, as discussed earlier, the domestic threat of militant Islam gave greater urgency to the Mubarak regime to address social and economic problems with the tools of the private sector, namely its knowledge, technology, and capital. The conditions of unemployment, inflation, poor schooling, and lack of housing are bases of the popular resentment, which feeds radical Islam. Additionally, Egypt felt that the United States would probably begin reducing Egypt's annual aid package of $2.1 billion because of the growing domestic demand in the United States to cut back on all foreign aid. Consequently, Egypt felt it needed to tap its own private sector for increased production.[102]

So with these reforms and financial rewards of its coalition alignment, who did benefit? According to Murphy, Egypt's slow retreat from socialism mainly benefited large businesses and the politically plugged-in upper classes, whose success is evident in the growing number of chic stores and luxury cars in Cairo. . . . By contrast, the majority of Egyptians have seen their standard of living deteriorate as a result of other economic reforms the government has made under pressure from the World Bank and the International Monetary Fund.[103]

Unfortunately, there is a perception among the well-to-do businessmen and ordinary people that official corruption has increased. Murphy observes that Egyptians openly and honestly complain about alleged activities of senior government officials, who alter the rules to leave a less-than-level playing field in the business community.[104] Making political and economic changes is not an easy task, but I think it is noteworthy that Egyptians do feel that they can openly complain about their government, which is not the case in Syria. This point is significant because without honest expression, change cannot happen because no one knows what to fix. In Egypt, at least there is a start point for change.[105]

Some of the economic frustration is due to rising expectations created by Nassar's rhetoric, the oil boom, American largesse, Sadat's infitah, and the disappointing decade of the 1980s. The post–1991 Gulf War further aggravated this disappointment because although the economy now reflects a dramatic improvement in its macroeconomic performance, it has suffered a sharp decrease in its microeconomic performance. Unfortunately for Mubarak, on the individual level, it is the microeconomic performance that influences attitudes and perceptions. Cassandra explains further that "while economists are persuaded by data on balance of payments, levels of indebtedness, budget deficits, and other macroeconomic indicators, such data mean little to ordinary people concerned about the scarcity of jobs, low wages, high prices, and inadequate profits."[106]

The success at this macrolevel is a result of the aid Egypt received after the Gulf War, including the May 1991 stabilization package agreed to with the IMF. This aid decreased Egypt's 1990 foreign debt of $50 billion to $26 billion by 1994. Fiscal reform reduced the budget deficit from 20 percent of Gross Domestic Product (GDP) in 1990 to approximately 3 percent in 1993, and inflation fell from 25 percent in 1991 to less than 10 percent in 1993. Furthermore, Egypt's foreign currency reserves increased from $2.7 billion to almost $12 billion in 1993.[107]

For Mubarak, the poor microeconomic performance has led to two politically relevant results, which are growing unemployment and a widening income gap between the rich and the poor. Cassandra notes that because it is primarily the unemployed who have been arrested for committing terrorist acts, some relief to joblessness would appear to be a precondition for addressing political violence.

Unfortunately, unemployment is steadily rising, reaching between 17 and 20 percent by 1993, while the 1994 numbers of unemployed Egyptians were between 1.5 and 2 million.[108] Just the perception that the state is inept or out of touch with the plight of the economically deprived helps broaden the gap between the government and the people.[109]

Mubarak must demonstrate governmental effectiveness in the economic realm in order to address rising discontent in the political realm. As Mary Morris observes, "The Egyptian economy is probably the most serious threat to the government's stability."[110] Andrew Album concurs: "For it is economic progress, rather than military crackdowns, which will ultimately ensure the long term survival of his regime and give it the support to see off the threat of Islamic militancy."[111]

Mubarak is trying to address Egypt's economy, and there is some cause for optimism. Admittedly, there are many observers who criticize Mubarak for being too slow on implementing reforms and lacking a market oriented strategy.[112] I think we must remember that Egypt is dealing with a population that produces one child every 27 seconds and one million new Egyptians per 10 months. It has seen the problems of Eastern Europe and the former Soviet Union in their transitions, so Mubarak has some cause to proceed gradually with reforms.[113] In the face of these challenges, Mubarak has been taking steps to slow down economic decline. For example, the economic restructuring progress under the first two stages of the IMF and World Bank reforms has surprised critics. Between 1990 and 1992, inflation decreased from 24 percent to about 12 percent, and Egypt cut its budget deficit from more than 20 percent of gross national product to 4.7 percent. Additionally, its foreign currency reserves rose to $17 billion, and the exchange rate remained stable.[114] Mubarak's stated goals are economic reform, security, social justice, unemployment, improved education, a decreased population growth, and a pared down state bureaucracy.[115]

Of significance is Mubarak's nomination of Ismail Hassan as the new governor of the Central Bank. He is a former chairman of the Bank of Alexandria and Misr American International Bank, who is widely respected in financial circles. Mubarak created a new ministerial post in charge of the public sector and administrative development for Atef Obeid, who has been the point person for the privatization program. Mubarak is trying to increase the momentum for reform by granting responsibility directly to Obeid. Other significant appointments are Mohmoud Mohammad Hahmoud, the former head of the Misr International Bank, as economy minister, and Ibrahim Fawzi Abdul Wahed as minister for industry in place of Mohammad Abdel Wahab who has not been a champion of wholesale privatization.[116]

Prime Minister Dr. 'Atif Sidqi described some of the economic reforms, to include plans to abolish subsidies gradually, except for the subsidy on basic commodities. [In an earlier report he said that the IMF and World Bank wanted the full abolishment of subsidies, but Egypt insisted that this be done gradually.[117] He explained that the state will compensate its citizens by other measures, such as increasing their incomes and salaries. He noted that the state had been subsidizing more than 150 commodities, but economic reform has made subsidies infeasible. The prime minister said that the state would increase its employees' and civil servants' salaries by up to 100 percent to face the increase in prices. He also expressed the state's goal to help landlords by re-looking at the law to try to increase revenue from property. For farmers, the state will attempt market pricing, except for cotton, which will be liberalized next year. He explained that the implementation of these reforms are designed to protect those citizens of low income.[118]

Other indications of some reform success occurred when the Egyptian delegation headed by Dr. Kamal al-Janzuri, deputy prime minister and planning minister, reached an agreement with the two financial institutions under which Egypt received a loan of $150 million, as well as 15 percent of its foreign debts written off. Dr. Tubar of the National Democratic Party's economic committee said that the IMF and the World Bank officials were convinced that the economic reform program was a success and that the economy achieved good results.[119]

Mubarak himself explains his concerns with economic reform, stating that "the economy was suffering from chronic ailments" that could have led to "a total collapse" if he had not decided to develop and implement the reform program "at the right time." He said:

> Our target will be to continue to liberate the economy; to develop and further liberate the public investments authority; to deal seriously with the enormous population increase; to work out a comprehensive program to supplement the economic reform program in order to increase production, both in terms of quality and quantity, and to enhance people's abilities and skills; and to take care of low-income groups during the reform periods.[120]

The article reported that Mubarak "stressed the need for cohesion and solidarity among all members of Egyptian society to maintain stability, overcome hatred, and develop gratitude among the low-income groups."[121]

Another indication that Mubarak felt a sense of support and legitimacy from his people is that he frankly talked about the problems Egypt faced. At an Alexandria University anniversary celebration Mubarak explains,

> We need to talk frankly about our internal affairs, the economic situation, peace process, our international relations with the East, the West, Africa, and Arab countries, because all these things are linked in one chain. One cannot carry out economic reform in Egypt without having strong and good relations with the outside world, because you simply need them. We need to have good relations with the entire world so we can overcome the crisis we are in the process of surmounting.[122]

As I mentioned earlier, I believe that it is a good sign when leaders and citizens can honestly assess regime performance, and Egypt does this. From a Western liberal perspective, admittedly Egypt does not compare in this arena, however, in the regional context I believe it does.

Mubarak also explains how he has tried to protect ordinary Egyptians as Egypt implements reforms: "When we started the five-year plan in 1982, many economists told me during our meetings: Mr. President, the situation requires a courageous step. What sort of courageous step? They said: Cancel subsidies, cancel free education, lay off 25 percent of the government's employees. Oh no!"[123] Here, Mubarak explains his dilemma of quick reform versus protecting the people from great hardships.

He continues to explain his rationale for not reducing the Army:

> The Egyptian army supports every citizen; it backs the Egyptian people. The Egyptian Army secures the country's existence. It is not an aggressive army that seeks to occupy other areas. The feeling that no one can attack our country fills us with pride and strength. . . . Who makes up the Army but our sons. If you were to reduce the Army, what would you really be doing? You would be dismissing your own sons. People have sons and brothers in the Army. These sons would have nothing to do outside the Army and would become unemployed. What would you do then? What would you do then? The Army employs people and gives them jobs. They earn their income to survive. If you were to discharge people from the Army, you would weaken it. Our self-esteem would drop.[124]

Finally, Mubarak explains the danger of reform and admits the burden it places on all Egyptians.

> We have initiated economic reforms and have made great progress. I have said on more than one occasion . . . that economic reform places a great burden on us all. We do not want to delay economic reform until things are destroyed, people cannot find anything to eat, and we reach a stage of collapse. That is exactly what happened in Russia.[125]

Mubarak talks about the importance of investment, but that entails stability. "Without stability, tourism and investment will go away. How can we live when we are multiplying at such a dreadful rate? Imagine; our population has increased by 14 million since 1982, equal to the population of the Gulf states."[126]

In sum, the coalition alignment provided an economic opportunity for Egypt. The actual beneficiaries appear to be big business and the upper classes. I do believe, however, that the intention of the economic reforms and aid was for the overall improvement of the economy that would have been felt throughout the population. Unfortunately, economic reform cannot proceed too quickly without causing great hardships for most Egyptians, as the preceding discussion on subsidies indicates. The problem is that Egypt is facing such great odds for improvement just by trying to keep up with its alarming population growth rate. Additionally, Mubarak recognizes that the source of domestic unrest is the economy, and so do Mubarak's opposition. The Muslim Brotherhood seeks to exploit this class differential in Egypt. Mubarak's task is to provide economic benefits for his people so that they do not look elsewhere for help, namely the Islamic groups. What is remarkable is that in the midst of such bad economic conditions and with the prospect of short-term microeconomic problems caused by the Gulf crisis, Mubarak still had great support at home. The challenge for Mubarak is to prevent a downward spiral of ineffectiveness because in the long term such ineffectiveness may eventually erode the regime's internal status.

INDICATOR: FOREIGN AID AND TRADE

As with our Syrian case, I will combine the issues for this indicator because they are so interrelated, and also, as before, I have already covered this indicator in my previous section. Again, there are differing interpretations of the hard data, such as the effectiveness of Mubarak's economic reforms. In my view, the difficulty in analyzing this indicator is that the outcome does not indicate the policy intentions for reasons already discussed. Here, I present hard data in the form of tables, but we must remember that a positive macroeconomic performance does not necessarily reach the individual, consequently, good macroeconomic performance does not diminish discontent as would an increase at the microeconomic level. I will still attempt to answer the question of who is benefiting here.

ISSUES: SECURITY, TERRITORY, HUMAN, AND NONHUMAN RESOURCES

Egypt was able to benefit from the peace treaty with Israel concerning its military spending. From 1973–1975, Egypt was spending 32 percent of its GNP on military forces; however, by the late 1980s, its spending dropped to 8–12 percent. Also, in 1973–1975, Egypt was spending over 50 percent of its central government's expenditures on the military, but by 1986–1988, this expenditure dropped to 20–22 percent. Even with this drop in military spending, Egypt's economy struggled.[127] According to Edward Atkeson, "Egypt has no apparent ambition for expanding its forces, but seeks to modernize through gradual transition to Western equipment."[128] Perhaps the economy prevented Egypt from thinking about expanding its forces.

Luckily, Egypt has been able to modernize its military with help from the United States. President Bush asked Congress in September 1990 to forgive Egypt's debt of $6.7 billion, which was approved in December 1990. Not only did this debt forgiveness ease Egypt's economic strain, it also helped with modernizing Egypt's forces. This debt servicing for past FMS loans would help with scheduled payments for the subsequent five years.[129]

Egypt needed such modernization assistance especially because of the challenge it has faced through the 1980s of integrating U.S. equipment with Soviet equipment and doctrine. Egypt made significant progress on this conversion, especially since 1985 when all of the FMS financing, which from 1987–1992 was an annual $1,300 million, was in the form of grant aid. The debt forgiveness described above was also instrumental. Consequently, Egypt has bought a great amount of U.S. equipment. By late 1991, Egypt operated 1,550 U.S.-made tanks, 1,361 other armored vehicles, and 532 TOW launchers. Air defense forces had 72 improved Hawk launchers and 8 TPS-63 2D radars. The Air Force had 144 U.S.-made combat aircraft and 101 other Western-made combat aircraft.[130] Refer to table 6.4.

It appears that militarily Egypt's coalition position allowed it to keep pace, if not improve the technological edge of its arsenal with U.S. assistance. While it does appear that the Army itself benefited from the alignment decision, I believe the Army offered Egypt two main benefits. First, a respectable military helped to provide Egypt with enough clout to be a key player in the region. As noted earlier, such status earned Egypt economic benefits. Second, the Army offered employment, as noted earlier by Mubarak, himself. The economy could not absorb a great influx of unemployed soldiers. Again, there is a tie-in to the economic imperative.

Table 6.4.   Military Spending Trend: Egypt (U.S. dollars)[131]

	Manpower (1,000s)	Tanks	Aircraft	Defense Spending ($ millions)	Arms Imports ($ millions)	Arms Exports ($ millions)
1967	220	530	400	0.3	204	1
1973	390	1,880	620	11.4	741	14
1982	447	2,100	429	7.2	1,900	360
1988	452	2,425	517	6.1	725	170
1991	420	3,190	495	5.2	—	—

Tables 6.5–6.7 explore the human and nonhuman resource issue, and they support our earlier assessment that the macroeconomic level of performance is better than the microeconomic level. Consequently, the ordinary citizen is not likely to feel as if he or she is benefiting from any of the economic rewards Egypt received for its participation in the Gulf War. Similarly, Mubarak's reforms in the face of such dire statistics concerning unemployment and population growth rates have a hard time even measuring on a Richter scale. The tables are rather deceiving because, as described earlier, the intentions to help all Egyptians do not match the outcome, which is little effect for many, but great effect for the privileged upper class few.

CONCLUSION

As I mentioned in the introduction, Egypt is a difficult case because it is our null set case. Consequently, we are showing the significance of a lack of ethnic divisiveness on the Persian Gulf War alignment decision. I believe, however, that there are significant indications of legitimacy enjoyed by Mubarak as a result of ethnic homogeneity. In other words, the fact that he had great support for his initial coalition stance in the face of tremendous economic woes combined with a growing anti-West sentiment in the region is significant and is linked to Egypt's ethnic homogeneity. The idea that the Egyptian

Table 6.5. Economic Data for Egypt, 1992–1993[132]

Per Capita GDP (U.S. $)	715	Annual GDP Growth Rate	2.4%
Population (thousands)	56,400	Annual Pop. Growth Rate	2.2%
GDP (billions of U.S. $)	40.3		

Table 6.6. Cost of Living: Egypt (Consumer Price Index base: 1980 = 100)[133]

	1988	1989	1990
Food	373.8	473.3	548.3
Fuel and Light	133.5	137.2	n.a.
Clothing	274.3	315.3	374.1
Rent	122.4	128.7	150.0
All Items (incl. others)	337.1	408.8	477.3

Source: ILO, Yearbook of Labour Statistics

Table 6.7. Principal Trading Partners: Egypt (Egyptian pounds, millions)[134]

	Imports				Exports		
	1989	1990	1991		1989	1990	1991
Australia	428.2	1,038.0	858.4	Belgium	140.8	164.8	162.8
Austria	128.0	216.6	284.2	Czech.	92.5	153.5	8.8
Belgium	363.9	468.5	502.7	France	408.0	278.4	695.3
China, PRC	133.0	276.9	n.a.	Germany	296.8	386.0	439.2
Czechoslovakia	160.2	249.9	338.3	Greece	131.3	104.5	448.2
France	920.7	1,355.7	824.2	Israel	364.8	451.5	1,186.8
Germany	1,613.4	2,621.0	2,631.0	Italy	792.8	849.3	1,743.8
Greece	169.5	174.3	182.9	Japan	206.2	189.0	165.1
Japan	642.6	923.6	1,026.0	Romania	7.7	75.2	399.3
Romania	496.5	256.0	210.3	SA	169.8	206.2	366.1
Saudi Arabia (SA)	102.1	205.9	433.8	Sudan	47.1	55.8	81.8
USSR	576.6	733.0	458.3	USSR	764.4	1,097.5	745.8
USA	2,930.7	3,502.9	4,056.7	USA	288.9	596.7	894.7
TOTAL (incl. others)	16,623.6	24,823.2	25,216.3		5,734.7	6,953.8	11,764.7

people will support the state and ask questions later provides the Egyptian leader with some room to maneuver in foreign policy. This contrasts with Asad, who is constantly trying to build a consensus before he makes a move. Ironically, the seemingly absolute ruler, Asad, apparently operates with tighter constraints, as we will see again in the next chapter, than does Mubarak in the foreign policy realm. I will discuss this point in greater detail in my concluding chapter.

This case demonstrated that the economic imperative seems to weave its way through the other issues. Security and status seem to be the means by which Egypt gains economic benefits. Admittedly, Egypt had some external security concerns with Israel, even with the treaty, and with the threat of Iranian hegemony in the region. However, it was evident that Egypt was more concerned with the postwar security arrangement than with the immediate external threats, especially in terms of laying the groundwork for the peace process. Numerous Egyptian officials saw the peace process as an opportunity for Egypt to build economically. Boutros-Ghali even called for a Marshall Plan for the region. Pelletier's view that "Egypt's security problem must be seen in context of its economic plight" is evident in this case.[135]

Also, Egypt seemed to have ensured a continuation of its military capabilities through its alignment because of continued U.S. assistance. Although Egypt does not seem to be harboring offensive designs or anticipating war with Israel, it does see a respectable military as essential for providing diplomatic clout. The issue of security for Egypt meant ensuring that Egypt remained a key regional and international player in the peace process, and aligning with the coalition allowed Egypt to do just that.

Increased regional and international status is valuable for Egypt because it can convert this status into economic benefits. The coalition alignment allowed Egypt to increase its status in both the regional and international communities, and both communities rewarded Egypt with economic benefits. These benefits, combined with the rise in Mubarak's stature helped to increase his status at home. What is remarkable is that Mubarak had great support from both his political supporters and the opposition parties. Also, the Egyptian people expressed support, even in the face of short-term economic hardships, that would be felt throughout the population. This point is significant, and I believe it is directly related to the Egyptian sense of national identity based on its ethnic homogeneity. It is this reservoir of legitimacy, resulting from this ethnic homogeneity, that allows for regime stability in the face of economic non-performance.

When we did look at the beneficiaries of the economic reforms and aid from the war, it was apparent that the majority of Egyptians were not the recipients. There are several reasons for this outcome. First, Egypt is facing almost insurmountable odds because of its skyrocketing population growth rate. Second, economic reforms at too quick a pace would cause tremendous hardships on the ordinary Egyptian, which makes reforms difficult to implement. Third, macroeconomic performance has increased as a result of the economic benefits from the coalition alignment, however, these benefits have yet to be felt at the microeconomic level. All these factors contribute to the mismatch between policy intentions and policy outcomes.

It is important, though, that we recognize the intention of the alignment decision in terms of economic benefits and reforms. That intention is to raise the standard of living for the average Egyptian. As mentioned earlier, the economy is at the root of Egypt's security, and we have discussed this point in terms of the Islamic opposition. In Egypt, the Islamic opposition does not have ethnic divisions to exploit, but rather the danger is the opposition's exploitation of class divisions. Again, we see the economic imperative for the regime itself. It is amazing to me that Mubarak feels comfortable to openly acknowledge this problem and not feel threatened. I think this is a healthy sign for Egypt's future, not only in the economic realm, but also in the political arena as it continues its path towards democracy.

It does appear that the post–Cold War era affects behavior in several ways. First, I agree with some scholars' views that pragmatism has become the guiding "ideology" for policy. The end of the Cold War did provide less room for maneuver; no longer can third world states play the superpowers off one another. In fact, reminiscent of Kenneth Waltz, there appears to be more uncertainty concerning the reliability of U.S. assistance in the absence of a comparable rival. Consequently, it appears that states have to look elsewhere for support, namely the region and themselves. For this reason, it appears that in the post–Cold War era, domestic variables are coming to the fore. For Egypt, that variable is the economy.

The other variable that Egypt has been able to tap is the seemingly intangible but highly significant variable of legitimacy based on its ethnic homogeneity. Ajami observes that:

> Egyptians who know their country so well have a way of reciting its troubles, then insisting that the old resilient country shall prevail. As an outsider who has followed the twists of the country's history and who approaches the place with nothing but awe for its civility amid great troubles, I suspect they are right. The country is too wise, too knowing, too tolerant to succumb to a reign of theocratic zeal. Competing truths, whole civilizations have been assimilated and brokered here; it is hard to see Cairo, possessed of the culture that comes to great, knowing cities turning its back on all that.[136]

It is this intangible variable of legitimacy based on ethnic homogeneity and subsequent strong sense of national identity that allows Egypt's leaders to take some risks because they can count on their people's support. Sadat did this, and Mubarak, in the face of an anti-West opposition and an economic crisis, chose to take a bold pro-U.S. stance—and his people cheered.

NOTES

1. The entire discussion on Mubarak's principles and the quotation are from Derek Hopwood, *Egypt: Politics and Society, 1945–1990* (Oxford: HarperCollins Academic, 1991), 184.

2. Gregory Aftandilian, *Political Change in the Arab World: A Report on the Deliberations of a Meetings Program Conference at the Council of Foreign Relations*, 24 April 1992, 27–28.

3. Hopwood, 191.

4. Ibid., 190.

5. Ibid., 191.

6. Harold H. Saunders, *The Other Walls: The Politics of the Arab-Israeli Peace Process* (Washington, D.C.: American Enterprise Institute for Public Policy Research, 1985), 103–104.

7. The Arab view of the USSR's demise and the quotation are from Aftandilian, 16.

8. Ibid., 17.

9. Ibid., 15–16.

10. Ibid., 68–70.

11. Ibid., 81.

12. *The Middle East* (Washington, D.C.: Congressional Quarterly, 1994), 204–205.

13. According to Anthony H. Cordesman, *After the Storm: The Changing Military Balance in the Middle East* (Boulder: Westview Press, 1993), 256, Syria contributed an armored division to the Persian Gulf War, which according to *Supporting Peace: America's Role in an Arab Israel-Syria Peace Agreement*, Report of a Washington Institute Study Group, p. 83, claims that Syria has a total of five armored divisions. It seems, then, that the Syrian contribution could not have been too far behind in Egypt's contribution in terms of numbers of personnel and tanks.

14. *The Middle East*

15. The effects of the invasion are from Aftandilian, 28–29, and the quotation is from p. 29.

16. Ibid., 29–30.

17. Nazih N. Ayubi, *The State and Public Policies in Egypt Since Sadat* (Reading: Ithaca Press, 1991), 291.

18. All the quotations are from Aftandilian, 32, and the discussion of Egypt as a regional power and leader is from pp. 31–32.

19. Edward B. Atkeson, *A Military Assessment of the Middle East, 1991–1996* (U.S. Army War College: Strategic Studies Institute, 1992), 36, and quotation on p. 37.

20. "Mubarak Discusses Peace Process, Domestic Issues," *FBIS*, NES (10 April 1990): 9 (quotation) and 10.

21. "Abu-Ghazalah on Expected Scenario, Gulf Security," *FBIS*, NES (17 January 1991): 5.

22. "Mubarak Discusses Peace Process, Domestic Issues," 9 (quotation) and 10.

23. 'Abd-al-Majid Issues Statement on Gulf War 17 Jan.," *FBIS*, NES (18 January 1991): 10.

24. The quotation and Mubarak's views on the peace process are from Mary Morris, 7–8.

25. "Mubarak Comments on Peace Conference, Gulf War," *FBIS*, NES (20 May 1991): 4–5.

26. Boutros Boutros-Ghali, "Egyptian Diplomacy: East–West Detente and North–South Dialogue," in *Contemporary Egypt: Through Egyptian Eyes*, ed. Charles Tripp (London: Routledge, 1993), 146.

27. "Mubarak Speaks at Alexandria University Event," 10.

28. Stephen C. Pelletiere, *Shar'ia Law, Cult Violence and System Change in Egypt: The Dilemma Facing President Mubarak* (U.S. Army War College at Carlisle Barracks: Strategic Studies Institute, April 1995), 1.

29. Egypt already had the Sinai, so for Egypt territory was not an issue. It was only an issue in terms of Egypt's support of Palestinian rights.

30. "Secretary Baker, Israel's Rabin to Pay Visits," *FBIS*, NES (20 July 1992): 11.

31. "Butrus Ghali Views Nonaligned Initiative," *FBIS*, NES (20 February 1991): 7.

32. "Palestine Issue to Draw Attention After War," *FBIS*, NES (31 January 1991): 5.

33. "Ghali Holds Press Conference on Gulf, Arab Ties," *FBIS*, NES (28 January 1991): 7.

34. "Ministerial Group Discusses Gulf War Developments," *FBIS*, NES (5 February 1991): 4.

35. "Ghali Examines Gulf Crisis, Palestinian Issue," *FBIS*, NES (19 December 1990): 6.

36. Steve Negus, "Mubarak's Diplomatic Coup," *Middle East Insight* (15 March 1996): 8.

37. Farwaz A. Gerges, "Egyptian–Israeli Relations Turn Sour," *Foreign Affairs* 74, no. 3 (May/June 1995): 78.

38. "Al-Baz Discusses Tripartite Efforts For Peace," *FBIS*, NES (19 December 1990): 5.

39. "Says Egyptian Forces Will Not Enter Iraq," *FBIS*, NES (31 January 1991): 4.

40. "Abu-Talib: Troops Not Subjected to 'Animosity,'" *FBIS*, NES (20 February 1991): 8.

41. "Views War, Israel's Involvement," *FBIS*, NES (9 January 1991): 1–3. One of the writers commented on the devastation on tourism and how long Egypt can endure this devastation; other concerns were food supply, lack of arable land.

42. Mary E. Morris, *New Political Realities and the Gulf: Egypt, Syria, and Jordan* (Santa Monica: Rand, 1993), 7.

43. Ibid.

44. Ibid., 7–8.

45. "People's Assembly Declares Support for Gulf Policy," FBIS, NES (28 January 1991): 9.

46. Ann M. Lesch, "Contrasting Reactions to the Persian Gulf Crisis: Egypt, Syria, Jordan, and the Palestinians," *The Middle East Journal* 14, no. 2 (Winter 1990): 39.

47. Ibid., 39–40.

48. "Wafd Party Stance on Gulf War Involvement Explained," *FBIS*, NES (1 February 1991): 8.

49. Ibid.

50. Lesch, 40.

51. Ibid., 38.

52. Aftandilian, 33.

53. Ibid., 34.

54. "Egypt's Elite Rate U.S., GCC States High; Iraq and Libya Low," *Research Memorandum* (Washington, D.C.: U.S. Information Agency), 1–2.

55. Ibid., 1.

56. Ibid., 5.

57. Ibid.

58. David Pollock, "The Arab Street"?: Public Opinion in the Arab World," *The Washington Institute Policy Paper*, no. 32 (Washington, D.C.: The Washington Institute for Near East Policy, 1992), 32.

59. Ibid.

60. Ibid., 57–58.

61. Ibid., 58.

62. Ayubi, 312.

63. Ibid.

64. Ibid., 313.

65. Hopwood, 184.

66. Paul Salem, "The Rise and Fall of Secularism in the Arab World," *Middle East Policy* 4, no. 3 (March 1996): 151–152.

67. Ibid., 152.

68. Ibid.

69. Ibid., 160.

70. "Editorial Analyzes Gulf War, Peace Prospects," *FBIS*, NES (19 December 1990): 7.

71. Ann M. Lesch, "Domestic Politics and Foreign Policy in Egypt," in *Democracy, War and Peace in the Middle East*, ed. David Garnham and Mark Tessler (Bloomington: Indiana University Press, 1995), 236–237.

72. Pelletiere, 23.

73. Lesch, "Domestic Politics and Foreign Policy in Egypt," 237.

74. "Journalists Stage Sit-In to Protest Gulf War," *FBIS*, NES (1 February 1991): 9.

75. "University Demonstrations Continue; City Calm, Protestors Kept Off Streets," *FBIS*, NES (26 February 1991): 4.

76. Pelletiere, 21–22.

77. Ibid., 22–23.

78. Robert D. Kaplan, "Eaten From Within," *Foreign Affairs* 73, no. 6 (November 1994): 28.

79. Ibid., 34.

80. Pelletiere, 17.

81. *The Middle East* (Washington, D.C.: Congressional Quarterly, 1994), 348 and 194.

82. George W. Gawrych, "Jihad in the Twentieth Century," in *Book of Readings: Modern Military History of the Middle East*, ed. George W. Gawrych (Fort Leavenworth: U.S. Army Command and General Staff College, 1995), 5–6.

83. Ibid., 6.

84. Mona Makram-Ebeid, "Egypt's 1995 Elections: One Step Forward, Two Steps Back? " *Middle East Policy* 4, no. 3 (March 1996): 135.

85. Morris, 10.

86. Makram-Ebeid, 136.

87. Morris, 8.

88. Lesch, "Domestic Politics and Foreign Policy in Egypt," 240.

89. Robert Springborg, "Approaches to the Understanding of Egypt," in *Ideology and Power in the Middle East: Studies in Honor of George Lenczowski*, ed. Peter J. Chelkowski and Robert J. Pranger (Durham: Duke University Press, 1988), 159.

90. Fouad Ajami, "The Sorrows of Egypt," *Foreign Affairs* 74, no. 5 (September/October 1995), 76.

91. "Abd-al-Majid Issues Statement on Gulf War

92. "Butrus Ghali Views Nonaligned Initiative," 6–7.

93. Aftandilian, 71.

94. "Egypt," *Background Notes*, U.S. State Department, 5, no. 7 (August 1994): 6.

95. Springborg, 140.

96. Shimon Shamir as cited in Ayubi, 342.

97. Hopwood, 193.

98. Ibid., 193–194.

99. Ibid., 197.

100. Tim Niblock, "Arab Losses, First World Gains,"in *Beyond the Gulf War: The Middle East and the New World Order*, ed. John Gittings (London: Catholic Institute for International Relations, 1991), 83.

101. "Says Egyptian Forces Will Not Enter Iraq," *FBIS*, NES (31 January 1991): 4.

102. Carlyle Murphy, "The Business of Political Change in Egypt," *Current History* 94, no. 588 (January 1995): 19.

103. Ibid.

104. Ibid.

105. The ability for self-examination was an important step for Egypt after the 1967 war. Egypt acknowledged its military's shortcomings and was able to take steps to correct them. This was not the case in Syria after the 1967 war. Consequently, Egypt's military was a more trained military than Syria's military for the 1973 war.

106. Cassandra, "The Impending Crisis in Egypt," *Middle East Journal* 49, no. 1 (Winter 1995): 11.

107. Ibid.

108. Quotation as cited in Casandra, 12, taken from Said El-Nagger, "Politics and Economic Reform in Egypt" (paper presented to the nineteenth annual symposium of the Center for Contemporary Arab Studies, Georgetown University, Washington, D.C., 7–8 April 1994).

109. Casandra, 13.

110. Morris, 10.

111. Andrew Album, "Egypt Faces its Moment of Economic Truth," *Business and Finance of The Middle East* (July/August 1995): 29.

112. Casandra, 14.

113. Morris, 11–12.

114. "Caution is the Watchword," *Business and Finance*, (December 1993): 29.

115. Ibid.

116. Ibid., 30.

117. "Prime Minister Discusses Economic Measures, Reforms, *FBIS*, NES (3 December 1992): 16.

118. "Sidiqi on Economic Liberalization, Subsidies," *FBIS*, NES (2 December 1992): 24–25.

119. "IMF Cancels 15 Percent of Foreign Debt," *FBIS*, NES (16 October 1992): 12.

120. "Mubarak Explains Reasons for Economic Reform," *FBIS*, NES (16 September 1992): 13.

121. Ibid.

122. "Mubarak Speaks at Alexandria University Event," 7–8.

123. Ibid., 8.

124. Ibid.

125. Ibid.

126. Ibid., 9.

127. Cordesman, 328–329.

128. Atkeson, 37.

129. Cordesman, 328.

130. Ibid., 331.

131. Cordesman, 322.

132. *The Middle East and North Africa, 1987* (London: Europa Publications Limited, 1988), 769.

133. Ibid.

134. Ibid.

135. Pelletiere, 1.

136. Ajami, 88.

Chapter Seven

Post–Cold War Case: Syria

This chapter examines Syria's Persian Gulf War alignment in the context of the post–Cold War era and analyzes how ethnic divisiveness in Syria affected this alignment. Furthermore, this examination of our last case will help determine how significant this domestic variable, that is, ethnic divisiveness, was in the Cold War versus post–Cold War eras. Two key points need mentioning: first, my discussion of the motivation for the alignment will include some reference to the post–Persian Gulf War peace process, a process which offered a window of opportunity for the collection of survey data. Second, after the war, Hafiz Asad continued to perform his balancing act among many interests as a means to ensure stability of his Alawi, minority-ruled regime. I will elaborate on this last point throughout this section. Generally, I find that while Syria's alignment with the West appears to be a radical departure, it really reflected Asad's cautious and calculating nature.

BACKGROUND

The 1980s saw the passing of the Cold War era. Soviet leader Mikhail Gorbachev initiated his "new thinking," which in the Middle East meant normalizing ties with Israel, creating close ties with pro-West Arabs, calling for moderation within the PLO, criticizing Syria's role in Lebanon, dropping the amount of Soviet arms sent to Syria, and calling for diplomatic, not military, means to resolve the Arab-Israeli conflict. This "new thinking" occurred as a result of the Soviets' internal focus, a desire to reverse past ineffective policies, and a desire to improve relations in the West. These new policies worsened relations between Syria and the Soviet Union, especially in 1987 when Gorbachev refused Syria's request for strategic parity with Israel. What caused this Soviet "new thinking" and the resultant changes in Soviet Middle East policies?[1]

Although much has been written on the reasons for the Soviet decline as a superpower, we will focus on three points. First, the United States' insistence on pursuing the Strategic Defense Initiative (SDI) broadened the definition of national power. Technology, not just numbers of missiles, defined power. The Soviets realized that, although they could quantitatively compete with the United States, they were unprepared to qualitatively compete on an entirely new technological level.[2] Second, the Soviets were experiencing severe economic hardships which made it impossible for them to even maintain their military strength, much less compete on economic fronts. Finally, attempts at democratization throughout Eastern Europe and the Soviet Union itself contributed to the Soviet Union's political instability. The Persian Gulf War confirmed what was already occurring: the decline of the Soviet Union as a world power and the United States' emergence as the sole world leader.

Syria's reasons for her initial participation as part of the coalition were based on Asad's promise to King Fahd of Saudi Arabia to help defend his territory, the prevention of the destruction of the holy places, the prevention of further fragmentation of the "Arab nation," and the belief that Arab forces would replace foreign forces. Asad denounced the Iraqi invasion because Iraq violated the basic codes of inter-Arab relations while also exposing the region to foreign intervention.[3] Asad further claimed that Saddam Hussein involved the Arabs with a peripheral issue just as he had done in his war with Iran, and that his focus should have been on Israel instead.[4]

Iraq's invasion also posed direct problems for Syria. Iraq's actions threatened some of Syria's resources, challenged Syria's commitment to Arab nationalism, threatened its own security and that of Lebanon, and increased the potential of Israeli involvement. Syria's participation reflected its concern for security. "Only if its needs and strategic interest against Iraq or Israel are at stake will it become a player in the Gulf, searching for friends who share its strategic conception of the world."[5] Syria also looked forward to some concrete and immediate benefits, to include funds from the Gulf Cooperation Council (GCC), aid from the European Community (EC), and renewed support from the Soviet Union. Perhaps Syria could look forward to American technological support, removal of Saddam Hussein, increased prestige, restoration of the Golan Heights, and a Palestinian solution. Syria realized that it would have more input to long-range Middle East plans as a member of the coalition, than as a member of the Iraqi-Jordanian-PLO alliance.[6]

Domestically, however, many groups disagreed with Asad's position. They based their opposition on the presence of foreign troops and the perception of Hussein as an Arab hero and pro-Palestinian. Even some Ba'th and military officers questioned Asad's alliance with the West. Asad would need some of those potential benefits realized to keep his detractors at bay.[7] Syria's blatant pro-West stance as a member of the coalition challenged long-standing anti-West and anti-Israeli sentiment. Could Asad afford to discard what seemed to be unifying sentiments in his society?

To answer this question, it is first necessary to fully understand the significance of the Persian Gulf War in the global post–Cold War era. This war was the first post–Cold War era war.[8] Specifically, "for the first time in recent history, a Middle East war has been fought with the two superpowers on the same side, no longer engaged in zero-sum struggles."[9] The Cold War "rules of the game" were no longer in place. These rules were implicitly acknowledged by the superpowers and served to deter a superpower war and maintain stability. These rules included a respect for each other's spheres of influence, avoidance of direct confrontation, use of nuclear weapons only as a last resort, preference for "predictable anomalies over unpredictable rationality"[10] (examples of anomalies include the division of Germany and Korea), and the refusal to undermine each other's leadership.[11]

Client states realized the significance of these missing "rules of the game."

> Traditional verities about the character of the old international order were shattered. Radical Third world leaders, the Ortegas . . . , the Saddams, Qaddafis and the Assads, long accustomed to the economic and military benefits of playing East against West, quickly recognized they would no longer loom as high on the international horizon.[12]

Perhaps if the Soviet Union had still been a superpower in August 1990, it would have prevented Iraq from invading Kuwait in order to avoid escalation and possible superpower confrontation. The Persian Gulf War, due in some degree to the demise of the Cold War rules, created the need for other "rules" to help stabilize the situation.

These rules included an active role for the United Nations, cooperation between the United States and the Soviet Union, and international cooperation.[13] The United States showed that technology on the battlefield is a critical component for victory. The United States proved its position as world leader due to its military, diplomatic, political, and economic powers.[14] Power is now the "political ability to change political environments and to build, guide, and sustain coalitions and relationships necessary to accomplish tasks that no one nation can accomplish alone."[15] Globally, the Persian Gulf War highlighted the critical elements of national power, as well as the power of collective security in the form of the United Nations and the international coalition.

Regionally, the Gulf War produced shifts in alliances, revealing a lack of cohesion among the political leftists and religious rightists, as well as disunity among the Arabs.[16] We have not seen internal changes in either Iraq or

Kuwait. Hussein still rules Iraq and the Emir rules Kuwait. The Kurds are still in desperate straits, and the gap between the haves and the have-nots remains. For Syria, the end of the war marked the end of Syria's regional isolation, established its consolidated hold over Lebanon, created closer ties to the West and the United States, and acquired subsidies from the Gulf countries and Saudi Arabia.[17] More significantly, Syria initiated a peace process to help resolve the Arab-Israeli conflict.

I believe that Syria's aggressive pursuit of a diplomatic settlement is not out of character. Asad was, once again, using the best means available to accomplish his goals. The Soviet Union, even before the war, refused to help Syria establish strategic parity with Israel. In fact, the Soviet Union's historical inability to influence Israel gravely limited its effectiveness in playing a major role in the Arab-Israeli conflict.[18] Only the United States had that ability, which explains why "Mr. Gromyko (never had) the freedom to shuttle between confrontation parties enjoyed by Dr. Kissinger or Mr. Vance."[19] Additionally, Syria's economy in the 1980s suffered, especially while it tried to build up its military.[20] Asad realistically turned to those new elements of power that proved themselves during the war, namely the diplomatic, political, economic, and technological elements. As a result, we see Asad becoming a major player in the Middle East through his peace initiative. Additionally, through his new alliances, Asad was receiving aid to bolster his economy, and perhaps he would now be able to divert funds from the military to other sectors of the economy by reducing both Israel and Iraq as regional threats.

We must not forget, however, that Asad is not afraid to antagonize his allies. His policies reflect his overriding concern for security and determination for independent decision-making. Asad's independence seems critical for his desired image as a leader who does not answer to foreigners, especially non-Arabs. Historically, he has made several policy decisions that clearly opposed Soviet interests. However, he showed great loyalty to the Soviet Union when he truly needed its aid. Asad used those available tools that best suited his interests, and his loyalty was to the security of his regime. Now that the Soviets can no longer offer the required aid due to their own demise, Asad must look elsewhere for support. He saw the West as the best source of support to help him acquire power economically, diplomatically, and technologically.

While Asad has been able to broaden his base of support beyond the Party and the military, it is still the Ba'th Party that centrally controls the Syrian education system. This type of control has hurt the quality of education, especially since it hinders initiative and flexibility. Additionally, the society rewards those students who become graduate civil servants, not skilled non-graduate technicians. Promotions occur through patronage and corruption, party membership, or Alawi loyalty.[21]

The problem is that effective policies and reform would flourish best in a more liberal, less ideologically determined atmosphere and with more incentives for private initiative. Strict adherence to central planning and a controlled public sector, together with a lack of political freedom, hinder, rather than encourage this progress.[22]

Although Syria will be able to advance somewhat technologically and economically by its westward looking policies, unless reforms occur internally, Syria will never achieve parity with Israel, nor reach its potential as a nation and society.[23]

However, Syria faces the challenge of transitioning from a socialist to a modern capitalist economy as it opens to the world, a challenge that a peace with Israel would bring. Such a transition would precipitate societal dislocations and upheavals, such as those which caused such havoc in the former states of the Soviet Union and the countries of the former Eastern Europe. Such change would threaten the stability of the Asad regime. Moreover, Syria would have to halt its U.S.-alleged drug trade, which would, no doubt, antagonize some of its most powerful citizens who are the chief beneficiaries of this trade.[24]

Robert Lifton's meeting with Asad explains the constraints that faced this seemingly absolute ruler:

> As I sat listening to him talk about the constraints upon him, I remember being told by an Arab leader of the limitations on Assad because he is a minority Alawite in a country dominated by Sunnis. Mubarak, too, told us about rejectionist factions in Syria limiting Assad's options. Moreover, it is no secret that there has been internal dissension in Syria that recently led to Assad firing four of his top military and intelligence commanders. . . . What is clear, and should be borne in mind by those concerned with the process, is that while the world thinks of Assad as having absolute power and therefore free to make peace on any terms he chooses, he does not see himself that way.[25]

Raymond Hinnebusch describes the importance for Asad to maintain his regime's autonomy as he attempted to create foreign policy in the midst of the dramatic changes ushered in by the post-bipolar and peace eras. Asad tried to maximize autonomy and stability by broadening the regime's internal bases of support. In essence

> He [continued] . . . to seek, with every bit of leverage at his disposal, to extract a settlement from Israel that would minimize the damage to the regime's legitimacy in the transition to peace, while simultaneously trying to alter the bases of this legitimacy. Thus, Asad [was] . . . "omni-balancing" between the elements of his internal coalition and between this coalition and the external arena.[26]

Our task is to determine the significance of ethnicity as a variable that affected Asad's foreign policy calculation, namely his Persian Gulf War alignment. Perhaps understanding his motivation for this alignment will help us better understand his motivation for the peace process, a peace that he was unable to achieve in his lifetime.

INDICATOR: ELITE ATTITUDES

I will rely heavily on elite attitudes as an indicator for the issues of security and territory, status, and human and nonhuman resources. Generally, I will use expert analyses of the elite views, but I will also examine the recent surveys conducted in Syria, as well as in those other Arab countries that may help us understand some of the differing views based on sectarian or ethnic groupings. Particularly, I found a striking correlation between Sunni professionals and students in Lebanon with Syrian professionals. Because urban businessmen are generally Sunni in Syria, I believe that Lebanese Sunni responses to surveys are an indicator of Sunni sentiment in Syria.

ISSUE: SECURITY AND TERRITORY

Security, both externally and internally, was a priority for Asad in the events leading up to, during, and after the Persian Gulf War. Asad saw the war as an opportunity to regain lost territories, but he never wavered in his belief that Israel was a major threat. Additionally, Asad continued to ensure the survival of his regime, and I will show how his Alawite minority rule influenced his alignment decision. First, we will examine the external threats which influenced Asad's decision concerning state alignment.

During the buildup to the war and the actual war, Syria clearly articulated its view that Israel remained the real threat. According to a highly informed source in Damascus,

> Though Syria and Washington agree in their insistence on Iraq's withdrawal from Kuwait, Syria does not accept that the United States use this crisis as a pretext to consolidate Israel's military capability and weaken Iraq's capability. . . . Syria continues to realize that a potential Arab-Israeli war must place it on the side of Iraq, which is seen as Syria's strategic depth in the absence of Egypt, which signed the Camp David accord with Israel, to face the Zionist enemy, which has never abandoned its aggressive intentions.[27]

Additionally, a Syrian radio commentary explained the fallacy of the pro-Iraqi supporters who claim that Iraq's actions are supportive of the Palestinians. The commentary explains that Iraq has only served to distract the Arab world from its real threat, Israel.

> Gentlemen: The latest thing invented by the intellect of those who are trying to justify and defend the Iraqi invasion of Kuwait is the proposition that this action will help liberate Palestine from the yoke of the Zionists and save the Arab homeland from the evil aggressive claws. Therefore, according to the logic of those people, the invasion should be viewed as an act of national liberation that should be welcomed and supported. We do not know how the occupation of Kuwait can become the basis for liberating Palestine. We have never heard of an enemy being defeated through seizing a brother's land, destroying his existence, and displacing him.[28]

Syria saw the Persian Gulf War as a means for obtaining security and territory by aligning against Iraq and pursuing its desire to militarily expand its influence in Lebanon as a consequence of its pro-coalition stance. Moreover, Syria was able to do this without the threat of international censure. It was understood that in return for Syria's participation in the U.S.-led multinational force, the United States exerted some pressure on Israel not to intervene in Lebanon, thus securing Syrian hegemony over Lebanon. Consequently, the Ta'if Agreement became completely Syrianized with the blessing of both Saudi Arabia and the United States.[29]

Additionally, Syria used this opportunity to address the occupied territories. Syria did not automatically favor the format of an international conference designed to address the Arab-Israeli conflict in the immediate aftermath of the Persian Gulf War. After a visit with U.S. Secretary of State James Baker in early April 1991, Foreign Minister Faruq al-Shara restated his government's position that the United Nations should play "a significant role" in such a conference, and that Resolutions 242 and 338 would be the bases for any negotiations. On the eve of the initial meetings in Madrid, Syrian officials announced that unless there were clear progress on the resolution of the occupied territories, they would not participate in follow-up talks with Israel on other regional, environmental, and economic issues.[30] A Damascus station commentary reminded its audience that

> The enemy of the nation in occupied Palestine has not changed. Moreover, the danger this enemy poses to our pan-Arab existence surpasses all dangers and its ambitions in our land and wealth are above all other ambitions. This enemy does not discriminate between the oil of Iraq and that of Kuwait, nor between Syrian or Egyptian soil. Why, then, are we ignoring this inarguable fact, and replacing the battle of pan-Arab existence with the Zionist enemy by an illusory war with the brother, whose victim this time was Kuwait.[31]

Here, the commentary links the issue of the occupied territories with the Zionist threat and pan-Arabism.

This linkage reflects Asad's external and internal security concerns. Harold H. Saunders explains that "For President Assad the top priority in his definition of the problem is organizing his neighborhood in a way that is secure for Syria and for his regime. Each decision he makes must be understood in light of his aim to establish Syria's influence over the course of events."[32] Asad's objectives for the peace process that followed the war provide some insights for his motivation for aligning with the coalition. These objectives were the following: recover the Golan; consolidate power in the Levant, especially Lebanon; obtain U.S. aid, trade, and technology; and ensure that nothing threatens the regime.[33] It appears that internal as well as external security concerns have entered into Asad's peace process equation. These two concerns are also linked, and this point will become more clear in the status section.

The importance of reclaiming territory, namely the Golan, has continued to assume great significance in the peace process. According to Muhammad Muslih, "the return of the Golan to Syria is pivotal to a solution of the Israeli-Syrian conflict, and, indeed, a sine qua non for peace between the two countries."[34] The Golan has external security value and has been an area of dispute since the armistice in 1949. Its strategic value stems from its high ground, with an average altitude of 1,000 meters, and its wealth of regional water sources.[35] For Syria, the Golan is especially important because Syria has no natural boundaries, and its loss of its superpower patron together with Israel's superior economy and military make the Golan even more significant.[36] We will find that the return of the Golan, for Asad, would be a personal as well as, if realized, a public coup. The disposition of the Golan, an external security and territorial issue, also affects the security of his regime. The return of the Golan would bolster Asad's domestic status, that is, his regime's legitimacy and stability. We will explore these ideas in the status section.

In my view, a look at the peace process will help us understand elite attitudes concerning the decision to align with the West. According to Hilal Khashan, political developments, rather than steadfast religious beliefs for those Sunnis who were self-defined religious moderates, play a critical role concerning attitudes towards key international issues, such as the peace with Israel.[37] This observation indicates that perhaps the international system's change was a key variable for these self-defined religious moderates. This also suggests, based on our definition of ethnicity of which religion is a component, that perhaps these Sunnis felt less ethnic loyalty than those Sunnis who felt highly religious. However, this observation is based on questions concerning peace with Israel. Ethnic loyalty may change when asked in the context of the Asad regime. I will explore this notion in the status section. Tables 7.1 and 7.2 reveal that those Sunnis in Lebanon and professionals in Syria (note the correlation here between Sunnis in Lebanon and Syrian professionals) who consider themselves as moderates feel more inclined towards a peace with Israel. Lebanese Sunni students, who define themselves as moderately religious, increased their support between 1993 and 1994 for peace from 31 percent to 71 percent, while Syrian professionals increased their support from 29 percent to 67 percent. Additionally, Lebanese Sunni professionals who define themselves as moderately religious increased their support from 34 to 68 percent.[38] On a domestic level, perhaps these people forsee economic rewards for establishing peace with Israel. Such a peace may instigate more of a true economic opening that would enhance business, in which the Sunnis in Syria have a stake. We will explore this point more fully in the human and nonhuman resources section.

Another interesting trend is that other surveys conducted in urban Jordan and Lebanon described the Arab-Israeli conflict as national, not religious, in nature. "The pragmatism this engenders may be similar to that encountered in surveys among Arab Muslims in the Persian Gulf, where the public predominantly characterized peace talks with Israel as at least 'somewhat un-Islamic' but nonetheless gave those talks some lukewarm support."[39] Additionally, in 1994, 64 percent of Lebanese surveyed viewed the Palestinian issue (the region's most critical political conflict) as a national, not religious, conflict.[40] This is an interesting phenomenon because it confirms Dr. Mahmud Faksh's view that the Persian Gulf War validated national boundaries. Perhaps when assessing an external threat or issue, nationalism is taking on a more prominent role. However, when assessing internal threats, perhaps ethnicity plays a prominent role, especially in a minority-ruled regime.

It is important to differentiate between peace and normalization. While peace may be somewhat acceptable, normalization may not be as readily welcomed. "Many Arabs perceive the diplomatic process as an act of *force majeure*, but believe they can resist normalization at the individual and societal levels."[43] An indication that political developments affect attitudes regarding normalization seem validated by two polls conducted in 1993 when 63 percent of Lebanese surveyed favored normalization, yet in 1995 when talks stalled, six in ten were opposed to it.[44] See Tables 7.3 and 7.4, which reveal that support among Lebanese Sunnis and Syrian professionals for the peace talks rose between 1993 and 1994/95 among moderate religious Sunnis. However, when it came to policies that stressed positive ties with the West, only one in ten Lebanese surveyed felt such a policy was a priority issue.[45]

Table 7.1. Degree of Religiosity and Support for the Peace Process Among Lebanese, Syrian, and Palestinian Groups in 1993 (percent support)[42]

Groups	N	Degree of Religiosity								
		High			Medium			Low		
		Yes	No	Unsure	Yes	No	Unsure	Yes	No	Unsure
Lebanese Shi'a Students (Beirut)	150	0	100	0	50	37	12	85	0	15
Lebanese Shi'a Professionals (Beirut)	100	0	100	0	38	54	8	80	10	10
Lebanese Sunni Students (Beirut)	150	11	82	7	31	54	15	73	14	14
Lebanese Sunni Professionals (Beirut)	100	14	86	0	34	56	10	82	14	5
Syrian Professionals (Damascus)	150	9	79	12	29	49	22	71	8	21
Syrian Laborers (Beirut)	100	28	41	31	68	29	2	60	7	33
Palestinian Professionals (Beirut)	100	9	82	9	21	58	21	56	17	28
Palestinian Professionals (Amman)	150	2	93	5	22	42	36	71	12	17

Table 7.2. Degree of Religiosity and Support for the Peace Process Among Lebanese, Syrian, Jordanian, and Palestinian Groups in 1994 (percent support)[42]

Groups	N	Degree of Religiosity								
		High			Medium			Low		
		Yes	No	Unsure	Yes	No	Unsure	Yes	No	Unsure
Lebanese Shi'a Students (Beirut)	125	5	89	7	82	14	4	87	10	3
Lebanese Shi'a Professionals (Beirut)	85	15	74	11	75	25	0	88	12	0
Lebanese Sunni Students (Beirut)	125	12	85	3	71	22	7	82	18	0
Lebanese Sunni Professionals (Beirut)	85	18	77	5	68	30	3	100	0	0
Syrian Professionals (Damascus)	245	18	79	4	67	25	7	73	14	14
Jordanian Professionals (Amman)*	150	14	81	5	97	3	0	100	0	0
Palestinian Professionals (Beirut)	90	5	86	8	14	81	5	70	30	0
Palestinian Professionals (Amman)	150	22	73	5	90	5	5	100	0	0

*Sample not included in 1993 poll

Table 7.3. Trend of "Medium" Religiosity and Support for Peace with Israel Among Lebanese, Syrian, and Palestinian Groups in 1993 (percent support)[46]

		N	Support Peace Talks	Oppose Peace Talks
Lebanese Shi'is:	Students	150	50	37
	Professionals	100	38	54
Lebanese Sunnis:	Students	150	31	54
	Professionals	100	34	56
Syrians:	Beirut Laborers	100	68	29
	Damascus Professionals	150	29	49
Palestinians:	Beirut Professionals	100	21	58
	Amman Professionals	150	22	42

Additionally, there are indications that not all of Syria's elite even supported the peace process. The Syrian columnist, Khayri Hama states, "The conflict with the Zionist enemy has never been a border issue nor an interstate conflict but rather a total confrontation concerning the survival of our nationalism . . . against threats posed by the Israeli entity."[48] Additionally, In'am Ra'd, Secretary of the Syrian Socialist National Party claims that Israel would economically and militarily dominate the "new Middle East."[49] The Union of Syrian Writers opposed the membership of a well-known poet because he supported "normalization with the Zionist enemy."[50] While the Arab publics and some elites may envision a cold peace, it appears, however, that a warm peace is not a short-term prospect. This sentiment is consistent with the sen-

Table 7.4. Trend of "Medium" Religiosity and Support for Peace with Israel Among Lebanese, Syrian, Jordanian, and Palestinian Groups in 1994/1995 (percent support)[47]

		N	Support Peace Talks	Oppose Peace Talks
Lebanese Shi'is:	Students	125	82	14
	Professionals	85	75	25
Lebanese Sunnis:	Students	125	71	22
	Professionals	85	68	30
Syrians:	Professionals	245	67	25
Jordanians:	Professionals	150	97	3
Palestinians:	Beirut Professionals	90	14	81
	Amman Professionals	90	90	5

timents expressed by some of the Arab officers who attended the Command and General Staff College with me in 1995–1996.

While there may be varying levels of support for peace and normalization among the elite, Asad seemed to use these varying views to his advantage. For example, it appears that Asad cleverly used his top officials to move cautiously and incrementally, while still leaving his options open in this peace process. Chief of Staff Shihabi, according to Moshe Maoz, was a key player in the peace process because he is Sunni, and 60 percent of the population is Sunni (he lends legitimacy to the peace process). Foreign Minister al-Shara (non-Alawi) projects a cosmopolitan image, and Vice President Abd al-Halim Khaddam (non-Alawi) is the tough guy. Long-time allies of Asad, Ali Duba (Alawi) and Muhammad Nasif (Alawi) coordinate the intelligence services. Mustafa Talas (non-Alawi), the defense minister is seen as a "buffoon." Shara's role is to cultivate relations with Israel and the West, while Khaddam is reassuring Iran. Khaddam responded to a question concerning Syria's minimal efforts towards building relations with Israel, "Our people are ready. They (the Israelis) are bombing South Lebanon, beating Palestinians. It's not up to us to win them over. We're clear about what we want: a pullout to the lines of June 4, 1967. When the last Israeli soldier leaves occupied territory, we'll start talking about normalization."[51]

Many observers, to include politicians from both sides of the Knesset, and academics all agree that Asad has made a pragmatic "strategic decision" to make peace—"not in his heart, but in his head." Maoz claims that with the breakup of the Soviet Union, Asad realizes that he can only retrieve the Golan through negotiations. Maoz claims that "apart from the Golan, he wants Israel out of southern Lebanon and confirmation of his rule there, and he wants investment and high-tech from the U.S. to develop his economy. It's not that he is seeking peace, but if that's the price he has to pay, so be it."[52]

Daniel Pipes agrees with this assessment. He concludes:

While Assad shares with other authoritarian leaders the goal of personal and regime survival, he stands apart from most of them in his willingness to resort to extreme means to achieve his ends. To keep himself and his fellow Alawis in power, he could do anything from destroy a Syrian city (as he did to Hama in 1982) to reverse a lifetime of anti-Zionism and sign a peace treaty with Israel.[53]

This motivation reflects his decision to align with the West. He saw it as an opportunity to gain stability, and, one may argue, internal security for his regime.

Asad seemed to have had genuine external security concerns, namely his belief that Israel was a threat. He has stated his desire to reclaim the Golan, as well as his desire to influence Lebanon. Asad saw the coalition as a means to derive territorial concessions, as well as an opportunity to defeat his historical enemy, Iraq, and gain the upperhand vis-à-vis Israel. Additionally, Asad's desire for internal security, and, thus his need to build domestic consensus for his policy, are reflected in the surveys which favor peace, and in some cases, normalization with Israel. The next two sections will analyze this point and expose the overlap of regime security and stability with Asad's quest for legitimacy in his minority-ruled regime.

ISSUE: STATUS

The task for this section is to determine how international versus regional versus domestic status affected Asad's alignment decision. Again, we will find some interaction among all three levels of status. The key will be to determine, especially for domestic status, if ethnicity played a role. The minority-led regime had to consider regime stability, and we will see that, especially for the peace process, Asad worked rather hard to gain public consensus. In fact, he was leery of moving too fast in this process for fear of domestic unrest, namely by the Sunni majority. We will look at the Gulf War, as well as the peace process that followed, in order to see how gaining status, namely legitimacy, was a motivating factor for Asad's decision to align with the coalition. Herein lies the difference between Asad and Mubarak. Whereas Mubarak's focus of internal status was on the economy, Asad's focus was on legitimacy—that is the lack thereof.

In June 1994, about one-third (35 percent) of the Lebanese and Jordanians surveyed chose "showing solidarity with all other Arabs" as the first priority or second most important national priority. Surveys on other Arab countries at the time were consistent with the above results. However, when the option was replaced by "promoting interests of all oppressed Muslim peoples" as a priority, then the ranking changed. In 1993, Jordanians and other Arab publics ranked that policy somewhat lower at 15 percent. "This difference suggests that Arab publics generally view solidarity based on ethnicity a bit more favorably than solidarity based on religion."[54]

This solidarity based on ethnicity seems to be most prevalent in Syria, where the Islamic movement is widely popular among Sunnis and has experienced a greater loss of life than similar movements in other countries. Daniel Pipes concludes that this movement "in Syria . . . is more anti-Alawi and anti-Ba'th, more communal than religious. Muslim Brethren literature, for example, hardly ever brings up the usual fundamentalist concern for applying the sharia. Rather its goals consist of the Sunni public agenda." The movement does, at times, threaten the Alawis, which causes the "Alawis to associate more with the regime, [thereby] . . . compelling the regime to make [ethnic] survival its top priority."[55] It is through this lens of ethnicity that Sunnis view the regime. "The passage of time has hardened the Sunni-Alawi divide to the point that it dominates the way Syrians interpret domestic politics, and the way they anticipate Syria after Assad's passing."[56]

Asad's concern for his minority-ruled regime's survival compels him to be a pragmatist and establish a consensus among his elite and the populace.[57] Stephen Cohen claims that, "Not only does Mr. Assad seek to maintain his monopolistic control over the multiplicity of military and security forces, he also strives to balance rival ethnic groups and regional interests against one another."[58] Asad's consensus building and desire for legitimacy or internal status is an important point for U.S. policy-makers. Dore Gold claims that the U.S. desire to have Syria cut its ties with Iran, thereby contributing to dual containment, is naïve: "Syria needs Iran not only for Israel, but as a counterweight to Turkey and as an instrument against any internal fundamentalist challenge. Since Shi'ite clerics recognize the Alawis as true Muslims, the connection with Iran affects the legitimacy of Assad's minority government."[59]

It is this domestic consensus-building that was the impetus, I believe, for Asad to reassert himself in regional affairs before, during, and after the Persian Gulf War by aligning with the coalition. The best way to neutralize the threat posed by the Sunni majority is "to take maximalist positions on all regional and international questions related to the Arab nation issue or to Muslim problems."[60] Asad did this in the past. "The Alawis were always — sometimes to the point of caricature — at the head of the pack on Arab-world causes, the last to make concessions in this domain, and even then only after all the Sunni leaders had preceded them."[61] Volker Perthes claims that Syria's regional status is a primary source of legitimacy for the regime on a domestic level. Consequently, "It has been essential for the regime, particularly so since it rules in the name of Ba'thist Arab nationalism, to demonstrate its adherence to what can be considered a national myth, namely the conviction that Syria is the heartland of Arab and specially Palestinian rights."[62] We will see that Asad and other Syrian officials' statements stress Syrian alignment with the coalition as a measure necessary to bolster the Arab cause. Would a pro-coalition or anti-Iraqi stand enhance Asad's domestic status?

According to Ghayth N. Armanazi, the Persian Gulf War greatly enhanced Syria's status in both the regional and international contexts. This increase in status represented a huge change for Asad's political, economic, and strategic fortunes, which only a year earlier were suffering due to diplomatic isolation, economic strangulation, and the prospects of increasing vulnerability, especially because its longtime patron, the Soviet Union, was no longer willing to support Asad's goal of strategic parity with Israel.[63] Syria's position looked grim by the summer of 1990, and it was considered an outcast by the other Arab countries.[64] Iraq and the PLO were championing Arab rights, not Syria. The Baghdad-PLO axis was gaining strength and increasingly closing ranks with Amman. This axis worried Syria, especially since a year earlier, it witnessed the inception of the Arab Cooperation Council, an Iraqi inspired organization which incorporated Egypt and Yemen in addition to Iraq and Jordan, but deliberately and conspicuously left out Syria. Syria felt isolated and threatened.[65]

Asad viewed the Iraqi invasion of Kuwait on August 2, 1990, as an opportunity for Syrian leadership to preside in the region. Syrian leadership in this case supported its longtime policy towards its historical enemy, Iraq, and "Overnight, the whole edifice of the regional status quo crumbled and Syria seized the occasion to establish for itself a new position of power and influence within the nascent system."[66] It was not just Syria who saw its new leadership role. The former Egyptian foreign minister and secretary general of the Arab League, Mahmoud Riyad stated,

> It is clear that the principal role in any future negotiations lies on the shoulders of Syria. Without her the conference will not convene, and without the recovery of the Golan no peace can be realised . . . the management of negotiations is not unlike directing a military battle, indeed it is more daunting, and the state best qualified to direct the negotiating battle is Syria.[67]

Additionally, other members of Asad's administration saw the importance of Syria's role in the Arab world, and they all stressed the importance of championing the Arab cause. Interestingly, many of these statements made by non-Alawis, such as those listed below, were, I believe, an attempt to attain support for policy among the Sunni majority. Foreign Minister Faruq al-Shara sent a letter to the Arab League secretary general Chedli Klibi:

> In view of accelerating developments in the wake of the Iraqi invasion of Kuwait and the potential Israeli and foreign intervention in the region; to confirm the call made by President Hafiz al-Asad in the first hours of the invasion when he was in touch with a number of Arab leaders with a view to convening an immediate Arab summit; and in accordance with the Arab League Council's resolution issued in Cairo on 3 August 1990 recommending the holding of an emergency Arab summit, the Syrian Arab Republic requests the convening of an emergency Arab summit in Cairo, the permanent seat of the Arab League, to weigh the consequences of the Iraqi invasion and to take whatever decisions and measures required to advance the objectives of the Arab nation and safeguard its supreme interests.[68]

Comrade 'Abdallah al-Ahmar, assistant secretary general of the Arab Socialist Ba'th Party, stressed Syria's national and pan-Arab responsibilities to defend Arab causes to regain invaded territory and to oppose foreign intervention and the Iraqi invasion.[69]

> The Central Command of the National Progressive Front (NPF) held a meeting this morning under the chairmanship of President Hafiz al-Asad. It reviewed the developments that resulted from the Iraqi forces' invasion of Kuwait and the efforts to convene an immediate emergency Arab summit to tackle the situation and avoid potential danger to the region. The Central Command supported the Syrian Arab activity and praised the personal efforts of President Hafiz al-Asad to handle the situation out of concern for pan-Arab interests.[70]

General al-Shihabi, chief of staff of the Army and Armed Forces, called the Iraqi invasion unprecedented; motivated by economics, and not by Arab interests; an excuse for foreign intervention by outside powers; and he reaffirmed Asad's efforts.[71]

Asad, however, had to weigh the pros and cons of supporting the coalition. If Saddam Hussein was perceived as the victor in this conflict, then Asad's regional and international status would have been seriously undermined, especially since he had aligned with Israel's primary patron, the United States, as well as with the conservative rulers of the Arabian Peninsula. His domestic status would have suffered also since he aligned against an Arab ruler whose sentiments of anti-Zionism and anti-imperialism were widely supported within Syria. However, Asad calculated that Saddam Hussein would not win this conflict. Instead, Asad saw this crisis as an opportunity to contribute to the downfall of his enemy, Saddam, as well as an opportunity to earn financial rewards from the oil-producing states of the Arabian Peninsula. Asad believed that the United States would welcome Syria's position, and perhaps help Syria regain the Golan Heights. There was a great deal at stake as a result of the conflict, but

> most important, the crisis provided him with an opportunity to confirm Syria's move back to center stage within the region and to strengthen Syria's ties with Egypt and Saudi Arabia, two key powers, at a time when its superpower backer was disengaging from the Middle East and openly opposing its strategy of achieving strategic parity with Israel.[72]

Asad, however, did not embrace the United States with his pro-coalition stance. In fact, Syria gave the coalition credibility because of its historical anti-West stand. Asad used caution and restraint in his criticism of Hussein. At the Cairo Summit Conference on August 9, Asad stated, "It is difficult for me to imagine that any leader in this hall arrived with the intention of leaning towards this party or that. We are all brothers. Iraq is a brother; Kuwait is a brother . . . we all cherish Iraq, I have no doubt, and we all cherish

Kuwait."[73] Syrian officials wanted Syrian troops to operate separately from foreign forces on Saudi soil, and they criticized the immense U.S. buildup, strongly opposed a U.S.-Iraqi military confrontation, and wanted economic and diplomatic pressure to force Saddam to find a political solution to the conflict.[74]

Asad's stand-off approach to the United States is evident in the statements made concerning foreign forces on Arab soil. "Syrian sources have informed the newspaper Al-Diyar that Damsacus is sticking to its basic position that Iraq should withdraw from Kuwait, as this will prevent foreign intervention. Syria rejects the idea of multinational forces."[75] Additionally, "Al-Safir cites a high-ranking Syrian source as saying that Syria will dispatch forces to Saudi Arabia, noting, however, that these will be token forces whose purpose is to emphasize the need for Arab presence to deal with the Gulf crisis and to affirm Arab responsibility for defending that area."[76]

Statements continued to remind the Syrian people that the country still considered the United States as a threat:

> Current events in the region leave no room for doubt at all. The United States, who today calls for rejecting the aggression of one country against another and the occupation of its land, is the one who supported, financed, and backed the Israeli occupation of the Arab lands.[77]

At the same time, the Asad regime emphasized the regional importance of Arab unity and Asad's leadership in the Arab world. For example, one commentary applauds Asad's efforts at the Arab summit and stresses the importance for Arab solidarity. It goes on to say that:

> The Arab summit's resolution condemning the Iraqi occupation and demanding the return of the status quo in Kuwait plainly shows the Arab masses who is really placing himself against the will of this nation and defying its charters and agreements, which organize Arab relations. Therefore, the resolution to dispatch Arab forces to Saudi Arabia and the Gulf countries to defend them debunks the pretexts for foreign intervention created by the Iraqi threats to these countries, keeps the risk of foreign aggression on the region at bay, and prevents the region's falling under direct foreign hegemony and control.[78]

The newspaper, *Al-Ba'th,* with the headline, "The Dangers of the Crisis and the Prelude To Addressing It," warns of the danger the conflict poses to the Arab world. The paper "affirms in its editorial today that it has become clear to everybody that Iraq's invasion of Kuwait, which created this explosive situation, has placed the entire region at the mouth of a raging volcano whose fire and damage, if it were to erupt, might reach everywhere in the Arab homeland and the countries surrounding it and perhaps other world arenas."[79]

Not everyone in Syria, however, was swayed by Asad and his officials' line of argument. The controller general of the Muslim Brotherhood in Syria, 'Adnan Sa'd al-Din, and member of the political Bureau of the National Front for the Salvation of Syria, declared his support of Iraq against the forces of the "American-Zionist-Atlantic invasion." Al-Din, "called on the sons of the Syrian Arab people—officers, soldiers, workers, students, and peasants—to assume their role to save the homeland and liberate it from treason and sectarianism in all its forms and names so that Syria can restore national unity, Arab unity, and Islamic jihad."[80] In other reports, there were claims of pro-Iraqi demonstrations in Syria.

> Travelers arriving in Jordan from Syria reported clear signs of high tension, but none who had visited the turbulent eastern part of the country was prepared to speak to reporters. . . . Diplomats and intelligence sources from other Arab states confirmed the information. . . . The sources regarded the outbreak of protests in Syria as a serious threat to al-Asad. . . . The diplomats also saw trouble as evidence of President Husayn's growing appeal to the Arab generally in his stand against the U.S. and allied forces in the Gulf.[81]

As mentioned earlier, Asad has always tried to build a consensus among his people and elite for his policies. As shown above, he seems to have stressed the importance of his pro-Arab stance in his decision to align with the coalition, although he was not always successful in persuading everyone. He used prominent non-Alawis to publicize support for his policy, such as Mustafa Talas, the minister of defense; Hikmat al-Shihabi, army chief of staff, and Abd-al-Halim Khaddam, minister of foreign affairs.[82] Even before the conflict, there is evidence that Asad tried to initiate some political reform in the hopes of gaining internal status or legitimacy, especially in light of the international events of 1989 and the collapse in Eastern Europe.[83] This point suggests that the changing international system did, in fact, affect Asad's behavior. It is important to note, however, that these changes were small and in no way reflected a change in the overall nature of Asad's authoritarian regime. The collapse of socialist Eastern Europe destroyed the international legitimacy which Syria previously enjoyed as a socialist regime itself. Even within the constraints of political expression in Syria, there has been some support for perestroika-like reforms, even within the ruling Ba'th party. The Party newspaper, *Al-Baath,* has acknowledged these sentiments. However, the collapse of Eastern Europe confronted the regime with a political challenge, as well. The collapse showed that popular movements were, in fact, able to topple the ruling communist parties. The idea of presidents for life, party elites, and the single-party regime, now looked vulnerable.[84]

All this provoked a defensive response from Asad, and in his annual revolution day speech, Asad blamed the communist collapse on the United States and Israel. Less widely reported was Asad's efforts to reassert regime legitimacy. His efforts consisted of three elements: first, he called for reinstitutionalizing politics and reaffirming popular organizations. He wanted Syrians to consider political institutions more seriously, to mobilize for greater levels of political participation, and finally to decrease some of the arbitrariness of Syrian politics. Second, he renewed and strengthened corporatist links between the regime and some of the more important popular organizations, such as the General Federation of Trade Unions, the Peasant's Federation, and the Youth Federation. Essentially, this meant that professional associations and civil society came under state direction.[85] Finally, Asad limited the scope of emergency regulations. "In doing this, the regime . . . coopted a plank from its critics and moved to defuse a long-standing source of popular complaints stemming from the arbitrary application of emergency decrees."[86]

Asad in his 1990 revolution-day speech said,

> restricting freedom tarnishes it, but regulating its practice makes it brighter. Restricting freedom means dwarfing it, but regulating its practice means developing it and making it healthy. . . . Freedom and its regulations belong side by side. They do not live apart. . . . Like everything else in this universe, freedom needs order.[87]

Steven Heydeman claims that

> Considering Assad's disregard for the practice of freedom, it would be easy to dismiss these thoughts. However, Assad's attention to such topics as pluralism and freedom in a speech marking Syria's most important political anniversary indicates how seriously the Syrian regime is challenged by the events of 1989.[88]

This point suggests that perhaps in this post–Cold War environment, domestic variables came to the fore. In particular, Asad, I feel, was moved to address the legitimacy of his minority-ruled regime by trying to broaden his support. Heydeman admits that Asad's actions did not constitute democratization, but they do indicate how important Asad regarded popular opinion and how popular opinion can affect policy and rhetoric.[89]

Syria's role in the peace process signified a great deal to Asad in terms of potential status. According to Ann Lesch, Asad wanted Syria in a strategically central position in the Middle East so that it mighty better influence events and resolve central issues. Asad viewed his alignment with Riyadh and Cairo as a means to a comprehensive agreement with Israel that would allow Syria to regain the Golan Heights, while resolving the Palestinian question in a manner acceptable to Syria. Lesch claims that for Asad this "triad was more appealing than the alternative alignment with Iraq, Jordan, and the PLO in which Iraq would be the dominant partner and the Palestinian movement would be beyond Syrian control."[90]

With the collapse of the Soviet Union, Asad saw the United States as the key to Syria's inclusion in the new regional order emerging after the Gulf War. According to Muhammad Muslih,

> Arab diplomats who are well-connected with al-Asad's inner circle explained to me that the Syrian president understood that the United States wanted Israel and the Arab states to make a lasting peace. He also understood that such peace, if it were anchored in a comprehensive settlement, including total Israeli withdrawal from the Golan, would offer Syria the best chance of playing the role that befits its central position in regional politics. Thus, Syria's politics of patience in this phase should be seen not as a diplomatic technique aimed at dividing a wedge between Israel and the United States, but rather as an exercise in the service of state interest and regional peace.[91]

However, Asad proceeded slowly with the peace process because he had to consider the effects of his negotiations at home. According to Stephen Zunes, "Those with ties to the Syrian government . . . have insisted that a separate agreement would not help anyone. . . . Finally, they fear that an Alawite president making a separate peace with Israel could conceivably provoke a reaction from hardline Sunnis."[92]

Ori Orr, chairperson of the Foreign Affairs and Defense Committee in the Israeli Knessett, claims that before Asad could actually make peace, he had to first believe that he would be able to control the effects of western exposure to his regime. Such exposure posed a grave threat to his closed, minority-led regime. Because of Asad's desire to ensure continued Alawite rule, Orr says that "Asad fears openness could bring it to an end." Consequently, "Asad can't afford to hurry. He needs to ensure he has the people with him, and can keep them with him. That's why he's still hesitating." Asad, who used Nicolae Ceaucescu's Romania as a model regime, was not anxious to share Ceaucescu's fate, and he well remembered the "Asadescu" graffiti in Damascus that coincided with Ceaucescu's demise.[93] Fathi Shikaki, the Damascus-based leader of Islamic Jihad, also believed that Asad would take his time to finalize a peace. Shikaki claims that he received messages that implied that he would be given a year's notice before Asad gave the nod for peace because it was planned that he and several other Islamic extremists and Palestinian rejectionists would be turned out. He cheerfully told the interviewer, "I haven't had the phone call yet."[94]

Asad needed to convince his people that peace would mean the return of the Golan. According to Syrian officials, the United States and Israel failed to understand this point. Asad had to consider the Syrian public consensus, especially concerning the Golan Heights "because the Syrian public will never accept conceding any part of the Golan to Israel. Thus, al-Asad believes that for him to spell out the exact nature of peace with Israel, and sell it to his people, he needs Rabin's explicit statement on the extent of Israeli withdrawal from occupied Golan."[95] The issue for Asad was that if he had laid out the Syrian position without Israel responding in kind, then his regime and his standing in the Arab world would be adversely affected.[96]

It is this need for Asad to gain a consensus that caused him to weigh very carefully the consequences of his actions. "For President Assad the top priority in his definition of the problem is organizing his neighborhood in a way that is secure for Syria and for his regime. Each decision he makes must be understood in light of his aim to establish Syria's influence over the course of events."[97] Orr explains, however, that Asad is "not impulsive, no Saddam Hussein, but Hamah proves he can be decisive."[98] Furthermore, Syria's unwillingness to define in advance the nature of peace has to do with Asad himself. "Unlike the late Anwar al-Sadat, the Syrian president plays his cards close to his chest because any blunder could seriously undermine his regime. He likes to move in a gradual manner in order to scrutinize the political fallout after every move he makes."[99]

It seems that the decision to align with the coalition greatly enhanced Asad's status on the regional and domestic levels, and one could argue that Asad's role in the peace process is evidence of his having attained a greater international status. Asad's enhanced regional status helped his status at home. As mentioned earlier, he stressed the importance of Arab unity throughout the conflict, a technique used by the Alawite leadership to gain Sunni support for its policies. Additionally, Asad primarily used his highly visible Sunni officials to publicize his coalition support — another tactic to increase his domestic support. He always ruled with the principle of gaining a public consensus at home, which caused him to create policy incrementally, cautiously, and carefully. The bottom line is that the Alawite regime benefited from the coalition alignment decision. Asad increased his status on the domestic, regional, and international levels, especially with the prospects of regaining the Golan Heights. The benefits for the Alawis will become more clear in the next section.

ISSUE: HUMAN AND NON-HUMAN RESOURCES

There is great debate concerning the health of Syria's economy prior to the Gulf War. What is clear, however, is that there has been a gradual, cautious approach towards opening the economy. It is this incremental approach in the economic sphere that reinforces Asad's goal towards maintaining both external and internal security. Again, we must answer the question of who is benefiting from the alignment decision, i.e., who is receiving the majority of the human and nonhuman resources as a result of this decision, and why are they recipients?

An analysis of the debate on the health of Asad's economy before the war will provide some insights concerning the economic changes that took place and their impact on Asad's alignment decision. Both David Waldner and Fred Lawson believe that the Syrian economy was not dismal prior to the war, and therefore it was not the driving force for Asad's decision to align with the coalition. According to Waldner, Syria had already taken steps to respond to its deteriorating economy at least five years prior to the decline of Soviet support, "and that by 1990, when, it is said, Syrian foreign policy underwent fundamental transformation, the Syrian economy, although plagued by numerous problems, was vastly improved in comparison to ten years earlier."[100]

Asad began to increase liberalization, especially in the mid 1980s. The new economic strategy was articulated during the Eighth Regional Congress of the Ba'th Party. The strategy had three components. First, the state would maintain control over the "commanding heights of the economy." Second, any economic reform would not hamper the regime's ability to use resources as a means to ensure its social support. Finally, within the limits posed by the above imperatives, private capital would be allowed greater latitude than in the past. The newly appointed minister of economy and foreign trade, Muhammad al-Imadi, implemented this strategy. Some of the allowances made for the increased latitude for private capital included the following: private exporters retained greater sums of earned foreign exchange, which in turn financed further imports; less restrictive import controls; encouraged exporting by devaluing the currency; and a 1986 legislative decree permitted the creation of joint-stock agricultural and tourist companies, in which the state would own 25 percent equity.[101] Syria began to experience trade surpluses in 1989. Law 10 of May 1991 further committed the regime to economic rationality and private sector participation. By the time of the fall of the Berlin Wall and the Gulf War, the Syrian economy was on the upswing. "Indeed, by the early 1990s, in a range of issues, the regime demonstrated its resolve to be more accountable to the grievances of the private sector and the larger public."[102] Syria still has a way to go, "but there is little or no evidence that recent Syrian foreign policy is driven by economic concerns."[103]

Lawson agrees that the economic situation in Syria was not the primary reason for Asad's coalition alignment. Syria's economic crisis did not threaten the regime. According to Lawson, "The country's persistent economic crisis—which, in fact, became somewhat less pressing beginning in early 1991 — posed almost no threat to the domestic political position of the most powerful forces within the dominant social coalition."[104]

However, Lawson acknowledges some of Syria's economic woes at the close of the 1980s. For example, external indebtedness rose to $4.9 billion by 1988, payment on foreign loans fell $100 million and $210 million in arrears by 1989 and 1990 respectively; the state had to ration hard currency because it became so scarce; oil revenues fell; bilateral and multilateral economic assistance dropped from 1982 through 1987 when Syria received $500 million annually in aid disbursements, but in 1988, it received only $80 million. The Organization for Economic Cooperation and Development claimed that Syria's repayments on loans exceeded new loans by $9 million dollars per year. However, by the beginning of 1990, the balance of trade was in the black. The Ministry of the Economy and Foreign Trade attributed this change to a 60 percent rise in non-petroleum exports in 1989, primarily consisting of private-sector manufactures and private- and mixed-sector agriculture produce. Also, 1990 saw a 6 percent rise in the Gross Domestic Product (GDP), and inflation dropped from 70 to 40 percent. The European Community in 1991 rescinded its freeze on economic assistance and released concessionary loans valued at $200 million. Japan announced grants worth $466 million. Arab nations in the Persian Gulf also contributed; the Kuwait Fund for Arab Economic Development (KFAED) provided $100 million for infrastructure projects in December 1990 and earmarked future funds.[105]

By August 1991, a prominent entrepreneur from Syria claimed that the private sector was growing at 20 percent. The World Bank and the International Monetary Fund (IMF) sent missions to Syria to convince Syria of its responsibility to resume payment on debt, an indication of Syria's wellness. By the dawn of the post–Cold War era, Syria's economic situation was improving enough to allow the Alawite regime to appease or at least successfully fend off the opposition.[106] This opposition consisted primarily of the Sunnis, who, as mentioned earlier, were the economically advantaged group.

Other scholars view the economic situation as being in more dire straits at the end of the Cold War. Armanazi claims that the picture for Syria in 1990 was grim, "especially against the background of the relentless depletion of the Soviet strategic reservoir upon which Syria depended, and the deterioration in the economic conditions of the country as its foreign exchange reserves were eroded, factories turned idle because of shortages of raw materials, and inflation and scarcities of essential products blighted the Syrian consumer."[107] Muslih seems to agree because he claims that the "Peace with Israel will also give Syria a good chance at stimulating more economic growth by shifting funds from the military to job-generating projects in the civilian sector. During the 1980s, Syria indulged in arms imports that had built up close to $12 billion in military debts to the former Soviet Union alone."[108]

Alon Ben-Meir agrees with Armanazi, as he examines the peace process after the Gulf War. He compares Syria to Egypt in 1977 when Sadat was forced to address his country's economic failings. Syria's economy needed outside help. Its defense spending exceeded 45 percent of the budget; it had high unemployment; salaries were low; and there were limited opportunities for its skilled professionals. Economically, Syria needed peace.[109] Additionally, Ben-Meir takes a systemic approach to Asad's decision to align with the coalition and pursue a peace process. Simply put, the end of the Cold War and the disintegration of the Soviet Union left Syria with no choice but to lean towards the United States.[110]

Whether or not Syria's economy was desperate in the summer of 1990, Syria did pursue some economic rewards for its role with the coalition. For example, one diplomatic source reported that during a Gulf states' meeting in Cairo, the Syrian and Egyptian regimes submitted a proposal that called for a regional security plan "under the two regimes' auspices in return for an annual sum of $15 billion."[111] Syria's alliance with the GCC did guarantee funds and investments for Syria's struggling economy. Additionally, its alliance meant renewed ties and aid from the European Community and support from the Soviet Union. There was potential for U.S. technology and commercial credits if Washington removed Syria from its blacklist for supporting terrorist groups.[112] According to Sylvia Polling, "Syria has capitalized on the change of tack in its foreign policy orientation. Siding with the Western alliance against Iraq triggered a renewed commitment by the Gulf states to abundantly reward its non-Gulf Arab coalition partners." While the original pledges of $10 billion developmental money ultimately decreased to $6.5 billion dollars, other significant disbursements, such as debt relief and cash payments, were made to Egypt, Morocco, and Syria. By the end of 1990, Syria received $1.5 billion in developmental aid from its Gulf coalition partners.[113]

Nabil Sukkar, who worked as an economist for the World Bank and now heads the Syrian Consulting Bureau for Development and Investment in Damascus, claims that "Syria's new foreign alliances will no doubt play a role enhancing the market element in the economy, but Syria is not likely to adopt doctrinaire market formulas. It will probably attempt to strike a balance between the roles of the market and the state."[114] Additionally, Sukkar explains that Syria requires a high growth strategy, which means a high investment rate and efficient allocation of resources in order to take care of its anticipated high population growth of 3.7 percent per annum for the next decade. An economic opening will allow Syria to pursue this strategy.[115] Polling concurs that Syria requires reform for the reasons Sukkar offers. However, big changes do not appear in the offing when one looks at the incremental, cautious reforms designed in the mid-1980s through the 1990s—reforms designed to avoid the upheavals experienced in the former Eastern European nations.[116]

Finally, Eberhard Kienle claims that Syria recognized its need to reform its economy due to the Soviet Union's rapid decline, collapse of its markets, and recalling of Syria's military debts that were once forgotten. The pro-coalition stance provided Syria "an opportunity to side openly with the winners of the Cold War who soon won the Kuwait war as well. New, external resources could thus be attracted into the country in order to give a new impetus to economic reform."[117] He also concludes that Syria's economic policy is reactive and incremental in nature.

> In a nutshell, the style of Syria's economic-policy making could be characterized as gradualist, reactive, and personalized with some corporatist, consultative elements. These combined features are inseparably linked to Syria's authoritarian system whose prime decision-maker, considers economic questions of secondary importance, while national security and regime stability hold primacy.[118]

The economic reforms were a means to regime stability, and the decision to align with the coalition expedited these needed reforms.

While there is some debate as to the health of the 1989–1990 Syrian economy, there is agreement that Syria was pursuing some economic reform, perhaps in anticipation of future economic requirements, but I and others argue that the reforms were necessary to help build broader regime support. It was another tactic used by Asad to build his public consensus for his policy towards the Gulf War and subsequent peace process. The speech by Prime Minister Mahmud al-Zu'bi to the delegation from the Syrian Arab Society in Britain reflects some of these reforms. He explained Syria's economic strategy to allow for a greater opportunity for investments. He appealed to Syrians at home and abroad to contribute to Syria's goal of increased agricultural and industrial advancement and trade.[119]

In a speech by Dr. al-'Imadi:

> The decisions made have contributed to the consecration of economic pluralism and also to opening up further horizons before it. The value of the contribution of the private and mixed sector to the gross national product has increased from 42.6 billion pounds in 1985 to 111 billion pounds in 1989. The total of the fixed capital in this sector increased from 6.519 billion to 15.229 billion over the same period. Its contribution to the commodity export operations increased from 6.373 billion in 1987 to 16.189 billion in 1989. We still believe that the latent capabilities of this sector are numerous. We are working and will continue to work to open up further horizons and further incentives for accommodating the savings and capabilities of this sector inside and outside.[120]

While al-Imadi talks about the virtues of economic liberalization in 1990, he ensures that ties with former allies such as the former Eastern European nations and Soviet Union remain:

Our country continues to work on developing its trade exchanges and technical and development cooperation with all countries, whether industrial or developing, in addition to the developed relations with the friendly Soviet Union, the East European countries, as well as economic groupings and international organizations, which serve to meet common interests.[121]

It appears that Syria wants to gradually and carefully open the economy, but it is not quick to embrace the West or the United States. We see this "stand-offish" approach towards the United States in the peace process.

There are other elites in Syria who are suspicious of economic normalization. The surveys conducted on Lebanese and Jordanian professionals reveal an "economic inferiority complex." Most of those surveyed feel that Israel would benefit the most from normalization. Many feel that Israel's economy is so huge in comparison to their nations' economies that competition would be one-sided. Yusuf Shibl claims that Israel's industrial output of $15 billion, which contributed 25 percent of its GNP in 1992, is four times greater than Lebanon's entire GNP. Additionally, a majority of those surveyed feel that Israel would not fully cooperate with Arab countries and would not share technology. Khashan believes that these views are not a result of hard analyses, but rather they reflect stereotyping and biased attitudes—products of five decades of hostility and an absence of meaningful interaction.[122]

It appears, however, that there is evidence that the economic elite, who are predominantly Sunni, do welcome normalization. The health of the economy seems to be paramount in the minds of the professional Lebanese Sunnis. In 1994, 85 percent of Lebanese surveyed (mostly Sunni) saw economic growth as their country's top priority, even more important than religious guidance.[123]

Some anecdotal evidence suggests that the business community is ready for economic normalization. One merchant claims that "People are tired [of the conflict]." Abu'l-Huda, a businessman, says that while Asad decides on matters of war, "when the door is open, we'll be ready for business." Walid, a dealer in embroidered tablecloths, told an Israeli-based journalist, "Please tell the Israelis that we have very good prices here. We want them to come." His brother added, "Peace will be good for Syria and Israel together." A shopkeeper in Damascus, Bassam al-Subayni, claims that "peace means more business." Travelers report that restaurants are offering menus in Hebrew, and merchants are looking forward to Israeli customers. Land investors are buying land on the border between Syria and Israel, thus creating a vested interest in peace.[124]

Who opposes the peace? According to Pipes, the strongest opposition comes from Ba'th Party members and the military. Viktor Posuvalyuk, the special Russian envoy for Middle Eastern issues, found "substantial centers of opposition at the highest echelons of the Syrian administration." Other elements of opposition come from fundamentalist Muslims, a weak force in Syrian politics, and intellectuals who harbor pan-Arabist ideals. However, it is the military and the Party, bastions of Alawite dominance, that oppose the peace. According to a Western diplomat, "the strongest voice resisting peace right now comes from people in the military and security apparatus who have been making fortunes [from the confrontation with Israel]."[125]

There are two divergent opinions on whether the public or the regime is ready for peace with Israel. Western diplomats in Syria suggest that the people are more ready for peace than the regime, while other observers feel that the regime is the supporter of peace. Syrian leaders support the latter view. Vice President Khaddam says that "We can only afford a just peace that is supported by the population." Syria's foreign minister, al-Shara, claims that "the Syrian government wants peace more than its population." Pipes feels that it is the business community which strongly supports peace, and that it is up to Asad to change the population's sentiments. Patrick Seale argues that Assad is "probably the only [Syrian leader] capable of turning around Syrian opinion and making his fellow citizens accept the strategic decision for peace with the historic enemy."[126]

It appears that it may have been more critical for Asad to convince his political elites, namely his fellow-Alawites, of the need for peace since it is perhaps the Sunnis who viewed peace as a means for not only an economic opening but also a political opening. Perhaps Asad was once again carefully balancing several interests—that of the Sunni business community who can help the nation's economy, his fellow Alawis who have a stake in the regime, and himself who is the center of the regime's power. This careful balancing produces incremental policy, a trademark of Asad.

According to Khashan, "Arab governments are fragile because they lack popular legitimacy. Thus, peace at the official level—though significant—is not sufficient. Until Arab regimes legitimize themselves by broadening the base of national politics and introducing liberalization and accountability, they can continue to lose ground to Islamic fundamentalists."[127] In Syria's case, it did not want to lose ground to the Sunnis, so we see an economic liberalization, but it is important to note that Asad would not do anything to jeopardize his Alawite regime. How, then, would any liberalizing of the economy safeguard Alawite power, especially since it is the business class, dominated by Sunnis, who would seemingly benefit from this liberalization?

According to Hinnebusch,

> The regime's autonomy has enabled it to shape its policies according to raison d'etat, that is, its own interests, not those of a dominant class. Preservation of internal security and the extraction of resources for the external power struggle have therefore taken precedence over the capital accumulation requisites of the bourgeoisie and these power requisites have obstructed economic liberalization.[128]

It appears, then, that the interests of the Alawite minority in power is what is holding back the pace of economic liberalization. Hinnebusch explains that the priority of the state is to protect its resources, which makes the public sector a key factor. Foreign currency is also critical as a resource source. A second priority is to satisfy the core elites.

> The fact that this elite is dominated by formerly propertyless minorities, especially 'Alawis, who use the state as a ladder of advancement, while the private economy is dominated by the majority of the Sunni community, gives the regime an exceptional stake in maintaining a large state role in the economy.[129]

This point suggests that those in the state bureaucracy and military view the peace process as a threat to their power. They would not want to see money taken from the military and state to address interests outside of their purview. This threat, however, may not have been that apparent at the time Syria decided to align with the coalition, but it does suggest an anti-Western sentiment that may have contributed to Asad's less-than-enthusiastic embrace of the coalition.

Finally, Hinnebusch claims that the Asad regime had to broaden its support among unionized workers, public employees, and small peasants by providing welfare and economic opportunities to them. These groups are primarily Alawi and are most threatened when steps are taken to liberalize the economy. The interests of the bourgeoisie (Sunni) and the statist elites (Alawi) are in a constant dynamic balance. Hinnebusch explains that

> To liberalize means that the authoritarian-populist state has significantly to shift its social base toward the bourgeoisie, a task made all the harder in Syria because of a certain overlap between the state/private and 'Alawi/Sunni cleavages. This contrasts with conservative authoritarian regimes whose social base is firmly rooted in the bourgeoisie, sectors of which typically welcome liberalization.[130]

The problem that faced, and still faces, the regime is that the state economic strategy failed to accumulate capital. The state is over-bureaucratized and politicized, for example with patronage. The politics of inclusion favored mass consumption, not capital accumulation; favored import substitution which led to a crisis in a balance of payments and foreign exchange; and, relied on short run oil rents, but when the rents declined, the state could not support its size and functions. Consequently, Syria had to take austere measures in public spending, contracts, and jobs. The state had no choice but to turn to the bourgeoisie in the mid-1980s. As a result, "the limits of the state's ability to maintain growth and create jobs needed to coopt the growing educated middle class have made it more politically dangerous to maintain the status quo than to alter it."[131]

Even with this liberalization, however, the bourgeoisie are politically weak because they are internally divided, have not forged alliances with other sectors, and remain outside the Alawite elite, e.g., there is little intermarriage between Alawites and Sunnis. "Therefore, the bourgeoisie currently lacks both the power and the will to push for more economic liberalization than the regime wants." Additionally, in this authoritarian regime, Asad is the decision-maker, and he is guided by raison d'etat, which leaned him towards liberalization. Following the collapse of the Soviet Union, he realized that he needed a foreign policy that was not in opposition to the United States, and this meant some internal liberalization. This point, in conjunction with his economic imperative for opening, allowed Asad to broaden regime support by coopting a portion of the bourgeoisie.[132]

Asad, however, was pragmatic and cautious and would never stray too far away from the elite consensus. What was that consensus? "As such, the extent of liberalization is being affected in good part by bureaucratic politics: an intra-regime struggle between liberalizing 'technos' and statist 'politicos'." Hinnebusch claims that the main actors were the economy minister, al-'Imadi, who was the liberalizer and had the trust of the president, and 'Izz al-Din Nasir, a member of the party regional command, head of trade union confederation, and an Alawi, who opposed liberalization. Again, this balancing of interests resulted in an incrementally driven economic liberalization policy. While al-'Imadi might have been the "liberalizer," in my view he certainly would not have promoted any program that did not meet Asad's approval. In other words, no economic liberalization program will conflict with regime stability; it is only there as a means to ensure stability. Hinnebusch concludes that

> until the social cleavage between state and bourgeoisie is fully bridged, the 'Alawi would be threatened by any return of power to the Sunni-dominated business establishmen. . . . The regime is determined to prevent the Algerian and East European scenarios and the security forces have the firepower and personal stake in the regime's survival to defend it.[133]

Perthers agrees with Hinnebusch's assessment and further describes the politically powerless Sunni business community as a divided community, a community that values individual over collective gains.[134] In sum, the decision to join the coalition allowed for a continuation of incremental economic reform, as long as such reforms benefited the Alawi minority-ruled regime. Additionally, this incrementalism was seemingly a product of Asad's careful, cautious policy-making trait based on a need to build a consensus while maintaining Alawite rule.

INDICATOR: FOREIGN AID AND TRADE

In this section, I will combine the issues because they are so interrelated, and also I have already covered a good deal of this indicator in my discussion in the previous section. The reason for this is that there are differing interpretations of hard data, such as the overall economic health of Syria prior to the Gulf war discussed earlier. Consequently, this chapter on Syria spends more time in the previous section analyzing the various interpretations. I will, however, attempt to answer the question of who is benefitting here.

ISSUES: SECURITY, TERRITORY, HUMAN AND NONHUMAN RESOURCES

Militarily, Syria has not seemed to suffer in its military hardware area (table 7.5). Its arms imports declined between 1984 and 1988, mainly due to the Soviets' denial of further military credits. Syria turned to Bulgaria, Czechoslovakia, the People's Republic of China, and North Korea. Additionally, the Soviets were more interested in helping with Syria's defensive capabilities rather than its offensive capabilities. However, by 1990 Syria's problems with arms imports eased. Kuwait, Saudi Arabia, the UAE, Germany, Japan, and other nations agreed to pay $2.5—$3.2 billion in return for Syria's support of the coalition. In 1990, Syria used $960 million to buy military hardware. This includes those arms listed in table 7.6, and they reflect an offensive capability.[135]

Not only did Asad secure arms required for security, but his alignment with the coalition secured his hold on Lebanese territory with the possibility of regaining the Golan Heights through negotiation. The Taif agreement permitted the deployment of Syrian forces in Lebanon to maintain security.

Table 7.5.   Military Equipment and Defense Spending: Syria (U.S. dollars)[136]

	Manpower (1,000s)	Tanks	Aircraft	Defense Spending ($ millions)	Arms Imports ($ millions)	Arms Exports ($ millions)
1967	80	430	150	313	58	0
1973	115	1,170	326	589	1,270	0
1982	300	3,990	450	1,907	2,600	120
1988	400	4,050	499	1,604	1,300	0
1991	404	4,350	650	3,330	0	0

Table 7.6.   Syrian Arms Orders After Iraqi Invasion in August 1991[137]

Country	Equipment
Czechoslovakia	250–300 T-72M1s (80–100 already delivered)
USSR	400–600 T-72s; MiG-23s, MiG-29s, and Su-24s
North Korea	30–60 Improved Scud missiles
Bulgaria	SP artillery

This requirement culminated, in May 1991, with the signing of a "fraternity, cooperation and coordination" treaty between Lebanon and Syria. The Syrian presence ignited controversy, but its hold on Lebanon has not diminished. By 1993, Syria had 35,000 troops in Lebanon.[138] We have already discussed the Golan Heights imperative for the peace process. Clearly, Asad's pro-coalition alignment was motivated by security and territorial issues.

Refer to tables 7.7–7.9 for an analysis of the human and nonhuman resource issue. There is evidence that Syria was the primary economic beneficiary from the war. Its GDP increased 5 percent in 1991, and it experienced a healthy trade surplus. Aid from members of the coalition, as well as some economic reforms, helped to bolster the Syrian economy. While some funds earmarked for public sector projects were impeded by bureaucratic procedures, and the financing of some private sector projects was hampered by cumbersome foreign exchange rules, Syria's real economic growth reached 10 percent in 1993.[139] Who is benefiting by the economic rewards gained by Syria's pro-coalition stand?

According to Lawson, the Arab Gulf states replaced Syria's funding and technical support previously provided by the former Eastern European nations and Soviet Union. This funding was designed to revitalize the public sector. For example, in July 1991, the Kuwait Fund for Arab Economic Development agreed to provide $60.5 million to build the Idlib cotton mill; Saudi Arabia took responsibility for funding, at a cost of approximately $500 million, the al-Zara iron and steel complex.[143]

This funding provided the military, party-state officials, and public sector managers with enough resources to enable them to maintain their ties with the nations of the former Eastern Bloc. Additionally, this alliance allowed these officials to maintain their positions in the face of growing wealth and influence of the country's private commercial and industrial entrepreneurs. The revenues produced by the state's oil and phosphate production, as well as those revenues from the illegal drug trade with

Table 7.7. Economic Data: Syria in 1993[140]			
Per Capita GDP (U.S. $)	710	Annual GDP Growth Rate	8 percent
Population (thousands)	14,300	Annual Pop. Growth Rate	3.8 percent
GDP (billions of U.S. $)	10		

Lebanon, facilitated the continuation of the regime's Eastern connection. Lawson claims that "The combination of intransigence towards Israel, internal economic recovery and continued ties to the former Eastern Bloc enabled the coalition of senior military and security officers, Ba'th Party and central administrative officials and mangers of public sector enterprises to retain a predominant position within the country's domestic arena."[144] Lawson also claims that on those occasions when Syria adopted a softer line concerning the peace process, it was a tactic to appease discontent at home by members of the private sector. Such a soft stance "concerning the peace talks suggests that the officer/party/state coalition [Alawi] was willing to run considerable external risks in an effort to undercut its internal challengers [Sunni]. It also indicates that the Asad regime enjoys a notable capacity to withstand outside pressure, so long as the home front remains quiescent."[145]

I already covered the many economic interpretations in the previous section, but I feel that the evidence presented in this section supports Lawson's claim that the regime was the chief beneficiary. Specifically, it seems that the Alawis ensured that their coercive instrument, i.e., the army, remained vital, and the economic opening ensured broad support among the Sunni business class. While members of this group economically benefited, it was not at the political expense of the Alawi regime.

Table 7.8. Cost of Living Data: Syria (Consumer Price Index for Damascus: base: 1980 = 100)[141]			
	1990	1991	1992
Food	795.5	823.9	851.6
Fuel and Light	493.7	544.7	766.8
Clothing	769.9	906.5	952.9
Rent	281.8	282.3	282.3
All items (incl. others)	715.4	770.2	843.5
Source: ILO, Year Book of Labour Statistics.			

Table 7.9. Principal Trading Partners: Syria (Syrian pounds, millions)[142]

	Imports				Exports		
	1990	1991	1992		1990	1991	1992
Austria	454.9	495.3	482.3	Bulgaria	391.6	892.6	829.2
Belgium	883.6	1,062.6	1,240.7	Egypt	534.7	152.5	189.8
Bulgaria	437.4	866.5	1,677.4	France	6,039.4	6,811.3	6,446.0
China	463.3	632.3	1,045.7	Germany	1,110.2	1,135.1	853.2
Cuba	246.0	253.2	218.2	Italy	9,845.9	8,622.6	12,163.7
Czechastovakia	217.1	377.1	620.6	Jordan	275.0	768.4	581.7
Egypt	227.2	295.1	481.4	Kuwait	138.9	188.3	692.1
France	3,425.2	2,090.5	2,479.4	Lebanon	2,988.0	3,695.2	4,516.3
Iran	365.7	16.9	135.4	Russia	15,445.8	7,259.6	534.0
Japan	890.8	1,403.8	3,899.6	SA	3,035.4	2,238.4	1,498.1
Kuwait	275.7	2.6	38.0	UK	935.7	729.3	647.0
Lebanon	188.3	330.4	519.4	USA	405.3	208.5	273.6
Russia	766.9	417.8	825.8				
Saudi Arabia (SA)	368.6	411.6	465.1				
UK	711.7	810.8	1,154.8				
USA	2,892.8	2,907.8	2,397.1				
TOTAL (incl. others)	26,936	30,794	39,178		47,281	38,501	34,719

CONCLUSION

There is great overlap among the issues discussed above and together they created a synergistic effect on Asad's status at home, in the region, and in the world. There is a tremendous amount of evidence that, for Asad there were external security and territorial factors motivating him to align with the coalition. Additionally, he received a great deal of monetary aid for his pro-coalition stance. What I think is most interesting, however, is how these factors bolstered Asad's status on all levels, which enabled him to build legitimacy at home. He crafted and executed policy carefully, cautiously, and incrementally in both his alignment decision and subsequent peace process. He never embraced the United States or the West, and he stressed the regional Arab benefits for his positions. In fact, it appears that the motivating factor for Asad's policy choices was survival of his Alawi-minority regime.

On an international level, he lost a substantial amount of status with the collapse of his former patron, the Soviet Union. He responded to this development in several ways. He did make some changes, though small, in his own one-party regime to avoid the fate of Ceaucescu. Additionally, he continued his incremental economic opening to appease the Sunni business class, as well as to bolster his economy. Finally, he did not embrace the West, but he did seek out Western ties, while maintaining his ties to the former Eastern Bloc. On a systemic level, then, Asad incrementally changed his state's behavior and looked inward to bolster his status and seek resources. He also looked outward to achieve these gains, and he primarily looked to bolstering his status in the region as a means to achieve legitimacy or internal status, security and territory, and economic benefits.

It does appear that Asad was constantly aware of his minority status. His policy reflected his careful balancing of interests between the Alawi political elite and the Sunni economic elite. So far, this balancing has worked since the Sunnis have yet to gain political elite status. Table 31 suggests that Alawis fill positions heading the critical, coercive instruments of the state, and the Sunnis holding high-visibility positions provide a degree of legitimacy for Asad among the Sunni majority. It was Asad's primary concern that his regime stay in power, and it was the constant potential threat of a Sunni majority that affects his policy moves.

He engaged in omnibalancing, and in this case he attempted to have the Sunnis, his potential internal threat, align with the state vis-à-vis Iraq. He encouraged Sunni support by highlighting the coalition's support for Arab rights. The coalition also suggested future economic openings with the West as well as territorial gains. Regionally, Asad balanced against Iraq by aligning with the majority of the Arab nations. In this context he aligned with the

Sunnis. On an international level, he aligned but did not embrace the West. This type of alignment allowed him to emphasize his regional alignment, which was more readily acceptable. However, such an alignment benefited the business community, which was dominated by Sunnis. Consequently, his regional and international alignments based on his pro-coalition stance broadened his domestic support among the Sunnis.

Although there was a great deal to be gained from the West, Asad approached the alignment much more cautiously than his fellow Arab leaders. He could not agree to tremendous economic opening because that would be too threatening to his fellow Alawis. As long as the Sunnis remained in the economic sphere and did not challenge his political power, then Asad could allow a gradual economic opening. In fact, if the Sunnis could bolster the economy, that would help alleviate economic pressures, while allowing Asad to continue to import military hardware to shore up his regime's coercive instruments. Any economic achievements were acceptable as long as they helped ensure regime stability.

It appears, then, that Asad aligned with the West and the Arab world as a means to bolster his regime support. In a sense, he diffused a potential threat at home through his regional and international alignment. The way in which he presented and incrementally executed this policy suggests that he was safeguarding his Alawi power at home. The coercive instruments of the state did not falter; he continued his ties to the former Eastern Bloc; he increased his own status on all levels; he was able to set himself up for possible territorial gains during the ongoing peace process; and he directed pro-coalition economic rewards to the public sector, which is dominated by the Alawis. Perhaps without the full support of his former Soviet patron, Asad had to pay closer attention to the potential Sunni threat and use more of the "carrot" rather than "stick" approach in order to gain legitimacy. His pro-coalition alignment allowed him to do just that.

NOTES

1. John P. Hannah, "At Arms Length: Soviet–Syrian Relations in the Gorbachev Era, " *The Washington Institute Policy Papers, no. 41* (Washington, D.C.: The Washington Institute for Near East Policy, 1989), xi–12.

2. This idea about technology and SDI is taken from Richard Smoke, *National Security and the Nuclear Dilemma: An Introduction to the American Experience* (New York: Random House, 1987), 277–278, and Robert Gilpin, *War and Change in World Politics* (Cambridge: Cambridge University Press, 1986), 182.

3. Ann Mosley Lesch, "Contrasting Reactions to the Persian Gulf Crisis: Egypt, Syria, Jordan, and the Palestinians," *The Middle East Journal* 14, no. 2 (Winter 1991): 41.

4. Ibid.

5. Bruce Stanley, "Drawing from the Well: Syria in the Persian Gulf," *Journal of South Asian and Middle Eastern Studies* 14, no. 2 (Winter 1990): 63–64.

6. Lesch, 42–43.

7. Ibid., 43.

8. Hermann Frederick Eitts, "The Persian Gulf Crisis: Perspectives and Prospects," *The Middle East Journal* 45, no. 1 (Winter 1991): 7.

9. Geoffrey Kemp, "The Middle East Arms Race: Can it be Controlled?" *The Middle East Journal* 45, no. 3 (Summer 1991): 443.

10. John Lewis Gaddis, "The Long Peace," *International Security* 10, no. 4 (Spring 1986): 132.

11. Ibid., 132–140.

12. Graham E. Fuller, "Moscow and the Gulf War," *Foreign Affairs* 70, no. 3 (Summer 1991): 64.

13. Robin Wright, "Unexplored Realities of the Persian Gulf Crisis," *The Middle East Journal* 45, no. 1 (Winter 1991): 29.

14. Charles Krauthammer, "The Unipolar Moment," *Foreign Affairs* 70, no. 1 (Winter 1991): 24.

15. Harold H. Saunders, "Political Settlement and the Gulf Crisis," *Mediterranean Quarterly: A Journal of Global Issues* 2, no. 2 (Spring 1991): 6.

16. Lesch, 48.

17. Peter W. Rodman, "Middle East Diplomacy," *Foreign Affairs* 70, no. 2 (Spring 1991): 5.

18. Peter Mangold, "The Soviet Record in the Middle East," in *Crisis Management and the Superpowers in the Middle East*, ed. Gregory Treverton (Westmead: Gower Publishing Company Limited, 1981), 91.

19. Ibid., 91–92.

20. Yosef Olmert, "Domestic Crisis and Foreign Policy in Syria: The Assad Regime," *Middle East Review* 20, no. 3 (Spring 1988): 20.

21. Delwin A. Roy and Thomas Naff, "Ba'thist Ideology, Economic Development and Educational Strategy," *Middle Eastern Studies* 25, no. 4 (October 1989): 471–477.

22. The idea concerning parity is taken from ibid., 476.

23. Ibid., 479.

24. Robert K. Lifton, "Talking with Assad: A Visit to the Middle East in Transition," *Middle East Insight* (September/October 1994): 10.

25. Ibid., 10–11.

26. Raymond A. Hinnebusch, "Syria: The Politics of Peace and Regime Survival," *Middle East Policy* 3, no. 4 (April 1995): 75.

27. "Nation Opposes U.S. Attempt to Weaken Iraq," *FBIS*, NES (29 October 1990): 53.

28. "Radio Commentary," *FBIS*, NES (12 October 1990): 50–51.

29. Fida Nasrallah, "Syria After Ta'if: Lebanon and the Lebanese in Syrian Politics," in *Contemporary Syria: Liberalization between Cold War and Cold Peace*, ed. Eberhard Kienle (London: British Academic Press, 1994), 135–136.

30. Fred H. Lawson, "Domestic Pressures and the Peace Process: Fillip or Hindrance?" in *Contemporary Syria*, 140–141.

31. "'Illusory War' Replacing Fight Against Israel," *FBIS*, NES (30 August 1990): 48.

32. Harold H. Saunders, *The Other Walls: The Politics of the Arab–Israeli Peace Process* (Washington, D.C.: American Enterprise Institutes for Public Policy Research, 1985), 86.

33. Dore Gold, "The Syrian–Israeli Track—Taking the Final Step: What Sacrifices Will Assad Make to Get Back the Golan?" *Middle East Insight* (September/October 1994), 15.

34. Muhammad Muslih, "The Golan: Israel, Syria, and Strategic Calculations," *Middle East Journal* 47, no. 4 (Autumn 1993): 611.

35. Ibid., 613–614 and 621.

36. Ibid., 626.

37. Hilal Khashan, "Partner or Pariah: Attitudes Toward Israel in Syria, Lebanon, and Jordan," *Policy Papers, No. 41* (Washington, D.C.: The Washington Institute for Near East Policy, 1996), 13.

38. Ibid., 14–15.

39. Ibid., 13.

40. Fred Huxley, "The Arabs," in *In the Eye of the Beholder: Muslim and Non-Muslim Views of Islam, Islamic Politics, and Each Other*, ed. David Pollock and Elaine El Assal (Washington, D.C.: Office of Research and Media Reaction, USIA, 1996), 7.

41. Khashan, 14.

42. Khashan, 15.

43. Khashan, 26.

44. Huxley, 8.

45. Ibid., 13 and 15. Also, see David Pollock, *The Arab Street? Public Opinion in the Arab World* (Washington, D.C.: The Washington Institute for Near East Policy, 1992), 52, which claims that two-thirds of the Lebanese surveyed (mix of Sunnis and Christians) supported the peace process, and a narrower majority supported normalization.

46. Huxley, 13.

47. Huxley, 13.

48. Khashan, 19.

49. Ibid., 21.

50. Ibid., 26.

51. David Horovitz, "Portrait of the Enemy," *The Jerusalem Report* 6, no. 6 (July 27, 1995): 27.

52. Ibid.

53. Daniel Pipes, "Syria Beyond the Peace Process," *The Washington Institute Policy Papers*, no. 40 (Washington, D.C.: The Washington Institute for Near East Policy, 1996), 3.

54. Huxley, 6.

55. All the quotations are taken from Pipes, 12–13.

56. Ibid., 11.

57. Ibid., 13.

58. Stephen P. Cohen, "A Not-So-Odd Mideast Couple," *New York Times* 25 (August 1994): sec. A, p. 21.

59. Gold, 17.

60. "Syria: Impact of Wielding Power on 'Alawi Cohesiveness,'" in the *Daily Report Supplement of Near East and South Asia, FBIS, NES*, 3 October 1995, 3.

61. Ibid.

62. Volker Perthes, *Economic Change, Political Control and Decision Making in Syria* (Germany: SWP, 1994), 239.

63. Ghayth N. Armanazi, "Syrian Foreign Policy at the Crossroads: Continuity and Change in the Post-Gulf Era," in *State and Society in Syria and Lebanon*, ed. Youssef M. Choueiri (New York: St. Martin's Press, 1993), 112.

64. Ibid., 113.

65. Ibid.

66. Ibid., 114.

67. Ibid., 112.

68. "Al-Shar' Requests Emergency Arab Summit," *FBIS*, NES (9 August 1990): 48.

69. "Al-Ahmar Reasserts 'Rejection' of Iraqi Invasion," *FBIS*, NES (9 August 1990): 49.

70. "NPF Supports Al-Asad Efforts in Gulf Crisis," *FBIS*, NES (10 August 1990): 60.

71. "Army Chief Calls Invasion 'Unprecedented Event'," *FBIS*, NES (10 August 1990): 60.

72. Alasdair Drysdale and Raymond A. Hinnebusch, *Syria and the Middle East Peace Process* (New York: Council on Foreign Relations, 1991), 92–93.

73. Armanazi, 114–115.

74. Lesch, 42.

75. "Nation Will Not Defend Iraq Against Israel," *FBIS*, NES (14 August 1990): 51.

76. "Troops Slated for Saudi Arabia Service," *FBIS*, NES (14 August 1990): 51.

77. "Paper Views U.S. Support of Israeli Occupation," *FBIS*, NES (14 August 1990): 51.

78. "Commentary Applauds Arab Summit Resolutions," *FBIS*, NES (14 August 1990): 51–52.

79. "Editorial Urges Return to Pre-Invasion Kuwait," *FBIS*, NES (14 August 1990): 53.

80. "Muslim Brotherhood Leader Voices Support for Iraq," *FBIS*, NES (30 January 1991): 48.

81. "INA Reports 30 Aug.," *FBIS*, NES (31 August 1990): 39.

82. "Power and 'Alawi Cohesiveness," 12, describes these Sunni officials as tokens.

83. Steven Heydeman, "Can We Get There From Here? Lessons From the Syrian Case," *American-Arab Affairs* 36 (Spring 1991): 27.

84. Ibid., 27–28.

85. Ibid., 28. While the source does not give the ethnic composition of these groups, the correlation between Lebanese Sunni professionals and Syrian Sunnis leads me to believe that the professional associations are primarily Sunni. Additionally, previous discussions in chapters 3 and 5 reveal that the Sunnis, while not politically powerful, still

are the economic elites. The public sector groups and those groups which rely on the state for their economic well-being, such as trade unions, peasants, and youth federations are most likely disproportionately Alawi. See Raymond A. Hinnebusch, "Liberalization in Syria: The Struggle of Economic and Political Rationality," in *Contemporary Syria*, 97–113, and this chapter, pp. 42–44.

86. Heydeman, 28.

87. Ibid., 29.

88. Ibid.

89. Ibid., 30.

90. Lesch, 42–43.

91. Muhammad Muslih, "Dateline Damascus: Asad Is Ready," *Foreign Policy*, no. 96 (Fall 1994): 150–151.

92. Stephen Zunes, "Israeli-Syrian Peace: The Long Road Ahead," *Middle East Policy* 2, no. 3 (1993): 63.

93. The whole discussion of Orr's views and the quotations are from Horovitz, 30.

94. Ibid.

95. The importance of public support regarding the Golan and the quotation are from Muslih, "Dateline," 155–156.

96. Muslih, "Golan," 629.

97. Saunders, *The Other Walls*, 86.

98. Horovitz, 26.

99. As cited from author's discussions with Syrian officials who did not want to be identified, in Muslih, "Golan," 629.

100. David Waldner, "More Than Meets the Eye: Economic Influence on Contemporary Syrian Foreign Policy," *Middle East Insight* 11, no. 4 (May–June 1995): 34.

101. Ibid., 35–36.

102. Ibid., 36.

103. Ibid., 37.

104. Fred Lawson, "Domestic Transformation and Foreign Steadfastness in Contemporary Syria," *Middle East Journal* 48, no. 1 (Winter 1994): 48.

105. Ibid., 48–51.

106. Ibid., 51.

107. Armanazi, 114.

108. Muslih, "Dateline," 153.

109. Alon Ben-Meir, "The Israeli-Syrian Battle For Equitable Peace," *Middle East Policy* 3, no. 1 (1994): 75.

110. Ibid.

111. "Egypt, Syria Said to Propose Gulf Security Plan," *FBIS*, NES (25 February 1991): 44.

112. Lesch, 42.

113. Sylvia Polling, "The Syrian Surprise: A New Spirit of Entrepreneurism and Diligent Program of Economic Reforms Are Transforming the Syrian Economy," *Middle East Insight* (July–August 1991/993): 8.

114. Nabil Sukkar, "The Crisis of 1986 and Syria's Plan for Reform," in *Contemporary Syria*, 42.

115. Ibid.

116. Polling, 6–7.

117. Eberhard Kienle, "Introduction: Liberalization between Cold War and Cold Peace," in *Contemporary Syria*, 2.

118. Perthes, 199–200.

119. "UK-Based Businessman Briefed on Economic Policy," *FBIS*, NES (7 November 1990): 41.

120. "Economy Minister Speaks at Damascus Fair," *FBIS*, NES (5 September 1990): 45–46. Because of the Alawi control of the state, Party, and military, I think it is fair to say that the Alawis disproportionately control the public sector, while the economic upperclass, the Sunnis, disproportionately control the private sector.

121. "Economy Minister Speaks at Damascus Fair," 45–50.

122. Khashan, 30–37.

123. Huxley, 5.

124. Daniel Pipes, 118.

125. Ibid., 119. I linked the Alawite description based on earlier accounts of Alawite power, as well as the "Provisional Classification of Syrian Nomenclatura" found in "Syria: Impact of Wielding Power on 'Alawi Cohesiveness,'" in the *Daily Report Supplement of Near East and South Asia, FBI S, NES*, 3 October 1995, 16.

126. Ibid., 121–122.

127. Khashan, 46.

128. Raymond A. Hinnebusch, "Liberalization in Syria: The Struggle of Economic and Political Rationality," in *Contemporary Syria*, 99.

129. Hinnebusch, "Liberalization in Syria," 99.

130. Ibid., 99, and quotation on p. 100.

131. Ibid., 110–101, and quotation on p. 101.

132. Ibid., 102–105, and the quotation is on p. 103.

133. Ibid., 105–106, and the quotations are found on p. 105 and 107.

134. Volker Perthes, "Stages of Economic and Political Liberalization," 60–68, and the quotation is on p. 68.

135. Anthony H. Cordesman, *After the Storm: The Changing Military Balance in the Middle East* (Boulder: Westview Press, 1993), 182–187 and 260–263.

136. Cordesman, 256.

137. Cordesman, 363. Note that these figures are not exact.

138. *The Middle East and North Africa, 1995: Forty-First Edition* (London: Europa Publications Limited, 1995), 846–847.

139. Ibid. 848–849.

140. *Background Notes: Syria*, U.S. Department of State, 5, no. 13 (November 1994).

141. *The Middle East and North Africa, 1995: Forty-First Edition*, 859.

142. Ibid, 860.

143. Lawson, "Domestic Pressures and the Peace Process: Fillip or Hindrance?" 151.

144. Ibid., 151, and the quotation is found on p. 154.

145. Ibid., 154.

Chapter Eight

Conclusion

What strikes me about this study is that it is one of many moving parts. The issues are extremely interrelated, and I recognize that by analyzing each issue separately some analytical points may have been lost. Nevertheless, I still believe that this study struck a good balance by telling the whole story while analyzing the issues in order to understand our variables. I also realize that this study touched on myriad topics. The bad news is that due to the scope of this project, I cannot address all of these topics in depth. The good news is that this study serves as a good springboard for further studies, which I will elaborate on later. At this point, I will put together some of these moving parts in order to address the questions first posed in chapter 1. Addressing these questions directly will help provide insights to our central question, that is how ethnicity affects state alignment decisions.

The line of logic presented here is that ethnicity feeds directly into the notion of legitimacy. This concept of legitimacy is a key ingredient to a regime's stability or, as Timothy Lomperis claims, its ability to rule well.[1] A state's level of legitimacy based on a shared ethnic identity influences that state's foreign policy decisions, specifically its state alignment decisions. Our four cases allowed us to examine the impact of ethnic divisiveness versus ethnic homogeneity on a state's alignment decision, demonstrating the relationship between these variables through Alek Holsti and John D. Sullivan's linkage politics model. This concluding chapter begins with a review of the core concepts and ideas that formulate our line of logic. Next, we will recall the specific state alignment decisions, review the theoretical definitions and put them in context of the cases, discuss the theoretical contributions of this study to both the international relations and comparative politics fields, and end with recommendations for further research and for future partnering among academics, military leaders, and policy-makers.

DOMESTIC REVIEW: THE ETHNIC VARIABLE
AND ITS LINK TO LEGITIMACY

Ethnicity is not a precise term, yet it describes a powerful force when it becomes politicized. For this study, I chose a balance between the all-inclusive definition and the all-exclusive definition, while adapting its meaning to the region presented in this study. Consequently, I adopted Robert J. Thompson and Joseph R. Rudolph's definition of ethnicity based on three overlapping traits: kinship, religion, and language.[2] Based on this definition, we established the Sunni population in Syria as one ethnic group, who are ruled by the minority Alawi ethnic group. We also established the Egyptian people as a single ethnic group. This point clarified, David Horowitz provided the criteria that enabled us to demonstrate the existence of ethnic divisiveness in Syria, and its nonexistence in Egypt.

Chapter 1 established the importance of ethnicity as a factor for legitimacy, which appendix A (Theory) further develops; however, legitimacy is not an easy concept to measure. Because of its centrality in the field of political science, it is critical that we still attempt to discover its significance on the polity and the international system. David Easton explains that "Given its long and venerable history as a central concept in political science, legitimacy has yet to receive the attention it merits in empirical research."[3] It is for this reason that I believe this study is important, if only to lay the groundwork for further study.

Simply put, legitimacy is the idea that the people believe that the regime is morally in the right. Many scholars have defined and elaborated on this critical concept. Easton's definition of legitimacy for a regime is

> that it is right and proper . . . to accept and obey the authorities and to abide by the requirements of the regime. It reflects the fact that in some vague or explicit way [a person] sees these objects as conforming to his own moral principles, his own sense of what is right and proper in the political sphere.[4]

Lomperis's view of legitimacy is threefold: first, it is multifaceted in its motives and, consequently, requires different appeals. Second, society must view the regime as having the moral authority to rule. Third, ". . . a state can rule without legitimacy, but not well."[5] Ted Robert Gurr and Muriel McClelland define legitimacy as "the extent that a polity is regarded by its members as worthy of support."[6] However, they claim that even a state with high legitimacy may have political violence: "neither civil order nor durability is primarily determined by legitimacy; both are also affected by decisional efficacy . . . notably the occurrence of severe societal strain."[7] For our Egyptian case, we saw this occurrence of civil strife, not based on the people's legitimacy for the regime, but rather based on "the severe societal strain" due to a poorly performing economy, combined with a skyrocketing population growth.

Michael Hudson explains that Arab states experience a legitimacy problem due to the lack of prerequisites for political modernity, which are authority, identity, and equality. "The legitimate order requires a distinct sense of corporate selfhood: the people within a territory must feel a sense of political community which does not conflict with other subnational or supranational identifications."[8] This point is critical and explains why ethnicity plays such a key role for regime legitimacy. Easton claims that there are three sources of legitimacy: ideology, structure, and personal qualities. For Easton, ideology refers to a sense of the regime being morally right; structure refers to the acceptance of norms and governmental apparatus; and personal qualities refers to the acceptance of leaders who fill the structural roles.[9] These sources correspond to Max Weber's view that legitimacy is derived from tradition, laws, and charisma.[10] What seems to be a critical component in all these definitions is the idea that the people have a shared sense of community and belief that the regime has the moral right to rule.

Ethnicity helps establish this shared sense of values and community. As our review of the ethnicity literature showed, ethnic loyalty is a powerful force. In Hudson's explanation of one of his models for understanding legitimacy in a context of social change, the role of ethnicity becomes clear. "The mosaic model emphasizes the persistence of primordial and parochial loyalties even during rapid modernization, and in some conditions even predicts their strengthening."[11] The impact of ethnicity is truly great, and it is for that reason that I have examined this variable. Hudson reviews Clifford Geertz's point concerning the criticality of primordial ties, to include ethnic, religious, racial, and linguistic ties to a state's political development, which according to Milton Esman "are likely to touch deeper emotional levels" than any other type of societal cleavage; consequently, modernizing regimes have a difficult time replacing these loyalties.[12] Finally, Augustus Richard Norton explains that the most important element for state survival is legitimacy, meaning "that authority which rests on the shared cultural identity of ruler and ruled."[13] Our case studies reveal that Egypt enjoys this legitimacy based on shared identity, while Syria does not.

Granted, there are other sources of legitimacy. Hudson explains that there are some external sources, one being the "all-Arab core concerns. The legitimacy of given leaders in a given state is determined to an important extent by their fidelity of these core concerns."[14] We observed the selective use of this external source for legitimacy in our cases. Interestingly, we saw leaders who disregarded this source, e.g., Sadat's loss of regional status when he realigned with the United States and signed the treaty with Israel, and during the 1980s, Syria chose to support Iran vis-à-vis another Arab country.

In sum, legitimacy is a key ingredient for regime stability, and when ethnic loyalties coincide with national loyalties, then that sense of a shared political community and values is a great commodity for the regime. Conversely, when these loyalties are in conflict, then the regime is in a dangerous position.

On the domestic level for Syria, ethnic divisiveness was a prominent factor in the political arena. Asad ruled, as Seale observed, with two guiding principles: he worked to gain a public consensus, and in the absence of this consensus, he relied on coercion. Additionally, we saw how dangerous the Muslim Brotherhood was in Syria because the Brotherhood was able to exploit these ethnic divisions. Pipes explains that "the passage of time has hardened the Sunni-Alawi divide to the point that it dominates the way Syrians interpret domestic politics, and the way they anticipate Syria after Asad's passing."[15] Moreover, Pipes explains that the Islamic movement "in Syria . . . is more anti-Alawi and anti-Ba'th, more communal than religious. Muslim Brethren literature, for example, hardly ever brings up the usual fundamentalist concern for applying the sharia. Rather its goals consist of the Sunni public agenda."[16]

In Egypt, the Brotherhood did not have this context in which to work. While it challenged the regime in the economic realm by providing social welfare activities, it did not challenge the people's identity. Everyone considered themselves Egyptian. This strong national identity and its resulting legitimacy has allowed Egypt to weather long periods of economic malaise and Islamic fundamentalism. Recall Fouad Ajami:

> Egyptians who know their country so well have a way of reciting its troubles, then insisting that the old resilient country shall prevail. As an outsider who has followed the twists of the country's history and who approaches the place with nothing but awe for its civility amid great troubles, I suspect they are right. The country is too wise, too knowing, too tolerant to succumb to a reign of theocratic zeal.[17]

The leaders of both countries face tremendous domestic challenges; however, in my view Egypt will successfully face its challenges. The legitimacy it enjoys allows its leaders and people to assess their condition honestly. While the fixes will not be easy, Egyptians are at least at a valid starting point to improve conditions. Admittedly, the fixes are being conducted incrementally because their implementation places a great strain on society. Syria is also proceeding incrementally in the domestic arena as it also tries to open its economy. This is where the similarity ends, however, because the countries handle their foreign policies much differently as a direct result of their differing levels of legitimacy based on ethnicity.

STATE ALIGNMENT REVIEW: CASE STUDIES

What do the state alignment decisions reveal? First, Syria in the Cold War era performed omnibalancing in accordance with Steven David's definition; that is, Syria bandwagoned with the superpower in order to balance against the internal threat, the Sunni majority. It is important to understand the nature of this alignment. First, Syria had a cordial but not warm relationship with the Soviet Union. Second, Syria used a combination of "carrots" and "sticks" in order to deal with its internal threat; however, for this decision, it appears that Syria chose to balance against the Sunni internal threat by using the stick, such as the case in Hama. Third, Asad chose to relinquish regional status when he signed the Treaty of Cooperation and Friendship with the Soviet Union and supported the Soviets when they invaded Afghanistan. He also turned his back on the region when he supported the non-Arabic state of Iran during the Iraq-Iran War. Finally, the treaty focused on military wares, not on economic tools, and his economy suffered. As this case study showed, Asad had great concern for the internal threat, the Sunni majority, and he chose to face this threat using the military tools from the Soviet Union.

Security, on both the regional and domestic levels, seemed to be a major concern for Asad. In fact, he linked the domestic threats with regional threats, thereby justifying his actions on other states based on his belief of their meddling within his country's borders. Asad explained that, "We were not just dealing with killers inside Syria, but those who masterminded their plans. The plot thickened after Sadat's visit to Jerusalem and many foreign intelligence services became involved. Those who took part in Camp David used the Muslim Brothers against us."[18] Mahmud Faksh explains that Syria's involvement with Lebanon was "a fear of [a] possible spillover"[19] of sectarian violence. According to Alasdair Drysdale, "It was further proof that the Alawis were not Muslim at all . . . it was only a matter of time before some of Lebanon's sectarian violence would be transmitted to Syria."[20] Asad's focus on security overshadowed his state's economic problems. The treaty with the Soviets was primarily for military wares. According to Umar F. Abd-Allah, "the chief purpose of the Soviet-Syrian 'friendship pact' was to strengthen Asad's position in the face of mounting popular opposition,"[21] and according to the Action Committee for the Liberation of Syria, the pact was designed "to protect Asad from the wrath of the Syrian people."[22]

Syria's alignment decision benefited a particular group, the Alawis. Not only did the treaty bolster the military, which is primarily in the hands of the Alawis, it also gave the minority-ruled regime the tools to repress the Sunni majority. In my view, it is more than just coincidence that the signing of the treaty and the subsequent military hardware came just before Asad's brutal massacre of

Hama. The lack of legitimacy of Asad's minority-ruled regime forced him to proceed cautiously in the foreign policy realm. He used a combination of carrots and sticks to deal with his internal enemies, and Hama was an example of his use of sticks. He did, however, try to build a public consensus for his policies, causing him to produce only incremental policy changes. While Asad's policies may look convoluted, they really were products of Asad's cautious calculations as he tried to balance the many competing interests in his society. While he may at first glance appeared to have been belligerent and radical, he really was, as Shlomo Avineri describes, a status quo leader.[23]

Egypt in the Cold War era also bandwagoned with a superpower, the United States, as well as with Israel. The realignment with these two countries was a radical departure from Egypt's previous alignment choices, since the beginning of the Cold War. This radical realignment, as with Syria's alignment, cost Egypt its regional status, but Egypt had great support from the people for this decision. As Thomas Lippman claimed:

> Sadat wanted to seize the moment. He was not crippled by the domestic weaknesses that hindered other Arab leaders—Egypt was not a precarious artificial state with an imposed monarchy, like Jordan, nor a pit of unrest run by a despised minority, like Syria—and he had established Egypt's freedom of action by breaking with the Soviet Union and attacking Israel in 1973.[24]

Sadat stressed an Egyptian-first credo, and he addressed Egyptian interests. As a result, Egypt was able to address a domestic variable—its economy—by aligning itself with the superpower that would help it address this domestic concern. This is what Syria could not do because of Asad's preoccupation with quelling the Sunni threat.

For Egypt, security was a secondary issue. Sadat believed that the 1973 war was the last war and that Egypt needed peace in order focus on its main concern, providing for its people. It does appear that Sadat wanted all of Egypt to prosper, not just a certain group. A ministry development plan document stated that:

> political wisdom and simple justice call for the alleviation of the burdens of the masses. They deserve respite, for they have given much when Egypt required it of them, socially, politically, and militarily. Political wisdom further recognizes the inherent danger in allowing the standard of living of the majority to deteriorate, when they can see around them luxurious consumption and special privileges. It is only human that they should feel discontent, fear, and envy.[25]

The problem, of course, is that this intention did not reflect the outcome, and the rich tended to get richer, while the poor got poorer. The point, however, is that

Sadat was able to address this growing domestic problem by taking a seemingly risky approach in his realignment decision. According to Ali E. Heikal,

> Sadat used to contrast Egypt's deep-seated unity with the sectarian, familial, and communal fragmentation of most Arab countries. According to Sadat, this unity allowed Egypt to pursue a purposeful foreign policy and to make hard decisions (e.g., peace with Israel) impossible for most Arab countries because of their domestic fragmentation.[26]

In the post–Cold War era, Syria's alignment behavior was still cautious and calculating, but its alignment concerning the domestic threat changed. First, it bandwagoned with the Sunnis in the form of offering carrots, not sticks. Asad realized he needed Sunni support in the economic realm and a means of diffusing the potential Sunni threat. Siding with the coalition provided an opportunity for Asad to gain some needed economic support, as well as a means to gain back status, both regionally and internationally. It is important to note that while Asad did address some of his state's economic concerns, security was still a primary issue, primarily the security of his regime:

> [Asad's] general attitude toward the private sector has always been positive, provided the representatives of this sector stuck to their business and did not oppose his regime. . . . For that reason, Asad has never favoured abandoning unnecessarily any element of state control and the means of patronage such control implies, nor introducing or envisaging farreaching changes that might be considered a challenge to parts of his political basis.[27]

Although he balanced against a regional threat and a fellow Arab state, it was a historical enemy. Now, Syria was eager to reenter the Arab fold, and its alignment with the coalition allowed it do just that. Syria did bandwagon with the lone superpower, the United States, but Syria gave it a cold embrace. Syria's motivation for stiff-arming the United States was to appease Asad's fellow Alawis. According to Pipes, it is the centers of Alawi power, the military and the Ba'th Party, who opposed the post-Persian Gulf War peace process.[28] Consequently, Syria seems to have adopted a pragmatic approach to its alignment behavior by carefully balancing the interests of the Sunni majority, thereby opening its economy, while continuing its bellicose rhetoric toward the United States and keeping the reins on the economic opening. In sum, Asad would not have done anything to endanger the survival of his regime. As Pipes suggested:

> While Asad shares with other authoritarian leaders the goal of personal and regime survival, he stands apart from most of them in his willingness to resort to extreme means to achieve his ends. To keep himself and his fellow Alawis in

power, he could do anything from destroy a Syrian city (as he did to Hama in 1982) to reverse a lifetime of anti-Zionism and sign a peace treaty with Israel.[29]

Finally, Egypt in the post–Cold War era continued its alignment with the now sole superpower, the United States, and with Israel. The difference with this superpower alignment from Syria's post–Cold War superpower alignment is that Mubarak chose to take a strong pro-U.S. stance. He was able to do this because he had support from the Egyptian people. Consequently, he was better able to address his economic situation than was Asad. Mubarak continued Sadat's pragmatic approach to foreign policy, perhaps even more so because he reentered Egypt into the Arab fold, while reestablishing ties with the Soviet Union. On the one hand, Mubarak demonstrated some risk-taking by embracing the United States in the midst of short term economic costs and regional anti-West sentiment—two key openings for Islamicist groups. On the other hand, his regional and international alignment allowed him to secure some economic benefits, which he had hoped to distribute throughout the population.

Mubarak looked past the Gulf crisis in hopes of establishing an arrangement that would benefit Egypt, primarily in the economic realm. All issues seemed to point toward the economic imperative. According to Stephen Pelletiere, "Egypt's security problem must be seen in context of its economic plight."[30] Status also was a means to gain economic benefits. Steve Negus explained that "Egyptian diplomats openly admit that as their diplomatic utility wanes, the money will start to dry up."[31] Boutros-Ghali felt that "the postwar period in the Arab world should correspond to the postwar period in Europe which gave rise to the Marshall Plan and the EEC. We have a similar opportunity 50 years later."[32]

One may argue that Egypt's motive for addressing its economy was to stifle the Muslim Brotherhood. I agree with this view to some extent, however, we must also remember the Egyptian people's willingness to forgo short-term economic benefits in support of Mubarak's coalition decision. Even the opposition groups, the Muslim Brotherhood included, supported Mubarak's decision. What seems to be a potential problem is the difference between the elite and public opinion. This gap is better addressed in a study focused on democratization. What I have uncovered, however, is an honesty in Egypt's self-assessment, by its leaders and people. Such a reassessment is an important start point on the path toward democracy. In fact, Egypt's ability to conduct honest self-assessments is what led to its effective military reforms and excellent performance on the battlefield in the October 1973 War, as discussed in chapter 4. Another critical factor, and the focus of my study, is Egypt's strong sense of national identity based on ethnic homogeneity. As noted earlier, Ajami explains this identity by observing that, "Egyptians who know their country so well have a way of reciting its troubles, then insisting that the old resilient country shall prevail."[33] This sense of nationalism may be helpful for Egypt on its path to democracy, or it may signify a political culture that seeks a more paternalistic regime or some variant thereof. This point, I feel, is worthy of further study.

DEFINITIONS

Recall our key definitions of balancing and bandwagoning:

1. If a weak state balances, then we will observe the state aligning against the threat.
2. If a weak state bandwagons, then we will observe the state aligning with the threat.

My cases support Randall L. Schweller's views that balancing and bandwagoning "are not opposite behaviors. The motivation for bandwagoning is fundamentally different from that of balancing. Bandwagoning is commonly done in the expectation of making gains; balancing is done for security and it always entails costs."[34] All my cases revealed that each country viewed the superpowers as sources of gain, not as threats. During the Cold War era, Sadat admits that the economy was the major reason for launching the October War, and Marc Cooper claims that "Mid-1977 begins to look a great deal like mid-1973. The economy was under a severe strain and going nowhere. There was nothing left to be tried in the polity." Moreover Cooper recounts an Egyptian phrase concerning Egypt's realignment: "The Soviets can give you only war, only the Americans give you peace, and the Soviets cannot give you economic development."[35] While Asad was not necessarily looking for economic gain in his decision to sign the 1980 treaty with the Soviets, he was looking for military hardware to primarily thwart ethnically based internal threats. The Soviet-Syrian alliance is characterized by Efraim Karsh as a "marriage of convenience," which he described "in terms of a mutually beneficial strategic interdependence between two allies: a relationship favoring each partner in accordance with the vicissitudes of regional and global affairs." Other scholars described Syrian policy in terms of having an independent character, tempered by Arab-Israeli and inter-Arab relations, as well as occurring only when Soviet and Syria relations converged.[36]

The post–Cold War era cases also support Schweller's definition of bandwagoning. Again, Egypt's motivation for its Persian Gulf War alignment was economically based. Boutros-Ghali described his country's expectations from the War in terms of the Marshall Plan and EEC, which followed World War II.[37] Everything was colored by Egypt's economic imperative. Mubarak viewed the United States as a source to address his country's economic woes. Asad's alignment with the United States and the Persian Gulf coalition also was economically motivated, not threat-based. The problem for Asad was that his superpower benefactor had collapsed. He had no other alternative but to turn to the United States, but as I will address later, the nature of Asad's alignment with the United States was much different than the Egyptian-American alliance. The point here is that bandwagoning, for my cases, was motivated by economics, not threat.

Using David's test for omnibalancing allows us to further refine the definition of bandwagoning and balancing. According to David, the strongest test for omnibalancing would be "if the leadership bandwagoned with an external threat in order to balance against an internal threat. This outcome would confirm the importance of internal threats (and) demonstrate the need to appease some threats to deal with others."[38]

Here again, I draw upon Schweller's view that bandwagoning and balancing are not opposite behaviors. The first part of the hypothesis is only partially corroborated by my cases. We observed both Egypt and Syria bandwagoning with a superpower, but as explained above, the motivation was not threat-based. Second, I contend that only Syria bandwagoned in order to balance against internal or regional threats during both time periods. In the Cold War era case, Syria balanced against an internal threat, i.e., the Sunni population, and in the post–Cold War case, it aligned, or bandwagoned, with its internal threat, while balancing against a regional threat. The nature of the alignment with the West allowed Asad to make gains, in terms of economic benefits, as well as status, but mostly this alignment allowed him to balance the interests of his Alawi coalition and Sunni population.

So what did my cases reveal about David's omnibalancing hypothesis? First, it worked best, except for the modification of bandwagoning explained above, for the Cold War era Syrian case. Syria bandwagoned with the Soviets to address its internal threat. Second, in the post–Cold War era, Syria bandwagoned with the United States and the West to address the internal threat, the Sunnis, as well as the regional threat, Iraq. Additionally, Asad bandwagoned with the Sunnis in order to gain greater regime support. Finally, Egypt did not balance against an internal threat. It sought gains in order to address its economic situation, but significantly, it did not have to address a legitimacy problem based on ethnic divisions. This is the significant point, which leads to our central question as it relates to Egypt's bold versus Syria's cautious foreign policy to which I referred in the preceding chapters.

Egypt, during both time periods was able to bandwagon with a superpower without having to balance against an internal threat. While Egypt obviously had to consider its dire economic conditions, both Sadat and Mubarak did not have to concern themselves with their state's legitimacy and, consequently, they both enjoyed great support from their people for their foreign policy initiatives. As Nazih N. Ayubi claims, "By political and legal tradition, both the State and the President (rayyes) are invested with much power and respect. One result is that both in domestic and external matters, 'regime' and 'policy' are often presented and/or perceived of as one and the same thing. The political instinct of most Egyptians would be first to support the state and then to find out why!"[39] Consequently, when Sadat and Mubarak embarked on a foreign policy course, they knew that they enjoyed a reservoir of legitimacy. They did not have to concern themselves with building a consensus, so they were able to make their alignment decisions without this constraint. These leaders had a great deal of maneuver room, which allowed them to embark on bold, purposeful foreign policy.

Asad, on the other hand, had to balance against an internal threat. Asad did not enjoy the legitimacy that the Egyptian leaders did. During the Cold War period, Asad had to gain military wares in order to address his internal Sunni opposition. While he did not use the same means to address this opposition in the post–Cold War era, he still had to address their interests. He did this by embarking on an incremental, cautious policy of economic liberalization, while establishing a very cold embrace for his Western alignment. Asad could not initiate bold, purposeful foreign policy because he was constrained by the lack of legitimacy at home. He did take bold action at home when he massacred the town of Hama, but it was a last resort after he was unable to build a domestic consensus, and his alignment with the Soviets was still "a marriage of convenience"—no bold foreign policy here.

I will further address my refinement of balancing and bandwagoning in the theoretical contribution section. The point I want to make now is that I did find that a state that is ethnically divided acts differently toward the international system than a homogeneous state. This difference, however, is more meaningful when described in terms of bold, purposeful behavior versus cautious, incremental behavior, rather than using the terms of bandwagoning and balancing. However, it is the presence of bandwagoning and balancing, as defined by Schweller, that may help us determine whether a state will embark upon bold versus cautious behavior toward the international system. Generally, I have found that a state that is ethnically divided will have to balance against or bandwagon with its internal (ethnic) threat. A homogeneous state does not have to do this, and, therefore, is less constrained from making bold, foreign policy.

ADDRESSING OUR QUESTIONS

What did our cases reveal concerning the systems level of analysis? In other words, did these states act differently in the Cold War versus the post–Cold War era? First, the preceding cases suggest that in the post–Cold War era, domestic variables come to the fore. Leaders must look within for fixes. What is interesting to me and what might help predict future alignment behavior is an analysis of Syria's alignment with its internal enemies in the post–Cold war era versus in the Cold War era. In the post–Cold War era, Asad bandwagoned with the Sunnis in order to build the economy. Specifically, he made in-roads to western technology, and he liberalized the economy. Both measures also helped to broaden support of his regime. In fact, it appears that he had to convince his own circle of fellow Alawis to accept the peace process, which was widely supported by the economically well-off Sunnis. Will the Sunnis be able to use their economic power to affect the regime now that Asad is gone? Egypt has continued its gradual economic and to some extent, political liberalization. The question for Egypt is whether economically it is doing too little too late. Will it be able to continue economic reform without causing too much hardship on its people? Will such hardship, then, spill into the political realm? The good news is that perhaps the post–Cold war era, with all its uncertainties, is forcing regimes to fix themselves from within. These fixes may be easier for ethnically homogeneous states because it provides an easier context in which to deal with opposition groups. For example, currently, the Muslim Brotherhood is a greater threat in Syria because of its ability to exploit ethnic divisions, than in Egypt where such divisions are minor in comparison. Additionally, fixes which come from within will perhaps have long-term effects, as compared to band-aid fixes imposed by the international arena. There is cause for optimism in the post–Cold War era, if this is indeed a trend.

This discussion leads us to the second point: these cases suggest that in the post–Cold War era there is great significance placed on the region, rather than on the international arena, concerning alignment decisions. Both countries chose to leave the Arab fold during the Cold War for their respective alignment decisions. However, in the post–Cold War era, both countries made deliberate efforts to renew their regional ties and gain regional status. During the Cold War era, I believe that Egypt's national sentiment combined with the status it gained in the international arena via its ties with the United States compensated for any lost regional status. For Syria, its ties with the Soviet Union also served to compensate for any regionally lost status. Additionally, its ties with the Soviets allowed it to gain the necessary military hardware to deal with any domestic unrest, so in Asad's view he was able to use coercion to gain internal support. The nature of this internal support is debatable, however.

Why did both states choose to turn their focus on the region in the post–Cold War era? This new focus supports Kenneth Waltz's view that there is a degree of more uncertainty in the other-than-bipolar world. During the Cold War era, both countries manipulated the Cold War rivalry for their own purposes. The rivalry ensured aid in some form or another. In the post–Cold war era, assistance and even alliances are less certain. Now countries are looking to their own neighborhood for future economic, security, and cultural arrangements. While Egypt already had ties with the United States, there was some uncertainty concerning future U.S. aid. The Syrians lost their superpower patron altogether. It was necessary for both Asad and Mubarak to look regionally for assistance.

What have we learned about foreign policy trends or alignment behavior? First, it appears that ethnic homogeneity does have an impact on foreign policy. It provides a wealth of legitimacy, thereby allowing that state's leader more maneuver room in foreign policy. Consequently, that leader is able to take risks, which leaders of ethnically divided states are unable to do. Such boldness enables leaders to make strong, purposeful alignments, as opposed to tentative, cautious alignments. In other words, the ability to make bold foreign policy causes the nature of alignments, whether they are balancing or bandwagoning type alignments, to be different from those alignments stemming from a cautious, tentative foreign policy. Practically, this point enables policymakers to adjust their expectations concerning the policies of ethnically divisive versus ethnically homogeneous states.

Second, it appears that the post–Cold war era promotes bandwagoning with internal enemies because there is a degree of uncertainty in the international system concerning a superpower's support. The state cannot count on support from the international system. The imperative now is to find fixes from within, which may in the longterm cause a state to better address its real concerns, such as the economy. This point is responsible for what observers call pragmatism in policy-making. Perhaps this bodes well for transitioning regimes on the road to democracy, a topic for further study. Finally, in the post–Cold War era, it appears that the region has become more significant than in the Cold War era. This may provide added prestige and functionality to regional organizations (again, a topic for further research).

THEORETICAL CONTRIBUTIONS

I have already touched on the theoretical implications of my project in both the international relations and comparative politics fields. Without overstating this point, I feel that my cases clearly show the importance of asking both international relations and comparative politics questions when trying to understand state alignment behavior. Specifically, this project furthers the discussion of balancing versus bandwagoning state alignment behavior. I have added to the critique of Stephen Walt's work by expanding on Schweller's definitions of balancing and bandwagoning and applying them to David's idea of omnibalancing. These behaviors are not opposites, as Schweller tells us, and bandwagoning is done for profit, not for security purposes. What I have discovered is that when a state does not have to balance against or bandwagon with an ethnically charged internal threat, then it can bandwagon and balance in a bold, unconstrained manner; there is more maneuver room for state alignment decisions in such states. Conversely, a state that must constantly balance against or bandwagon with an ethnically charged internal threat as a means to gain legitimacy can only conduct state alignment decisions in a cautious, incremental manner. There is no maneuver room for state alignment decisions in such states that lack legitimacy due to ethnic divisiveness, where group and state loyalties do not coincide. In sum, balancing and bandwagoning alignment behavior are not polar opposites; bandwagoning is for profit, while balancing is for security purposes, and the absence of internal bandwagoning/balancing engenders bold, purposive state alignment behavior, while the presence of internal bandwagoning/balancing fosters cautious, incremental alignment behavior.

This point begs the question on what is bold, purposive behavior versus cautious, incremental behavior. Bold, purposive behavior may take the form of realignments and strong commitments to allied partners. These actions may seem risky because they are new and challenge perhaps former policies. Cautious, incremental behavior reflects more of a status quo in terms of alliances as well as weak commitments. These actions are risk-adverse because they are not new, and the luke-warm commitments allow for balancing and bandwagoning at home should regime support not be forthcoming.

The domestic variable that causes internal bandwagoning or balancing is the lack of legitimacy due to ethnic divisiveness. This variable is tremendously significant, however, when examined in its positive state. In other words, when ethnic and state loyalties coincide, there is a great reservoir of legitimacy, and a leader of such a state can generally count on great domestic support concerning state alignment decisions. Egypt highlights the significance of this variable, i.e., the presence of great legitimacy because while it was suffering from great economic inefficiencies, both Sadat and Mubarak were still able to count on great domestic support. While one may argue that Syria's economy was in much better condition than Egypt's, Asad could not count on broad regime support due to the state's lack of legitimacy. My cases suggest that legitimacy based on ethnic homogeneity can be a more powerful variable than economic efficiency for the state in terms of gaining support for state alignment decisions. Clearly, my cases demonstrate the importance of continued research on legitimacy studies, even though it is not a tangible, easily quantifiable variable, for indeed, "the issue of support and opposition, legitimacy and illegitimacy . . . stands at the crux of all political study."[40]

While I feel that this study's biggest contribution concerns the link between the domestic variable and alignment behavior, my cases also reveal the importance of understanding the international system in which states make alignment decisions. The primacy of the region and the state became clear in the post–Cold War era. In this regard, Waltz's claim concerning the uncertainties of a multipolar world is justified. If the rewards from the international system are unclear, then a state must look inward or to its immediate neighborhood for fixes. Additionally, these cases reveal that the certainty of a hegemon to take care of the international system, as Robert Gilpin explains, is unclear. What this work adds to Waltz and Gilpin is an other-than-great power approach. Such an approach, as other scholars claim, require an understanding not only of the international system, but also of the region and the state, especially since the idea of "statehood" for Third World countries is different than the Western notion.[41] Consequently, scholars must understand the state as well as the international system in order to further understanding of state alignment behavior.

SUGGESTED FURTHER RESEARCH

While I have a learned a great deal from researching this project, there is a great deal yet to be done. The problem with studying this area of the world is that some data are either not available or too sensitive for publication. This point is especially an issue for the Cold War cases, specifically Syria. However, I do believe there are ways to overcome either the unavailability of data or its inaccessibility. First, it is important to take advantage of windows of opportunity for data-gathering. Such a window occurred after the Gulf War. Second, we must build bridges within the academic world, e.g., between comparativists and international relations scholars. No longer may these fields develop independently from one another, and I believe that this study is proof of their interrelationship. Third, we must build bridges between the governmental and military intelligence organizations. Each organization offers a great deal, and I believe the intelligence assessments of our nation would be tremendously enhanced with more cross-talk, a topic for another book. Most importantly, it is critical that there is cooperation and understanding among academia, the military, and the policy-making world. I realize that this point may sound naïve, but in the course of my research, I was struck by how critical such cooperation may be in pursuit of theoretical break-throughs, policy-making, or the appropriateness of the use of force.

Bridges must be made among these three areas because in pursuit of truth, whether in policy-making or theory, open-mindedness is paramount. While we may never rid ourselves of biases or parochialisms, we must never strive for less of a goal. It is not easy to do this because all three fields have grown to cherish their organizational essences, and to a point this is necessary. It becomes a problem when it prevents cooperation and the sharing of ideas. Practically, each area offers a great deal to each other, as I found in my research.

With this in mind, other areas of further research have already been addressed, but I will restate them here. Democratization, consensus-building, ethnicity studies, etc., are all touched on here and are worthy of further study in the context of the cases presented here or in other cases. Additionally, such studies will enhance the politically important, yet empirically difficult concepts of legitimacy and ethnicity. Moreover, we need more Cold War era versus post–Cold War era cases to validate, refute, or build upon the points presented in this study. Further use of the linkage model between domestic variables and foreign policy used here will help sharpen the model itself. Other linkage models may also provide insights and better understanding of the relationship between the domestic and foreign realms.

The policy implications concerning such topics as democratization, multilateral organizations, and the role of force versus aid need further review and hard study. The implication here is that as regimes look inward in this post–Cold War era, the United States may want to engage in self-help type policies for these regimes. This implies that we understand the regime and the nature of its challenges. There may be some regimes who would adopt a variant of democracy, and we will need to resist the temptation to judge them against the American or even western model.

While the post–Cold War era may be rife with uncertainty, it may also hold for us tremendous possibilities. What this means for scholars, policy-makers, and military leaders is that understanding regions and regimes has become at least as important as understanding the international system. While the challenge is great, there is cause for much hope, not only in broadening our understanding of the world, but also in designing policies that will bring happiness and prosperity, too. We are in exciting and uncertain times. Let us face this future together, sharing ideas and dreams.

NOTES

1. Tim Lomperis, *From People's War to People's Rule: Insurgency, Intervention, and the Lessons of Vietnam* (Chapel Hill: The University of North Carolina Press, 1996), 30–32.

2. Robert J. Thompson and Joseph R. Rudolph, "Ethnic Politics and Public Policy in Western Societies: A Framework for Comparative Analysis," in *Ethnicity, Politics, and Development*, ed. Dennis L. Thompson and Dov Ronene (Boulder, Colorado: Lynne Reinner, 1986), 27–28. See chapter 1 for the literature concerning the people of the Middle East.

3. David Easton, "A Reassessment of the Concept of Political Support," *British Journal of Political Science* 5, part 4 (October 1975): 451.

4. Ibid.

5. Lomperis, 32.

6. Ted Robert Gurr and Muriel McClelland, "Political Performance: A Twelve Nation Study," in *Comparative Politics Series*, ed. Harry Eckstein and Ted Robert Gurr, vol. 2, no. 01–018 (Beverly Hills: Sage Publications, 1971), 30.

7. Ibid., 32.

8. Michael C. Hudson, *Arab Politics: The Search for Legitimacy* (New Haven: Yale University Press, 1977), 4.

9. Easton, "A Reassessment of the Concept of Political Support," 452.

10. Max Weber, "Politics As A Vocation," in *From Max Weber: Essays in Sociology*, ed. H. H. Gerth and C. Wright Mills (New York: Oxford University Press, 1946), 78–79.

11. Hudson, 7.

12. Hudson cites Clifford Geertz, "The Integrative Revolution: Primordial Sentiments and Civil Politics in the New States," in *Old Societies and New States*, ed. Clifford Gertz (New York: Free Press of Glencoe, 1963), 105–157, and Milton Esman, "The Management of Communal Conflict," *Public Policy* 21, no. 1 (Winter 1973): 49–78, 54, in Hudson, 9.

13. Augustus Richard Norton, "The Security Legacy of the 1980s in the Third World," in *Third World Security in the Post–Cold War Era*, ed. Thomas G. Weiss and Meryl A. Kessler (Boulder: Lynne Reinner Publishers, 1991), 24.

14. Hudson, 5.

15. Daniel Pipes, "Syria Beyond the Peace Process," *The Washington Institute Policy Papers*, no. 40 (Washington, D.C.: The Washington Institute for Near East Policy, 1996), 11.

16. Ibid., 12–13.

17. Fouad Ajami, "The Sorrows of Egypt," *Foreign Affairs* 74, no. 5 (September/October 1995): 88.

18. Seale, 335.

19. Mahmud A. Faksh, "Syria's Role and Objectives in Lebanon," *Mediterranean Quarterly* 3, no. 2 (Spring 1992): 87.

20. Alasdair Drysdale, "Syria's Troubled Ba'thi Regime," *Current History* 80, no. 462 (January 1981): 33.

21. Dr. Umar F. Abd-Allah, *The Islamic Struggle in Syria* (Berkeley: Mizan Press, 1983), 75.

22. Ibid., 76.

23. Shlomo Avineri's view is taken from Fouad Ajami, "The Arab Road," in *Pan-Arabism and Arab Nationalism: The Continuing Debate*, ed. Tawfic E. Farah (Boulder: Westview Press, 1987), 126.

24. Thomas W. Lippman, *Egypt After Nasser: Sadat Peace and the Mirage of Prosperity* (New York: Paragon House, 1989), 9–10.

25. Ibid., 91.

26. Ali E. Hillal Dessouki, "The Primacy of Economics: The Foreign Policy of Egypt," in *The Foreign Policies of Arab States: The Challenge of Change*, ed. Bahgat Korany and Ali E. Hillal Dessouki (Boulder: Westview Press, 1991), 160.

27. Volker Perthes, *Economic Change, Political Control and Decision Making in Syria* (Germany: SWP, 1994), 203–204.

28. Pipes, 118.

29. Ibid., 3.

30. Stephen C. Pelletiere, *Shar'ia Law, Cult Violence and System Change in Egypt: The Dilemma Facing President Mubarak* (U.S. Army War College at Carlisle Barracks: Strategic Studies Institute, 5 April 1995), 1.

31. Steve Negus, "Mubarak's Diplomatic Coup," *Middle East Insight* (15 March 1996): 8.

32. "Butrus Ghali Views Nonaligned Initiative," *FBIS*, NES (20 February 1991): 6–7.

33. Ajami, 88.

34. Randall L. Schweller, "Bandwagoning for Profit: Bringing the Revisionist State Back In," *International Security* 19, no. 1 (Summer 1994): 106.

35. See chapter 4, pp. 191 and 192, which cite R. D. McLaurin, Don Peretz, and Lewis Snider, pp. 34–35, and Marc Cooper, pp. 250 and 252.

36. See chapter 5, p. 218, which cites Karsh, pp. 1 and 21, and paraphrases Golan and Rabinovich, 228.

37. See chapter 6, p. 308, which cites Boutros-Ghali in "Butrus Ghali Views Nonaligned Initiative," *FBIS*, NES (20 February 1991): 6–7.

38. Steven R. David, *Choosing Sides: Alignment and Realignment in the Third World* (Baltimore The Johns Hopkins University Press, 1991), 8.

39. See chapter 6, p. 296, that cites Nazih N. Ayubi, *The State and Public Policies in Egypt Since Sadat* (Reading: Ithaca Press, 1991), 312.

40. Lomperis cites Harry Eckstein in, *From People's War to People's Rule*, 31.

41. See appendix A (Theory) for a full discussion of these viewpoints.

Epilogue

Implications For A Post-9/11 World

The next set of questions must focus on the applicability of the previously discussed findings to the post-9/11 world. At first glance, it appears that such questions would derive from the assumption that something has changed from the post–Cold War era to the post-9/11 era. I contend that the trends observed in the post–Cold War era cases describe what we are witnessing now and for the foreseeable future. For now, it is important to bring forward some of the conclusions discovered from our previous cases to the current and foreseeable future of our post-9/11 world. In short, does the region play an increasingly significant role in determining state behavior? Does ethnic homogeneity versus ethnic heterogeneity continue to play a role in each state's legitimacy formula, thereby affecting alignment decisions? Should we expect continued bandwagoning and balancing behaviors we observed in our previous post–Cold War cases? Or more to the point, will we continue to observe cautious, incremental alignments from Syria and bold alignment behavior from Egypt? Will domestic factors continue to play an increasingly significant role in a state's alignment decisions?

Still, at the crux of the story is the concept of legitimacy. Yet, to fully understand state legitimacy, once again one must identify the driving forces in the domestic, regional, and global environments. Even more so today, these environments are inextricably linked. One cannot understand alignment decisions without first understanding these connections. Observations of the current security environment require discussion of what appears to be emerging fundamentalist Islamic challenges to secular authority in Egypt, Syria, and in the region overall, and regimes cannot ignore these threats; perhaps these forces have changed each state's threat perception, thereby changing the state's legitimacy formula. If so, how does the existence of ethnic homogeneity versus ethnic diversity affect threat perception and the evolution of the fight for legitimacy between the state and the challenges posed by these groups?

Stephen M. Walt explains that "there is an inescapable link between the abstract world of theory and the real world of policy. We need theories to make sense of the blizzard of information that bombards us daily."[1] Yet, lately, it seems as if reality has outpaced theory, which bodes poorly for both policymakers and academics. It is important, then, to help advance theory by first observing those forces in the security environment that may help us anticipate behaviors. Subsequently, the next sections will identify the driving forces in the global, regional, and domestic security environments during the past decade leading up to 9/11 and post-9/11 events. Since our last two cases focused on the alignment decisions concerning the Persian Gulf War, it is important to reflect on the post–Gulf War trends of the past decade, as well as the post-9/11 events. When we put together the confluence of forces and events in these security environments, we can hope to better understand the threat and anticipate state behaviors. Perhaps we may also gain some insights on the behavior of nonstate actors, namely militant fundamentalists, an unexplored realm of inquiry. This is the first step in theory building in what appears to be a chaotic and incoherent world.

GLOBAL SECURITY ENVIRONMENT

Our conclusion from the post–Cold War cases is that the international system influences state behavior. With only one superpower, there is uncertainty, and states cannot afford to ignore their region. This point discovered in previous chapters has gained prominence today, which we will explore shortly. What is the post-9/11 world? Is it really different from the post–Cold War era? After all, there is still one superpower. To address these questions, it is necessary to determine if the driving forces identified in the post–Cold War chapters are prevalent today. Are there other driving forces in the forefront that require attention? If we hope to advance theory, which indeed is lacking now, then approaching the security environment in this manner is a first step in theory development. It is perhaps too soon to say whether 9/11 marks a systemic shift. However, 9/11 and the events that have so far followed have changed the way the international community and, specifically, the Middle East view the security environment. According to Shibley Telhami:

> What has changed in the past two years is not al-Jazeera. It is the world. What has changed in the past two years is that there has been a complete transformation of the environment. We had a world in the 1990s that had a seemingly work-

ing Israeli-Palestinian peace process. People could point to it, and when a moderate in the Arab world debated an extremist on al-Jazeera or anywhere else, they could not only reject the extremist method, but they could put forth a positive alternative. They could say look, we have a peace process, peace is around the corner. We're going to have an agreement.[2]

Embedded in the above quote are some of the effects of the "conceptual anchor" for understanding today's and tomorrow's world: globalization.[3] As a process, globalization's opposite is localization or fragmentation. James Rosenau explains: "In short, globalization is boundary-broadening and localization is boundary heightening."[4] These forces are powerful, and the U.S. Commission on National Security/21st Century describes these forces as "two contradictory trends ahead: a tide of economic, technological, and intellectual forces that is integrating a global community, amid powerful forces of social and political fragmentation."[5] The Arab world has even developed the term "al-awlama" to identify globalization.[6] The effects of this globalization appear numerous as do the interpretations, both normative and empirical. According to Hans-Henrik Holm and Georg Sorensen, the unevenness of globalization causes variations among regions:

> We need to study the effects of uneven globalization . . . as they are "filtered through" different regions. It is . . . the combined effect of uneven globalization and the end of the Cold War [that causes] increased variation, not only between North and South but also among different regions of the world.[7]

Globalization not only affects the region, but it also has a direct effect on the individual and vice versa. "Globalization increases risks and opportunities for individuals, who become both objects and participants in global processes, and individual actions may have dramatic consequences for international relations."[8] It is not a big leap to observe the fact that the continued hunt for Osama Bin Laden and Saddam Hussein underscores this point.

Jessica Mathews argues that indeed globalization has changed the character of the significant players in the international system. She argues that there has been a "power shift" away from nation states and toward non-state actors. The increased accessibility and sophistication of information technologies has displaced the government's monopoly on information. "In every sphere of activity, instantaneous access to information and the ability to put it to use multiplies the number of players who matter and reduces the number who command authority."[9] She also explains that this information revolution has changed communal relations, established new groups, altered state-societal relations, and established new communal connections across state borders.[10] Bruce Hoffman predicted that the end of the Cold War era would unleash forces, primarily terrorism: forces "long held in check or kept dormant by the cold war may erupt to produce even greater levels of non-state violence."[11] Moreover, these non-state actors, namely terrorist groups, have greater accessibility to the materials, technologies, and experts required for acquiring and using weapons of mass destruction.[12] And terrorism is not the only force to be unleashed. The U.S. National Security Strategy describes a list of transnational forces that must be seriously addressed:

> [These are transnational] threats that do not respect national borders and which often arise from non-state actors, such as terrorists and criminal organizations. . . . Examples include terrorism, drug trafficking and other international crime, illicit arms trafficking, uncontrolled refugee migration, and trafficking in human beings. . . . We also face threats to infrastructures, which increasingly take the form of cyberattack in addition to physical attack or sabotage.[13]

With the end of the Cold War, there appeared to be no ideological competitor to democracy. The dialogue of competition between democracy and communism had been secular. However, the end of communism as a viable alternative to democracy seemed to bolster religion as a political solution.[14] Moreover, democracy and other secular forms of governing have not been effective everywhere. Many western institutions and experiments with democracy proved disastrous in the Third World. In fact,

> some of the most poignant cases of disenchantment with secularism are to be found among educated members of the middle class who were raised with the high expectations propagated by secular nationalist political leaders. . . . One Muslim leader described Egypt's policies as "an economic, social, and moral failure."[15]

As a result of corruption, political and economic underdevelopment, the conditions for failing states, have been on the rise. It is more than ineffectiveness; it is a loss of legitimacy. Many perceive secular nationalism as a failure. They no longer believe in its institutions, and more importantly, they no longer "believe in it. In their own way they are experiencing what Jurgen Habermas has dubbed a modern 'crisis of legitimation,' in which people's respect for political and social institutions has been deflated throughout the world."[16] In these circumstances, religion has emerged as a powerful, transnational, and alternative force. It has a built-in organization that crosses boundaries; it is a ready-made force that, when used by extremists, can motivate members, mobilize resources to include recruits, provide moral justification for increasingly lethal acts of violence, and become what Bruce Hoffman describes as a political movement.[17]

These powerful transnational forces with their accompanying effects on state legitimacy have led to increasing numbers of failed states, which wreak havoc on a failing state's regional neighbors that can quickly have global consequences. Michael Brown argues that intra-state conflicts can quickly become regional and global in nature. One cannot ignore the spill-over effects of intra-state conflict, given the forces of globalization. Intra-state conflicts demand attention not only due to the magnitude of human suffering, but also due to the effects on the region and the world, namely on "distant powers."[18] In short, what happens in Egypt and Syria, the Middle East, and the world are interconnected.[19]

What these scholars anticipated, as a result of driving forces—accessibility of information technologies, the Islamic militant response as the only alternative ideology to Western, secular thought, the effects of globalization and fragmentation on state-societal relations in the underdeveloped world, and the availability of weapons of mass destruction outside state control—in the global security environment in what is now the post-9/11 world, was a high level of violence conducted by non-state actors with greater consequences than ever witnessed previously. Interestingly, Louise Richardson argues that due to these changes, we must re-look at the relationship between states and non-state actors, primarily terrorist groups.[20] In other words, there are new relationships between terrorist groups and their statesponsors. She describes a five-part continuum of possible relationships. First, there is total state control vis-à-vis the terrorist group, where the state directs the killing of dissidents. The second stage describes the state's recruitment and training responsibilities of the group for particular missions. The third stage still reflects state control through its direct instructions concerning the group's activities. In the fourth stage, we observe a group's operational autonomy, but the group still receives a state's financial, training, and safe-haven support. Finally, in the fifth stage, state-sponsorship occurs, but the state's expectations are only based on common diffuse interests. For example, Libya supported the IRA, not because of Muammar al-Qaddafi's specific interest concerning the situation in Northern Ireland, but due to the IRA's efforts against Britain.[21] At an extreme, given recent revelations about Al-Qaeda's operations in Afghanistan, we may have indeed witnessed a terrorist-sponsored state. In any event, Richardson's argument compels us to rethink alignments not only among states, but also with non-state actors. In our cases, we observed Syria bandwagoning with segments of the population, and Egypt has taken, at times, a balancing approach toward the Muslim Brotherhood and in other times a bandwagoning approach. Richardson provides a start point for further study on alignment theory that would include non-state actors.

Richardson also describes networks among terrorist groups, absent of any state involvement. These networks know no boundaries and are international in scope.[22] This feature requires intense study beyond the scope of this book; however, again, further study of state alignment theory cannot ignore the expanding scope of these terrorist networks. Another global trend that must be addressed is what Jessica Stern refers to as the "protean nature" of terrorist groups.[23] Terrorist groups change and adapt in order to survive and stay ahead of their adversaries. Groups will even change their missions and forge unlikely alignments. As an example, there is evidence that al Qaeda, a Sunni-based group, has ties with Hizballah, a Shi'a group.[24] These innovations and adaptations along with the counter-intuitive quality and scope of networks or alignments require close scrutiny in the post-9/11 world. Not only must states anticipate the actions of other states, it is clear that states must consider these non-state actors just as carefully as state actors. If one considers the confluence of these driving forces, such as networking, accessibility to information technologies, including weapons of mass destruction, and religious ideology, then the trend can only be one of increased lethality. "The volatile combination of religion and terrorism has been cited as one of the main reasons for terrorism's increased lethality."[25] At the end of the day, the terrorist requires public support. The issue of legitimacy is central. This becomes a key point in the following sections where we revisit the Muslim Brotherhood.

REGIONAL SECURITY ENVIRONMENT[26]

On a regional level, the forces described above combined with the U.S. war on terrorism, the Israeli-Palestinian conflict, and post-conflict Iraq, reflect the interconnectedness of the global and regional security environments. The increase of information technologies in the form of the media, continued political and economic despair in the region, and the growing youthful and unemployed population, has created a more volatile Arab street. Thomas Friedman explained:

> We are seeing the convergence of three historical trends. . . . The first is this terrible intifada, this Israeli-Palestinian violence that is of a level of intensity and depravity we've never seen in this conflict before. . . . From another direction, we have a huge pig in a python, [namely] a huge population explosion going on in the Arab-Muslim world. . . . Fifty percent of the Muslim world under 20 . . . or 25. . . . So a huge population explosion marching toward the workplace. And from a third direction we have an explosion of multimedia, Jazeera,[27] satellite TV, Internet, and basically, what is going on is that the media is taking these images of this Intifada and feeding it to this population explosion coming up the road.[28]

This growing despair in the region reflects illegitimate and authoritarian regimes that most of the population live under, the regimes' dysfunctional economies, and their foreign policies as it relates to the region itself.[29] One cannot ignore the effects of the Israeli-Palestinian conflict, the U.S. war on terrorism, and the current post-Iraq conflict situation on Arab sentiment toward the United States. Augustus Norton warned that Arab leaders expected the Arab street to mobilize with the war on Iraq (and it is interesting to see how each Arab leader handled the situation), and perhaps these leaders must be even more concerned about their populations should the post-conflict Iraq situation linger without tangible improvement.[30] Increased significance of the Arab street occurred, for example, in Egypt where large demonstrations turned out to protest the situation on the Israeli-Palestinian front: "While they say their enemy is Israeli leader Ariel Sharon, the protesters appear uncertain and confused about who their allies are."[31] Zogby International recently polled Arab adults from Egypt, Israel, Jordan, Lebanon, Kuwait, Morocco, the United Arab Emirates, and Saudi Arabia about political issues. While civil and personal liberties and health care were rated the highest in priority, the next two priority issues were Palestine and rights of Palestinians.[32] Telhami also argues that the issues concerning Palestine resonate throughout the region. He explains that the Palestinian issue "is central to the collective consciousness in the region, to the collective Arabic and Islamic identity. . . . And thus when an Arab or Muslim makes a judgment about the world, subconsciously he or she makes a judgment through the prism of the Palestinian issue."[33] Additionally, an indication of sentiment toward the war on terrorism was captured in a Gallup poll where 77 percent of Islamic respondents believed that military force in Afghanistan was unjust.[34] Zogby polls support the Gallup findings with most Arab countries (Egypt, Saudi Arabia, Lebanon) responding negatively toward the U.S. war on terrorism. The only Arab country that had a favorable rating was Kuwait, and the United Arab Emirates had 38–39 percent split between those that viewed the war on terrorism favorably and unfavorably, respectively.[35]

As mentioned previously, globalization seems to affect regions differently. The despair felt throughout the Middle East was a primary concern reflected in the United Nations Arab Human Development Report (UNDP). According to the report, "Securing a better future for all requires putting the attack on poverty at the top of national agendas in Arab countries."[36] According to the World Bank's estimates, the populations of the Middle East and North Africa grew from 174 million in 1980 to 295 million in 2000. By 2015, that number may be as high as 389 million. Moreover, per capita income rose only by one-third the population rate, and, even using optimistic assumptions, the estimate projected that per capita income would grow at only half the rate through 2010.[37] Politically, the UNDP identified the Arab world as lagging behind most other regions "in terms of participatory governance," and called for more accountability mechanisms, transparencies, a free press, civil society, and political participation as the means required for real socioeconomic development progress. [38]

Regime ineffectiveness and illegitimacy have taken a toll across the region. The response has been a "power shift" and the rise of non-state actors in the region, specifically, Islamists. Michael Hudson explains this tendency in the Arab world:

> The persistent authoritarianism of their regimes has come to indicate the hollowness of their entire political order. At the same time, societies began to display greater vitality than before, with associations and NGOs. . . . But it was far from clear where the new societal energy would lead. . . . The far more rooted societal tendency belonged to Islamists.[39]

These transnational networks are a critical structural characteristic of both the new global and regional environments, and they are significant "agents of change."[40]

Regionally, the network of Islamist groups is evident. The Arab Muslim Brotherhood has tremendous political clout, and the branches, theoretically, have roots to the Brotherhood's Egyptian leader.[41] There have been attempts to bring ideological groups together. For example, The Solidarity Conference in Tehran, October 1991, was an attempt to bring disparate groups together to include the Muslim Brotherhood, Ba'thists, and communists. Olivier Roy describes this alliance as

> one chapter in the anti-imperialist struggle, which is occurring today under the green banner instead of the red. Essentially, it is the Third World, anticolonialist sensibility, always present in the history of Islamism, that is reemerging today in what is an undoubtedly temporary alliance with secular currents of the same sensibility.[42]

The ability to network has been a powerful resource for many extremist groups. As mentioned earlier, al-Qaeda, a Sunni off-shoot, and Hizballah, a Shi'a group, are cooperating. Hizballah has truly gone transnational, with presence in Lebanon, South America, and the United States. The U.S. presence is mainly for financing purposes, but the CIA recently reported that the group has been conducting surveillance on U.S. facilities. Interestingly, in South America, specifically the tri-border region defined by the borders of Paraguay, Brazil, and Argentina, there are reports of truly diverse groups, such as Marxist Colombian rebels, American white supremacists, Hamas, and Hizballah. George Tenet describes this phenomenon as "mixing and matching of capabilities, swapping of training, and the use of common facilities."[43] With access to information technologies and the rewards of networking, these terrorist groups are finding ways to acquire and develop weapons of mass destruction.[44]

The driving forces in the region seem to reflect our observations of the global environment. Namely, that through the process of globalization and localization, the forces that play a significant role in the region include rampant despair; illegitimate authoritarian regimes; economic underdevelopment; a growing youthful population; the rise of extremist and transnational Islamic groups; and, the access to information beyond state control to include media availability to the Arab street. These forces combined with the U.S. war on terror, the Palestinian-Israeli conflict, and post-conflict Iraq have created a regional dynamic that highlights the importance of the region as a level of analysis. Arab leaders must calculate regional dynamics into their threat perception. Each state's Arab street is affected by events and forces in the region. Consequently, leaders have to reevaluate their legitimacy formula as they consider regime survival and alignment decisions in particular.

EGYPT: DOMESTIC

In the context of Steven David's omnibalancing, states that must deal with internal threats must either bandwagon with or balance against those threats. A state that must address internal threats that challenge its legitimacy has less maneuver room for its foreign policies, specifically its state alignment decisions, than a state that enjoys internal legitimacy. How a state addresses internal threats to its legitimacy also matters, and therefore, requires analysis of the domestic environment.

The last case on Egypt discussed events leading up to the Oslo peace process. The findings suggest that the idea of being Egyptian provides the Egyptian regime, namely Mubarak, with a level of legitimacy to make bold alignment decisions. Also, we discovered that the threat for Egypt is its dire economic conditions. How have the regional and global environments affected the Mubarak regime? Is maneuver space contracting? Do we see Mubarak balancing or bandwagoning with internal threats? After the Gulf War, there was hope for political liberalization and economic development for Egypt. The economy posed the greatest challenge for Mubarak, and it appeared that he would have to meet the problems of his own regime head-on. What happened?

In short, Egypt reflects the problems specified in the United Nations Arab Development Report mentioned earlier. What needs to be watched carefully for the future is Egypt's legitimacy formula. While it is a paternal state, and the people tend to support their leader's decisions, other forces, especially in the region, have impacted this support. One cannot talk about Egypt without understanding the regional context. According to Dr. Said Aly, the director of

Al-Ahram Center, "I think bilateral and regional are linked. . . . Nobody invests in a country; they invest in a region. And tourism is very vital to us and highly sensitive to developments in Palestine and Israel."[45]

The main shift in Mubarak's legitimacy formula is the rise of the Arab street due to the forces inherent in globalization described earlier: the people have more information; they are affected by events in the region; there has been continued economic despair and political de-liberalization; and extreme Islamic fundamentalism is on the rise. This does not indicate that there will be a revolution in the style of 1979 Iran, but rather the elite, namely Mubarak's support base, are affected.[46] What we will see in the future is a narrowing of his base of support, which will have an effect on his decisions and behavior.

Economically, what happened after the first Gulf War? According to Genieve Abdo, "The regime in the 1990s had no goals for the future beyond its own survival, no demonstrable interest improving the living standard for the average Egyptian, and no plans for pursuing policies that reflected the increasing importance of society's religious values."[47] The middle class has been hit especially hard and can easily be considered in a state of anomie. For example, those professionals who earned degrees decades ago are now finding that as civil engineers, they can only expect a monthly salary of approximately 336 Egyptian pounds, which equates to less than $100. As doctors, they can expect monthly salaries at 332 Egyptian pounds, and as lawyers, about 292 Egyptian pounds, or $85.[48] Abdo recounts that:

> Wherever I went I encountered the deep disillusionment of Egypt's professionals. Most represented the first generation in their families to be educated, and they had made huge sacrifices to get a university degree. They thought it would make a difference. But what was the point of higher education if you could earn more money driving a cab.[49]

While once again Egypt's macroeconomic numbers are positive, they have not been felt by the masses. The lower class's wretched conditions have created a climate of alienation throughout this group as well as in the professional class. This alienation has been exploited by fundamentalists and moderates alike, especially by the Muslim Brotherhood, which represents a moderate political alternative.[50] While the economy revealed growth rates of 5 percent, it did not match the population growth rate. As a result, the per capita income decreased, and by 2001, unemployment was reported at 9 percent, all of which fueled more radicalism.[51]

Furthermore, several events adversely impacted the economy by causing a downturn in tourism. For example, the attacks on tourists in 1997 by Islamic militants in Luxor caused a decrease in tourism. The Asian crisis also exacerbated Egypt's economy. Egypt lost revenues from the Suez Canal due to regional conflict that made the area unattractive for insurance and investment companies. Of course the September 11 attacks caused further decline in tourism for Egypt. A decline in tourism significantly impacts the Egyptian economy; some estimates indicate that tourism represents 10 percent of the country's GDP and project future income from tourism to decline at least by 50 percent.[52] And for Egypt, the timing of the Iraq war came at a very bad time. The economy, which has been depressed for five years, sank even lower a month before the Iraq War, with its currency experiencing a 20 percent devaluation that has increased prices.[53]

With a declining economy, people are looking elsewhere for answers. Some found answers in Saudi Arabia during the 1980s and 1990s when they were forced to look for employment outside Egypt. While working in Saudi Arabia, many were exposed to the extreme conservative religious beliefs in Saudi society and brought those extreme views back to Egypt.[54] The public has overtly criticized the regime, which in some cases has been met by aggressive responses from the Egyptian police. At one point, a crowd attempted to tear down a large picture of Mubarak in front of his party's headquarters.[55] And for the celebrations marking Egypt's fiftieth anniversary in July 2002, "The government had to strain to drum up the carnival atmosphere, however, with cynicism and lack of faith in the system currently at a high because of economic woes made worse after the September 11 attacks and an ossified political system."[56] There still is no succession plan other than speculation that Gamal, Mubarak's son, or Omar Suleiman, Mubarak's intelligence chief, are the contenders.[57] While Mahmud Faksh contends that the historical strength of the state, especially with its military backing, will prevent regime failure, one can only wonder how long Mubarak can play both sides against the middle.[58] According to Saleh Issa, an Egyptian historian and editor of the *al-Qahira*, a weekly paper, "The shelf life of this system has passed, and it doesn't fit with the global system now present in the world."[59]

As the current postwar situation in Iraq continues, the region will continue to suffer. It is the major states in the region—Egypt, Syria, Saudi Arabia, and Iran—that are most concerned about the post-conflict situation in Iraq.[60] Even before 9/11, one observer commented that U.S. policymakers viewed the Arab street as a significant political force and a "new phenomenon of public accountability, which we seldom had to factor into our projections of Arab behavior in the past."[61] George J. Tenet, the Director of Central Intelligence, in February 2001 stated that the "right catalyst—such as the out-break of Israeli-Palestinian violence—can move people to act. Through access to the Internet and other means of communication, a restive public is increasingly able of taking action without any identifiable leadership or organizational structure."[62] The Arab leaders are not only concerned about the power of their people, they are also concerned about what the United States will do next. According to Emad Shaheen, a political science professor at the American University in Cairo, "Arab regimes have a feeling that they may be next."[63]

How Mubarak handles the situation in his own country will be critical to his survival as Egyptians continue to witness post-conflict events in Iraq. But he will also want to receive his usual $2 billion of U.S. aid. Mubarak's middle ground has been to allow anti-American sentiment without alienating the United States.[64] Even with his security apparatus, Mubarak is concerned about internal unrest, so he has encouraged anti-American sentiment in the public. His son, Gamal, even led an antiwar rally of approximately 300,000 participants.[65] However, according to Fouad Ajami,

> The more pro-American the regime, the more anti-American the political class and the political tumult. The United States could grant generous aid to the Egyptian state, but there would be no dampening of the anti-American fury of the Egyptian political class. Its leading state-backed dailies crackled with the wildest theories of U.S.-Israeli conspiracies against their country.[66]

And this point is key to the emerging political significance of the Arab street's influence on the elite. Not only are the political classes affected, but also the very reliable Mubarak support base found in the military. Among junior officers there is growing discontent with Egyptian policies, especially concerning Israel. The junior officers are affected by the public's anti-regime sentiment.[67]

What are the alternative political options for Egyptians—those of the impoverished masses and those of the alienated professional classes—who are fed up with the status quo? Unfortunately, the government's reaction to militant groups has had a de-liberalizing effect on society by suppressing legitimate organizations that could provide a vibrant civil society for Egypt. According to Issa, "The struggle now in the Arab world is between despotic authoritarian regimes and the religious trend. There is no real civilian force with political vitality."[68]

For Egypt, Makram-Ebeid explains, "Relations between the Muslim Brotherhood and the regime will be the most important dynamic to watch."[69] The Brotherhood not only is indigenous to Egypt, but is a powerful regional force. It has branches and followers throughout the Middle East, making it resemble a "transnational, pan-Islamic movement." It is a political movement that protests modernity, corruption, injustice on both a social and economic level, and western influence.[70] In the 2000 preliminary Egyptian parliamentary elections the Muslim Brotherhood did well, perhaps due to the ongoing Palestinian intifada at the time.[71] It was particularly successful at the grassroots level and well-organized, especially in the provincial towns.[72] And Mubarak's party, the NDP, suffered enough of a decline in the 2000 elections to embarrass the regime, though it by no means signaled the regime's downfall.[73] The bottom line is that the Muslim Brotherhood has become woven into the socioeconomic and political life of the region, and specifically in Egypt.[74] And while the mainstream Brotherhood represents a moderate voice, it has grown extremists and radical off-shoots over the years.[75]

In the aftermath of the first Gulf War, there was a rise in violent acts by extremists, namely from Islamic Jama'a and the Jihad organization. Their targets included government officials, Coptic Christians, writers, and tourists. In fact, the targeting of tourism created economic effects that in 1991–1992 resulted in a loss between $700 million to one billion dollars.[76] According to Faksh, there was also a rise in "Islamized spaces" where militants, not the state, control neighborhoods. "These Islamized spaces not only were moral puritan enclaves, but also provided competing networks of social and economic support services that rivaled and even supplanted the inefficient government system."[77] These militants carried and continue to carry an antiregime message. In its pamphlet, "Neglected Duty," the Egyptian Islamic Jihad (EIJ) names the rulers of the Islamic world as its main enemies and challenges the legitimacy of these regimes by calling for mass resistance against them.[78] Rohan Gunaratna refers to Al Qaeda's organization as "the natural off-shoot of the Muslim Brotherhood, a consequence of its political agenda . . . it built on the Brotherhood, drawing on its committed followers, its structures and its experience."[79] He further explains the links among EIJ, Islamic Jihad, and Osama Bin Laden.[80] The networking among these radicalized groups are perhaps the second and third order effects of the Egyptian regime's failure to address its socioeconomic and political underdevelopment. Moreover, as the regime cracked down at home, these groups had to look elsewhere for support. In essence, Egypt exported its terrorists.[81]

The regime's response at home was not limited to militants, but also included legitimate opposition groups. The government used special police forces, relied on military tribunals, and conducted mass executions.[82] In fact, some of the restrictions have hampered secular groups more than the religiously based groups due to loopholes. The religious groups have advantages over secular groups due to availability of mosques and grass-roots network.[83] Also, interestingly, Mubarak has adopted a form of state-sponsored Islam as a counter to the fundamentalists.[84] In the past, forces of nationalism and liberalism tended to counterbalance Islamic revivalism.[85] Mubarak's use of state-sponsored Islamism looks oddly similar to Hafiz Asad's legitimacy formula. Except for Mubarak, in the long term, this may back-fire as he continues to court the United States, but encourage anti-American sentiment. He has helped shift the debate away from secularism, himself. Fawaz Gerges warns that:

Egypt might witness low intensity strife for the foreseeable future unless the government . . . liberalizes further and tackles the roots, not just the symptoms of violence. For now, all that may be said with certainty is that the Egyptian state has militarily defeated this last wave of Islamist insurgency, though with considerable socioeconomic and political costs.[86]

It is true that by 1997, Egypt crushed the militant opposition.[87] But this is more than a military fight; it is a war of ideas. And though al-Jama'a and Jihad militarily lost, they exposed a weak, illegitimate regime that cannot seem to address its people's desperate economic condition and must rely on U.S. aid. In the interim, there has been a shift in state-society; specifically, the culture and, perhaps more significantly for Egypt, many of the elite have been Islamized. If this is true, then the militants have "lost the war but won the debate."[88]

Even with the estimated economic costs of the recent war in Iraq ($6–$8 billion [10 percent of GDP] from the drop in tourism, Suez canal tolls, and exports to Iraq),[89] Mubarak still characteristically took a strong stance on his country's position concerning the United States and the Iraqi war. According to the *Economist*, Mubarak seemed

> to wash his hands of Iraq's fate. . . . Egypt's president has courted American favour even more boldly by inviting Israel's newly returned prime minister, Ariel Sharon, to come on a visit. The move, unprecedented given Mr. Sharon's infamy among Arabs, shocked the Egyptian people.[90]

Interestingly, Mubarak has, again, taken a firm stand on his alignment with the United States concerning the recent war in Iraq. Egypt still strives to be a primary regional player: "Egypt's involvement in the Palestinian-Israeli negotiation has been a vital ingredient of every Palestinian-Israeli agreement since 1993 . . . [and the] Egyptian–Israeli peace treaty remains the cornerstone of the peace process."[91] How long can Egypt rely on U.S. aid and earn its status as regional leader given its dire conditions at home? The dynamics at the global and regional level have a much greater influence on the state legitimacy formula than ever before. The Arab street matters because it is affecting the elite in Egypt. And what happens inside Egypt has grave consequences on the region and the world as well. Mubarak's harsh crackdowns tactically yield results, but in the long term, his actions only further radicalize opposition groups that have brought their fight to the regional and global level. With a contracting support base and a public that is seeking answers, the Mubarak regime is at a crossroads. Winning the war of ideas will require reform at home. As previously noted, the domestic factors must be addressed, but now, it is evident that more is at stake than the Egyptian state and people; the regional and global dynamics make Egyptian reform a regional and global concern.

SYRIA: DOMESTIC

The last case on Syria also discussed events leading up to the Oslo peace process. The findings suggest that whenever he made alignment decisions, Asad had to take into account his country's ethnic divisions and the fact that Syria appeared to be a minority-ruled regime . Subsequently, Asad's decisions really were of a status quo nature, and his decisions were very calculated, cautious, and incremental. Unlike Mubarak, Asad could not rely on a reservoir of legitimacy at home to support bold decisions. Asad, however, proved to be extremely cunning and skilled in managing competing interests, and his Gulf War decision reflected David's concept of omnibalancing. A great deal has happened through the 1990s and the post-9/11 period. Most of all for Syria, Bashar, Asad's son, has taken over as President. This is perhaps the single most significant legitimacy factor for which to account; however, we cannot assess Bashar alone. Once again, it is critical to ask the following: How have the regional and global environments affected the Syrian regime, particularly its legitimacy formula? Do we see Hafiz and then Bashar Asad balancing or bandwagoning with internal threats? After the Gulf War, there was a sense that Syria was opening economically and there were hopeful signs of economic improvement. Could the Sunnis translate economic power into political power? What happened?

Unfortunately, Syria also reflects the problems specified in the United Nations Arab Development Report mentioned earlier. While Syria remains a closed society, it seems that it would be hard pressed to prevent a spill-over effect. In other words, what is happening in the region matters. It is interesting to note, however, that in the course of my research, Syria's citizens once again seem to be omitted from polls and surveys. The excellent Zogby, Gallup, and Pew polls do not include Syria. The opening that seemed to occur right after the first Gulf War appears to have been shut down. The conclusion one could draw from this point is that Bashar is carefully controlling the access to his elite circle and is shutting down avenues for any opposition. How has the confluence of domestic, regional, and international factors affected Syria's legitimacy formula? Can Bashar hold off the regional and global forces?

Before examining Syria under Bashar, it is important to briefly review what occurred through the 1990s. Ray Hinnebusch argues that Hafiz Asad genuinely desired peace as the prime motivation in the 1990s.[92] Patrick Seale explains that for Asad, the regional and international changes that occurred during the 1980s and 1990s, especially Iraq's defeat in 1991, made life difficult for Asad.[93] Asad's view of the peace process was that it should be comprehensively struck on all fronts, not conducted bilaterally, so it was with much reluctance that he entered into the Madrid formula.[94] When Asad witnessed agreements struck by the PLO, Jordan, Morocco, Tunisia, Oman, and Qatar, he wanted to ensure his own regional status. Subsequently, he clenched his fist on Lebanon, reached out to Iran, and worked to sustain his alliance with Egypt and Saudi Arabia. On the international front, he wanted to have an open line with the United States, which he knew was key in the peace process.[95] Asad's position since Madrid had been Israel's complete withdrawal to the pre-1967 war boundaries. And in March 2000, Asad and President Clinton met, but with no results.[96] Syria is one of two countries since Madrid that has not struck an agreement with Israel. Although Lebanon finds itself in this category as well, it has at least seen Israel's unilateral withdrawal during the summer of 2000.[97] Hafiz Asad has remained a mystery. Was peace his main motivation or regime survival? Anthony Cordesman criticizes Asad harshly:

> Hafiz al-Asad was a disaster in every sense for the Syrian people. He spent decades weakening the Syrian economy, failing to come to grips with Syria's population and water problems, wasting vast amounts on arms and engaging in futile military adventures. He then refused a deal with Barak's Israel that would have given him virtually all of the Golan and have inevitably led to a far more stable future for Lebanon. It is easy to forget Asad's prelude to the second intifada, but he must share much of the blame.[98]

Once again, it is difficult to ascertain his motivation, but his regime indeed survived the 1990s. But does it have staying power?

Economically, the early 1990s reflected positive signs. There were new discoveries of oil fields in eastern Syria, Syria received grants after the first Gulf War ($2–$3 billion), and the peace process encouraged foreign investment.[99] But by 1994 these signs became signs of stagnation. Syria's estimated trade deficit stood at $1 billion, and there was a discernible decline in oil revenues, exploration, and international oil prices. A major oil fire at Dayr az-Zur further degraded the oil sector. The economy continued its decline due to decreased subsidies, increased world prices on imports, and an unreliable supply of electricity, which negatively impacted Syria's industry.[100] The main challenge to the economy has been and continues to be Syria's explosive population growth rate of 3.3–3.5 percent. Syria's lack of social services, shortages in water and electricity, and corroding infrastructure all contribute to the increasing signs of extreme poverty on the streets.[101] Unemployment is estimated at approximately 15 percent, which will likely rise given increased regional instability; currently there are 250,000–500,000 Syrians employed in the Gulf states, and 500,000 employed in Lebanon.[102] Moreover, the economy reflects a widening gap between the rich, many of whom are Sunni urban elites, and the poor.[103] With expected decreases in oil revenues and a population growth that has the dubious distinction of being one of the highest in the world, prospects for the economy are grim.[104] And while the recent polls from Zogby do not include Syria, the Lebanese scored the lowest among the other Middle Eastern countries polled (Jordan, Kuwait, Saudi Arabia, United Arab Emirates, Morocco, Egypt, and Israel) in terms of their socioeconomic outlook for the future.[105] The Lebanese response reflects a mood in Syria due to the two countries' close ties and Syrian influence.

Also, Syria's economic policies do not seem to be helping. The government is protecting areas of high rents; in other words, the government is protecting those sectors that support the governing elites and their circles. These sectors have not undergone market reform, allowing key groups, namely the Alawites, peasantry, the Ba'th party, government bureaucrats, and the army and security elites, to benefit.[106] For these groups, reform has come in the form of corruption and has blocked the progress of rational economic policy. Instead, "the game is fixed, with licenses doled out as favors to friends of the regime."[107] Even the Syrian ambassador to France, Ilyas Najamh, boldly criticized the extent of government corruption and Law Number 10, which was designed to encourage foreign investment.[108] What does the future hold? Some Syrian officials look to China as their model of economic reform without political reform; however, whereas in China, there has been less party involvement in economic policy-making and positive outreach to the global market, neither has happened in Syria. While it appears that economic liberalization will pressure the regime for more political openness, some of the elite seem to be operating with blinders.[109] Others believe that economic change, a requirement for peace, will occur slowly and regionally and therefore Lebanon, with its economic potential, will play a key role in Syria's eventual transition and road to economic development.[110]

Has the economic situation affected the composition of the elite? Raymond Hinnebusch claims that after the first Gulf War, the Ba'th Party lost its ideological essence and became a party of patronage, losing much of its autonomous power and influence.[111] The liberalization of the 1990s allowed for more economic and personal freedoms for the bourgeoisie, although without the accompaniment of political power.[112] Asad tried to broaden the support for his regime by including or coopting more businessmen.[113] In fact, many of them, most of whom are Sunni with urban background, have been elected as independents in the People's Assembly. Forty percent of the Assembly's seats are reserved for independents, and the Assembly has taken a larger role in economic policy. This "new" elite group has focused its efforts toward promoting the economic interests of both individuals and groups in ways that coincide with the regime's attempts to advance a more liberal economic agenda.[114]

There have been slight shifts at the elite level beyond the growing role for Sunni elites in the economy, though the tradition of passing power on to sons remains. For example, Alawite officers now represent a new generation at the intermediate level (division command level); these new commanders represent support for Bashar, who is responsible for their promotions. These officers have the "right" family, tribe, and/or religious ties.[115] It appears that corruption has perhaps cemented the ties among the elite and the "new" elite. Eyal Zisser explains that "The predominant trend is still one of continuity coupled with little change. . . . It is equally obvious that, aside from promoting their own sons and confidants as potential successors, the Syrian leadership is not doing very much to address the issue of the 'next generation'."[116] Without real reform, the regime's long-term political stability is at risk.[117] To understand why, one must seriously consider the Arab street, given the global, regional, and domestic forces described earlier.

While it difficult to assess changes among the elite, which appear to be incremental, it is also extremely hard to assess changes occurring among Syria's Arab street. Again, what makes assessment hard is a result of a closed society. However, due to forces described earlier, one can get a glimpse of things to come at least in terms of their impact on Bashar's legitimacy formula. *The Economist*'s recent report showcases the cascading effect of these forces:

> Arab audiences have also been surprised to find that, in contrast to previous wars in the region, their own news channels are proving at least as reliable as western ones. Round-the-clock news stations, such as al-Jazeera, Saudi-owned al-Arabia and Abu Dhabi TV, maintain larger networks of correspondents inside Iraq and rarely flinch from airing graphic content. . . . The second factor is the failure of many Arab governments to provide adequately for their own people. Demonstrators in impoverished Syria are too afraid to criticize their own corrupt regime, whose only proven competence, in any case, seems to lie in diverting criticism to foreign affairs.[118]

Bashar seems to realize the importance of the Arab street, and he is wary of showing too much favor toward the United States. A recent report commented that "As Syria's leader, Bashar Assad, said recently, being America's enemy these days may be dangerous, but being its friend could prove fatal."[119]

Even with Syria's repressive regime, still 500,000 Syrians during poor weather marched through Damascus to protest the 2003 Iraqi war.[120] With the Arab media reporting on regional events, declining socioeconomic conditions, and rising unemployment, it is no wonder that Bashar is concerned about being America's friend. While his father enjoyed the help of the Soviet Union and for awhile the benefits emanating from the first Gulf War, Bashar has neither. Even his military seems questionable. Recently, the *Economist* recounted the joke that Syria cannot withdraw its 20,000 "peacekeeping" troops "because the vintage Soviet trucks cannot make it up the hill." And for its economy, "the main construction activity in the past two decades has been the extension of slums around Damascus."[121] As a frontline state, Hafiz Asad incorporated the Arab-Israeli issue into his legitimacy formula, and with increased media reporting of regional events and the current post-Iraq situation, Bashar has had to consider regional events and their impact on public sentiment. While it is hard to gauge public sentiment, there have been reports, even among elites, that tie the Arab-Israeli situation directly to Syrian legitimacy. Syrian officers and businessmen have lectured or expressed extreme dissatisfaction with the developments concerning the Arab-Israeli situation and feel that Syria has been most affected by what they perceive as U.S. bias toward Israel. Moreover, protests have erupted in Damascus even before the 2003 Iraqi War, especially in response to the second intifada. In fact, the Syrian government, trying to appease the protestors without angering the United States, organized some of these demonstrations in an attempt to keep them more peaceful. Whether or not people were ordered into the streets to demonstrate or simply encouraged, these protests had the blessings of the government as a way to allow the public to vent its anger.[122]

So, is Bashar relying on his father's legitimacy formula? For Hafiz Asad, it had been, as Seale commented, one of creating public consensus, but in its absence, cracking down. And as we discovered in the earlier chapters, Hafiz deftly used a combination of Islam, Arabism, and national sentiment to elicit public support. Arabism is still a more viable sentiment than Syrian nationalism, and regime legitimacy is still tied to Arab nationalism regarding Israel.[123] While being Egyptian for Egypt coincided with its state borders, Syria has always referred to its collective identity beyond state borders. Eberhard Kienle further claims that even with "the cautious attempts more recently to imagine and construct a community of Syrians, [they] will have a long way to go before creating a sense of collective identity similar to that of the Egyptians."[124] Bashar and neighboring King Abdullah in Jordan, who both succeeded their fathers at roughly the same time, were experiencing rising domestic tension when the events of 9/11 occurred. While both leaders initially took measures to politically liberalize their states, they have since cracked down and increased repression by arresting regime opponents and closing political offices. Interestingly, while Syria has edged closer to the United States, it has remained on the U.S. list of terrorist states.[125] For now, it appears that Bashar will have trouble replicating his father's formula without a superpower's aid in the midst of declining socioeconomic conditions, a degraded military, and regional conflict. Definitely, the dynamic of rising extremism or at least the global impact of rising extremism continues to impact Syria, which Bashar must seriously consider as he assesses his regime.

While 9/11 revealed the impact of extremism on the global stage, it certainly is not a new phenomenon to the Middle East and especially to Syria. How has Syria dealt with public sentiment and the extremist Islamic trend in the region? Over the 1990s, there appears to have been some reconciliation between the Islamic movement and the regime through the following: the regime has allowed for greater religious expression; released prisoners of the Islamic movement; allowed elections of Islamic, moderate clerics; and, allowed the return of many who had once fled Syria. Some security officials, though, have worried about the return of former Muslim Brotherhood members. This rapprochement between extremists and the Syrian regime may reflect a growing solidarity of sorts. Syria still represents a firm anti-Israeli and, to some extent, anti-Western stance. Damascus has been a place where leaders of extremist groups could go. Visitors have included Hasan Nasrallah, the secretary general of Hizballah; Husayn Fadlallah, Hizballah's spiritual leader; Hasan Turabi, the leader of the Sudanese Islamic movement; and other radical leaders from around the region. In January 1997, a working paper signed by Ishaq Farhan, the Secretary General of the Jordanian Islamic Action Front, described cooperation between the Ba'th Party and Islamic forces in Jordan. This paper was signed in Damascus. Damascus is also a center for several Palestinian Islamic movements, headquartering the Islamic Jihad and allowing a place for Hamas's information bureau.[126]

Why would a secular regime be so open to religious extremists? Why would extremists want to align with a secular regime? Here, we can recall Louise Richardson who describes the changing nature of state-terrorist group alliances. This alliance may be tactical in nature, and it may be, for the time being, supporting each party's interests. Richardson's ideas about who is controlling whom becomes most interesting if one considers the fact that Syria has very little means in terms of conventional state power to influence the domestic and foreign arenas. Hizballah and the Palestinian groups in Damascus provide Syria with some leverage.[127] From the Syrian view, these organizations are not terrorist groups but liberation groups. Hizballah especially evokes much pride from the Syrian people. It is seen to have caused Israel's unilateral withdrawal, and is therefore a much more effective entity than any state in the region. As one observer noted on a trip through the Bekaa Valley in 2001, "several well-to-do Syrians . . . eagerly donated cash along the roads to youths waving Hizballah flags and collecting money for the group . . . no other group . . . attracted the same level of admiration on the part of private Syrian citizens."[128]

Conflicting views on terrorism is a significant driving factor that has caused perplexing relations between the United States and Syria lately. Patrick Seale's description, and really criticism, of U.S. policy is telling: The U.S. "denounced Hizballah and Hamas as 'terrorist' organizations—rather than recognizing them to be legitimate national resistance movements to Israeli occupation—and refused to remove Syria itself from the State Department list of states allegedly sponsoring terrorism."[129] Herein lie the shades of gray that mark U.S.-Syrian relations. It is a relationship marked by ambiguity: cooperation and denunciation.

Generally, Syrians had a mixed reaction to the news of the 9/11 events. While many felt that the atrocities visited on the Palestinians finally made their way to the United States, there was sympathy for the innocent victims. This reaction came from many who witnessed the effects of radicalism in 1982, as discussed in chapter 5. Interestingly, Syria and the United States started sharing intelligence on Al-Qaeda members, many of whom were once members of the Syrian Muslim Brotherhood. Specifically, Syria shared information on Ma'mun Al-Dirkizili, a former Muslim Brotherhood member, who controlled Al-Qaeda money in Hamburg and met Marwan al-Shehi, one of the hijackers. Syria arrested the Syrian-born Mohammad al-Zumr, one of the recruiters for the 9/11 attacks. The FBI even traveled to Aleppo as part of its investigation of Mohammad Atta, who at one time lived in Syria. Bashar expressed support for the U.S. war on terror, and the United States agreed to Syria's position on the UN Security Council as a rotating member.[130]

Other signs of cooperation included Syria's favorable vote on Resolution 1441. Asad visited London in December 2002, which was the first time a Syrian president visited Great Britain since 1946. Perhaps Asad was preparing for a post-Saddam world; he had low-key discussions with the United States, and he has shown some indication of helping Syria's own Kurdish population. Perhaps he felt he had to offset the negative effects of his continuing support of Palestinian extremists and Hizballah in Lebanon.[131] However, other factors have put negative pressure on U.S.-Syrian relations: the U.S. failure so far to capture Osama Bin Laden; the continuing Israeli-Palestinian conflict; and, Bush's request that Syria crack down on Hizballah and other "resistance" groups centered in Damascus. But as Bush urges Bashar to choose sides, Bashar has allowed operations of these groups to continue.[132] While the United States sees the region and choices in black and white, for Bashar, he is balancing many interests, groups, and issues such that he cannot afford, for his own survival, to view the world in such stark terms.

Before the actual start of the war, Syria was Iraq's only neighboring country to support the idea of a fair trial for Saddam. Some observers feel that Syria's outlook was greatly influenced by its $2 million-per-day oil smuggling operation with Iraq.[133]

But there are other reasons why Syria had an antiwar stance. Syria also had good reason to worry about the Kurds' desire for autonomy; Turkey's actions during the course of the war and postwar; U.S. presence and its effect on Syria's ability to influence Israeli actions; and the effects of regional instability overall.[134] Although Syria and Iraq have had their share of antagonistic relations, they share a great deal in terms of geography, people, secularism, and Arab nationalism. Each country's relationship with the United States has been inconsistent over the years, as well.[135] And it is possible that Bashar feared that his regime would be next after Iraq's defeat.[136]

And perhaps Bashar had good reason to worry. The U.S. Senate passed the Enhanced Border Security and Visa Entry Reform Act, which prevents citizens from terrorist states to study, work, or visit the United States. These countries are Cuba, Iran, Iraq, Libya, Sudan, North Korea, and Syria. Diplomatically, the United States showed disfavor when Vice President Cheney's trip in March 2002 to the Middle East did not include a stop in Damascus; Syria's response was its treatment of Colin Powell; namely, he was not shown the usual respect, and his Syrian counterpart did not display the proper diplomatic protocol to see him off at the airport. And Bush responded by not meeting with Foreign Minister Farouq al-Sharaa when he visited the United States. Furthermore, the United States' reevaluation of its annual $35 million of aid to Lebanon has been another pressure point aimed at Syria.[137]

With these mixed signals of cooperation and denunciation on both sides, it is hard to assess U.S.-Syrian relations. Murhaf Jouejati, a visiting scholar at the Middle East Institute, recently explained that the difficulty of understanding Bashar's decisions is a result of the power struggles within Syria between Bashar and the old guard from the days of his father. According to Jouejati, alignment decisions under Bashar do not reflect the rationality displayed by his father.[138] While there are some reports that Syrians helped Iraq during the war, other reports claim that any such help was not backed by Syria.[139] However, with the fall of Saddam, Syria has responded to U.S. demands. Hamas and Islamic Jihad offices in Damascus are now closed; Syria is turning over suspected Iraqis to the United States, and it is now grudgingly accepting the U.S.-sponsored roadmap.[140] In any case, Bashar seems to be balancing many interests and groups. Whether this balancing act is a reflection of his father's skill or the push and pull of power centers, I believe he will reach a crossroads similar to Mubarak's. *The Economist* sums up the balancing act in terms of Syrian cooperation with America:

> In recent years, Syria has been able to mute American criticism—of the succour it gives to extremist guerilla groups and of its role in Lebanon, among other things—by providing useful intelligence against al-Qaeda. It has also balanced pro-Iraqi rhetoric with quieter support for Iraq's foes, both in backing Resolu-

tion 1441, in the United Nations Security Council and in giving sanctuary to the Iraqi opposition. But Syrian room for manoeuvre, already small, is likely to shrink further.[141]

At the end of the day, it is hard to know exactly what has changed within the Syrian regime. With the confluence of global, regional, and domestic forces, it is doubtful that Bashar will be able to continue his father's status quo approach to regime survival. The continuing socioeconomic despair, regional instability, and a trend toward Islamic extremism can only embolden the Arab street, even in Syria. Just as in Egypt, where internal dynamics have grave effects for the world, Syria is a trouble spot as well. It may not be visible right now, but if the dynamics between state and terrorist groups are changing as Richardson argues, then we should be concerned about Syria, not as a state sponsoring terrorism, but more as a terrorist-sponsored state. Bashar may be forced to make tactical alignment decisions that may keep him in power for the short term, but for the longer term, these decisions may be replicating a Taliban-type situation.

CONCLUSION: PART DEUX

Theoretically, the dynamics observed in the post-9/11 era seem to validate the earlier findings. Regional dynamics directly affect state behavior, specifically by influencing each state's legitimacy formula. Due to the driving forces described earlier, both leaders recognize the Arab street as a potential political force, and they both have found ways to allow their publics to vent anger, especially anti-U.S. sentiment. Both leaders have looked to religion as a means to legitimize their regimes. Unfortunately, this move has increasingly reduced the political dialogue to the religious sphere instead of bolstering the idea of secular government, an alternative, in word and deed.

Asad is continuing his father's cautious, incremental behaviors, with careful (or some would say ambiguous) bandwagoning and balancing behaviors among old guard, coopted Sunni elite, the United States, regional neighbors, and extremist Islamic groups. The challenge for Bashar is that he no longer wields significant military power (or other elements of state power), and he has no superpower or great power backing. In other words, for Bashar, his elements of state power . . . economic, diplomatic, informational, and military . . . are bankrupt. Bashar, I believe, is in a dangerous position. He must still consider the sectarian nature of his regime and populace in the midst of renewed regional conflict and chaos. His leverage to address his internal and external security challenges seems to be his hold on groups such as Hizballah and other militant Islamic groups. The worst scenario for Syria, the region, and the world is to have a Taliban-like situation develop where the terrorist group-state relationship gets turned on its head. This possibility makes the domestic situation in Syria a serious matter for all.

For Mubarak, he is able to take a more firm stand concerning alignment decisions when compared to Syria, but, he too has had to be wary of the regional and global effects on his public and elements of his elite. Mubarak can still count on U.S. aid, and one can argue that Egypt's behavior post-9/11 and the run-up to the 2003 Iraqi war has been one of omnibalancing. Egypt has been able to apply U.S. aid to its economic situation, but mostly to its military and security forces which have cracked down on internal opposition or militant groups. For the short term, these behaviors may seem viable; however, both the crackdowns and the tie to the United States are eroding Mubarak's support base. First, the crackdown has extended beyond the extremist groups, affecting any development of civil society. Second, Mubarak's tie to the United States runs contrary to the public's anti-U.S. sentiment when placed in the context of the regime's legitimacy. While the political community, that is, people feeling Egyptian, continues to be an important factor for Mubarak, it is a resource that cannot be taken for granted. With continued state ineffectiveness and changing challenges to legitimacy, ethnic homogeneity as an important basis for legitimacy may be overwhelmed in the near future. Mubarak and Asad are both at crossroads that have domestic, regional, and global implications.

What 9/11 demonstrated is that what happens on the domestic scene not only affects the proximate region, but it has now a direct global effect. Understanding messy concepts such as state legitimacy is not just an academic exercise. Hardened authoritarian regimes' response to illegitimacy can be harsh crack-downs and/or the embracing of extremist groups. For the region and the world, this means an exportation of terrorism and a safe haven for terrorism, respectively. The problem is that these behaviors are not addressing the roots of the problems. Cordesman contends that "Terrorism, asymmetric warfare and ideological warfare are the symptoms of far more serious population and economic problems, not the disease."[142] I agree with Cordesman, but I also believe that the war of ideas is central. Ideas are critical to building political community, a political culture, and currently that political culture is being Islamized. The problem is that this shift of the political culture does not address the deficits described in the UN's Arab Human Development: "the freedom deficit; the women's empowerment deficit; and, the human capabilities/knowledge deficit relative to income."[143] As addressed earlier, more critical study and policy initiative are required concerning paths toward democracy. For these regimes, the path may not be a U.S.-style path, but it must be one that addresses these tragic deficits.

The rub is that the current regimes may not want to address these deficits because that would require political reform. What they must realize, however, is that political reform is not just a normative quality, it is a "security imperative."[144] It is, therefore, a U.S. interest to facilitate such reform. However, the means to that facilitation is just as important as the ends. There are powerful tools other than force that can help provide incentives for reform. Understanding the basis for regime legitimacy or illegitimacy is a start point to knowing where to begin to at least gain some traction. The United States, if serious about the root causes of terrorism, must reevaluate how best to integrate short-term counterterrorism strategy with long-term foreign policy that addresses these root causes. Ideas, disease, poverty, etc., must be met head-on with soft rather than hard power, but this will take time. It will also require leaders of great courage to stay the course without reaping short-term political benefits. As the world's sole superpower, the United States is best suited for this task, and it surely is the only country that can take such a courageous step. While it may seem only altruistic, at the end of the day it really is key to U.S. national security.

NOTES

1. Stephen M. Walt, "International Relations: One World, Many Theories," *Foreign Policy* (Spring 1998): 1. Accessed on 21 July 2003 at proquest.umi.com.

2. Shibley Telhami, "Understanding the Challenge," *Middle East Journal* (Washington: Winter 2002): 5. Accessed on 1 August 2002 from proquest.umi.com.

3. Michael C. Hudson, "Imperial Headaches: Managing Unruly Regions in an Age of Globalization," *Middle East Policy* (December 2002): 3. Accessed on 21 March 2003 at proquest.umi.com.

4. James Rosenau, "The Complexities and Contradictions of Globalization," in *Understanding International Relations*, ed. Daniel J. Kaufman, Jay Parker, and Kimberly C. Field (New York: McGraw-Hill, 1999), 758–759.

5. "Seeking a National Strategy: A Concert for Preserving Security and Promoting Freedom," *The U.S. Commission on National Security/21st Century* (April 15, 2000), 5.

6. Hudson, "Imperial Headaches," 3.

7. Hans-Henrik Holm and Georg Sorensen, *Whose World Order? Uneven Globalization and the End of the Cold War* (Boulder: Westview Press,), 6–7.

8. Ibid., 5.

9. Jessica T. Mathews, "Power Shift," in *Strategy and Force Planning, 3rd edition*, ed. Strategy and Force Planning Faculty (Newport, RI: Naval War College Press, 2000), 94.

10. Ibid., 94–95.

11. Bruce Hoffman, "Low Intensity Conflict: Terrorism and Guerilla Warfare in the Coming Decades," in *Terrorism: Roots, Impacts, and Responses*, ed. Lance Howard (New York: Praeger, 1992), 139.

12. Jessica Stern, "Will Terrorists Turn to Poison," *Orbis* 37, no. 3 (Summer 1993): 5. Accessed on 23 November 2001 at ehostvgw6.epnet.com. In this article Stern primarily addresses biological and chemical weapons.

13. "A National Security Strategy for a New Century," The White House, December 1999, 2.

14. Mahmud Faksh explains that the 1990–1991 Gulf crisis exposed the illegitimacy and ineffectiveness of past ideologies based on Marxism, liberalism, and secular nationalism. The resultant ineffective policies "turned Muslims inward in search of indigenous ways of life and governance. This, of course, in the context of these societies could only mean Islamization." These points are discussed in Faksh, *The Future of Islam in the Middle East: Fundamentalism in Egypt, Algeria, and Saudi Arabia* (Westport: Praeger, 1997), 24.

15. Mark Jurgensmeyer, *The New Cold War?: Religious Nationalism Confronts the Secular State* (Berkeley: University of California Press,), 23.

16. The failure of secular nationalism's institutions and legitimacy, and the following quote is taken from Jurgensmeyer, 24.

17. This idea of terrorism becoming a political movement comes from Bruce Hoffman, Lecture to the Terrorism Seminar," at West Point, April 2002.

18. Michael Brown, "Introduction," in *The International Dimensions of Internal Conflict*, ed. Michael E. Brown (Cambridge: The MIT Press, 1996), 3.

19. Some of these driving forces were first presented in Cindy R. Jebb, "The Fight for Legitimacy: Liberal Democracy Versus Terrorism," *Journal of Conflict Studies* 23, no. 1 (Spring 2003).

20. There is much written about the debate of what constitutes terrorism. For our purposes here, terrorist activities "have a political purpose, and they are conducted outside normal political bounds, involving symbolic violence usually perpetrated against innocent victims in order to weaken the bonds between the legitimate government and society." See Jebb, 129–130, for further explanation.

21. Louise Richardson, "Global Rebels: Terrorist Organizations as Trans-National Actors," in *Terrorism and Counterterrorism: Understanding the New Security Environment* ed. Russell Howard and Reid Sawyer (Guilford: McGraw-Hill, 2002), 69–71.

22. Richardson, 72–73.

23. Jessica Stern, "The Protean Enemy," *Foreign Affairs* 82, no. 4 (July/August 2003), 28.

24. Ibid., 29 and 32.

25. Bruce Hoffman, "Holy Terror: The Implications of Terrorism Motivated by a Religious Imperative," *Studies in Conflict and Terrorism* 18, no. 4 (October 1995): 280.

26. The application of identifying driving forces in the Middle East was first presented in Ruth M. Beitler and Cindy R. Jebb, "Egypt as a Failing State: Implications for U.S. National Security," *Occasional Paper #51*, Institute of National Security Studies, July 2003. The authors used Peter Schwartz, "The Art of the Long View," *Strategy and Force Planning*, 2nd edition, ed. Strategy and Force Planning Faculty (Newport: Naval War College Press, 1997): 29–44. Schwartz explains the process of scenario development by identifying driving forces, predetermined elements and critical uncertainties in a business environment so as to better anticipate second and third order effects of one's decisions and actions.

27. According to "Al-Jazeera: Arabs Rate its Objectivity," Gallup Tuesday Briefing, 23 April 2002, 1. Accessed 10 July 2002 from www.gallup.com, "Al Jazeera boasts a regular viewership of some 35 million Arabs in its primarily Middle East market, as well as hundreds of thousands of viewers in the United States and Europe."

28. "Tom Friedman and Bill Kristol Discuss Violence in the Middle East," interview by Tim Russert on *Meet the Press*, 17 March 2002. Accessed on 6 August 2002 from web.lexis-nexis.com.

29. Telhami, 2.

30. Augustus Richard Norton discusses the Arab street's sentiments, especially with, at the time of his writing, the prospects for war in Iraq, in Norton, "America's Approach to the Middle East: Legacies, Questions, and Possibilities," *Current History: A Journal of Contemporary Affairs* 101, no. 651 (January 2002): 5.

31. Philip Smucker, "Egypt's Unrest a Two-Edged Sword," *Christian Science Monitor* (8 April 2002): 2. Accessed on 22 July 2002 at ehostvgw.com.

32. James J. Zogby, *What Arabs Think: Values, Beliefs and Concerns* (Zogby International/Arab Thought Foundation, September 2002), 33.

33. Telhami, 4.

34. Tim Russert cites this poll in "Tom Friedman and Bill Kristol Discuss Violence in the Middle East," 2.

35. "The Ten Nation Impressions of America Poll," Zogby International, 11 April 2002, 68. Accessed 31 July 2002 at interactive.zogby.com/clickon/products.dbm. Note that in this same poll, Iran had almost no support at all.

36. *Arab Human Development Report 2002: Creating Opportunities for Future Generations* (New York: United Nations Development Programme), 11. Accessed on 28 July 2002 from www.undp.org/rbas/ahdr/bychapter.html.

37. Anthony Cordesman, "Arab-U.S. Strategic Cooperation: A Net Assessment," *Middle East Policy* (December 2002): 5. Accessed on 21 March 2003 at proquest. umi.com.

38. *Arab Human Development Report*, 2.

39. Hudson, 5–6.

40. Ibid., 6.

41. Oliver Roy, *The Failure of Political Islam* (Cambridge: Harvard University Press, 1994), 110. Note that Roy's argument is that the nation-state structure will prevail over ideological forces: "Thus the impact of Islamism . . . is essentially socio-cultural: it marks the streets and customs but has no power relationship in the Middle East," in Roy, 131. Also, the Egyptian leader of the Muslim Brotherhood since 1986 is Muhammad Hamid Abu-Nasr, found in Roy, 111.

42. Ibid., 122.

43. The evidence of alliances is from Stern, "The Protean Enemy," 32, and the quote is from ibid, 33.

44. Jessica Stern explains that Al-Qaeda is close to developing such weapons, and will most likely work with other groups toward that end in Stern, "The Protean Enemy," 39.

45. Abdel Moneim Said Aly and Robert H. Pelletreau, "U.S.-Egyptian Relations," *Middle East Policy* (June 2001): 10. Accessed on 10 June 2003 at proquest.umi.com.

46. This argument was first made in Beitler and Jebb.

47. Geneive Abdo, *No God But God: Egypt and the Triumph of Islam* (Oxford: Oxford University Press, 2000), 76.

48. Ibid., 82.

49. Ibid.

50. Farwaz Gerges, "The End of the Islamist Insurgency in Egypt?: Costs and Prospects," *The Middle East Journal* (Autumn 2000), 5. Accessed on 10 June 2003 at proquest.umi.com.

51. Beitler and Jebb, 21.

52. Ibid., 22.

53. "Special Report: Damning and Damned; Arab Protest," *The Economist*, March 29, 2003, 2. Accessed 30 March 2003 at proquest.umi.com.

54. Diane Singerman, "The Politics of Emergency Rule in Egypt," *Current History: a Journal of Contemporary Affairs* 101, no. 651 (January 2002): 34.

55. "Special Report: Damning and Damned; Arab Protest," 2.

56. Andrew Hammond, "Egypt's Deep-Sixed 1954 Constitution a Reminder of What Might Have Been," *The Washington Report on Middle East Affairs* (September/October 2002), 1–2. Accessed on 10 June 2003 at proquest.umi.com.

57. Hammond, 3.

58. Faksh, 57.

59. Hammond, 3.

60. Stanley Reed, Susan Postlewaite, and Neal Sandler, "How the Arab World is Already Changing Governments are Scurrying to Ride Out—or Profit from—Saddam's Fall," *Business Week*, March 24, 2003, 2. Accessed on 30 March 2003 at proquest.umi.com

61. Author cites Edward S. Walker, "The New U.S. Administration's Middle East Policy Speech," *Middle East Economic Survey* 44, no. 26 (June 25, 2001), in Dale F. Eickelman, "Bin Laden, the Arab 'Street,' and the Middle East's Democratic Deficit," *Current History: A Journal of Contemporary World Affairs* 101, no. 651 (January 2002): 38.

62. Eikelman, 38.

63. Reed, Postlewaite, and Sandler, 2.

64. Ibid.

65. Ibid.

66. Fouad Ajami, "The Sentry's Solitude," *Foreign Affairs* 80, no. 6 (November/December 2001): 9.

67. As first cited in Beitler and Jebb, 48, interviews of several high ranking officials and analysts by Beitler and Jebb confirm this point. Also authors' interviews of Sarah Daly, analyst at Rand, interviewed 25 July 2002, and Mr. Muhammad Hakki, former editor of the Egyptian paper *Al-Ahram*, interviewed 26 July 2002, confirms this erosion of Mubarak's elite support base.

68. Hammond, 2.

69. Mona Makram-Ebeid, "Egypt's 2000 Parliamentary Elections," *Middle East Policy* (June 2001): 8. Accessed 10 June 2003 at proquest.umi.com.

70. Faksh, 43.

71. Makram-Ebeid, 4.

72. Ibid.

73. Ibid., 8. The author provides an optimistic view that "These losses may in fact offer a convenient opportunity to undertake 'housecleaning' that the younger generation of party leaders, specifically President Mubarak's son Gamal, has called for."

74. Gerges, 6. The author describes the Brotherhood in terms of its socioeconomic influence.

75. Faksh, 44.

76. Ibid., 49.

77. Ibid., 49–50, quote from ibid., 50.

78. Michael G. Knapp, "The Concept and Practice of Jihad in Islam," *Parameters* (Spring 2003), 5. Accessed on 1 July 2003 at proquest.umi.com.

79. Rohan Gunaratna, *Inside Al-Qaeda: Global Network of Terror* (New York: Berkeley Books, 2002), 128–129.

80. Gunaratna, 34.

81. This idea of exporting terrorists is from Sarah Daly, political analyst at Rand, 25 July 2002, Washington, D.C., as first cited in Beitler and Jebb, 31–32. She also commented that as these terrorists are hunted down outside Egypt, at some point, they will return. Also, Singerman states that "Despite Egyptian and Saudi claims that they have vanquished the violent Islamist threat, they have also fragmented, radicalized, and militarized the movement, inducing any survivors to leave the country," in Singerman, 34.

82. Faksh, 50.

83. Makram-Ebeid, 7.

84. Faksh, 52–53.

85. Faksh, 43.

86. Gerges, 5.

87. Ibid., 1.

88. Ibid., 5.

89. "International: Saddam's Summer Friends: Iraq's Neighbors," *The Economist*, February 8, 2003, 2. Accessed on 21 March 2003 at proquest.umi.com.

90. Ibid.

91. Ambassador Pelletreu as quoted in, "U.S.-Egyptian Relations," *Middle East Policy* 8, no. 2 (June 2001). Accessed on 23 July 2002 at proquest.umi.com.

92. Raymond A. Hinnebusch, "Does Syria Want Peace? Syrian Policy in the Syrian-Israeli Peace Negotiations," *Journal of Palestine Studies* 26, no. 1 (Autumn 1996), 42.

93. Patrick Seale, "Obituary: Hafez al-Assad: Feared and Respected Leader who Raised Syria's Profile but was Ultimately Unable to Contain Israel," *The Guardian* (June 12, 2000), 3. Accessed 29 July 2003 at proquest.umi.com (1–4).

94. Ibid.

95. Ibid.

96. "Israel, Syria and that Sliver of the Galilee Shore," *The Economist*, 30 May 2000, 1. Accessed on 18 July 2003 at www.economist.com.

97. P. R. Kumaraswamy, "The Israel-Syrian Peace Talks: 1991–1996 and Beyond," *Journal of Third World Studies* 19, no. 2 (Fall 2002): 1. Accessed on 29 July 2003 at proquest.umi.com.

98. Cordesman, "Arab-U.S. Strategic Cooperation: A Net Assessment," 3.

99. Eyal Zisser, "Syria at a Crossroads," *Syria: Domestic Political Stress and Globalization: Data and Analysis Series,* Moshe Dayan Center for Middle East and African Studies, Paper #64 (February 2002), 22.

100. Hisham Melham, "Syria Between Two Transitions," *Middle East Report: Lebanon and Syria: The Geopolitics of Change,* no. 203 (Spring 1997), 3.

101. Zisser, "Crossroads," 21.

102. Ibid., 24.

103. Ibid., 23.

104. Melham discusses the high population growth in Melham, 3, and Paul Rivlin discusses the reasons for pessimism in Rivlin, "The Syrian Economy in the 1990s," *Syria: Domestic Political Stress and Globalization: Data and Analysis Series,* Moshe Dayan Center for Middle East and African Studies, Paper #64 (February 2002), 59.

105. Zogby, 44.

106. Rivlin, 60.

107. Melham, 3. Melham cites John Lancaster, "Syria's Economy Starting to Slow," *The Washington Post,* October 9, 1994.

108. Ibid., 6.

109. Rivlin makes the comparison with China in Rivlin, 59. Melham, 2.

110. Melham, 5.

111. Hinnebusch, 45.

112. Ibid., 46.

113. Ibid.

114. Zisser, "Crossroads," 12.

115. Ibid., 11.

116. Zisser, "Crossroads," 13.

117. Ibid., 14.

118. "Special Report: Damning and Damned; Arab Protest, 2.

119. Ibid.

120. Ibid., 1.

121. "Fierce Words, Tied Hands," *The Economist,* 3 April 2003, 2. Accessed on 18 July 2003 at www.economist.com.

122. Michael B. Meyer, in interviews or in broader forums, describes Syrian officers' and businessmen's views concerning the Arab-Israeli situation, and he provides several accounts of significant demonstrations in Damascus in Brent J. Talbot and Michael B. Meyer, "View From the East: Arab Perceptions of the United States Presence and Policy," *INSS Occasional Paper #48,* February 2003, 51–53 and 62–64.

123. Hinnebusch, 48.

124. Eberhard Kienle, "Arab Unity Schemes Revisited: Interest, Identity, and Policy in Syria and Egypt," *International Journal of Middle East Studies* 27, no. 1 (February 1995): 53. The quote is from Kienle, 68.

125. Mustapha Kamel Al-Sayyid, Bahman Baktiari, Michael Barnett, Sonja Hegasy, et al., "The Impact of 9/11 on the Middle East," *Middle East Policy* (December 2002), 10. Accessed on 21 March 2003 at proquest.umi.com.

126. Zisser, "Crossroads," 16–17.

127. The idea of these groups providing Syria with some leverage is taken from P. R. Kumkaraswamy's review of Helena Cobban's book, *The Israeli-Syrian Peace Talks: 1991–1996 and Beyond,* in Kumkaraswamy, 2.

128. These perceptions and the quote are taken from Meyer, 57.

129. Seale, 4.

130. Sami Moubayed, "Yesterday's Friends Today are the Enemies of America," *The Washington Report on Middle East Affairs* 21, no. 9 (December 2002): 2. Accessed on 29 July 2003 at proquest.umi.com.

131. "International: Mr. Assad Goes to London: Syria, Iraq, and Britain," *The Economist,* December 14, 2002, 2. Accessed on 21 March, 2003 at proquest.umi.com.

132. Moubayed, 3.

133. "International: Saddam's Summer Friends: Iraq's Neighbors," 2.

134. Homayra Ziad, "Syrian Policy Expert Says U.S. Threat Not Serious," *The Washington Report on Middle East Affairs* 22, no. 6 (July/August 2003), 1–2. Accessed on 29 July 2003 at proquest.umi.com.

135. "Fierce Words," 1.

136. Reed, Postlewaite, and Sandler, 4.

137. Moubayed, 3.

138. Ziad, 2.

139. Reports of Syrian aid are from "Please Sir, We Really Didn't," *The Economist,* 29 May 2003, 2. Accessed on 18 July 2003 at www.economist.com, and claims that any help was not sanctioned by the Syrian regime are from Ziad, 2.

140. "Please Sir, We Really Didn't," 2.

141. "Fierce Words," 1.

142. Cordesman, 5.

143. *Arab Human Development Report 2002,* 27.

144. Jebb, "The Fight for Legitimacy," 143.

Appendix

Theory

The purpose of this appendix is to provide the theoretical underpinnings of this study. It will demonstrate the theoretical bridge between the international relations and comparative politics fields, which will help us better understand state alignment. I found that drawing upon literature from complementary fields academically exciting because of the insights gained by viewing an issue from multiple perspectives. Steven R. David's theory of omnibalancing provides a nice bridge between the international and comparative politics fields, thus demonstrating the significance of the nature-of-the-state level of analysis and the systems level of analysis. I begin with the systems theorists and trace the theoretical critiques and developments from the systems level of analysis to the comparativists' analyses of the state, concluding with the literature on ethnicity and legitimacy.

David's theory of omnibalancing draws heavily from Steven M. Walt's theory of state alignment, which is rooted in NeoRealism. Consequently, the next section begins with a discussion on Kenneth N. Waltz, Robert Gilpin, and Walt, as the premier Cold War era systems theorists. Next, I will look at Jack Snyder's *Myths of Empires* and Barry Posen's *Sources of Military Doctrine* because both works modify Realism's assumption that the state is a unitary, rational actor; however, these authors confine their cases to the great powers. Paul Schroeder, and Randall L. Schweller as they provide some thoughts on how best to explain state behavior in the post–Cold War era. Specifically, their work calls for analyses of the nature of the state. These authors focus on weak states rather than the great powers, and thus they challenge Realism's superpower bias. I will pay particular attention to David's work on omnibalancing.

My focus on weak, nonwestern states will lead to a brief review of some of the comparative literature before I focus my discussion on ethnicity as the basis for internal threats to a regime. Here, I expand on David's work because he stresses the importance of internal threats without clearly defining those threats. I explore the definitions of ethnicity because it is an imprecise and ambiguous term, and I clarify, for the purposes of this study, its definition. Finally, I end my theoretical discussion by demonstrating the relationship between ethnicity and state legitimacy.

COLD WAR SYSTEMS THEORISTS

As mentioned earlier, I will focus my discussion on Waltz, Gilpin, and Walt as they form the basis of systems theory and state alignment. This section reviews the characteristics of the Cold War and post–Cold War eras because understanding these contexts may help us determine the significance or relevance of systems theory vis-à-vis nature-of-the-state or comparative politics theories.

It is important to start this discussion with a brief reminder of the definition and purpose of theory. Although at first glance this process may seem elementary, it is really the key to any further analysis. One must have a firm understanding of theory as an analytical tool before any meaningful analysis can occur. According to Waltz, "theories explain laws."[1] Laws are "facts of observation" and theories ". . . are speculative processes introduced to explain them. . . . Laws remain, theories come and go."[2] Waltz takes a Kantian approach, and claims that a theory's explanatory power increases as the theory moves away from reality. "A theory, though related to the world about which explanations are wanted, always remains distinct from the world."[3] Finally, Waltz admits that theory does not explain everything, only those things of the utmost importance.[4] Specifically, "within a system, a theory explains continuities. . . . not change."[5] As we shall see, Waltz's view of theory becomes his strongest and weakest asset as we apply his systems theory to the post–Cold War era.

To determine a theory's usefulness, I will use J. David Singer's requirements of theory: that it provide description, explanation and prediction.[6] A theory's ability to satisfy these theoretical requirements will vary for many reasons. I will specifically look at systems theory's viability in the Cold War and post–Cold War eras. Systems theory may help us understand state behavior without explaining the reason for that behavior. Finally, we may find that in the context of the post–Cold War era, the theories on the nature of the state may become more useful for description, explanation, and prediction than the systems theory.

COLD WAR ERA

John Lewis Gaddis's article, "The Long Peace," provides a good description of the Cold War era.[7] Gaddis's description of the Cold War era is from a superpower perspective. I recognize and appreciate the arguments against such a perspective, especially concerning the "peacefulness" of this era, but one cannot discount the tremendous influence the superpowers have had on world affairs as compared to any other nations.[8] Regardless of one's perspective, however, there are still concrete facts that are indisputable. Gaddis points to the bipolar nature of the era with the United States and the Soviet Union as the dominant powers. This bipolarity began after World War II and continued for the next four decades. Nuclear weapons characterize this era as does the durable alliance system.[9]

Gaddis describes this period as stable. He cites Karl Deutsch and Singer, who describe stability as "the probability that the system retains all of its essential characteristics: that no single nation becomes dominant; that most of its members continue to survive; and that large-scale war does not occur."[10] The stabilizing factors include nuclear weapons which deter war and allow the United States and the Soviet Union to solve crises without going to war with each other. Gaddis coins the phrase, "reconnaissance revolution"[11] to describe the ability of the superpowers to know each other's capabilities. This knowledge also contributes to stability by making a surprise attack almost unfeasible, and, therefore, highly unlikely. The superpowers adhere to the "rules of the game"[12] which are implicitly acknowledged behavioral norms that encourage stability. These norms include a respect for spheres of influence, avoidance of direct confrontation, use of nuclear weapons only as a last resort, preference for "predictable anomaly over unpredictable rationality"[13] (examples of anomalies include the division of Germany and Korea), and the refusal to undermine each other's leadership.[14]

Gaddis also claims that the maintenance of the Cold War era system, bipolarity, was in the interest of both superpowers, so they encouraged those actions that fostered the status quo. Lastly, the superpowers were able to lay aside ideological differences in order to preserve order.[15] John J. Mearsheimer agrees with Gaddis concerning the stability of the Cold War era. He sees bipolarity, an equal balance of military power, and nuclear weapons as contributors to peace. Additionally, he cites the rigid alliance system and the lack of hypernationalism as essential factors to the maintenance of peace.[16] I will use these authors' views as a baseline, although I acknowledge the concerns of those scholars who challenge the assertion that the Cold War era was peaceful.

POST–COLD WAR ERA

What is the post–Cold War era? It appears to be unsettled. Certainly, we can say that bipolarity has diminished and we are in a unipolar world, with the United States as the major world power, a multipolar world, or a uni-multipolar world.[17] We are seeing a change in the nature of the alliance system with the end of the Warsaw Pact. Eastern Europe is attempting to democratize itself, and the fate of the republics of the former Soviet Union is yet to be determined. We engaged in our first post–Cold War era war in the Persian Gulf, with that region still searching for some sort of stability. President Bush called for a new world order, using vague notions of a peaceful family of nations providing a secure, peaceful world, and President Clinton has searched for a defining view of the world, with mixed results. How does theory help us understand our world and help predict state behavior?

THEORETICAL CONSIDERATIONS

Waltz, through his theory of NeoRealism, provides one way to view state behavior. NeoRealism's three assumptions are that the international system is anarchic; the basic unit of analysis is the state and it is a unitary, rational actor; and power and survival are the overriding concerns of these states. Specifically, Waltz defines international politics by its anarchical nature, the sameness of the states' functions, and the distribution of capabilities among the states. Let us look at each assumption. First, for Waltz, anarchy is not chaos, but rather that none of the units or states ". . . is entitled to command; none is required to obey. International systems are decentralized and anarchic."[18] There is no world government that enforces law and order. Waltz assumes that in this anarchical system states seek survival. "The survival motive is taken as the ground of action in a world where the security of states is not assured."[19] Waltz does not say that states act only to preserve their survival; instead, they may prefer amalgamation with other states.[20] I feel this is a fair assumption because as Waltz claims, "Survival is a prerequisite to achieving any goals that states may have."[21]

Part two of the definition concerns the function of states. The states that are the units of international-political systems are not formally differentiated by the functions they perform. Anarchy entails relations of coordination among a system's units, and that implies their sameness. So, international anarchy causes the function of the states to be the same. Waltz defends the use of the state as a unit of the international system because it is its interaction that forms the structure of the international system. He recognizes the existence of non-state actors, but asserts that the state, being the major actor, defines the structure of the system. Non-state actors, such as transnational movements, are among the processes that exist within the system; they do not constitute structure. The functions of the states are the same; their capability to perform those functions is what varies.[22]

Finally, because states are functionally the same, we must look to their differing capabilities as their mark of distinction. This systemic distribution of capabilities determines the structure of the system as well as its behavior and outcomes. This structure is Waltz's guiding principle. It is the core of Waltz's theory since it is the only characteristic of the system that varies; anarchy and states' functions are not as vulnerable to change.[23] From this point, Waltz goes on to discuss balance of power and polarity as the behavior and outcomes of the system because all states strive for power and survival.

According to Waltz, a balance of power occurs ". . . wherever two, and only two, requirements are met: that the order be anarchic and that it be populated by units wishing to survive."[24] Waltz's definition of the system fulfills these requirements, so the balance of power is an inevitable occurrence. This balance occurs differently in a bipolar world than in a multipolar world. The great powers in a bipolar system balance each other using internal methods: that is, relying on themselves. Great powers of multipolar systems rely on external methods of balancing, namely the realignment of coalitions. Self-reliance is a more reliable method of balancing than the external method, which relies on others.[25] This notion coincides with Gaddis and Mearsheimer's views concerning the rigidity of the bipolar Cold War alliance system. The alliance system of the Cold War was not fluid; nations did not cross over from one alliance to another. This rigidity of alliances and the superpowers' internal method of balancing, both contributed to the stability of that era.

Waltz links the system's stability with the great powers of the system and claims that the bipolar system provides the most stability of any other system. Waltz's justification for this stability is similar to those reasons as cited above by Gaddis and Mearsheimer. Waltz claims that, "with only two great powers, both can be expected to act to maintain the system."[26] It is easier to deal with just one other power than with many.[27] Each power knows its adversary; this knowledge is not evident in a multipolar world.[28] Waltz also claims that nuclear weapons do not alone set the great powers apart, rather, their ". . . ability to exploit military technology on a large scale and at the scientific frontiers" sets them apart.[29] Clearly, Waltz does not see nuclear weapons constituting a systems change. Certainty, rather than uncertainty, distinguishes the bipolar system from the multipolar system.

It is easy to see how Waltz's bipolar system reflects the Cold War era. How does it help us look at the post–Cold War era? Surely, there has been a redistribution of capabilities, with the United States seemingly more power-ful than its former Cold War adversary. If we assume the continuing anar-chical nature of the international system described by Waltz, then a world government cannot exist due to its inherent hierarchical nature. The end of the Persian Gulf crisis marked the rise of the United States as the sole world leader, but this temporary unipolar situation does not suggest the existence of world government. Surely, we have not reached that stage. In fact, it ap-pears that the glimpse of unipolarity now will soon pass into multipolarity.[30] Perhaps the balance of power, which naturally occurs in an anarchical sys-tem, prevents the permanence of a unipolar world. The balance of power would ensure that no one nation would become too powerful. According to Waltz's argument, multipolarity characterizes the post–Cold War era. The United States faces competition, namely on the economic front, from Japan and Europe. Surely, they have the technology and are on the "scientific fron-tiers" to challenge the United States. Due to the temporal nature of unipo-larity and the imminence of multipolarity, we will focus our discussion on multipolarity in the post–Cold War era.

What does a multipolar world hold for us? According to Waltz, it is an un-certain world and, therefore, an unstable world. Recent events support this claim of instability. The Persian Gulf War did not cause the usual bipolar op-posing alignments of the United States and the Soviet Union. The Soviet Union's minimal involvement failed to temper Iraq's actions, which may have contributed to the United States' inability to anticipate Iraq's actions correctly. The lack of "rules of the game" and uncertainty marked this con-flict. The old bipolar alignments might have prevented this crisis, or at least perhaps its escalation. Both superpowers, adhering to the rules of the game, would have worked to keep their respective clients under control. It would have been in neither power's interest to provoke a situation that might esca-late to either superpower confrontation or, as a worst case scenario, nuclear war.

A multipolar world suggests changing coalitions. Already we have seen the dissolution of the Warsaw Pact, and the future of NATO to include criteria for membership and missions is an ongoing debate. We have witnessed fluid coalitions in the Middle East, with the United States courting Syria, a notable past enemy, during the Gulf crisis. This new courtship was especially unique since Syria had been the Soviet Union's staunchest Middle Eastern ally dur-ing the Cold War era.[31] Will the United States be fighting Syria in the next Gulf crisis? The end of the Cold War perhaps facilitated the United States's flexibility to court Syria because either the Soviet Union did not feel threat-ened by this action or it could not respond to it. These changing coalitions, or reliance on external balancing, is less reliable than the internal balancing inherent in a bipolar world. This flexible alliance system is another element of uncertainty in the post–Cold War era.

Uncertainty also plagues the non-superpowers. Client nations of the Cold War era could count on their superpower's support. They could safely assume that nuclear weapons would not be used, as their nonuse was one of the rules of the game. A superpower's involvement in a smaller nation's affairs would not escalate into a world war for fear of nuclear reprisals. Generally, the superpowers acknowledged each other's spheres of influence. This acknowledgment is not present in a multipolar world. Does this mean that escalation is more probable? Outcomes seem more unpredictable for non-superpowers as in the case with Iraq, discussed earlier.

Clearly, Waltz provides us with a suitable context in which to work, that context being the uncertainties of a multipolar world in the post–Cold War era. It is as important, though, to understand what Waltz fails to provide. Just as Waltz's definition of theory may help to describe, explain, and predict events on a large scale (although he did not help us predict the end of the Cold War or the collapse of the Soviet Union), it fails, by its own definition, to describe, explain, and predict particular events. Additionally, also through self-definition, it fails to describe, explain, and predict change, thus perhaps failing to properly analyze events leading to the end of the Cold War.[32] Waltz claims that theory needs to be removed from reality to best explain it. Although this break from reality serves its purpose well on a grand scale and also benefits both scholars and policymakers by contributing to their world views with its profound tenets of realism, it fails to provide Singer's requirements on a small scale; it misses reality, that is, specific events that impact the international system. It is these particular events that concern us because it is in these particular or "small" scale events that lives are lost, nations destroyed, and tears shed. While it is important to understand the big picture, it is equally important to understand the smaller picture because this smaller picture is changing the big picture.

Waltz's NeoRealism fails on another account: it fails to provide policymakers with manipulable variables.[33] While he does suggest change based on a change in the system's distribution of capabilities, he does not provide us with a way of evaluating such change. Waltz's theory is one of continuity, not change. The system constrains behavior; it does not offer a plan of action. We expect policymakers to actively pursue our nation's interests, not sit back and let the system determine state behavior. We need manipulable variables to make a positive impression on world events. Also, policymakers need to know how systems change. Waltz only explains why systems remain and continue. Policymakers of non-superpowers who are unsatisfied with the status quo want to specifically know how and what makes a system change. They need to know more than that a change in the distribution of capabilities occurred; they need to know how that change occurred and what its impact will be.

Another systems theorist, Gilpin, helps us understand why systems change, whereas Waltz only deals with system continuity. Gilpin, although a realist, does look to the internal workings of the state to determine system change. Gilpin sees the relationship between the public and private sector in a state as being crucial to the potential cause for international change. "If the growth and expansion of the state and the interests of powerful groups are complementary, then there exists a strong impetus for the state to expand and try to change the international system."[34] Secondly, a society might encourage individuals or groups to contribute to the state in such a way as to influence that state's tendency to expand its control in the international system. Also, the nature of the regime may determine the character of its citizenry; this character may influence a state's success in the international arena.[35]

Gilpin, perhaps, helps better understand the change from the Cold War to post–Cold War eras by asking questions about the state. For example, as we search for answers about the Persian Gulf War, we might ask, Did the interests of Iraq's elite complement that state's expansion? Perhaps they did, although Iraq was most likely seeking to change the region, not the international system. A post–Cold War era question might be, Does Japan's competitiveness encourage its citizens to contribute to the state through their hard work, especially in business? Other incentives, such as nationalism, ideology, and religion, promise rewards for their adherents. For example, nationalism can persuade people to sacrifice their lives for the good of the state.[36] Additionally, a fanatically religious regime can promise martyrdom for those loyal subjects who die in battle. These domestic attributes may influence a state's growth and expansion and perhaps even change in the international system.

Gilpin also describes domestic factors that cause political decline, thus influencing a system change: ". . . every society eventually declines following the erosion of its economic base."[37] The economy may decline due to the rising cost of the military. Public and private consumption may outpace the gross national product. The service sector may develop as the predominant sector of the economy, thus lowering the rate of productivity. We only needed to look at the Soviet economy to understand its problems, especially in the 1980s. The Soviet State Planning Committee in 1990–91 predicted that the Soviet GNP would decline 11.6 percent in 1991; the previous year, the GNP fell by 3 percent. Additionally, the committee predicted that industrial production would fall 15 percent and agricultural output by 5 percent.[38] Perhaps if we had better understood this economic decline, we would have been able to predict the demise of the Soviet state.

Gilpin views the loss of control of economic, political and social developments, and the inability of a superpower to play a balancing role as destabilizing factors in the international system. He views the domestic stability of the superpowers as essential to a stable international system.[39] Clearly, the economic problems with which Gorbachev wrestled created difficult political problems for him. Nationalism was on the rise, and the Soviet Republics were demanding independence or at least a loosening of Kremlin control. Additionally, the United States's insistence on pursuing the Strategic Defense Initiative (SDI) emphasized the relationship of technology and power. Technology, not just numbers of missiles, is a critical component of national power. The Soviets realized that although they could quantitatively compete with the United States, they were unprepared to qualitatively compete on an entirely new technological level.[40] These developments in the Soviet Union may have helped explain the system change or the end of bipolarity in the post–Cold War.

Walt expands upon Waltz's idea of balance of power in his book *Origins of Alliances*. Walt uses alliances in the Middle East to explain his theory. Key to Walt's theory on balancing versus bandwagoning is his definition of the threat. According to Walt, "By defining the basic hypotheses in terms of threats rather than power alone, we gain a more complete picture of the factors that statesmen will consider when making alliance choices."[41] Walt provides four factors that affect threat level: aggregate power, geographic proximity, offensive power, and aggressive intentions.[42] Threat perception is a critical notion. Perhaps ethnicity affects a nation's predisposition in its threat assessment of another state. Threat assessment is critical for understanding balancing and bandwagoning behaviors. I will discuss this point in my *Indicators of Causality* section.

Through his case study analysis, Walt develops several hypotheses which help explain and predict a state's tendency to either balance against a threat or bandwagon with the threat. Walt claims that the conditions for balancing are the following:

1. Balancing is more common than bandwagoning.
2. The stronger the state, the greater its tendency to balance. Weak states will balance against other weak states but may bandwagon when threatened by great powers.
3. The greater the probability of allied support, the greater the tendency to balance. When adequate allied support is certain, however, the tendency for free-riding or buck-passing increases.
4. The more unalterably aggressive a state is perceived to be, the greater the tendency for others to balance against it.
5. In wartime, the closer one side is to victory, the greater the tendency for others to bandwagon with it.[43]

The bottom line is that balancing occurs more often than bandwagoning, which of course has many foreign policy implications, i.e., if a country does not want others to balance against it, then it will have a benevolent and restraining type of foreign policy. If a country sees bandwagoning as the predominant form of alignment, then the country will have an aggressive, competitive foreign policy.[44] As with Waltz, Walt has a superpower bias that we must address.

Theories that examine the nature of the state may help fill the gaps left by systems theory. Additionally, these theories may help us overcome the superpower bias of the systems or NeoRealist theorists. Waltz provides an uncertain multipolar world as the context for world politics. How do states behave in this multipolar system, and how does state behavior affect that system? Gaddis advocates the "consumerist" approach, that is, to critically choose those theories that together help explain events.[45] Other scholars are modifying Realism's assumptions to describe, explain, and perhaps even better predict state behavior.

MODIFYING REALISM'S ASSUMPTIONS

Both Snyder and Posen offer approaches to the study of state behavior which modify Realism's assumption that the state is a unitary, rational actor. In Snyder's *Myths of Empire*, he attempts to explain why some great powers tend toward overextension. He discusses the central myth of overexpansion, which is that expansion enhances state security. This myth actually benefited certain domestic coalitions. This discovery of a domestic source as the basis for a policy of overextension, is Snyder's great contribution to the international relations field. "These groups, including economic sectors and state bureaucracies, logrolled their various imperialist or military interests, using arguments about security through expansion to justify their self-serving policies in terms of a broader public interest in national survival."[46]

Snyder explores this myth's underlying premises: gains and losses are cumulative, the offense has the advantage, and others cooperate in the face of offensive threats.[47] This third idea is similar to Walt's bandwagoning behavior.[48] What Snyder discovers is that Realism does not explain this behavior, not logically nor empirically.

> The logical difficulty that Realists themselves claim that states typically form balancing alliances to resist aggressors. Therefore, at least in the long run, the balance of power that arises out of international anarchy punishes aggression; it does not reward it. Consequently, strategies of security through expansion violate the basic principles of international politics that the Realists themselves have articulated.[49]

Posen also challenges Realism's assumption that the state is a unitary, rational actor. He tests organizational theory with balance of power theory in his analysis of France, Britain, and Germany's military doctrine. While he finds that balance of power theory has more explanatory power, both theories are useful. He argues that ". . . it is clear that substantively the two theories provide complementary explanations of a complicated and important aspect of state behavior."[50]

Posen explains that organizational theory's explanatory power is based on three factors: purpose, people, and environment. Organizations exist for specific purposes. They pursue those purposes with people, and the environment "spawns the organization; it produces the purpose that calls the organization into being."[51] Additionally, Posen describes people as "a great source of uncertainty. . . . People seldom approach the perfect rationality assumed in classical economics."[52] Clearly, Posen provides us with a modification of Realism's assumption that the state is a unitary, rational actor, yet, he confines his cases to the great powers.

INTERNAL THREATS AND THE NATURE OF THE STATE: CHALLENGING SYSTEMS THEORY'S SUPERPOWER BIAS

Holsti in "International Theory and War in the Third World" attacks the superpower perspective of the Cold War systems theorists. He examines the Cold War period from a Third World perspective and reveals that "Most wars did not initially involve two or more regular armed forces of states," and they did not have the conventional features of Great Power war.[53] Most casualties during war in this period occurred in the Third World.[54] While the system theories of the Cold War focus on the great powers, they ignored the activities of the Third World which is where war mainly occurred. How can we call the Cold War period stable? Additionally, Holsti mentions that all the literature on the causes of war are primarily written by U.S. or European writers. In Jack Levy's survey of the literature, he cites 441 authors of whom only one was from the Third World.[55]

Holsti takes Gilpin to task, specifically his hegemonic view of state behavior and his sole use of western cases. According to Gilpin, hegemons provide stability by performing several functions in the international system. They provide public goods, long term finance, security, enforcement of rules, and crisis management. Without the hegemon, there would be no cooperation among states. Of course, the hegemon performs all these functions because it is in its own interest to do so. The bottom line here is that the hegemon is necessary to provide stability: without it there is chaos and war. The problem is that hegemons inevitably rise and fall in cycles, and it is the decline of the hegemon that causes war.[56]

Holsti argues that Third World nations do not behave as Gilpin's great powers have.[57] We have not seen hegemonic behavior in the Third World. This leads to the problems associated with the concept of a state. Statehood is a western notion, not a Third World notion. "The basis of statehood for most [western] European countries is a distinct nationality. [For] others, mostly the 'old' states, rest secure on historic (inheritance, war, and marriage) foundations."[58] The majority of new states in the Third World are made up of many different ethnicities and nationalities.[59] Statehood has a different meaning for these Third World states. Consequently, these states behave differently from western states. Deductive theories or theories based solely on western cases do not work for the states of the Third World. It is critical that we study the nature of the state to better understand its behavior. Third World states act differently from western states which I will address later. The point is that the universal laws designed by Gilpin, Waltz, and Walt are not appropriate for understanding the behavior of Third World states. Holsti calls for future collaboration between students of international relations and area experts.[60]

Buzan addresses the importance of examining the nature of the state in his book, *People, States, and Fears*. Buzan's work takes elements from Waltz and shows the importance of understanding level II. The importance of understanding the nature of the state, as well as its groups and individuals of the state, stems from his discussion of weak versus strong states. Weak states are fundamentally different from strong states. The difference is so significant that the idea of national security takes on a whole new meaning.[61] Weak states must calculate international relations based on internal as well as external threats; whereas strong states primarily look at external threats.[62] Strong and weak states function differently. Buzan claims that ". . . it is probably more appropriate to view security in weak states in terms of the contending groups, organizations, and individuals as the prime objects of security."[63]

Since weak states base behavior primarily on internal threats, it is important to understand those threats. Buzan acknowledges the importance of understanding the international system, but not in exclusion of understanding levels I (nature of man) and II (nature of the state). With the end of the Cold War, Buzan's ideas strike a recognizable chord. Regime instability is a threat to rulers among many states in the Third World, and it undoubtedly drives foreign policy. Buzan makes the same call as Holsti does, which is for the collaboration of comparative and security studies. Buzan awakens us to the need to take the weak state perspective as we advance the security field.[64]

David takes Walt to task by claiming that Walt does not understand Third World alignment. Walt ignores other considerations that these states have when assessing the threat. These nations must consider internal threats, and these threats then become part of the equation as they determine alignments. His idea of omnibalancing considers internal and external threats.[65] Labs challenges Walt on the same point. He found that weak states will choose sovereignty over security as they make their alignment choices. In other words, weaker states will choose to fight for their territorial or governance rights rather than surrender some of those rights in exchange for physical well being.[66] Schroeder criticizes Walt's use of history. Schroeder claims that historically, bandwagoning is a more common behavior, not balancing as Walt claims.[67] In fact, he criticizes NeoRealists in general for approaching history with a theoretical bias.[68] Finally, Schweller also criticizes Walt for his great-power perspective. Schweller claims that security is not the only concern for states; there are other reasons for alignment behavior.[69] "Simply put, balancing is driven by the desire to avoid losses, bandwagoning by the opportunity for gain."[70] Clearly, these scholars challenge Walt's interpretation of his case studies, claiming that he analyzed them with a superpower bias.

OMNIBALANCING

As mentioned earlier, David presents the theory of omnibalancing. He states that omnibalancing is a better theory for understanding Third World state behavior. His theory calls for the assessment of external and internal threats with respect to the leader's political survival, not the state's survival.[71] David offers three significant departures from systems theory. "First, rather than just balancing against threats or power, leaders of states will appease secondary adversaries to focus their resources on primary adversaries. . . . It must align with one threat to address the other and it does."[72] For weak states, the primary threat is often a domestic threat, and the secondary threat is often another state. Second, for Third World states internal threats are more dangerous than external threats. Finally, Third World leaders act in their own interests as opposed to their states' interests.[73] In sum,

> Omnibalancing incorporates both the need to appease secondary adversaries and the need of leaders to balance against both internal and external threats in order to survive in power. It is conditional on regimes being weak and illegitimate, and on the stakes for domestic politics being very high.[74]

David tests balancing, bandwagoning, ideology, and omnibalancing between Third World states and the superpowers. His hypotheses are: 1) If a state balances, then we should observe that state aligning away from the threat or superpower. 2) If a state bandwagons, then we should observe that state aligning with the superpower. 3) If ideology determines alignment, then we should observe a change in the Third World leader's ideology preceding the change in superpower alignment.[75] 4) Finally, David states that the strongest test for omnibalancing would be ". . . if the leadership bandwagoned with an external threat in order to balance against an internal threat. This outcome would confirm the importance of internal threats [and] demonstrate the need to appease some threats in order to deal with others."[76]

David justifies the Third World as an analytic category because all Third World states have a combination of characteristics:

> their cumulative impact makes virtually all Third World leaders more vulnerable to overthrow—particularly from internal threats—than other leaders. Thus while the leaders of all states must be concerned about threats, in the Third World such concerns assume an urgency and priority that is rarely matched elsewhere.[77]

David limits his test to Third World states—superpower alignments, which necessarily limits him to the Cold War era. Additionally, he does not fully develop or explain internal threats.

DEFINING INTERNAL THREATS: ETHNICITY

Theories of comparative politics may help us understand the nature of the state and its behavior. For that reason, I will briefly discuss the modernization school, political culture, statist school, rational choice theory, and new institutionalism before my discussion of ethnicity and legitimacy. I quickly survey this literature because it provides some of the foundations for thoughts on ethnicity. Modernizationist scholars felt that as society modernized, tradition would decline and mass participation in governmental matters would increase.[78] Modernization, however, has not led to participation or reduced ethnic conflict.[79] This is evident in Syria. Although modernization has alleviated the plight of the Alawis, it does not explain why the Alawis, and not some other minority, gained power. Additionally, the urban Sunnis, who seem to be in a good power position, have yet to regain their dominance. Modernization theory only offers correlative, not causative, explanations. It does, however, bring to our attention the availability or unavailability of resources to political entrepreneurs and societal groups. Clearly, the Alawis gained resources, albeit initially military resources, that helped propel them to power.

The literature on political culture provides useful insights for our study of Syria. Lucian Pye claims that political systems differ based on different societal cultures. He examines traditional and societal values as indicators of national goals. Specifically, he differentiates societies based on their bias toward trust versus distrust; hierarchy versus equality; liberty versus coercion, and loyalty.[80] Clearly, an examination of Syria's predominantly Muslim society will reveal that society's bias concerning the above values, thus helping us to understand the nature of its politics.

Sidney Verba claims that national identification is a critical element for social mobilization. Syria does not have a strong national identity.[81] Perhaps this weakness is a major cause for Asad's repressive regime. Verba also claims that

> in the absence of an established identity one is likely to engage in identity-creating acts—be these aggressions against other nations or other expressions of nationalism. And indeed wars and revolutions—if against the proper enemy and for the right cause—can be a major way of suddenly switching loyalties from parochial groups to the nation-state and of building political commitment in a hurry.[82]

Can Syria stir up nationalism without Israel? Will the Soviet Union's demise affect Syria's ability to obtain weapons, not only for aggression toward other nations but also as means of repressing its own people? While Verba and Pye help us understand the nature of Syrian society which provides us with insights regarding its political development, they fail to explore the politics of development. How do leaders make choices? Specifically, why did Asad sometimes choose repression, while at other times he chose to compromise? Why do individuals join a group or offer support for it? Specifically, why do Alawis act collectively as opposed to other groups in society?

Samuel Huntington offers some political explanations in his version of political culture. He emphasizes the importance of strong institutions as a means of stabilizing heterogeneous societies.[83] Without these institutions, corruption will occur because the private interests of the ruling elite will subdue the public interest.[84] Huntington accurately describes Syrian society under Asad.[85] Corruption, namely in the form of patronage, is rampant in Syria. There are no clear institutions except for Asad's family. While Huntington introduces institutions as a critical factor for political development, he does not explain how political consciousness occurs. Why does the individual become politically active or support a politically active group? Why do certain groups form and others dissolve?

Theda Skocpol uses a statist approach as she examines the cause for social revolution. She adopts a structural perspective, introducing the state as an autonomous actor, and analyzes its actions in the international context. She argues that the state, faced with military competition from economically superior nations, will break down if it cannot gain the resources necessary to compete effectively in the international arena.[86] Skocpol provides some keen

insights for our study of Syria. First, Syria may have difficulty gaining the resources necessary to compete with an economically and militarily superior
foe now that aid from the defunct Soviet Union is nonexistent. Will Syria look
elsewhere for resources, or will it try to make the necessary internal reforms
so that it can compete? Second, Skocpol introduces an autonomous state with
its own interests. An analysis of Syrian political development demands an
analysis of the state, as its policies have a profound impact on its society.

While this view of the state as an autonomous actor is helpful, it also creates
problems. By viewing the state as a unitary actor, Skocpol leaves out the politics. In Syria's case, the leadership style of Asad is critical in understanding policy and state actions. Another problem with Skocpol is her non-purposive perspective. While she insists upon the importance of state-building and
mobilization, she never reveals how that mobilization and state-building will occur.[87] Additionally, she only deals with class mobilization, rather than considering other groups in this light. I find this aspect of her argument lacking with respect to Syria. As asked earlier, why do individuals choose to mobilize? Why do
certain groups mobilize while others do not?

Political economists or rational choice theorists analyze the state based on
microfoundations. They view the individual as a profit maximizer who bases
decisions on self-interest. Barry Ames provides a useful argument for our
analysis of Asad. Ames argues that leaders make policies that will enhance or
maintain their power. Specifically, leaders will build coalitions and fight political struggles in the budgeting process with the aim of their own political
survival.[88] While this argument is useful, it is not clear to the observer which
of Asad's policies were solely for survival and which were substantive policies. Asad made policy that directly antagonized his regional allies and the
Soviet Union. Some scholars believe that Asad made seemingly bad policy
just to demonstrate his independence and autonomy from the Soviet Union.[89]
Rationality seems to be a relative concept. Perhaps we need to view rationality in the context of political culture.

Robert Bates links the rational actor perspective to ethnic competition. He
argues

> that ethnic groups represent, in essence, coalitions which have been formed as
> part of rational efforts to secure benefits created by the forces of moderniza-
> tion—benefits which are desired but scarce.[90]

This argument implies that modernization does not lead to a decline of ethnic
conflict; rather it increases ethnic conflict.[91] However, Bates claims that
groups which are urbanized, educated, and wealthy tend to sustain power.[92]
How did the Alawis gain power from the powerful Sunnis? Why did the Sunnis lose power? Even though the Alawis have gained power and achieved

some modernization, the Alawis are still sociologically and economically disadvantaged, yet they continue to hold power. Perhaps we need to consider the ethnic factor on its own merits, separate from economic ties, as we analyze Syrian society.

A brief discussion of new institutionalism literature will help us examine and measure the extent that ethnicity permeates politics in Egypt versus Syria. According to James G. March and Johan P. Olsen,

> In recent years . . . a new institutionalism has appeared in political science. It is far from coherent or consistent; it is not completely legitimate; but neither can it be completely ignored. This resurgence of concern with institutions is a cumulative consequence of the modern transformation of social institutions and persistent commentary from observers of them. Social, political, and economic institutions have become larger, considerably more complex and resourceful, and *prima facie* more important to collective life.[93]

Consequently, "new institutionalism insists on a more autonomous role for political institutions." In essence, "the organization of political life matters."[94]

Peter J. Katzenstein explains that new institutionalism took two forms: thick and thin. Thin institutionalism uses a rationalist approach to explain how institutions help solve coordination problems. Thick institutionalism looks at both state and social structures and examines political institutions and coalitions, social sectors, and ideological constraints. Katzenstein explains that these two forms mutually reinforce each other. Thick institutionalism

> does a good job of illuminating a broad variety of political settings, but it is less successful at connecting what it has to say about states, social structures, political coalitions, and ideologies to individual decision makers. . . . Thin institutionalism tells us much about the microfoundations of individual policy choices and politics, but it is much weaker in generalizing from the specific to the general.[95]

He, too, sees some shortcomings with this approach, yet notes its value.

Similarly, Sven Steinmo explains the shortcoming of new institutionalism as the ambiguity of the definition of institutions themselves, as well as the lack of accountability for the varying levels of autonomy by state actors. He cites Peter Hall's definition of institutions as

> the formal rules, compliance procedures, and standard operating practices that structure the relationship between individuals in various units of the polity and economy. As such, they have a more formal status than cultural norms, but one that does not necessarily derive from legal, as opposed to conventional standing.[96]

Steinmo believes that the importance of this approach is understanding the interactive role institutions have with the public policy they produce, as well as
understanding that the decision-making authority across polities may differ
with respect to its loci in a specific policy arena.[97]

Donald C. Williams explains the importance of the institutionalist approach in
examining weak states, namely Third World states. This approach helps provide
an understanding of the relationship between state and society. "In order to reconcile the untenable image of an autonomous state and the fragmented nature of
society, the patrimonial state model needs to be refined with an analytical tool
that adequately assesses the variable weight and influence of competing forms
of authority." Williams chooses to examine the crisis of the African state by examining the interaction of various institutions. He explains that institutions

> are viewed as collections of interrelated rules and routines that define appropri-
> ate or rational action in the larger context of norms and values. . . . In summary,
> state-society relations are really an encounter between a structural arrangement
> of rule-bearing institutions, of which the state is only one.[98]

This institutional approach will be useful for understanding ethnicity as a fac-
tor in the political development of our cases, both of which are weak states.
Before we do this, we must first examine ethnicity and its link to legitimacy.
Let us now turn to Joseph Rothschild's ethnicity framework.

Rothschild combines some of the elements of the theories described above
as he explains the role of ethnicity in political development. He claims that

> the contemporary rise of ethnic individual identification and the trend toward
> ethnic group politicization do not mean that all other orientations, affiliations,
> differentiations, segmentations, or conflicts have been neutralized or eliminated.
> They interact with ethnicity—within individuals, within states, and across
> states. But the ethnic dimension has become increasingly salient in an increas-
> ing number of political conflict situations in modern and transitional societies.
> It refuses to be dissolved into another dimension, such as class, and demands to
> be faced on its own political plane.[99]

Ethnicity cannot always be politicized, but it is more likely to occur if there
are structural inequalities within society and if there is a leadership willing to
direct ethnicity into the political arena. This process is more likely to occur in
a modern or transitional society.[100]

Rothschild uses a cross-patterned reticulate model to represent society in
which ". . . ethnic groups and social classes cross-populate each other—but the
distribution is not random or symmetrical or egalitarian . . . a certain amount
of overrepresentation and underrepresentation of ethnic groups within economic classes and political power clusters is possible."[101] Rothschild examines

the availability of resources to ethnic groups and the state as they fight their political battles. This balance can change, and Rothschild emphasizes this dynamic nature of his model and society. He highlights the fact that politics of ethnicity are a function of proportional resources and qualities.[102] Also, the model allows for individual choice, an element of rational choice theory. Individuals may join a politicized ethnic group if they feel that membership may be beneficial (not all ethnic groups are politicized, nor is ethnicity a factor in every aspect of societal life).[103] Rothschild recognizes ethnicity as a coping mechanism for individuals experiencing change, especially change wrought by the modernization process.[104] Perhaps individuals look at the spiritual as well as the material benefits when deciding on membership. Overall, the cross-patterned reticulate model is a good tool for analyzing Syrian society.

Ethnic consciousness does not necessarily require primordial roots. Political entrepreneurs can create ethnicity to further a particular political agenda.[105] Political entrepreneurs may use "fault lines" or "hot issues" to help build ethnic consciousness by using "the most accessible and yielding fault line of potential cleavage available, given the historic circumstances and the prevailing stratification."[106] Is the Alawi leadership successful because it knows how to choose an effective fault line? What about the Sunni leadership?

Rothschild provides a useful first step toward understanding how social mobilization occurs. He builds upon the existing comparative literature: he shows how modernization can provide mobilizational resources; the importance of understanding the history of ethnic conflict (political culture); the influence of the international system on state decisions (statist literature); and the importance of individual decision-making based on self-interest (rational choice). Rothschild's emphasis on political entrepreneurship, substantive ethnic issues, and fault lines as part of a mobilization strategy helps us analyze social mobilization—a phenomenon that the other theories fail to explain.

The situation in Syria, however, demands further research and analysis concerning the nature of ethnicity and its role with influencing state behavior, but what is ethnicity? The rise of the Alawi under-class in Syria suggests that ethnicity be viewed separately from other classifications such as economic class. This notion contradicts the neo-Marxist notion of ethnicity. Richard Thompson examines Oliver Cox's and Michael Reich's arguments, and he claims that "both see the race problem as inextricably tied to the class system."[107] Thompson himself argues that the economic structure is the primary framework when studying ethnicity.[108] Further analysis of Syrian political development may undercut this neo-Marxist perspective. Walker Connor suggests that future literature on ethnicity reflect its psychological and emotional aspects.[109] Abdul Said also believes that ethnicity has a strong psychological character.

Conflict is not necessarily irrational but the roots of cultural expression that produce conflict are psychosociological. Cultures and ethnic groups have an inner logic that determines behavior, values, and attitudes that confound objective description or absolutism.[110]

Nathan Glazer concurs that ethnicity is unique and constitutes more than an interest; it is a tie. Furthermore, ethnicity is critical for mobilization.[111] Donald Horowitz agrees that ethnicity can overwhelm rational and economic interests.[112] According to these scholars, ethnicity needs to be studied as a stand-alone factor that influences political development, a condition Syria offers.

Saul Newman argues that we should use religion to study political development, based on his critique of Fouad Ajami's book, *The Vanished Imam: Musa al Sadr and Shia of Lebanon*. Religious political movements have a tactical advantage over ethnic political movements because their religious leadership and organization can be applied to their mobilization efforts. Additionally, they have a ready-made ethical and moral code that may help define a political agenda. The Alawi-Sunni conflict may warrant a religious-based analysis. Perhaps we can apply this religious difference to Rothschild's "fault-line" concept.

Said claims that ethnicity overwhelms the importance of the nation-state.[113] Will Syria's ethnic diversity challenge her continuing existence as a nation-state? Ethnicity offers a challenge to the nation-state as a unit of analysis. Finally, Daniel Bell discusses the role of hate and ethnicity. He claims that "cohesion derives not only from some inner 'consciousness of kind,' but from some external definition of an adversary as well."[114] Will a peace with Israel diminish what is left of Syrian nationalism?

DEFINING ETHNICITY FOR THIS STUDY

How does one define ethnicity? As discussed earlier, there are many versions of the definition. Does one use an inclusive or exclusive definition? Horowitz chooses an inclusive definition for his study. Horowitz defines groups ". . . by ascriptive differences, whether the indicium is color, appearance, language, religion, some other indicator of common origin, or some combination thereof. This is an inclusive conception of ethnicity."[115] Rothschild also uses an inclusive definition because he claims that "After all, if religious, linguistic, racial, and other primordial criteria and markers were to be peeled off, it is difficult to see what precisely would be left to, or meant by, the residual notion of ethnicity or ethnic groups."[116] Robert J. Thompson and Joseph R. Rudolph Jr. explain, however, that

The broad inclusive approach raises questions about analytical precision. It seems so inclusive that it is difficult to conceive of what is not, or cannot be, an ethnic characteristic. . . . Yet the more exclusive approach is not without its problems. When the concept is used restrictively, to denote distinctions between such concepts as racial and ethnic groups, then one is forced to overlook the fact that the boundaries between the distinctions noted above have been intellectually and historically fuzzy. Seldom does any example of an ethnic group possess a clear set of these traits, particularly given the fact that group distinctiveness is derived from its ascriptive qualities. The usual pattern is for a group to possess an overlapping set of traits, such as language, religion, and culture, while sharing others with the rest of the society, with group distinctiveness becoming manifest only in various forms of social, economic, and political interaction.[117]

I will base my definition of ethnicity, therefore, on these overlapping sets of traits, thereby acknowledging this overlap, but also maintaining analytical precision. Consequently, I will describe what ethnicity is and what it is not for purposes of this study. For my purposes, ethnicity is a group identity based on religion, language, and kinship. It will not include such attributes as class, ideology, and region. This definition will allow me to analyze ethnicity as a variable, as well as other domestic variables, such as class, mentioned above. While Egypt may be divided along class lines, this variable may not serve to reinforce other societal cleavages; whereas in Syria, class and region, for example, serve to reinforce the ethnic cleavage between Alawis and Sunnis. However, the Alawi-Sunni cleavage is primarily based on religion and kinship.

ETHNICITY: LANGUAGE, RELIGION, AND KINSHIP

These traits—language, religion, and kinship—are suitable for this study because they are the terms primarily used by the peoples of the Middle East to describe group identification and cohesion. Also, they offer a best solution between the all-inclusive and all-exclusive definitions, as described above. Don Peretz echoes this problem of ambiguity. "It is difficult, if not impossible, to divide them into precise, scientific categories. Terms such as race, nationality, and religion often have meanings in the Middle East that differ from those of the Western world."[118] It is easier to describe what an Arab is not. "Arab national leaders are more and more associating the term [Arab] with language, with culture, and with a vague, intangible emotional identification with 'the Arab cause'. This is not an incontestable definition."[119]

Language serves two purposes. It is a mode of communication, and it symbolizes group identity.[120] Peretz classifies the people of the Middle East as Semitic, Turkish, and Iranian linguistic groups.[121] E. A. Speiser uses language in his study of Middle Eastern peoples as a critical criterion for group identity.[122] Both Bernard Lewis and Michael Hudson use the factors of language, culture, and religion in their attempts to understand and define the Arabic people.[123] Additionally, Hudson claims that, "Ethnographers look upon language as a key defining characteristics of ethnic communities."[124]

While I do not use culture as a variable of ethnicity, I do want to provide a few views on what culture is because some scholars consider religion and culture intertwined. Also, these views support my contention that culture is just too imprecise and all-inclusive a term to use as a variable for this study. According to Ronald Inglehart, culture describes the attitudes, values, and skills of a society.[125] Halim Barakat claims that culture in the social sciences encompasses three facets: it is the total way of life, artistic achievements, knowledge, thought, and the sciences. The distinctiveness of a people's culture is based on that people's uniqueness in social formations, living patterns, modes of production, socialization, and adaptations to the environment. "In other words, culture represents the complete design for living of a community of people inhabiting a particular environment."[126] David Easton defines culture as, "the body of customary beliefs, social forces, and material traits constituting the distinct traditions of . . . a social group."[127]

As mentioned above, some scholars closely relate religion and culture. Daniel Bates and Amal Rassam discuss Islam as a cultural tradition. They claim that, "Islam remains the single most important source for the ethos that distinguishes the area and imparts to its bewildering complexity and variation a measure of unity and cultural identity."[128] Hudson categorizes the people of the Middle East using religion as a critical distinguisher.[129] Also, religion is intertwined with language. Albert Hourani explains that the Arabic language in written form was ". . . preserved by the Qur'an, the book sent down in the Arabic language. . . . The religion carried the language with it."[130]

Kinship describes common blood ties and ancestry of a people, as usually claimed by tribes, clans, and even nations. If the kinship group coincides with a state's population, the political system's legitimacy is strengthened. When kinship groups are subunits of the state or are outside the boundaries of the state, then they may have a disruptive effect on the regime.[131] Common ancestry is a critical component of ethnicity.[132] According to Bates and Rassam, in order ". . . to understand Middle Eastern society, even its higher level of political organization, one has to understand the nature of the primary groupings into which the individual is born and how men and women subsequently fashion and use 'primordial' ties and relationships [kinships] throughout their lifetime."[133]

It is the reinforcement of ethnic cleavages, especially in the political arena, that serves to pose legitimacy problems for the nation. In Egypt, divisions exist, but they are not reinforcing. Consequently, Egypt enjoys a national identity that does not compete with strong ethnic identities and loyalties. The chapter describing political development will clarify this point. I will assess ethnic divisiveness based on Horowitz's claims that where ethnicity significantly permeates sectors of social life, we see deeply divided societies.[134]

> In severely divided societies, ethnicity finds its way into a myriad of issues: developmental plans, educational controversies, trade union affairs, land policy, business policy, tax policy. Characteristically, issues that elsewhere would be relegated to the category of routine administration assume a central place on the political agenda of ethnically divided societies.[135]

Another indication of a deeply ethnically divided society is the organization of activities, economically and politically, along ethnic lines.[136] "In divided societies, ethnic conflict is at the center of politics. Ethnic divisions pose challenges to the cohesion of states and sometimes to peaceful relations among states."[137] Here is where the institutionalist approach will help me assess the extent of ethncity's permeation in the political development of each of my cases; thus, the degree of permeation will, based on Horowitz's view, establish whether or not my case, or state is ethnically divided.

I think with the analysis of ethnicity and its role with omnibalancing, we will find a residual effect, that is that the study of Syrian and Egyptian political development can only enhance ethnic studies by, at the very least, adding to the data base on ethnicity. The rise of the Alawi under-class may serve to isolate ethnicity as a factor influencing political development, particularly social mobilization, thereby allowing scholars to better analyze the nature of ethnicity itself.

LEGITIMACY

Chapters 2 and 3 describe the link between ethnic homogeneity and legitimacy as well as ethnic divisiveness and illegitimacy in the cases of Egypt and Syria, respectively. The idea of legitimacy directly affects a regime's stability, or as Timothy J. Lomperis claims, its ability to rule well.[138] Here, I explain that relationship through the theoretical literature, but before we examine that link, I will turn to the concept of legitimacy itself. While it is a concept that eludes measurement, it is worthy of study because of its significance in the field of political science; therefore, it is critical that we still attempt to discover its impact on the polity and the international system. David Easton explains that "Given its long and venerable history as a central concept in political science, legitimacy has yet to receive the attention it merits in empirical research."[139] Lomperis cites Harry Eckstein's claim that "the issue of support and opposition, legitimacy and illegitimacy . . . stands at the crux of all political study."[140] It is for this reason that I pursue the links among ethnicity, legitimacy, and regime stability, at the very least by making a first cut at the centrality of these concepts and perhaps providing a start point for further study.

Simply put, legitimacy is the idea that the people believe that the regime is morally in the right. Easton's definition of legitimacy for a regime is:

> it is right and proper . . . to accept and obey the authorities and to abide by the requirements of the regime. It reflects the fact that in some vague or explicit way [a person] sees these objects as conforming to his own moral principles, his own sense of what is right and proper in the political sphere. . . . It is not unreasonable to assume that, where we consider a state of affairs morally proper or right, we are likely to view it in highly favorable terms. This positive nature in the belief in legitimacy usually carries with it the implication that we have an obligation to accept the acts of those considered legitimate to be binding on us. The converse is equally probable. With regard to those considered to rule illegitimately, we are relieved of all obligation; support is considered to be totally withdrawn or to be withdrawable.[141]

Lomperis believes that a key component of the concept of legitimacy is that "there must be a normative or moral judgment in favor of the regime's right to rule. . . . This central moral component to legitimacy, then, is something every government or regime needs to sustain its power and long-term ability to rule."[142] Ted Robert Gurr and Muriel McClelland define legitimacy as

> the extent that a polity is regarded by its members as worthy of support. This is not the same as citizens' compliance with laws and directives, but refers to a basic attitude that disposes them to comply in most circumstances. . . . To the extent that legitimacy is low or nonexistent, people are likely to support and obey authorities only out of fear or convenience, which means that rulers must rely expensively on coercion or risk political collapse. . . . No polity is likely to command the loyalty of all of its citizens all the time; what is crucial for high performance is that no large or vital segment of the population remain alienated for any length of time.[143]

Ralf Dahrendorf explains legitimacy in the context of stability. He claims that there are two keys to regime stability, effectiveness and legitimacy. He argues that for governments to work

> two things have to be present: effectiveness and legitimacy. Effectiveness is a technical concept. It simply means that governments have to be able to do things which they claim they can do . . . they have to work. Legitimacy, on the other

hand, is a moral concept. It means that what governments do have to be right. . . . A government is legitimate if what it does is right both in the sense of complying with certain fundamental principles, and in that of being in line with prevailing cultural values.[144]

Dahrendorf claims that there is a relationship between these two concepts, effectiveness and legitimacy. That relationship is asymmetrical. Governments may be effective without being legitimate. Totalitarian regimes are such an example.[145] However, "Over time, ineffectiveness will probably erode legitimacy."[146] Dahrendorf is most concerned about the erosion of legitimacy because for democracies ". . . there is a great danger that the response to a crisis of legitimacy will be authoritarianism and illiberty."[147]

Easton, in his article "The Analysis of Political Systems," stresses the importance of legitimacy. According to Easton,

When the basic political attachments become deeply rooted or institutionalized, we say that the system has become accepted as legitimate. Politicization therefore effectively sums up the way in which legitimacy is created and transmitted in a political system. And it is an empirical observation that in those instances where political systems have survived the longest, support has been nourished by an ingrained belief in the legitimacy of the relevant governments and regimes.[148]

Philip Norton's book, *The British Polity*, supports the criticality of legitimacy for regime stability. His thesis is that the political culture of Great Britain has been so strong that it has allowed the regime to survive periods of ineffectiveness, thereby remaining stable for several hundred years.[149] Additionally, Max Weber tells us that, "If the state is to exist, the dominated must obey the authority claimed by the powers that be. When and why do men obey? Upon what inner justifications and upon what external means does this domination rest?"[150] According to Weber, that inner justification is a state's legitimacy, which may be based on tradition, a leader's charisma, and legal statutes.[151]

The comparative politics literature helps us further explore the link between ethnic divisiveness and state legitimacy, which affects regime stability. First, Augustus Richard Norton claims that the Third World will play a more significant role now that the Cold War era is over. "The disappearance of the bipolar superpower-dominated security system will foster a much more unruly international regime in which Third World players may be prone to try to throw their weight around"[152] Clearly, understanding Third World state behavior has taken on a critical urgency with the end of the Cold War era. Norton tells us, however, that

it is not that interstate war is a minor problem, but . . . it pales in significance alongside the potential for intrastate violence." . . . The central problem for developing and developed countries in the 1990s will be the growing inability of governments to meet the psychopolitical, cultural, and economic needs of their constituents. The legacy of the 1980s is the crisis of legitimacy and political coalescence that is going to shake, rattle, and roll around the globe.[153]

Norton claims that the most important element for state survival is legitimacy, meaning "that authority which rests on the shared cultural identity of ruler and ruled."[154] States base legitimacy on a "political formula" which justifies a leader's rule.

As Gaetano Mosca notes, political formulas are not "mere quakeries aptly invented to trick the masses into obedience. . . . The truth is that they answer a real need in man's social nature; and this need, so universally felt, of governing and knowing that one is governed not on the basis of mere material or intellectual force, but on the basis of moral principle, has . . . a practical and a real importance."[155]

He further adds that "A political formula ceases to be compelling when the ruler or rulers, through neglect, incompetence, design, malfeasance, or happenstance fail consistently or spectacularly to meet the cultural or material needs of citizens."[156] When legitimacy dissolves, the regime is vulnerable to change.[157] According to Norton, modernization strengthens family, village, religious, and ethnic ties. These ties become significant when they are politicized. The resultant conflicts "illustrate a major danger of the 1990s, the spreading of interethnic and intercommunal combat exacerbated by the unpredictable, but unavoidable process of modernization. . . . The result is the breakdown of the state."[158]

Hudson also links the idea of ethnicity with legitimacy. He states: "If the population within given political boundaries is so deeply divided within itself on ethnic or class lines . . . then it is extremely difficult to develop a legitimate order."[159] He claims that this

legitimate order requires a distinct sense of corporate selfhood: the people within a territory must feel a sense of political community which does not conflict with other subnational or supranational communal identifications. . . . There must as well be a strong authoritative vertical linkage between the governors and governed. Without authoritative political structures endowed with 'rightness' and efficacity, political life is certain to be violent and unpredictable.[160]

Hudson argues that the main problem for Arab states is their lack of legitimacy.[161] Hudson offers a mosaic model for understanding the challenges to legitimacy. His mosaic model describes a society based on primordial and parochial ties, and modernization strengthens these ties.[162] This model does not lend itself to legitimacy, "Because ethnicity is so deep-rooted, the possibilities for the integration of new polities along modern lines, let alone revolutionary transformation are remote."[163] Hudson ultimately argues that a social mobilization model is a more accurate tool for analyzing society. This model views modernization as a process that helps develop a tolerant and educated society.[164]

Perhaps my analysis will shed more light on Norton and Hudson's opposing views. Both scholars, however, view repressive regimes as illegitimate.[165] Melvin Richter concurs and states that "All governments know that force has no title. As long as they have no other foundation than violence, they are entirely destitute of right." Richter continues to cite Guizot and claims that political legitimacy requires governments "to disclaim violence as a source of authority, and to associate it with a moral notion . . . of justice, of right, of reason."[166] This view of repressive regimes proves significant for my analysis, especially for my case study on Syria.

Norton and Hudson explain the link between ethnicity and legitimacy, as do all the scholars mentioned above who express the importance of a political community for establishing legitimacy. Ethnic homogeneity helps establish this shared sense of values and community. As this review of the ethnicity literature illustrated, ethnic loyalty is a powerful force. Ethnicity is a significant variable affecting state legitimacy, thus challenging regime stability. As all these scholars claim, a loss of legitimacy for the state is a prescription for instability. Clearly, states that lack legitimacy are vulnerable to change. In sum, legitimacy is a key ingredient for regime stability, and when ethnic loyalties coincide with national loyalties, then that sense of a shared political community and values is a great commodity for the regime. Conversely, when these loyalties are in conflict, then the regime is in a dangerous position. A regime in such a position affects its leader's decisions, policies, and actions much differently than does a legitimate, stable regime. I will analyze these differences as they affect the international system.

I provided a comprehensive review of the literature that both directly and indirectly affects my project. The discussions of ethnicity and legitimacy helped reveal the difficulty of using these terms, but at the same time revealed their importance, nevertheless. I believe that it is important to address these terms in our study of political science, even though they are a bit "messy." Further study will help refine these concepts, and, I believe, generate a better understanding of state behavior. Additionally, I found that the institutional literature provided an analytical framework in which to discuss the centrality of ethnicity and legitimacy, as they pertained to the political development of my case studies.

The international relations literature of Waltz, Walt, Schweller, and David provided me with the tools to help understand my cases. Waltz provided me with a systemic view, which helped me assess the impact of the international system change on my cases. Walt provided the basis of state alignment theory that caused such a great and interesting dialogue and critique of his theory. In fact, it was these critiques, by such scholars as Buzan and Schweller, that piqued my interest in this project. It was, however, David's idea of omnibalancing that provided the springboard for me. I not only wanted to examine his idea of omnibalancing, but I also used his case study approach. Holsti and Sullivan provided me with the analytical tool, which helped analyze the link between the domestic variables and state alignment behavior. The preceding comprehensive literature review helped form the logic between the domestic variables and state behavior in the international system. I hope to provide some theoretical insights through this study.

NOTES

1. Kenneth N. Waltz, *Theory of International Politics* (Reading, Massachusetts: Addison-Wesley Publishing Company, 1979), 6.

2. Ibid., 6.

3. Ibid., 6.

4. Ibid., 10.

5. Ibid., 69.

6. J. David Singer, "The Level of Analysis Problem in International Relations," in *International Politics and Foreign Policy: A Reader in Research and Theory*, ed. James N. Rosenau (New York: The Free Press, 1969), 21–22.

7. John Lewis Gaddis, "The Long Peace," *International Security* 10, no. 4 (1986): 99–142.

8. See Michael Brecher and Jonathan Wilkenfeld, "International Crises and Global Instability: The Myth of the 'Long Peace'" in *The Long Postwar Peace*, ed. Charles W. Kegley Jr. (New York: HarperCollins Publishers, 1991), 85–104, and John A. Vasquez, "The Deterrence Myth: Nuclear Weapons and the Prevention of Nuclear War," in *The Long Postwar Peace*, 205–223.

9. These points concerning bipolarity summarize Gaddis, 105–109.

10. Gaddis cites Karl Deutsch and J. David Singer for this definition in ibid., 103.

11. Ibid., p. 123.

12. Ibid., 132.

13. Ibid.

14. This paragraph summarizes ibid., 132–140.

15. Ibid. 126–128.

16. John J. Mearsheimer, "Why We Will Soon Miss the Cold War," *The Atlantic Monthly*, August 1990, 35–40.

17. Samuel Huntington introduces the idea of a "uni-multipolar" world in Samuel P. Huntington, "The Lonely Superpower," *Foreign Affairs* 78, no. 2 (March/April 1999): 36.

18. Waltz, 88.

19. Ibid., 92.

20. Ibid.

21. Ibid., 91.

22. Ibid., 93, 95–97.

23. Ibid., 97–99.

24. Ibid., 121.

25. Ibid., 168.

26. Ibid., 204.

27. Ibid., 193.

28. Ibid., 170.

29. Ibid., 181.

30. The idea of the temporary condition of unipolarity and the eventuality of multipolarity is taken from Charles Krauthammer, "The Unipolar Moment," *Foreign Affairs* 70, no. 1 (Winter 1991): 23.

31. Efraim Karsh, "A Marriage of Convenience: The Soviet Union and Asad's Syria," *The Jerusalem Journal of International Relations* 11, no. 4 (December 1989): 3.

32. Please note that there is much debate concerning the static versus dynamic nature of systems theory. Waltz responds to his critics and claims that systems theory does account for change: "Changes in, and transformation of, systems originate not in the structure of a system but in its parts . . . through variation, unit-level forces contain the possibilities of systemic change," in Kenneth N. Waltz, "Reflections on Theory of International Politics: A Response to My Critics," *NeoRealism And Its Critics,* ed. Robert O. Keohane (New York: Columbia University Press, 1986), 343. For more insight into systems change, see the *festschrift* for Robert C. North in Ole R. Holsti, Randolph M. Siverson, and Alexander L. George, eds., *Change in the International System* (Boulder, Colorado: Westview Press, 1980).

33. The idea of manipulable variables is taken from Jack Levy, "The Causes of War: A Review of Theories and Evidence," in *Behavior Society and Nuclear War Volume I,* ed. Philip E. Tetlock, Jo L. Husbands, Robert Jervis, Paul C. Stern, and Charles Tilly (New York: Oxford University Press, 1989), 279.

34. Robert Gilpin, *War and Change in World Politics* (Cambridge: Cambridge University Press, 1986), 97.

35. Ibid., 97–100.

36. The discussion concerning other incentives is from ibid., 98.

37. Ibid., 161.

38. Bruce W. Nelan, "Boris vs. Mikhail," *Time,* 24 March 1991, 29.

39. Gilpin, 237.

40. This idea about technology and SDI is taken from Richard Smoke, *National Security and the Nuclear Dilemma: An Introduction to the American Experience* (New York: Random House, 1987), 277–278, and Gilpin, 182.

41. Steven M. Walt, *The Origins of Alliances* (Ithaca: Cornell University Press, 1987), 26.

42. Ibid., 24.

43. Ibid., 33.

44. These points summarize ibid., 27–33.

45. John Lewis Gaddis,"Great Illusions, the Long Peace, and the Future of the International System," in *The Long Postwar Peace*, ed. Charles W. Kegley Jr. (New York: HarperCollins Publishers, 1991), 26.

46. Jack Snyder, *Myths of Empire: Domestic Politics and International Ambition* (Ithaca: Cornell University Press, 1991), 2.

47. bid., 3.

48. Ibid., 5.

49. Ibid., 11.

50. Barry Posen, *Sources of Military Doctrine: France, Britain, and Germany Between the World Wars* (Ithaca: Cornell University Press, 1984), 9.

51. The discussion about organizational theory and the quotation is from Ibid., 43.

52. Ibid.

53. K.J. Holsti, "International Theory and War in the Third World," in *The Insecurity Dilemma: National Security of Third World States*, ed. Brian L. Job (Boulder: Lynne Reinner, 1992), 38.

54. Ibid., 37.

55. Ibid., 39.

56. Robert Gilpin, *The Political Economy of International Relations* (Princeton: Princeton University Press, 1987), 72–80.

57. Holsti, 39.

58. Ibid., 53.

59. Ibid., 54.

60. Ibid., 57–59. I added Walt to Holsti's examples of systems theorists.

61. Barry Buzan, *People, States, and Fears: An Agenda For International Security Studies In The Post–Cold War Era* (Boulder, Colorado: Lynne Reinner Publishers, 1991), 97.

62. Ibid., 100–101.

63. Ibid., 101.

64. Ibid., 360.

65. Steven R. David, "Explaining Third World Alignment," *World Politics* 43, no. 2 (January 1991): 233.

66. Eric J. Labs, "Do Weak States Bandwagon?" *Security Studies* 1, no. 3 (1992): 407.

67. Paul Schroeder, "Historical Reality vs NeoRealist Theory," *International Security* 19, no. 1 (Summer 1994) takes Walt to task on p. 114 and makes his claim concerning bandwagoning on p. 117.

68. Ibid., 147–148.

69. Randall L. Schweller, "Bandwagoning for Profit: Bringing the Revisionist State Back In," *International Security* 19, no. 1 (Summer 1994): 82 for the point on Walt, p. 86 on the point of security, and p. 7 for the point concerning different alignment behavior.

70. Ibid., 7.

71. Steven R. David, *Choosing Sides: Alignment and Realignment in the Third World* (Baltimore: The Johns Hopkins University Press, 1991), xi.

72. Ibid., 6.

73. Ibid., 6–7.

74. Ibid., 7.

75. Ibid., 7.

76. Ibid., 8.

77. Ibid., 15.

78. See Karl Deutsch, "Social Mobilization and Political Development," *American Political Science Review* 55, no. 3 (September 1961): 499 for a detailed discussion of modernization and social mobilization and their positive effects for mass participation.

79. Saul Newman, "Does Modernization Breed Ethnic Political Conflict?" *World Politics* 43, no. 3 (April 1991): 451.

80. Lucian W. Pye, "Introduction," in *Political Culture and Political Development*, ed. Lucian W. Pye and Sidney Verba (Princeton: Princeton University Press, 1960), 19–23.

81. As the political development chapter on Syria will show, Syrian society consists of strong, reinforced ethnic cleavages. These reinforced cleavages create loyalties to ethnic groups which challenge loyalties to the state.

82. Sidney Verba, "Conclusion," in *Political Culture and Political Development*, 533.

83. Samuel P. Huntington, *Political Order in Changing Societies* (New Haven: Yale University Press, 1968), 9–12.

84. Ibid., 71.

85. Note that Syria's regime is not a bureaucratic authoritarian regime because Asad does want mass support, not apathy, as his repeated calls for Arab nationalism indicate.

86. Theda Skocpol, *States and Social Revolutions* (Cambridge: Cambridge University Press, 1979), 1–42.

87. Skocpol's emphasis on mobilization and state-building is taken from ibid., 161–169.

88. Barry Ames, *Political Survival: Politicians and Public Policy in Latin America* (Berkeley: University of California Press, 1987), 1.

89. Galia Golan and Itamar Rabinovich, "The Soviet Union and Syria: The Limits of Cooperation," in *The Limits to Power: Soviet Policy in the Middle East*, ed. Yaacov Ro'I (London: Croom Helm Ltd, 1979), 226.

90. Robert H. Bates, "Modernization, Ethnic Competition, and the Rationality of Politics in Contemporary Africa," in *State Versus Ethnic Claims: African Policy Dilemmas*, ed. Donald Rothchild and Victor Olorunsola (Boulder; Westview Press, 1983), 152.

91. Ibid., 165.

92. Ibid., 159.

93. James G. March and Johan P. Olsen, "The New Institutionalism: Organizational Factors in Political Life," *American Political Science Review* 78, no. 3 (September 1984): 734.

94. Ibid., 738, 747.

95. Atul Kohli, Peter Evans, Peter J. Katzenstein, Adam Przeworski, Susanne Hoeber Rudolph, James C. Scott, and Theda Skocpol, "The Role of Theory in Comparative Politics: A Symposium," *World Politics* 48, no. 1 (October 1995): 12.

96. Sven Steinmo, "Political Institutions and Tax Policy in the United States, Sweden, and Britain," *World Politics* 41, no. 4 (July 1989): 502.

97. Ibid., 503.

98. Both quotations are from Donald C. Williams, "Reconsidering State and Society in Africa: The Institutional Dimension in Land Reform Policies," *Comparative Politics* 28, no. 2 (January 1996): 208, 210.

99. Joseph Rothschild, *Ethnopolitics: A Conceptual Framework* (New York: Columbia University Press, 1981), 8.

100. Ibid., 248.

101. Ibid., 81–82.

102. Ibid., 81–85.

103. Ibid., 85–86.

104. Ibid., 5.

105. Ibid., 87–96.

106. Ibid., 96.

107. Richard A. Thompson. "Neo-Marxian Explanations and a Reformulation," in *Theories of Ethnicity: A Critical Appraisal*, ed. Richard A. Thompson (New York: Greenwood Press, 1989), 156.

108. Ibid., 145–157.

109. Walker Connor, "Ethnonationalism," in *Understanding Political Development*, ed. Myron Weiner and Samuel Huntington (Boston: Little, Brown and Company, 1987), 218.

110. Abdul A. Said and Luiz R. Simmons, "The Ethnic Factor in World Politics," in *Ethnicity in an International Context*, ed. Abdul A. Said and Luiz R. Simmons (New Brunswick: Transaction Books, 1976), 21.

111. Nathan Glazer and Daniel P. Moynihan, "Introduction," in *Ethnicity: Theory and Experience*, ed. Nathan Glazer and Daniel P. Moynihan (Cambridge: Harvard University Press, 1983), 18–19.

112. Newman cites Horowitz in Newman, 463–464.

113. Said, 10.

114. Daniel Bell, "Ethnicity and Social Change," in *Ethnicity: Theory and Experience*, 174.

115. Horowitz, 17–18.

116. Rothschild, 9.

117. Robert J. Thompson and Joseph R. Rudolph, "Ethnic Politics and Public Policy in Western Societies: A Framework For Comparative Analysis" in *Ethnicity, Politics, and Development* ed. Dennis L. Thompson and Dov Ronen (Boulder, Colorado: Lynne Reinner, 1986), 27–28.

118. Don Peretz, *The Middle East Today*, 5th ed. (New York: Praeger Publishers, 1988), 10.

119. Ibid., 12.

120. Rothschild, 89.

121. Peretz, 10.

122. E. A. Speiser, "Cultural Factors in Social Dynamics in the Near East," in *Social Forces in the Middle East*, ed. Sydney Nettleton Fisher (Ithaca: Cornell University Press, 1955), 19.

123. Bernard Lewis, "What is an Arab?" in *Peoples and Cultures of the Middle East*, ed. Ailon Shiloh (New York: Random House, 1969), 4, and Michael Hudson, *Arab Politics: The Search For Legitimacy* (New Haven: Yale University Press, 1977), 34. I chose not to include culture as a variable because of it is too inclusive and imprecise.

124. Hudson, *Arab Politics*, 38.

125. Ronald Inglehart, *Culture Shift in Advanced Industrial Society* (Princeton: Princeton University Press, 1990), 3.

126. The quotation and the points made are from Barakat, 41.

127. David Easton as quoted by Hudson, 33.

128. Daniel Bates and Amal Rassam, *Peoples and Cultures of the Middle East* (Englewood Cliffs: Prentice Hall, 1983), 81.

129. Michael Hudson's categories are 1. Arab and Shi'ite Muslims, 2. Arab and non-Muslim, 3. Muslim and non-Arab, and 4. Non-Arabs and non-Muslims in Hudson, 59.

130. Albert Hourani, *A History of the Arab Peoples* (Cambridge: The Belknap Press of Harvard University Press, 1991), 48.

131. Rothschild, 87.

132. Barakat, 40.

133. Bates and Rassam, 189.

134. Horowitz, 6–7.

135. Ibid., 8.

136. Ibid.

137. Ibid., 12.

138. Timothy J. Lomperis, *From People's War to People's Rule: Insurgency, Intervention, and the Lessons of Vietnam* (Chapel Hill: The University of North Carolina Press, 1996), 32.

139. David Easton, "A Reassessment of the Concept of Political Support," *British Journal of Political Science* 5, no. 4 (October 1975), 451.

140. Lomperis, 31.

141. Easton, "A Reassessment of the Concept of Political Support," 451.

142. Lomperis, 32.

143. Ted Robert Gurr and Muriel McClelland, "Political Performance: A Twelve Nation Study," in *Comparative Politics Series*, ed. Harry Eckstein and Ted Robert Gurr, vol. 2, no. 01–018 (Beverly Hills: Sage Publications, 1971), 30.

144. Ralf Dahrendorf, "On the Governability of Democracies," in *Comparative Politics: Notes and Readings*, ed. Roy C. Macridis and Bernard Brown (Pacific Grove, California: Brooks/Cole Publishing Company, 1990), 285–286.

145. Ibid., 286.

146. Ibid.

147. Ibid., 293.

148. David Easton, "The Analysis of Political Systems," in *Comparative Politics: Notes and Readings*, 58.

149. Philip Norton, *The British Polity* (New York: Longman, 1991), 65. Norton does not use the term, "legitimacy" here. Instead he argues that culture has given Great Britain the "breathing space" to work on its economic and social problems. The British

support for the regime is based on the British political culture. This argument implies that the political culture has positively influenced the legitimacy of the British regime.

150. Max Weber, "Politics As A Vocation," in *From Max Weber: Essays in Sociology*, ed. H. H. Gerth and C. Wright Mills (New York: Oxford University Press, 1946), 78.

151. Ibid., 78–79.

152. Augustus Richard Norton, "The Security Legacy of the 1980s in the Third World," in *Third World Security in the Post–Cold War Era*, ed. Thomas G. Weiss and Meryl A. Kessler (Boulder, Colorado: Lynne Reinner Publishers, 1991), 20.

153. Ibid., 23.

154. Ibid., 24.

155. Ibid.

156. Ibid.

157. Ibid.

158. Ibid., 30.

159. Hudson, 389–390.

160. Ibid., 4.

161. Ibid., 2.

162. Ibid., 7.

163. Ibid., 9–10.

164. Ibid., 7.

165. Norton, 24 and Hudson, 4.

166. Melvin Richter, "Toward a Concept of Political Legitimacy: Bonapartist Dictatorship and Democratic Legitimacy," *Political Theory* 10, no. 2 (May 1982), 198.

Bibliography

Abd-Allah, Umar F. *The Islamic Struggle in Syria*. Berkeley: Mizan Press, 1983.

Abdo, Genieve. *No God But God: Egypt and the Triumph of Islam*. Oxford: Oxford University Press, 2000.

Aftandilian, Gregory L. *Egypt's Bid For Arab Leadership: Implications For U.S. Policy*. New York: Council on Foreign Relations Press, 1993.

Ajami, Fouad. "The Arab Road." In *Pan-Arabism and Arab Nationalism: The Continuing Debate*, ed. Tawfic E. Farah, 115–132. Boulder: Westview Press, 1987.

Ames, Barry. *Political Survival: Politicians and Public Policy in Latin America*. Berkeley and Los Angeles: University of California Press, 1987.

Ansari, Hamied. *Egypt: The Stalled Society*. Albany: State University of New York Press, 1986.

Arab Human Development Report 2002: Creating Opportunities for Future Generations. New York: United Nations Development Programme, 2002. Accessed on 28 April 2002 at www.undp.org/rbas/adhr/bychapter.html.

Armanazi, Ghayth N. "Syrian Foreign Policy at the Crossroads: Continuity and Change in the Post-Gulf Era." In *State and Society in Syria and Lebanon*, ed. Youssef M. Choueiri, 112–119. New York: St. Martin's Press, 1993.

Atkeson, Edward B. *A Military Assessment of the Middle East, 1991–1996*. U.S. Army War College: Strategic Studies Institute, 1992.

Ayubi, Nazih N. "Government and the State in Egypt Today." In *Egypt Under Mubarak*, ed. Charles Tripp and Roger Owen, 1–20. London: Routledge, 1990.

Ayubi, Nazih N. *The State and Public Policies in Egypt Since Sadat*. Reading: Ithaca Press, 1991.

Ayubi, Shaheen. *Nasser and Sadat: Decision Making and Foreign Policy, 1970–1972*. Wakefield: Longwood Academic, 1992.

Baker, Raymond William. *Sadat and After: Struggles for Egypt's Political Soul*. Cambridge: Harvard University Press, 1990.

Barakat, Halim. *The Arab World: Society, Culture, and State*. Berkeley: University of California Press, 1993.

Barth Frederick. "Introduction." In *Ethnic Groups and Boundaries: The Social Organization of Cultural Difference*, ed. Frederick Barth, 10–15. Boston: Little, Brown and Company, 1969. Quoted in Dale F. Eikelman. *The Middle East: An Anthropological Approach*, 209, 2d ed. Englewood Cliffs: Prentice Hall, 1989

Bates, Daniel, and Amal Rassam. *Peoples and Cultures in the Middle East*. Englewood Cliffs: Prentice Hall, 1983.

Bates, Robert H. "Modernization, Ethnic Competition, and the Rationality of Politics in Contemporary Africa." In *State Versus Ethnic Claims: African Policy Dilemmas*, ed. Donald Rothchild and Victor Olorunsola, 152–171. Boulder: Westview Press, 1983.

Bell, Daniel. "Ethnicity and Social Change." *In Ethnicity: Theory and Experience*, ed. Nathan Glazer and Daniel P. Moynihan, 141–174. Cambridge and London: Harvard University Press, 1983.

Bill, James A., and Robert Springborg. *Politics in the Middle East*. New York: HarperCollins College Publishers, 1994.

Boutros-Ghali, Boutros. "Egyptian Diplomacy: East-West Détente and North-South Dialogue." In *Contemporary Egypt: Through Egyptian Eyes*, ed. Charles Tripp, 142–150. London: Routledge, 1993.

Brecher, Michael, and Jonathan Wilkenfeld. "International Crises and Global Instability: The Myth of the 'Long Peace'." *In The Long Postwar Peace*, ed. Charles W. Kegley Jr., 85–104. New York: HarperCollins Publishers, 1991.

Brown, Michael. "Introduction." In *The International Dimensions of Internal Conflict*, ed. Michael Brown, 1–31. Cambridge: The MIT Press, 1996.

Buzan, Barry. *People, States, and Fear: An Agenda For International Security Studies in the Post–Cold War Era*. Boulder, Colorado: Lynne Reinner Publishers, 1991.

Carter, Jimmy. *Keeping Faith: The Memoirs of a President*. Toronto: Bantam Books, 1982.

Comptons's Interactive Encyclopedia. Compton's NewsMedia, Inc., 1994.

Connor, Walker. "Ethnonationalism." In *Understanding Political Development*, ed. Myron Weiner and Samuel Huntington. Boston and Toronto: Little, Brown and Company, 1987.

Cooper, Marc N. *The Transformation of Egypt*. Baltimore: The Johns Hopkins University Press, 1982.

Cordesman, Anthony H. *After the Storm: The Changing Military Balance in the Middle East*. Boulder: Westview Press, 1993.

Dahrendorf, Ralf. "On the Governability of Democracies." In *Comparative Politics: Notes and Readings*, ed. Roy C. Macridis and Bernard Brown, 283–293. Pacific Grove, California: Brooks/Cole Publishing Company, 1990.

David, Steven R. *Choosing Sides: Alignment and Realignment in the Third World*. Baltimore: The Johns Hopkins University Press, 1991.

Dessouki, Ali E. Hillal. "The Primacy of Economics: The Foreign Policy of Egypt." In *The Foreign Policies of Arab States: The Challenge of Change*, ed. Bahgat Korany and Ali E. Hillal Dessouki, 156–185. Boulder: Westview Press, 1991.

Devlin, John F. *Syria: Modern State in an Ancient Land*. Boulder: Westview Press, 1983.

Drysdale, Alasdair, and Raymond A. Hinnebusch. *Syria and the Middle East Peace Process*. New York: Council on Foreign Relations, 1991.

Dupuy, T. N. *Elusive Victory: The Arab-Israeli Wars 1947–1974.* Fairfax: Hero Books, 1984.

Easton, David. "The Analysis of Political Systems." In *Comparative Politics: Notes and Readings,* ed. Roy C. Macridis and Bernard Brown, 48–57. Pacific Grove, California: Brooks/Cole Publishing Company, 1990.

"Egypt." *Middle East Economic Digest,* 23 February 1979, 24–26.

"Egypt." *Middle East Economic Handbook.* London: Euromonitor Publications Limited, 1986.

Eickelman, Dale F. *The Middle East: An Anthropological Approach.* 2nd ed. Englewood Cliffs: Prentice Hall, 1989.

Faksh, Mahmud A. *The Future of Islam in the Middle East: Fundamentalism in Egypt, Algeria, and Saudi Arabia.* Westport: Praeger, 1997.

Firro, Kais. "The Syrian Economy Under the Asad Regime." In *Syria Under Assad: Domestic Constraints and Regional Risks,* ed. Moshe Ma'oz and Avner Yaniv, 36–68. New York: St. Martin's Press, 1986.

Fleming, William G. "Sub-Saharan Africa: Case Studies of International Attitudes and Transactions of Ghana and Uganda." In *Linkage Politics: Essays on the Convergence of National and International Systems,* ed. James N. Rosenau, 94–121. New York: The Free Press, 1969.

Gaddis, John Lewis. "Great Illusions, the Long Peace, and the Future of the International System." In *The Long Postwar Peace,* ed. Charles W. Kegley Jr., 25–55. New York: HarperCollins Publishers, 1991.

Gawrych, George W. "Jihad in the Twentieth Century." In *Book of Readings: Modern Military History of the Middle East,* ed. George W. Gawrych, 1–9. Fort Leavenworth: U.S. Army Command and General Staff College, 1996.

Gilpin, Robert. *The Political Economy of International Relations.* Princeton: Princeton University Press, 1987.

Gilpin, Robert. *War and Change in World Politics.* Cambridge: Cambridge University Press, 1986.

Glazer, Nathan, and Daniel P. Moynihan. "Introduction." In *Ethnicity: Theory and Experience,* ed. Nathan Glazer and Daniel P. Moynihan, 1–26. Cambridge and London: Harvard University Press, 1983.

Golan, Galia. *Soviet Policies in the Middle East From World War II to Gorbachev.* Cambridge: Cambridge University Press, 1990.

Golan, Galia, and Itamar Rabinovich. "The Soviet Union and Syria: The Limits of Cooperation." *The Limits of Power: Soviet Policy in the Middle East,* ed. Yaacov Ro'i, 213–231. London: Croom Helm Ltd, 1979.

Gunaratna, Rohan. *Inside Al-Qaeda: Global Network of Terror.* New York: Berkeley Books, 2002.

Gurr, Ted Robert, and Muriel McClelland, "Political Performance: A Twelve Nation Study." In *Comparative Politics Series,* vol. 2, nos. 01–018, ed. Harry Eckstein and Ted Robert Gurr, 395–413. Beverly Hills: Sage Publications, 1971.

Haddad, Wadi D. *Lebanon: The Politics of Revolving Doors.* Washington, D.C.: Praeger Special Studies, 1985.

Halpern, Manfred. *The Politics of Social Change in the Middle East and North Africa.* Princeton: Princeton University Press, 1963.

Herzog, Chaim *The War of Atonement, October 1973: The Fateful Implications of the Arab-Israeli Conflict.* Boston: Little, Brown and Company, 1975.

Hinnebusch, Raymond A. "Liberalization in Syria: The Struggle of Economic and Political Rationality." In *Contemporary Syria: Liberalization Between Cold War and Cold Peace,* ed. Eberhard Kienle, 97–113. London: British Academic Press, 1994.

Hinnebusch, Raymond A. "Revisionist Dreams, Realist Strategies: The Foreign Policy of Syria." In *The Foreign Policies of Arab States: The Challenge of Change,* ed. Bahgat Korany and Ali E. Hillal Dessouki, 374–409. Boulder: Westview Press, 1991.

Hinnebusch, Raymond A. Jr. *Egyptian Politics Under Sadat: The Post-Populist Development of an Authoritarian-Modernizing State.* Cambridge: Cambridge University Press, 1985.

Hitti, Philip K. *Syria: A Short History.* New York: The MacMillan Company, 1959.

Hoffman, Bruce. "Low-intensity Conflict: Terrorism and Guerilla Warfare in the Coming Decades." In *Terrorism: Roots, Impacts, and Responses,* ed. Lance Howard, 139–154. New York: Praeger, 1992.

Holm, Hans-Henrik, and Georg Sorensen. *Whose World Order? Uneven Globalization and the End of the Cold War.* Boulder: Westview Press, .

Holsti, K. J. "International Theory and War in the Third World." In *The Insecurity Dilemma: National Security of Third World States,* ed. Brian Job, 37–60. Boulder: Lynne Reinner Publishers, 1992.

Holsti, Ole R., and James D. Sullivan. "National-International Linkages: France and China as Nonconforming Alliance Members." In *Linkage Politics: Essays on the Convergence of National and International Systems,* eds. James N. Rosenau, 147–195. New York: The Free Press, 1969.

Holsti, Ole R., Randolph M. Siverson, and Alexander L. George, ed. *Change in the International System.* Boulder: Westview Press, 1980.

Hopwood, Derek. *Egypt: Politics and Society 1945–1990.* London: HarperCollins, 1991.

Hopwood, Derek. *Syria 1945–1986: Politics and Society.* London: Unwin Hyman, 1988.

Horowitz, Donald L. *Ethnic Groups in Conflict.* Berkeley: University of California Press, 1985.

Hourani, Albert. *A History of the Arab Peoples.* Cambridge: The Belknap Press of Harvard University Press, 1991.

Hudson, Michael C. *Arab Politics: The Search For Legitimacy.* New Haven: Yale University Press, 1977.

Huntington, Samuel P. *The Political Order in Changing Societies.* New Haven: Yale University Press, 1968.

Hurewitz, J. C. *Middle East Politics: The Military Dimension.* New York: Praeger Publishers, 1969.

Inglehart, Ronald. *Culture Shift in Advanced Industrial Society.* Princeton: Princeton University Press, 1990.

Jurgensmeyer, Mark. *The New Cold War?: Religious Nationalism Confronts the Secular State.* Berkeley: University of California Press.

Kanovsky, Eliyanhu. "Egypt's Economy Under Sadat: Will the Peace Agreement be Followed by Prosperity?" In *Middle East Contemporary Survey 1978–1979*, ed. Colin Legum, Haim Shaked, and Daniel Dishon, 353–376. New York: Holmes and Meier Publishers, 1981.

Kaplan, Robert D. *The Arabists: The Romance of an American Elite.* New York: The Free Press, 1995.

Kessler, Martha Neff. *Syria: Fragile Mosaic of Power.* Washington, D.C.: National Defense University Press, 1987.

Kienle, Eberhard. "Introduction: Liberalization Between Cold War and Cold Peace." In *Contemporary Syria: Liberalization Between Cold War and Cold Peace*, ed. Eberhard Kienle, 1–13. London: British Academic Press, 1994.

Kissinger, Henry A. "Domestic Structure and Foreign Policy." In *International Politics and Foreign Policy: A Reader in Research and Theory*, ed. James N. Rosenau, 261–275. New York: The Free Press, 1969.

Koury, Enver M. *The Crisis in the Lebanese System: Confessionalism and Chaos.* Washington, D.C.: American Enterprise Institute for Public Policy Research, 1978.

Lawson, Fred. "Domestic Pressures and the Peace Process: Fillip or Hindrance?" In *Contemporary Syria: Liberalization Between Cold War and Cold Peace*, ed. Eberhard Kienle, 139–154. London: British Academic Press, 1994.

Legum, Colin, Haim Shaked, and Daniel Dishon, eds. *Middle East Contemporary Survey, 1979–1980.* New York: Holmes and Meier Publishers, 1981.

Lesch, Ann M. "Domestic Politics and Foreign Policy in Egypt." In *Democracy, War, and Peace in the Middle East*, ed. David Garnham and Mark Tessler, 223–243. Bloomington: Indiana University Press, 1995.

Levy, Jack. "The Causes of War: A Review of Theories and Evidence." In *Behavior Society and Nuclear War Volume 1*, ed. Philip E. Tetlock, Jo L. Husbands, Robert Jervis, Paul C. Stern, and Charles Tilly, 209–333. New York: Oxford University Press, 1989.

Lewis, Bernard. "What is an Arab?" In *Peoples and Cultures of the Middle East*, ed. Ailon Shiloh, 3–9. New York: Random House, 1969.

Lijphart, Arend. Democracies: *Patterns of Majoritarian and Consensus Government in Twenty-One Countries.* New Haven: Yale University Press, 1984.

Lippman, Thomas W. *Egypt After Nasser: Sadat, Peace, and the Mirage of Prosperity.* New York: Paragon House, 1989.

Lomperis, Timothy J. *From People's War to People's Rule: Insurgency, Intervention, and the Lessons of Vietnam.* Chapel Hill: The University of North Carolina Press, 1996.

Ma'oz, Moshe. "The Emergence of Modern Syria." In *Syria Under Assad: Domestic Constraints and Regional Risks*, ed. Moshe Ma'oz and Avner Yaniv, 9–35. New York: St. Martin's Press, 1986.

Ma'oz, Zeev. "The Evolution of Syrian Power, 1948–1984." In *Syria Under Assad: Domestic Constraints and Regional Risks,* ed. Moshe Ma'oz and Avner Yaniv, 69–82. New York: St. Martin's Press, 1986.

Macridis, Roy C., and Steven L. Burg. *Introduction to Comparative Politics: Regimes and Change.* New York: HarperCollins Publishers, 1991.

Mangold, Peter. "The Soviet Record in the Middle East." In *Crisis Management and the Superpowers in the Middle East*, ed. Gregory Treverton, 89–95. Westmead: Gower Publishing Company Limited, 1981.

Mathews, Jessica T. "Power Shift." In *Strategy and Force Planning, 3rd Edition*, ed. Strategy and Force Planning Faculty, 93–106. Newport: Naval War College Press, 2000.

Mayer, Thomas. *The Changing Past: Egyptian Historiography of the Urabi Revolt, 1882–1983*. Gainesville, University of Florida Press, 1988.

McDermott, Anthony. *Egypt From Nasser to Mubarak: A Flawed Revolution*. London: Croom Helm, 1988.

McLaurin, R. D., Don Peretz, and Lewis W. Snider. *Middle East Foreign Policy: Issues and Policies*. New York: Praeger Publishers, 1982.

The Middle East and North Africa, 1987. London: Europa Publications Limited, 1995.

The Middle East and North Africa, 1995. London: Europa Publications Limited, 1995.

Migdal, Joel. *Strong Societies and Weak States: State-Society Relations and State Capabilities in the Third World*. Princeton: Princeton University Press, 1988.

Morris, Mary E. *New Political Realities and the Gulf: Egypt, Syria, and Jordan*. Santa Monica: Rand, 1993.

Nasrallah, Fida. "Syria After Ta'if: Lebanon and the Lebanese in Syrian Politics." In *Contemporary Syria: Liberalization Between Cold War and Cold Peace*, ed. Eberhard Kienle, 132–138. London: British Academic Press, 1994.

Niblock, Tim. "Arab Losses, First World Gains." In *Beyond the Gulf War: The Middle East and the New World Order*, ed. John Gittings, 77–85. London: Catholic Institute for International Relations, 1991.

Norton, Augustus Richard. "The Security Legacy of the 1980s in the Third World." *Third World Security in the Post–Cold War Era*, ed. Thomas G. Weiss and Meryl A. Kessler, 19–33. Boulder: Lynne Reinner Publishers, 1990.

Norton, Philip. *The British Polity*. New York: Longman, 1990.

Olson, Mancur. *The Rise and Decline of Nations*. New Haven and London: Yale University Press, 1982.

Pelletiere, Stephen C. *Shari'a Law, Cult Violence and System Challenge in Egypt: The Dilemma Facing President Mubarak*. U.S. Army War College at Carlisle Barracks: Strategic Studies Institute, 5 April 1994.

Peretz, Don. *The Middle East*. New York: Praeger Publishers, 1988.

Perthes, Volker. *Economic Change, Political Control and Decision Making in Syria*. Germany: SWP, 1994.

Perthes, Volker. "Stages of Economic and Political Liberalization. In *Contemporary Syria: Liberalization Between Cold War and Cold Peace*, ed. Eberhard Kienle, 44–71. London: British Academic Press, 1994.

Pipes, Daniel. *Greater Syria: The History of an Ambition*. New York: Oxford University Press, 1990.

Posen, Barry. *Sources of Military Doctrine: France, Britain, and Germany Between the World Wars*. Ithaca: Cornell University Press, 1984.

Pye, Lucian W. "Introduction." In *Political Culture and Political Development*, ed. Lucian W. Pye and Sidney Verba, 3–26. Princeton: Princeton University Press, 1960.

Quandt, William B. *Camp David: Peacemaking and Politics*. Washington, D.C.: The Brookings Institution, 1986.

Richardson, Louise. "Global Rebels: Terrorist Organizations as Trans-National Actors. In *Terrorism and Counterterrorism: Understanding the New Security Environment*, eds. Russell Howard and Reid Sawyer, 67–73. Guilford: McGraw-Hill Press, 2002.

Rosenau, James N. "The Complexities and Contradictions of Globalization." In *Understanding International Relations*, ed. Daniel J. Kaufman, Jay Parker, and Kimberly C. Field, 756–760. New York: McGraw-Hill, 1999.

Rosenau, James N., ed. *Linkage Politics: Essays on the Convergence of National and International Systems*. New York: The Free Press, 1969.

Rothschild, Joseph. *Ethnopolitics: A Conceptual Framework*. New York: Columbia University Press, 1981.

Roy, Oliver. *The Failure of Political Islam*. Cambridge: Harvard University Press, 1994.

Sadat, Anwar. *In Search of Identity: An Autobiography*. New York: Harper & Row, Publishers, 1978.

Sadowski, Yahya. "Ba'thist Ethics and the Spirit of State Capitalism: Patronage and the Party in Contemporary Syria." In *Ideology and Power in the Middle East*, ed. Peter J. Chelkowski and Robert J. Pranger, 160–184. Durham: Duke University Press, 1988.

Safran, Nadav. "Dimensions of the Middle East Problem." In *Foreign Policy in World Politics: States and Regions*, ed. Roy C. Macridis, 374–419. Englewood Cliffs: Prentice Hall, 1989.

Said, Abdul A., and Luiz R. Simmons. "The Ethnic Factor in World Politics." In *Ethnicity in an International Context*, ed. Abdul A. Said and Luiz R. Simmons, 15–45. New Brunswick: Transaction Books, 1976.

Saunders, Harold H. *The Other Walls: The Politics of the Arab-Israeli Peace Process*. Washington, D.C.: American Enterprise Institute for Public Policy Research, 1985.

Schwartz, Peter. "The Art of the Long View." In *Strategy and Force Planning, 2nd Edition*, ed. Strategy and Force Planning Faculty, 29–44. Newport: Naval War College Press, 1997.

Seale, Patrick. *Asad: The Struggle for the Middle East*. Berkeley: University of California Press, 1979.

Seale, Patrick. *Asad of Syria: The Struggle For The Middle East*. Berkeley: University of California Press, 1988.

Singer, J. David. "The Level of Analysis Problem in International Relations." In *International Politics and Foreign Policy: A Reader in Research and Theory*, ed. James N. Rosenau, 20–29. New York: The Free Press, 1969.

Skocpol, Theda. *States and Social Revolutions*. Cambridge: Cambridge University Press, 1979.

Smoke, Richard. *National Security and the Nuclear Dilemma: An Introduction to the American Experience*. New York: Random House, 1987.

Snyder, Jack. *Myths of Empire: Domestic Politics and International Ambition*. Ithaca: Cornell University Press, 1991.

Spechler, Dina. "The Soviet Union in the Middle East: Problems, Policies and Prospective Trends." In *The Limits to Power: Soviet Policy in the Middle East*, ed. Yaacov Ro'I, 331–365. London: Croom Helm Ltd., 1979.

Speiser, E. A. "Cultural Factors in Social Dynamics in the Near East." In *Social Forces in the Middle East*, ed. Sydney Nettleton Fisher, 1–22. Ithaca: Cornell University Press, 1955.

Springborg, Robert. "Approaches to the Understanding of Egypt." In *Ideology and Power in the Middle East: Studies in Honor of George Lenczowski*, ed. Peter J. Chelkowski and Robert J. Pranger, 137–159. Durham: Duke University Press, 1989.

Springborg, Robert. *Mubarak's Egypt: Fragmentation of the Political Order*. Boulder: Westview Press, 1989.

Sukkar, Nabil. "The Crisis of 1986 and Syria's Plan for Reform." In *Contemporary Syria: Liberalization Between Cold War and Cold Peace*, ed. Eberhard Kienle, 26–43. London: British Academic Press, 1994.

Thompson, Robert J., and Joseph R. Rudolph. "Ethnic Politics and Public Policy in Western Societies: A Framework For Comparative Analysis." In *Ethnicity, Politics, and Development*, ed. Dennis L. Thompson and Dov Ronen, 25–63. Boulder: Lynne Reinner, 1986.

Thompson, Richard H. "Neo-Marxian Explanations and a Reformulation." In *Theories of Ethnicity: A Critical Appraisal*, ed. Richard H. Thompson, 141–174. New York: Greenwood Press, 1989.

Vasquez, John A. "The Deterrence Myth: Nuclear Weapons and the Prevention of Nuclear War." In *The Long Postwar Peace*, ed. Charles W. Kegley Jr., 205–223. New York: HarperCollins, 1991.

Vatikiotis, P. J. *The Modern History of Egypt*. New York: Frederick A. Praeger, 1969.

Verba, Sidney. "Conclusion." In *Political Culture and Political Development*, ed. Lucian W. Pye and Sidney Verba, 512–560. Princeton: Princeton University Press, 1965.

Walt, Stephen M. *The Origins of Alliances*. Ithaca: Cornell University Press, 1987.

Waltz, Kenneth N. *Man, the State, and War*. New York: Columbia University Press, 1959.

Waltz, Kenneth N. "Reflections on Theory of International Politics: A Response to My Critics." In *NeoRealism and Its Critics*, ed. Robert O. Keohane, 322–346. New York: Columbia University Press, 1986.

Waltz, Kenneth N. *Theory of International Politics*. Reading, Massachusetts: Addison-Wesley Publishing Company, 1979.

Weber, Max. "Politics As A Vocation." In *From Max Weber: Essays in Sociology*, ed. H. H. Gerth and C. Wright Mills, 23–29. New York: Oxford University Press, 1946.

World Tables, 1989–90 Edition: From the Data Files of the World Bank. Baltimore: The Johns Hopkins University Press, 1990.

Yorke, Valerie. *Domestic Politics and Regional Security: Jordan, Syria, and Israel*. Aldershot U.K.: Gower, 1988.

Zogby, James J. *What Arabs Think: Values, Beliefs and Concerns*. Zogby International: Arab Thought Foundation, September 2002.

GOVERNMENT DOCUMENTS, POLICY PAPERS, LECTURE, AND SPEECH

Beitler, Ruth M., and Cindy R. Jebb. "Egypt as a Failing State: Implications for U.S. National Security." Occasional Paper #51, Institute of National Security Studies, July 2003.

Department of Social Sciences. "Briefing to Alumni." Lecture given in June 1999 at the United States Military Academy, West Point, New York.

"Egypt's Elite Rate U.S., GCC States High; Iraq and Libya Low." *Research Memorandum*. Washington, D.C.: U.S. Information Agency, 1991.

Hannah, John P. "At Arms Length: Soviet-Syrian Relations in the Gorbachev Era." *The Washington Institute Policy Papers*, no. 8. Washington, D.C.: The Washington Institute for Near East Policy, 1989.

Hoffman, Bruce. Lecture to the Terrorism Seminar given in April 2002 at the United States Military Academy, West Point, New York.

Huxley, Fred. "The Arabs." In *In The Eye of the Beholder: Muslim and Non-Muslim Views of Islam, Islamic Politics, and Each Other*, ed. David Pollock and Elaine El Assal, 1–16. Washington, D.C.: Office of Research and Media Reaction, U.S. Information Service, 1996.

"Interview with Muhammad Hakki, former editor of *Al-Ahram*." Conducted by Ruth M. Beitler and Cindy R. Jebb on 26 July 2002 in Washington, D.C.

"Interview with Sara Daly." Conducted by Ruth M. Beitler and Cindy R. Jebb on 25 July 2002 at Rand, Washington, D.C.

Khashan, Hilal. "Partner or Pariah: Attitudes Toward Israel in Syria, Lebanon, and Jordan." *Policy Papers, No. 41*. Washington, D.C.: The Washington Institute for Near East Policy, 1996.

Meyer, Michael B., and Brent J. Talbot. "View From the East: Arab Perceptions of the United States Presence and Policy." Occasional Paper #48, Institute of National Security Studies, February 2003.

The Middle East. 8th ed. Washington, D.C.: Congressional Quarterly Inc., 1994.

"A National Security Strategy for a New Century." The White House. December 1999.

Pipes, Daniel. "Syria Beyond the Peace Process." *The Washington Institute Policy Papers, No. 40*. Washington, D.C.: The Washington Institute for Near East Policy, 1996.

Pollock, David. "The Arab Street?: Public Opinion in the Arab World." *The Washington Institute Policy Papers, No. 32*. Washington, D.C.: The Washington Institute for Near East Policy, 1992.

Sadat, Anwar. Speech to Israeli Knesset on November 20, 1977. Quoted in William B. Quandt. *Camp David: Peacemaking and Politics*, 346, Washington, D.C.: The Brookings Institution, 1986.

Saunders, Harold. "Changing Paradigms for the 1990s." Lecture given on 3 April 1991 at Duke University.

"Seeking a National Strategy: A Concert for Preserving Security and Promoting Freedom." *The U.S. Commission on National Security/21st Century* (April 15, 2000).

Supporting Peace: America's Role in an Arab Israel-Syria Peace Agreement. Washington, D.C.: Washington Institute Study Group.

"Tom Friedman and Bill Kristol Discuss Violence in the Middle East." Interview by Tim Russert on "Meet the Press" (17 March 2002). Accessed on 6 August 2002 at proquest.umi.com.

U.S. Department of State, Bureau of Public Affairs, Office of Public Communication. *Background Notes, 5, No. 7.* Washington, D.C.: U.S. Government Printing Office, August 1994.

U.S. Department of State, Bureau of Public Affairs, Office of Public Communication. *Background Notes, 5, No. 13.* Washington, D.C.: U.S. Government Printing Office, November 1994.

JOURNAL, MAGAZINE, AND NEWSPAPER ARTICLES

Ajami, Fouad. "The Phantoms of Egypt." *U.S. News and World Report*, 10 April 1995, 55.

Ajami, Fouad. "The Sentry's Solitude." *Foreign Affairs* 80, no. 6 (November/December 2001): 2–16.

Ajami, Fouad. "The Sorrows of Egypt." *Foreign Affairs* 74, no. 5 (September/October 1995): 72–88.

Album, Andrew. "Egypt Faces its Moment of Truth." *Business and Finance of the Middle East*, July/August 1995, 28–29.

Aly, Abdel Moneim Said, and Robert H. Pelletreau. "U.S.-Egyptian Relations." *Middle East Policy* (June 2001): 1–11. Accessed on 10 June 2003 at proquest.umi.com.

Baker, Pauline, and John A. Ausink. "State Collapse and Ethnic Violence: Toward a Predictive Model." *Parameters* 26, no. 1 (Spring 1996): 19–31.

Batatu, Hanna. "Some Observations on the Social Roots of Syria's Ruling Military Group and the Causes for its Dominance." *The Middle East Journal* 35 (Summer, 1981): 331–344.

Beinin, Joel. "Labor, Capital, and the State in Nasserist Egypt, 1952–1961." *International Journal of Middle Eastern Studies* 21, no. 1 (February 1989): 71–90.

Ben-Meir, Alon. "The Israeli-Syrian Battle for Equitable Peace." *Middle East Policy* 3, no. 1 (1994): 71–83.

Brown, Nathan. "Peasants and Notables." *Middle Eastern Studies* 26, no. 2 (April 1990): 145–160.

Campbell, John C. "Soviet Policy in the Middle East." *Current History* 80, no. 462 (January 1981): 1–9 and 42–43.

Casandra, "The Impending Crisis in Egypt." *Middle East Journal* 49, no. 1 (Winter 1995): 9–27.

Casandra. "The Impending Crisis in Egypt." *Middle East Journal* 49, No. 1 (Winter 1995): 9–27.

"Caution is the Watchword." *Business and Finance*, December 1993, 29.

Choueiri, Y. "Two Histories of Syria and the Demise of Syrian Patriotism." *Middle Eastern Studies* 23, no. 4 (October 1987): 496–511.

Cohen, Stephen. "A Not-So-Odd Mideast Couple." *New York Times*, 25 August 1994, 21(A).

Cordesman, Anthony. "Arab-U.S. Strategic Cooperation: A Net Assessment." *Middle East Policy* (December 2002): 1–8. Accessed on 21 March 2003 at proquest .umi.com.

David, Steven R. "Explaining Third World Alignment." *World Politics* 43, no. 2 (January 1991): 233–256.

Deutsch, Karl. "Social Mobilization and Political Development." *American Political Science Review* 55, no. 3 (September 1961): 493–514.

Drysdale, Alasdair. "The Succession Question in Syria." *The Middle East Journal* 39, no. 2 (Spring 1985): 246–258.

Drysdale, Alasdair. "Syria's Troubled Ba'thi Regime." *Current History* 80, no. 462 (January 1981): 32–35 and 37–38.

Easton, David. "A Reassessment of the Concept of Political Support." *British Journal of Political Science* 5, no. 4 (October 1975): 435–457.

Eikelman, Dale F. "Bin Laden, the Arab 'Street,' and the Middle East's Democratic Deficit." *Current History: A Journal of Contemporary World Affairs* 101, no. 651 (January 2002): 36–39.

Eitts, Hermann Frederick. "The Persian Gulf Crisis: Perspectives and Prospects." *The Middle East Journal* 45, no. 1 (Winter 1991): 7–22.

Faksh, Mahmud A. "The Alawi Community of Syria: A New Dominant Political Force." *Middle Eastern Studies* 20, No. 2 (April 1984): 133–153.

Faksh, Mahmud, A. "Syria's Role and Objectives in Lebanon." *Mediterranean Quarterly* 3, no. 2 (Spring 1992): 81–95.

"Fierce Words, Tied Hands." *The Economist*, 3 April 2003, 1–3. Accessed on 18 July 2003 at www.economist.com.

Fuller, Graham E. "Moscow and the Gulf War." *Foreign Affairs* 70, no. 3 (Summer 1991): 55–76.

Furtado, Charles F. Jr. "Nationalism and Foreign Policy in Ukraine." *Political Science Quarterly* 109, no. 1 (Spring 1994): 81–104.

Gaddis, John Lewis. "The Long Peace." *International Security* 10, no. 4 (1986): 99–142.

Gerges, Farwaz A. "Egyptian-Israeli Relations Turn Sour." *Foreign Affairs* 74, no. 3 (May/June 1995): 69–78.

Gerges, Farwaz A. "The End of the Islamist Insurgency in Egypt?: Costs and Prospects." *The Middle East Journal* (Autumn 2000): 1–14. Accessed on 10 June 2003 at proquest.umi.com.

Gold, Dore. "The Syrian-Israeli Track—Taking the Final Step: What Sacrifices Will Asad Make to Get Back the Golan?" *Middle East Insight*, September/October 1994, 14–17.

Gordon, Joel. "The False Hopes of 1950: The Wafd's Last Hurrah and the Demise of Egypt's Old Order." *International Journal of Middle Eastern Studies* 21, no. 2 (May 1989): 193–214.

Goudsouzian, Tanya. "We Are All Angry: Interview With Egypt's Foreign Minister Amre Moussa." *Middle East Insight* 16, No. 1 (January–February 2001): 29–33.

Hammond, Andrew. "Egypt's Deep-Sixed 1954 Constitution A Reminder of What Might Have Been." *The Washington Report on Middle East Affairs* (September/October 2002): 1–3. Accessed on 10 June 2003 at proquest.umi.com.

Heikal, Mohamed Hassanein. "Egyptian Foreign Policy." *Foreign Affairs* 56, no. 4 (July 1978): 714–727.

Heydeman, Steven. "Can We Get There From Here? Lessons From the Syrian Case." *American-Arab Affairs* 36 (Spring 1991): 27–30.

Hinnebusch, Raymond A. "Does Syria Want Peace? Syrian Policy in the Syrian-Israeli Peace Negotiations." *Journal of Palestine Studies* 26, no. 1 (Autumn 1996): 42–57.

Hinnebusch, Raymond A. "State and Civil Society in Syria." *Middle East Journal* 47, no. 2 (Spring 1993): 243–257.

Hinnebusch, Raymond A. "Syria: The Politics of Peace and Regime Survival." *Middle East Policy* 3, no. 4 (April 1995): 74–87.

Hoffman, Bruce. "Holy Terror: The Implications of Terrorism Motivated by a Religious Imperative." *Studies in Conflict and Terrorism* 18, no. 4 (October 1995): 271–284.

Horowitz, David. "Portrait of the Enemy." *The Jerusalem Report* 6, no. 6 (27 July 1995): 24–30.

Hudson, Michael. "Imperial Headaches: Managing Unruly Regions in an Age of Globalization." *Middle East Policy* (December 2002): 1–10. Accessed on 21 March 2003 at proquest.umi.com.

Hunter, F. Robert. "Self-Image and Historical Truth: Nubar Pasha and the Making of Modern Egypt." *Middle Eastern Studies* 26, no. 2 (April 1990): 363–375.

"International: Mr. Assad Goes to London: Syria, Iraq, and Britain." *The Economist*, 14 December 2002, 1–2. Accessed on 29 July 2003 at proquest.umi.com.

"International: Saddam's Summer Friends: Iraq's Neighbors." *The Economist*, 8 February 2003, 1–3. Accessed on 21 March 2003 at proquest.umi.com.

"Israel, Syria and that Sliver of the Galilee Shore." *The Economist*, 30 May 2000, 1–4. Accessed on 18 July 2003 at www.economist.com.

"Al-Jazeera: Arabs Rate its Objectivity." Gallup Tuesday Briefing, 23 April 2002. Accessed on 10 July 2002 at www.gallup.com.

Jebb, Cindy R. "The Fight for Legitimacy: Liberal Democracy Versus Terrorism." *Journal of Conflict Studies* 23, no. 1 (Spring 2003): 126–154.

Jebb, Cindy R. "The Fight for Legitimacy: Liberal Democracy Versus Terrorism." Paper presented at the International Studies Association National Conference in Chicago, 23 February 2001.

Karsh, Efraim. "A Marriage of Convenience: The Soviet Union and Asad's Syria." *Jerusalem Journal of International Relations* 11, no. 4 (December 1989): 1–26.

Kaufman, Chaim. "Possible and Impossible Solutions to Ethnic Civil Wars." *International Security* 20, no. 4 (Spring 1996): 136–175.

Kemp, Geoffrey. "The Middle East Arms Race: Can it be Controlled?" *The Middle East Journal* 45, no. 3 (Summer 1991): 441–446.

Kienle, Eberhard. "Arab Unity Schemes Revisited: Interest, Identity, and Policy in Syria and Egypt." *International Journal of Middle East Studies* 27, no. 1 (February 1995): 53–71.

Knapp. Michael G. "The Concept and Practice of Jihad in Islam." *Parameters* (Spring 2003): 1–9. Accessed on 1 July 2003 at proquest.umi.com.

Kohli, Atul, Peter Evans, Peter Katzenstein, Adam Przeworski, Susanne Hoeber Rudolph, James C. Scott, and Theda Skocpol. "The Role of Theory in Comparative Politics: A Symposium." *World Politics* 48, no. 1 (October 1995): 1–49.

Krauthammer, Charles. "The Unipolar Moment." *Foreign Affairs* 70, no. 1 (Winter 1991): 23–33.

Kumaraswamy, P. R. "The Israel-Syrian Peace Talks: 1991–1996 and Beyond." *Journal of Third World Studies* 19, no. 2 (Fall 2002): 1–3. Accessed on 29 July 2003 at proquest.umi.com.

Labs, Eric J. "Do Weak States Bandwagon?" *Security Studies* 1, No. 3 (1992): 383–415.

Lancaster, John, and Dana Priest. "U.S. Assures Egypt on Foreign Aid: Defense Secretary Makes No Promises About Cuts After 1996." *Washington Post*, 9 January 1995, 8–9.

Lapidus, Gail Warshofsky. "Ethnonationalism and Political Stability: The Soviet Case." *World Politics* 36, no. 4 (July 1984): 555–580.

Lawson, Fred H. "Domestic Transformation and Foreign Steadfastness in Contemporary Syria." *Middle East Journal* 48, no. 1 (Winter 1994): 47–64.

Lawson, Fred H. "From Neo-Ba'th to Ba'th Nouveau: Hafiz al-Asad's Second Decade." *Journal of South Asian and Middle Eastern Studies* 14, no. 2 (Winter 1990): 1–22.

Lesch, Ann Mosley. "Contrasting Reactions to the Persian Gulf Crisis: Egypt, Syria, Jordan, and the Palestinians." *The Middle East Journal* 14, no. 2 (Winter 1990): 32–50.

Lifton, Robert K. "Talking with Assad: A Visit to the Middle East in Transition." *Middle East Insight*, September/October, 8–11.

MacFarquhar, Neil. "Syria Reaches Turning Point, But Which Way Will it Turn." *New York Times*, 12 March 2001, 1–4 (A).

Mackie, Alan. "Cairo is Now Looking to Washington as a Major Source of Aid." *Middle East Economic Digest*, 5 January 1979, 5–7.

Makram-Ebeid, Mona. "Egypt's 1995 Elections: One Step Forward, Two Steps Back?" *Middle East Policy* 4, no. 3 (March 1996): 117–136.

Makram-Ebeid, Mona. "Egypt's 2000 Parliamentary Elections." *Middle East Policy* (June 2001): 1–10. Accessed on 10 June 2003 at proquest.umi.com.

Malik, Ifikhar H. "World Politics and South Asia: Beginning of an End?" *Journal of South Asian and Middle Eastern Studies* 19, no. 3 (Spring 1996): 40–70.

March, James G., and Johan P. Olsen. "The New Institutionalism: Organizational Factors in Political Life." *American Political Science Review* 78, no. 3 (September 1984): 734–749.

McIntosh, Mary E., Martha Abele MacIver, Daniel Abele, and David B. Nolle. "Minority Rights and Majority Rule: Ethnic Tolerance in Romania and Bulgaria." *Social Forces* 73, no. 3 (March 1995): 939–967.

Mearsheimer, John J. "Why We Will Soon Miss the Cold War." *The Atlantic Monthly*, (August 1990): 35–50.

Melham, Hisham. "Syria Between Two Transitions." *Middle East Report: Lebanon and Syria: The Geopolitics of Change* 0, no. 203 (Spring 1997): 2–7.

Moubayed, Sami. "Yesterday's Friends Today are the Enemies of America." *The Washington Report on Middle East Affairs* 21, no. 9 (December 2002): 1–4. Accessed on 29 July 2003 at proquest.umi.com.

Murphy, Carlyle. "The Business of Political Change in Egypt." *Current History* 94, no. 588 (January 1995): 18–22.

Muslih, Muhammad. "Dateline Damascus: Asad is Ready." *Foreign Policy* 96 (Fall 1994): 145–163.

Muslih, Muhammad. "The Golan: Israel, Syria, and Strategic Calculations." *Middle East Journal* 47, no. 4 (Autumn 1993): 611–632.

Negus, Steve. "Mubarak's Diplomatic Coup." *Middle East Insight*, 15 March 1996, 8–9.

Nelan, Bruce W. "Boris Vs. Mikhail." *Time* (24 March 1991), 26–31.

Newman, Saul. "Does Modernization Breed Ethnic Political Conflict?" *World Politics* 43, no. 3 (April 1991): 451–478.

Norton, Augustus Richard. "America's Approach to the Middle East: Legacies, Questions, and Possibilities." *Current History: A Journal of Contemporary Affairs* 101, no. 651 (January 2002): 3–7.

Olmert, Yosef. "Domestic Crisis and Foreign Policy in Syria: The Assad Regime." *Middle East Review* 20, no. 3 (Spring 1988): 17–25.

Paskar,' P. "The Soviet People—A New Social and International Community of People." *Kommunist Moldavii*, no. 12 (December 1982): 82. Quoted in Gail Warshovsky Lapidus. "Ethnonationalism and Political Stability: The Soviet Case." *World Politics* 36, no. 4 (July 1984): 556.

Perthes, Volker. "The Syrian Economy in the 1980s." *Middle East Journal* 46, no. 1 (Winter 1992): 37–58.

Pincus, Joseph. "Syria: A Captive Economy." *Middle East Review* 12, no. 1 (Fall 1979): 49–60.

Pipes, Daniel. "The Alawi Capture of Power in Syria." *Middle Eastern Studies* 25, no. 4 (October 1989): 429–450.

"Please Sir, We Really Didn't." *The Economist*, 29 May 2003, 1–4. Accessed on 18 July 2003 at www.economist.com.

Polling, Sylvia. "The Syrian Surprise: A New Spirit of Entrepreneurism and a Diligent Program of Economic Reforms are Transforming the Syrian Economy." *Middle East Insight* (July/August 1993): 6–11.

Ramet, Sabrina. "Eastern Europe's Painful Transition." *Current History* 95, no. 599 (March 1996): 97–102.

Reed, Stanley, Susan Postlewaite, and Neal Sandler. "How the Arab World is Already Changing Governments are Scurrying to Ride Out—or Profit from—Saddam's Fall." *Business Week*, 24 March 2003, 1–5. Accessed on 30 March 2003 at proquest.umi.com.

Richter, Melvin. "Toward a Concept of Political Legitimacy: Bonopartist Dictatorship and Democratic Legitimacy." *Political Theory* 10, no. 2 (May 1982): 185–214.

Rivlin Paul. "The Syrian Economy in the 1990s." *Syria: Domestic Political Stress and Globalization: Data and Analysis Series*. Moshe Dayan Center for Middle East and African Studies, Paper #64 (February 2002): 29–62.

Rodman, Peter W. "Middle East Diplomacy." *Foreign Affairs* 70, no. 2 (Spring 1991): 1–17.

Roy, Delwin A., and Thomas Naff. "Ba'thist Ideology, Economic Development and Educational Strategy." *Middle Eastern Studies* 25, no. 4 (October 1989): 451–480.

Sadowski, Yahya. Review of *Authoritarian Power and State Formation in Ba'thist Syria: Army, Party, and Peasant*, by Raymond A. Hinnebusch. In *Middle East Journal* 45, no. 2 (Spring 1991): 341–342.

Salem, Paul. "The Rise and Fall of Secularism in the Arab World." *Middle East Policy* 4, no. 3 (March 1996): 151–160.

Saunders, Harold H. "Political Settlement and the Gulf Crisis." *Mediterranean Quarterly; A Journal of Global Issues* 2, no. 2 (Spring 1991): 1–16.

Al-Sayyid, Mustapha Kamel, Bahman Baktari, Michael Barnett, Sonja Hegasy, et al. "The Impact of 9/11 on the Middle East." *Middle East Policy* (December 2002): 1–23. Accessed on 21 March 2003 at proquest.umi.com.

Schroeder, Paul. "Historical Reality vs. NeoRealist Theory." *International Security* 19, no. 1 (Summer 1994): 108–148.

Schweller, Randall L. "Bandwagoning For Profit: Bringing the Revisionist State Back In." *International Security* 19, no. 1 (Summer 1991): 72–107.

Seale, Patrick, "Obituary: Hafez al-Assad: Feared and Respected Leader who Raised Syria's Profile but was Ultimately Unable to Contain Israel." *The Guardian*, 12 June 2003, 1–4. Accessed on 29 July 2003 at proquest.umi.com.

Singerman, Diane. "The Politics of Emergency Rule in Egypt." *Current History: A Journal of Contemporary Affairs* 101, no. 651 (January 2002): 29–35.

Smucker, Philip. "Egypt's Unrest a Two-Edged Sword." *Christian Science Monitor*, 8 April 2002, 1–3. Accessed on 22 July 2002 at ehostvgw.com.

"Special Report: Damning and Damned: Arab Protest." *The Economist*, 29 March 2003, 1. Accessed on 30 March 2003 at proquest.umi.com.

Stanley, Bruce. "Drawing from the Well: Syria in the Persian Gulf." *Journal of South Asian and Middle Eastern Studies* 14, no. 2 (Winter 1990): 45–64.

Steinmo, Sven. "Political Institutions and Tax Policy in the United States, Sweden, and Britain." *World Politics* 41, no. 4 (July 1989): 500–535.

Stern, Jessica. "The Protean Enemy." *Foreign Affairs* 82, no. 4 (July/August 2003): 27–40.

Stern, Jessica. "Will Terrorists Turn to Poison?" *Orbis* 37, no. 3 (Summer 1993): 1–16. Accessed on 23 November 2001 at ehostvgw6.epnet.com.

Telhami, Shibley. "Camp David II: Assumptions and Consequences." *Current History: A Journal of Contemporary Affairs* 100, no. 642 (January 2001): 10–14.

Telhami, Shibley. "Understanding the Challenge." *Middle East Journal* (Washington, D.C.: Winter 2002): Accessed on 21 March 2003 at proquest.umi.com.

"The Ten Nation Impressions of America Poll." *Zogby International*, 11 April 2002. Accessed 31 July 2002 at interactive.zogby.com/clickon/products.dbm.

Waldner, David. "More Than Meets the Eye: Economic Influence on Contemporary Syrian Foreign Policy," *Middle East Insight*, May/June 1995, 34–37.

Walt, Stephen M. "International Relations: One World, Many Theories." *Foreign Policy* (Spring 1998): 1–9. Accessed on 21 July 2003 at proquest.umi.com.

Webber, Mark. "Coping With Anarchy: Ethnic Conflict and International Organizations in the Former Soviet Union." *International Relations* 18, no. 1 (April 1996): 1–28.

Williams, Donald C. "Reconsidering State and Society in Africa: The Institutional Dimension in Land Reform Policies." *Comparative Politics* 28, no. 2 (January 1996): 207–224.

Wright, Robin. "Unexplored Realities of the Persian Gulf Crisis." *The Middle East Journal* 45, no. 1 (Winter 1991): 23–29.

Ziad, Homayra. "Syrian Policy Expert Says U.S. Threat Not Serious." *The Washington Report on Middle East Affairs* 22, no. 6 (July/August 2003): 1–3. Accessed on 29 July 2003 at proquest.umi.com.

Zisser, Eyal. "Heir Apparent." *The New Republic* 221, no. 15 (11 October 1999): 1–3. Accessed on 29 July 2003 at proquest.umi.com.

Zisser, Eyal. "Syria at a Crossroads." *Syria: Domestic Political Stress and Globalization: Data and Analysis Series*. Moshe Dayan Center for Middle East and African Studies, Paper #64 (February 2002): 7–27.

Zunes, Stephen. "Israeli-Syrian Peace: The Long Road Ahead." *Middle East Policy* 2, no. 3 (1993): 62–67.

FOREIGN BROADCAST INFORMATION SERVICE

"Abd-al-Majid Issues Statement on Gulf War 17 Jan." *FBIS*, NES (18 January 1991):.

"Abu-Ghazalah on Expected Scenario, Gulf Security." *FBIS*, NES (17 January 1991): 5.

"Abu-Talib: Troops Not Subjected to 'Animosity'." *FBIS*, NES (20 February 1991): 8.

"Al-Aharam Praises Reagan Support of Camp David." *FBIS*, NES (8 December 1980): D1-D2.

"Al-Ahmar Reasserts 'Rejection' of Iraqi Invasion." *FBIS*, NES (9 August 1990): 49.

"Ali Denies Coordination With U.S., Israel." *FBIS*, NES (8 December 1980): D3.

"Army Chief Calls Invasion 'Unprecedented Event'." *FBIS*, NES (10 August 1990): 60.

"Al-Asad Congratulates Iran's Bani-Sadr." *FBIS*, NES (30 January 1980): H5.

"Al-Asad Interviewed by Kuwaiti Newspaper." *FBIS*, NES (8 December 1980): H1-H19.

"Ash-Sha'B Fears Zionist Influence." *FBIS*, NES (30 January 1980): D7.

"Ba'th Moroccan Socialist Party Delegations Hold Talks." *FBIS*, NES (30 January 1980): H2.

"Ba'th Official Receives Visiting Soviet Delegation." *FBIS*, NES (30 January 1980): H4.

"Ba'th Party Delegation to Visit GDR, USSR." *FBIS*, NES (30 January 1980): H2.

"Al-Ba'th: Syrian Presence in Lebanon Necessary." *FBIS*, NES (19 November 1982): H2.

"Al-Baz Discusses Tripartite Efforts For Peace." *FBIS*, NES (19 December 1990): 5.

"Al-Shar Requests Emergency Arab Summit." *FBIS*, NES (9 August 1990): 48.

"Butrus Ghali Views Nonaligned Initiative." *FBIS*, NES (20 February 1991): 6–7.

"Cairo Papers Report U.S. to Speed Arms Delivery." *FBIS*, NES (8 December 1980): D1.

"(Clandestine) Voice of Lebanon." *FBIS*, NES (): H2.

"Commentary Applauds Summit Resolutions." *FBIS*, NES (14 August 1990): 51–52.

"Damascus Domestic Service." *FBIS*, NES (30 January 1980): H3.

"Damascus Radio Carries Al-Asad's Der Spiegel Interview." *FBIS*, NES (30 August 1979): H2.

"Damascus Radio on Significance of Al-Asad's Visit to Moscow." *FBIS*, NES (16 October 1979): H1.

"Damascus Reports Khaddam's Cyprus Speech." *FBIS*, NES (20 July 1982): H2.

"Defense Minister Meets with USSR Deputy Minister." *FBIS*, NES (17 March 1982): H1.

"Economy Minister Speaks at Damascus Fair." *FBIS*, NES (5 September 1990): 45–46.

"Editorial Analyzes Gulf War, Peace Prospects." *FBIS*, NES (19 December 1990): 7.

"Editorial Urges Return to Pre-Invasion Kuwait." *FBIS*, NES (14 August 1990): 53.

"Egypt, Syria Said to Propose Gulf Security Plan." *FBIS*, NES (25 February 1991): 44.

"Foreign Minister Khaddam Returns From Iran." *FBIS*, NES (17 March 1982): H1.

"FRG Foreign Minister, Economic Delegation Visit." *FBIS*, NES (28 August 1979): H1.

"Ghali Examines Gulf Crisis, Palestinian Issue." *FBIS*, NES (19 December 1990): 6.

"Ghali Holds Press Conference on Gulf, Arab Ties." *FBIS*, NES (28 January 1991): 7.

"Illusory War Replacing Fight Against Israel." *FBIS*, NES (30 August 1990): 48.

"IMF Cancels 15 Percent of Foreign Debt." *FBIS*, NES (16 October 1992): 12.

"INA Reports 30 Aug." *FBIS*, NES (31 August 1990): 39.

"Journalists Stage Sit-In to Protest Gulf War." *FBIS*, NES (1 February 1991): 9.

"Lawyer Denounces Normalization." *FBIS*, NES (30 January 1980): D8.

"Minister of State Ghali Interviewed in Paris." *FBIS*, NES (16 October 1979): D2–D4.

"Ministerial Group Discusses Gulf War Developments." *FBIS*, NES (5 February 1991): 4.

"Mubarak Comments on Peace Conference, Gulf War." *FBIS*, NES (20 May 1991): .

"Mubarak Discusses Peace Process, Domestic Issues." *FBIS*, NES (10 April 1990): 8–10.

"Mubarak Explains Reasons for Economic Reform." *FBIS*, NES (16 September 1992): 12–14.

"Mubarak Speaks at Alexandria University Event." *FBIS*, NES (20 July 1992): 10.

"Muslim Brotherhood Leader Voices Support for Iraq." *FBIS*, NES (30 January 1991): 48.

"Nation Opposes U.S. Attempt to Weaken Iraq." *FBIS*, NES (29 October 1990): 53.

"Nation Will Not Defend Iraq Against Israel." *FBIS*, NES (14 August 1990): 51.

"NPF Supports Al-Asad Efforts in Gulf Crisis." *FBIS*, NES (10 August 1990): 60.

"Palestine Issue to Draw Attention After War." *FBIS*, NES (31 January 1991): 5.

"Paper Views U.S. Support of Israeli Occupation." *FBIS*, NES (14 August 1990): 51.

"People's Assembly Declares Support for Gulf Policy." *FBIS*, NES (28 January 1991): 9.

"Prime Minister Discusses Economic Measures, Reforms." *FBIS*, NES (1 December 1992): 15–16.

"Progressive National Front Meets Under Al-Asad." *FBIS*, NES (17 March 1982): H1.

"Radio Commentary." *FBIS*, NES (12 October 1990): 50–51.

"Says Egyptian Forces Will Not Enter Iraq." *FBIS*, NES (31 January 1991): 4.

"Secretary Baker, Israel's Rabin to Pay Visits." *FBIS*, NES (20 July 1992): 11.

"Sidiqi on Economic Liberalization, Subsidies." *FBIS*, NES (2 December 1992): 24–25.

"Syria: Impact of Wielding Power on 'Alawi Cohesiveness'." *Daily Report Supplement of Near East and South Asia. FBIS*, NES (3 October 1995).

"Tishrin Scores Lack of Arab Support For Lebanon." *FBIS*, NES (4 January 1983): H3.

"Troops Slated for Saudi Arabia Service." *FBIS*, NES (14 August 1990): 51.

"UK-Based Businessman Briefed on Economic Policy." *FBIS*, NES (7 November 1990): 41.

"University Demonstrations Continue; City Calm, Protestors Kept Off Streets." *FBIS*, NES (26 February 1991): 4.

"Views War, Israel's Involvement." *FBIS*, NES (9 January 1991): 1–3.

"Wafd Party Stance on Gulf War Involvement Explained." *FBIS*, NES (1 February 1991): 8.

"Yugoslav Paper Rilindja Interviews Al-Asad." *FBIS*, NES (29 August 1979): H4–H5.

Index

About the Author

Cindy R. Jebb is the Director of Comparative Politics and Security Studies in the Department of Social Sciences, where she oversees the Comparative Politics course electives and teaches Comparative Politics, International Security, and Terrorism: New Challenges for Security Professionals. Recent professional highlights include duty as the USMA Fellow at the Naval War College (2000–2001), where she taught the graduate-level course on Strategy and Force Planning; interviews by International CNN, MSNBC, and Dutch National News; recent articles published in *Parameters, European Security*, and *Journal of Conflict Studies*; and, three books, *Bridging the Gap: Ethnicity, Legitimacy, and State Alignment in the International System*, *The Fight for Legitimacy: Democracy Versus Terrorism* (coauthored with P. H. Liotta), and *The Last Best Hope: Legitimacy and the Fate of Macedonia* (coauthored with P. H. Liotta), due in 2004.

Colonel Jebb has served in numerous command and staff positions in the United States and overseas, to include tours with the 1st Armored Division, III Corps, and the National Security Agency. Before reporting to the United States Military Academy, she served as the Deputy Commander of the 704th Military Intelligence Brigade, which supported NSA.

Colonel Jebb received a Ph.D. in Political Science from Duke University in 1997, a MA in Political Science from Duke in 1992, an MA in National Security and Strategic Studies from the Naval War College in 2000, and a BS from the United States Military Academy in 1982. Her husband is Major Joel E. Jebb, and they have three children.